Indian Coast Guard

Section-I For Navik (GD/DB) & Yantrik

Latest Edition
Practice Kit

25 Tests

15 Sectional Test
10 Mock Test

Based On Real Exam Pattern

✓ Thoroughly Revised and Updated

✓ Detailed Analysis of all MCQs

Title : Indian Coast Guard Section-I For Navik (GD/DB) & Yantrik
Author Name : Mr. Rohit Manglik
Published By : EduGorilla Community Pvt. Ltd.
Publishers Address : 12/651, First Floor Opp. Arvindo Park, Near Jama Masjid, Indira Nagar, Lucknow, Uttar Pradesh-226016, India

Copyright EduGorilla

ISBN : 978-93-91464-41-7
Second Edition

Disclaimer EduGorilla

Although the author and publisher have made every effort to ensure the accuracy of information in this book, we do not assume any responsibility to errors and hereby disclaim any liability to any party for any loss, damage, or disruption caused by errors or omissions, whether such errors or omissions result from negligence, accident, or any other cause.

Compiled and created by EduGorilla Community Pvt. Ltd

Printed By EduGorilla Community Pvt. Ltd.

ROHIT MANGLIK
CEO, EduGorilla

Dear Applicants,

People say *"Success comes to those who work hard."* But I've seen people working hard for their exams day in and day out for marginal success. While others succeed in their examinations by putting in just half the work. So are they God Gifted? No! I believe that it's because they work *smart* and not just *hard*. Similarly, for your exams, you should strategize your preparation so as to increase the likelihood of success. Well with EduGorilla get ready to increase your *chances of selection* in your exam by *16x*.

EduGorilla helps you in not only working *hard* but also working in a *smart and strategic* manner. With EduGorilla's preparation package, you get a chance to make your exam preparation easy, and a fun learning path towards selection. Finding the right path to your preparations can be difficult if you don't know in which direction to head. Don't worry, we have you covered! EduGorilla will be your guide to success in your journey. With our Preparation Package, you can prepare strategically and beat the exam in just one attempt.

EduGorilla's Preparation Package includes-

- **Test Series**
- **Books**

Our preparation package is handcrafted as per the latest changes, expert opinions, and students' discretion. Thus, enabling you to get through each stage of the selection process for your exam.

Our Books are designed by the teachers and experts of the respective exam with a combined 150+ years of experience; to provide you with easy, efficient, and effective learning. Our books are smart, in the sense that not only do they give you the answers to the questions but also provide similar questions for practice.

EduGorilla's competent Test Series gives you real-time experience and confidence through which you can clear your offline or online exam in just one attempt. We currently host 83,000+ mock tests for 1,440+ competitive and academic exams.

Thus, EduGorilla misses no chance to assist you in your preparation and covers all stages of the exam, so that you don't have to look anywhere else.

We provide complete preparation packages for defense, banking, teaching, and other National & State-Level exams. Hence, it doesn't matter which exam you aspire to because you will reach your success.

ALL THE BEST !

Let EduGorilla be your Guide to Success.

Rohit Manglik,
Founder and CEO, EduGorilla

Editor's Note

INTRODUCTION

EduGorilla focuses on guiding students to succeed in their examinations. With that in mind, our book, titled "Indian Coast Guard : Section-I For Navik (GD/DB) & Yantrik", has been drafted through the collective efforts of our distinguished experts with 150+ years of combined experience. This book consists of questions that are created following the latest changes in the syllabus and exam pattern. We compiled the book on the basis of questions that are most likely to appear in the Indian Coast Guard Navik (DB). Through EduGorilla's "Indian Coast Guard : Section-I For Navik (GD/DB) & Yantrik" your chances of success will increase 16x.

EduGorilla does this through our Complete Preparation Package. This package consists of well-conceptualized and structured content in the form of questions that are tailor-made according to your needs and will help you practice for exams in a smart way by pinpointing all the necessary information. It also provides hints and solutions, along with a smart answer sheet for your self-evaluation. You can assess your shortcomings and work accordingly on areas that may require more of your attention.

EduGorilla promises to help you succeed in your examination and accomplish your dream goals. We believe in our aspirants and see them at the top of the merit list. And the first step towards the top is to start preparing with us. EduGorilla's "Indian Coast Guard : Section-I For Navik (GD/DB) & Yantrik" includes the following attributes.

- Well-Researched Content
- Top-Notch Quality
- Detailed Answers and Analysis
- Smart Answer Sheet
- Exam Relevant Questions

Therefore, EduGorilla fortifies your preparation and makes it durable enough to help you stand tall and beat the examination.

Indian Coast Guard Navik (DB)

Scan QR code for Eligibility, Exam Pattern, Syllabus and more.

Book ID: 0818

TABLE OF CONTENTS

Mock Test 01

English

Q.1 Direction: Choose the option that is the passive form of the given sentence.

Who has given permission to enter the garden?

A. By whom has permission been given to you to enter the garden?
B. By whom had been permission given to you to enter the garden?
C. By whom was permission given to you to enter the garden?
D. By whom is the permission being given to you to enter the garden?

Q.2 Direction: In the question below the sentence has been given in Direct/Indirect speech. From the given alternatives, choose the one which best expresses the given sentence in Indirect/Direct speech.

She said, "Take the test next year instead."

A. She advised them to take the test next year instead.
B. She advised them that take the test next year instead.
C. She advised them took the test next year instead.
D. She advised them take the test next year instead.

Q.3 Direction: In the following question, out of the four alternatives, select the word opposite in meaning to the given word.

Gigantic

A. Mediocre **B.** Tiny
C. Big **D.** None of the above

Q.4 Direction: In the following question, out of the four alternatives, select the word same in meaning to the given word.

Mirth

A. Glee **B.** Anger **C.** Mistrust **D.** Sarcasm

Q.5 Direction: Choose the most appropriate preposition and fill in the blank.

I think my best friend is talking badly about me ____ my back.

A. across **B.** over **C.** in **D.** behind

Q.6 Direction: Spot the erroneous parts, if any, in the following sentences.

We visited (a)/the beach and the seawater (b)/felt warmly. (c)/No error (d)

A. (a) **B.** (b) **C.** (c) **D.** (d)

Q.7 Direction: Select the most appropriate Pronoun to fill in the blank in the given sentence.

The professor shouted at ____ for not submitting the desired documents.

A. my **B.** I **C.** me **D.** mine

Q.8 Direction: In the following question, out of the four alternatives, select the word opposite in meaning to the given word.

Allure

A. Repulse **B.** Attract **C.** Rewind **D.** Revive

Q.9 Direction: Choose the correct adjective for the following sentence.

The weather this summer is as _______ as last year.

A. worse **B.** worst
C. bad **D.** None of these

Q.10 Direction: Select the most appropriate Tense to fill in the blank in the given sentence.

We _______ the City Palace in the afternoon as per the schedule.

A. are visiting **B.** will visiting
C. will be visit **D.** visiting

Q.11 Direction: Fill in the blank with the most appropriate phrasal verb.

Did you remember to ______ the water and gas before you left the house?

A. put on **B.** put off **C.** shut off **D.** drop off

Q.12 Choose the correctly punctuated sentence.

A. I need to buy pens, pencils and books for the children.
B. I need to buy pens, pencils; and books for the children.
C. I need to buy, pens, pencils and books for the children.
D. I need to buy pens; pencils and books for the children.

Q.13 Direction: Choose the preposition in the given sentence.

He was walking along the main road.

A. He **B.** Along **C.** The **D.** Main

Ques (14-15):Direction: Read the following passage and answer the questions that follow it.

I worked for a brief while in a college in Delhi, and among my more uncomfortable memories is a language exercise, I gave a group of eight undergraduates: I asked them to imagine that they had already graduated and wanted them to write an application for a suitable job. Seven of the eight students wrote applications for the jobs of clerks. Even in one of the good universities, and in a college that had a reputation for its academic standards, the system has snuffed out all youthful ambitions.

Q.14 According to the author, the system has:

A. killed the students' ambitions.
B. motivated the students ambitions.
C. taught them to write apllications.
D. inspired them to become scholars and scientists and statesmen.

Q.15 The number of students who wrote applications for the jobs of clerks was:

A. One **B.** Eight **C.** Five **D.** Seven

General Knowledge

Q.16 Which state government has partnered with the Federation of Indian Chambers of Commerce & Industry (FICCI) in August 2022?

A. Odisha **B.** Jharkhand
C. Goa **D.** Karnataka

Q.17 The northernmost point of India is known as:

A. Indira Heights **B.** Indira Col
C. Indira Point **D.** None of the above

Q.18 Who was the first Indian to receive a Nobel Prize?

A. Mother Teresa
B. Hargobind Khorana
C. CV Raman
D. Rabindranath Tagore

Q.19 Who among the following was the first editor of 'Kesari' the journal started by Bal Gangadhar Tilak?

A. Gopal Krishna Gokhale
B. Srinivasa Shastri
C. MG Ranade
D. Gopal Ganesh Agarkar

Q.20 The capital of Afghanistan ______.

A. Kabul **B.** Herat
C. Kandahar **D.** Ghazni

Science

Q.21 Weber is the unit of ______.

A. electric conductance
B. magnetic flux
C. magnetic flux density
D. capacitance

Q.22 Gravitational force is maximum at which of the following place?

A. At equator
B. At tropic of cancer
C. At tropic of capricorn
D. At poles

Q.23 According to Newton's third law of motion, the action-reaction forces act on:

A. Same body
B. Two different bodies
C. Both (A) and (B)
D. None of these

Q.24 A current of 0.5 A is drawn by a filament of an electric bulb for 20 minutes, find the amount of electric charge that flows through the circuit.

A. 300 Coulomb **B.** 600 Coulomb
C. 2400 Coulomb **D.** 20 Coulomb

Q.25 If the current in the wire is doubled then the heat produce will become:

A. Half **B.** One fourth
C. Double **D.** Four times

Q.26 Radioactive substances do not emit:

A. Photons
B. Electrons
C. Helium nuclei
D. Electromagnetic waves

Q.27 The earth, while rotating around the sun, always keeps its axis pointed towards which one of the following?

A. Venus **B.** The Moon
C. The Pole Star **D.** The Saturn

Q.28 A long spring is stretched by 2 cm and its potential energy is U. If the spring is stretched by 10 cm, then its potential energy would be:

A. 25 U **B.** 5 U **C.** $\frac{U}{5}$ **D.** $\frac{U}{25}$

Q.29 Name the characteristic of the sound which distinguishes a sharp sound from a grave or dull sound?

A. Intensity **B.** Echo
C. Pitch **D.** Resonance

Q.30 Which metal is extracted from sea water?

A. Potassium **B.** Magnesium
C. Aluminium **D.** Beryllium

Reasoning

Q.31 Letters of the words given below have been jumbled up and you are required to construct the words. Each letter has been numbered and each word is followed by four options. Choose the option which gives the correct order of the letters as indicated by the numbers to form words.

V A R S T E
1 2 3 4 5 6

A. 2, 3, 1, 6, 4, 5 **B.** 3, 2, 4, 5, 6, 1
C. 4, 5, 2, 3, 1, 6 **D.** 6, 3, 4, 5, 2, 1

Q.32 If in a certain code language "SORE" is coded as "2861" and "CHAIR" is coded as "37546", then how will "SEARCH" be coded in that code language?

A. 215637 **B.** 261537 **C.** 251367 **D.** 637251

Q.33 Direction: A word with letters jumbled has been given. Choose the correct order of letters that are required to form the correct word.

MYOECD

A. 3, 1, 4, 6, 2, 5 **B.** 5, 3, 1, 4, 6, 2
C. 5, 3, 2, 4, 1, 6 **D.** 4, 3, 1, 6, 2, 5

Q.34 Arrange the words given below in a meaningful sequence.

1. Probation
2. Interview
3. Selection

4. Appointment
5. Advertisement
6. Application

A. 5, 6, 3, 2, 4, 1 **B.** 5, 6, 4, 2, 3, 1
C. 5, 6, 2, 3, 4, 1 **D.** 6, 5, 4, 2, 3, 1

Q.35 If '+' means '×', '-' means '÷', '×' means '-' and '÷' means '+' then

18 × 9 ÷ 3 + 8 - 4 = ?

A. 15 **B.** 3 **C.** 1 **D.** 0

Q.36 Which one of the given responses would be a meaningful order of the following?

1. Add oil in the frying pan.
2. Peel the potatoes.
3. Remove and place the potato fries on a plate with paper towels to absorb the leftover cooking oil.
4. Add the sliced potatoes to the oil in the frying pan.
5. Cut potatoes into thin straw-like pieces.

A. 4, 1, 5, 3, 2 **B.** 2, 5, 1, 4, 3
C. 1, 2, 5, 3, 4 **D.** 4, 2, 1, 5, 3

Q.37 In the question below, which one of the given responses would be a meaningful order of the following words? (Depending upon their value in meters in ascending order)

1. Foot
2. Yard
3. Inch
4. Mile
5. Meter

A. 2, 3, 5, 1, 4 **B.** 3, 2, 5, 4, 1
C. 3, 1, 2, 5, 4 **D.** 3, 2, 1, 5, 4

Q.38 A cube is made by folding the given sheet. In the cube so formed, which number will be on the face opposite to the face having the number '6'?

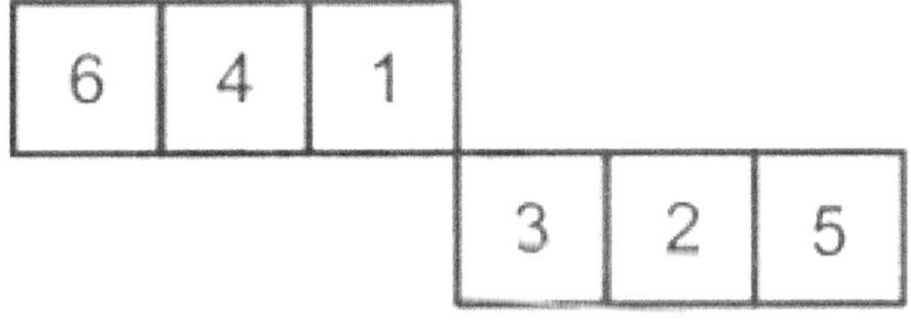

A. 3 **B.** 5 **C.** 2 **D.** 1

Q.39 What will be the next figure in the series?

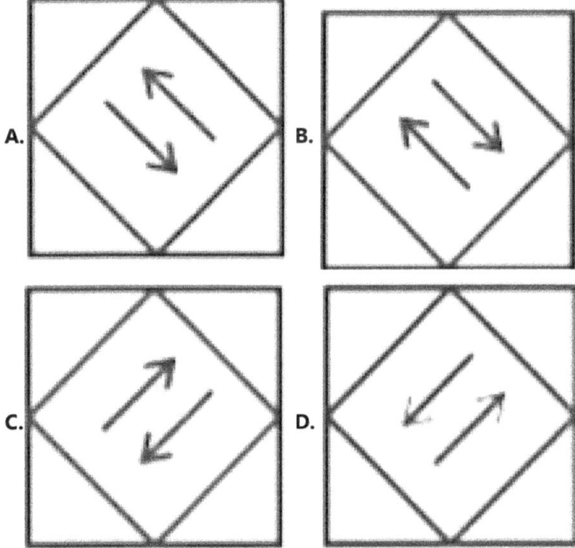

Q.40 In a certain code FIRE is coded DGPC. What is the last letter of the coded word for SHOT?

A. R **B.** S **C.** P **D.** Q

Mathematics

Q.41 By selling a piece of writing for Rs. 540, a person incurs a loss of 20%. At what price should he sell it so that he makes a profit of 40%?

A. Rs. 890 **B.** Rs. 105 **C.** Rs. 1256 **D.** Rs. 945

Q.42 30% of the number is 86 less than the $\frac{7}{9}$th of that number, what is the number?

A. 100 **B.** 180 **C.** 90 **D.** 120

Q.43 If a certain sum of money becomes doubles at simple interest in 12 years, what would be the rate of interest per annum?

A. $8\frac{1}{3}$ **B.** 10 **C.** 12 **D.** 14

Q.44 What is the value of $\frac{\sqrt[5]{27\times\sqrt[2]{81}}}{\sqrt[3]{125}}+\frac{\sqrt[2]{49}}{\sqrt[4]{256}}$.

A. $\frac{2498}{95}$ **B.** $\frac{3981}{39}$ **C.** $\frac{47}{20}$ **D.** $\frac{33}{76}$

Q.45 Find the value of following expression.

$$(\tan 45^\circ \times \cot 30^\circ)^2 + \sin 30^\circ \times \tan 30^\circ \times \cos 90^\circ$$

A. 0 **B.** 1 **C.** 2 **D.** 3

Q.46 In a ΔPQR, PQ = QR, ∠Q = x and ∠P = 3x – 15°. Then ∠Q is:

A. 40° **B.** 15° **C.** 30° **D.** 50°

Q.47 The length, breadth, and height of a cuboid are 12 cm, 9 cm, and 8 cm respectively. What is the length of the longest diagonal of the cuboid?

A. 16 cm **B.** 13 cm **C.** 17 cm **D.** 14.5 cm

Q.48 If $x = 3$ is a root of the polynomial, $f(x) = 4x^3 + 2x^2 + 5x - a$. Find the value of a.

A. 123 **B.** 141 **C.** 136 **D.** 189

Q.49 The mean of the data is 13, then find the value of x.

$8,12,7,15,9,21,x$

A. 9 **B.** 29 **C.** 17 **D.** 19

Q.50 A boy runs 20 km in 2.5 hrs. How long will he take to run 32 km at double the previous speed?

A. $2\frac{1}{2}$ hrs **B.** $4\frac{1}{2}$ hrs **C.** 5 hrs **D.** 2 hrs

Q.51 If A can do $\frac{2}{5}$ of the work in 24 days and B can do 60% work in 18 days, then find in how many days they can do the work together.

A. 15 days **B.** 20 days **C.** 25 days **D.** 30 days

Q.52 If A : B = 3 : 7 and B : C = 7 : 9, then A : C is equal to:

A. 3 : 7 **B.** 2 : 3 **C.** 3 : 1 **D.** 1 : 3

Q.53 If $a + b = 13$ and $ab = 42$, then find the value of $a^3 + b^3$?

A. 595 **B.** 565 **C.** 559 **D.** 556

Q.54 Simplify:

$$\sqrt[3]{138 - \sqrt[2]{181 - \sqrt[2]{324 - 180}}}$$

A. 8 **B.** 7 **C.** 6 **D.** 5

Q.55 A sum of money becomes six times in 10 years at simple interest then find the rate of interest.

A. 10% **B.** 20% **C.** 30% **D.** 50%

Q.56 A sphere has a total surface area of 9π cm ^{2}. Its volume is:

A. 36π cm ^{3} **B.** $\frac{9}{2}\pi$ cm ^{3}

C. 18π cm ^{3} **D.** $\frac{4}{3}$cm ^{3}

Q.57 Find the mean and median of the given data respectively:
{21, 22, 24, 25, 25, 18, 26}

A. 23, 24 **B.** 24, 23 **C.** 22, 25 **D.** 25, 22

Q.58 If $a^3 + b^3 + c^3 = 3abc$. Find the value of $a + b + c$?

A. 4 **B.** 6 **C.** 2 **D.** 0

Q.59 What is the simplified value of $(\cos A + \sin A)(\cot A + \tan A)$?

A. $cosecA + \sec A$ **B.** $\sin A + \cos A$

C. $\tan A + \cot A$ **D.** $secA - cosecA$

Q.60 If the mean and median of a statistical data be 5 and 6 respectively, then the value of mode is:

A. 11 **B.** 9 **C.** 8 **D.** 7

// Smart Answer Sheet //

Correct Percentage of students who answered correctly. **Skipped** Percentage of students who skipped.

Q.	Ans.	Correct / Skipped	Q.	Ans.	Correct / Skipped	Q.	Ans.	Correct / Skipped	Q.	Ans.	Correct / Skipped	Q.	Ans.	Correct / Skipped	Q.	Ans.	Correct / Skipped
1	A	31.55 % / 13.37 %	11	C	29.41 % / 13.91 %	21	B	39.57 % / 8.56 %	31	C	36.36 % / 9.09 %	41	D	35.29 % / 8.56 %	51	B	39.04 % / 11.76 %
2	A	43.85 % / 10.16 %	12	A	45.99 % / 13.37 %	22	D	42.25 % / 8.55 %	32	A	59.36 % / 10.16 %	42	B	43.32 % / 9.09 %	52	D	46.52 % / 11.77 %
3	B	41.18 % / 13.9 %	13	B	58.29 % / 13.37 %	23	B	40.64 % / 8.56 %	33	B	52.94 % / 9.09 %	43	A	43.85 % / 9.63 %	53	C	41.18 % / 10.69 %
4	A	22.99 % / 12.3 %	14	A	29.41 % / 8.02 %	24	B	44.92 % / 9.09 %	34	C	32.62 % / 10.16 %	44	C	43.32 % / 12.29 %	54	D	43.85 % / 7.49 %
5	D	45.99 % / 13.9 %	15	D	37.43 % / 10.16 %	25	D	37.43 % / 9.09 %	35	A	47.06 % / 9.09 %	45	D	25.67 % / 10.16 %	55	D	27.81 % / 12.3 %
6	C	32.09 % / 11.76 %	16	A	36.36 % / 11.23 %	26	A	24.06 % / 8.56 %	36	B	63.1 % / 11.23 %	46	C	42.25 % / 8.02 %	56	B	34.76 % / 8.02 %
7	C	53.48 % / 13.9 %	17	B	37.97 % / 10.69 %	27	C	30.48 % / 8.56 %	37	C	48.66 % / 8.56 %	47	C	37.43 % / 8.56 %	57	A	33.69 % / 9.63 %
8	A	27.27 % / 13.91 %	18	D	50.8 % / 10.7 %	28	A	17.65 % / 9.09 %	38	D	43.32 % / 10.16 %	48	B	54.01 % / 8.02 %	58	D	29.41 % / 10.16 %
9	C	34.22 % / 13.91 %	19	D	22.99 % / 10.7 %	29	C	39.04 % / 9.09 %	39	C	70.59 % / 10.16 %	49	D	34.22 % / 10.7 %	59	A	33.69 % / 9.09 %
10	A	39.04 % / 13.37 %	20	A	74.33 % / 10.7 %	30	B	41.71 % / 8.56 %	40	A	55.61 % / 10.7 %	50	D	36.9 % / 6.95 %	60	C	26.74 % / 7.48 %

//Hints and Solutions//

1. The passive form of the given sentence is 'By whom has permission been given to you to enter the garden?'.

We need to follow these instructions while changing the voice of an interrogative sentence.

- 'who' is changed to 'by whom' in the passive voice.
- Now, interchange the places and the forms of subject and object.
- When the active voice is in the present perfect tense (has/have + V_3), 'has/have been' will be used in the passive voice.
- Always use the third form of the main verb.
- At last line up the remaining part.

Hence, the correct option is (A).

2. The given sentence is an Imperative sentence and it is in direct speech.

The rule for changing an imperative sentence from direct speech to indirect speech:

- We will use 'to' as a joining clause before the reported command or request, and the reported verb will be changed according to the moods of the sentence (e.g., ordered, requested, urged, advised, forbade, or begged).
- Structure for indirect speech for an imperative sentence: reporting verb (e.g., ask, tell) + noun/pronoun + to infinitive

Therefore, the correct sentence is 'She advised them to take the test next year instead.'

Hence, the correct option is (A).

3. Gigantic: extremely huge

Tiny: very small

Mediocre: of not very high quality

Big: large

Hence, the correct option is (B).

4. Mirth: a mood characterized by high spirits and amusement and often accompanied by laughter

Glee: great delight, especially from one's own good fortune or another's misfortune

Anger: a strong feeling of annoyance, displeasure

Mistrust: lack of trust; suspicion

Sarcasm: the use of irony to mock or convey contempt

Hence, the correct option is (A).

5. I think my best friend is talking badly about me **behind** my back.

Speaking behind someone's back is used to say that someone intentionally says or does something when another person is not there and cannot know about it, usually ill words.

Example: I can't believe you said those things about me behind my back.

Hence, the correct option is (D).

6. The error lies in Part (c) of the sentence.

'Felt' is the verb of sensation.

Therefore, an adjective is used after it and not an adverb.

Warm is an adjective and warmly is an adverb.

Hence, the use of 'warmly' in Part (c) of the sentence should be replaced with 'warm' to make it grammatically correct.

Correct sentence: We visited the beach and the seawater felt warm.

Hence, the correct option is (C).

7. We use objective cases (me, him, her, them, us, etc.) of pronouns after all the prepositions.

Example:

I believe in him. (Him-Objective case of 'He')

As per the rule given above, 'me' will be used in the underlined part of the sentence.

Hence, the correct option is (C).

8. Allure: powerfully attract or charm; tempt

Repulse: cause to feel intense distaste and aversion

Attract: cause to come to a place or participate in a venture by offering something of interest or advantage

Rewind: to go back, or to make something go back, to an earlier time

Revive: restore to life or consciousness

Hence, the correct option is (A).

9. The weather this summer is as **bad** as last year.

'Worse' and 'worst' are comparative and superlative degrees of the word 'bad'.

The positive degree of the adjective is used between the phrase 'as.......as'.

Hence, the correct option is (C).

10. The structure is given below:

Subject + is/am/are + V1 + ing + Object

For events that will take place in the near future, Present Continuous Tense is used.

Complete sentence: We are visiting the City Palace in the afternoon as per the schedule.

Hence, the correct option is (A).

11. Put on: to move something you wear onto your body

Put off: to delay or move an activity to a later time, or to stop or prevent someone from doing something

Shut off: to stop the operation of a machine or system

Drop off: to take someone or something, esp. by car, to a particular place

Hence, the phrasal verb 'shut off' should be used to make the sentence grammatically correct.

Correct sentence: Did you remember to **shut off** the water and gas before you left the house?

Hence, the correct option is (C).

12. The correct answer is 'I need to buy pens, pencils and books for the children'.

- The punctuation 'comma (,)' is used to give a short pause. It is also used to separate elements in a list.
- When there is a list of two elements, we don't use 'comma' before 'and'.
- When there is a list of more than two similar elements, we use 'comma' before 'and'.
- In the given sentence, the list consists of three stationery items.

Hence, the correct option is (A).

13. A preposition is a word used before a noun/pronoun and denotes the relationship between a noun/pronoun and other words of the sentence.

The word 'along' means 'moving in a constant direction and line on a road or a path'.

So, in the given sentence, 'along' is the preposition.

Hence, the correct option is (B).

14. Let's have a look at the last sentence from the paragraph:

"Even in one of the good universities, and in a college that had a reputation for its academic standards, the system has snuffed out all youthful ambitions."

Upon perusal of the above statement, it can be concluded that the system has killed the students' ambitions.

Hence, the correct option is (A).

15. Let's have a look at the third sentence from the paragraph:

"Seven of the eight students wrote applications for the jobs of clerks."

Upon perusal of the above statement, it can be concluded that seven students wrote applications for the jobs of clerks.

Hence, the correct option is (D).

16. Odisha and the Federation of Indian Chambers of Commerce & Industry (FICCI) signed an MoU making FICCI the National Industry Partner for the Make in Odisha (MIO) Conclave 2022.

To attract investors & entrepreneurs from around the world, the 3rd edition of the MIO conclave is scheduled to be held from November 30th to December 4th, 2022.

Hence, the correct option is (A).

17. The northernmost point of India lies in the state of Jammu and Kashmir and it is known as Indira Col. The Indira Col (altitude 5,764 meters) is a mountain pass located on the Indira Ridge in the Siachen Muztagh in the Karakoram Range.

Hence, the correct option is (B).

18. Rabindranath Tagore was the first Indian ever to receive a Nobel Prize. Popularly known as Gurudev, India's Poet Laureate Tagore was born on 7th May 1861, in Kolkata. He was awarded the Nobel Prize for Literature in recognition of his work Geetanjali, a collection of poems, in 1913.

Hence, the correct option is (D).

19. Gopal Ganesh Agarkar was a social reformer and freedom fighter from Maharashtra. He co-founded the New English School, Deccan Education Society, and Fergusson College. He also served as the Principal of Fergusson College till his death in 1895. He was the first editor of Kesari. He also started his own periodical 'Sudharak' through which he campaigned against untouchability and the caste system.

Hence, the correct option is (D).

20. The capital and currency of Afghanistan are Kabul and Afghani respectively. Afghanistan is a land-based country in South Asia. Afghanistan became the eighth member of SAARC in April 2007.

Hence, the correct option is (A).

21. Magnetic flux is a measurement of the total magnetic field which passes through a given area. Magnetic flux is the product of the average magnetic field times the perpendicular area that it penetrates. The SI unit of magnetic flux is Weber (Wb).

Hence, the correct option is (B).

22. The result is that the weight of a body on the Earth's surface increases slightly as it moves away from the equator and toward the poles. This is because the Earth's gravitational force is slightly less at the equator than at the poles.

The gravitational field between two bodies is in versa proportional to the square of the distance between their centers of gravity, i.e. the higher the distance between the bodies, the lower the gravitational field. The Earth is not a perfect sphere and its radius varies at the poles and the equator, the radius being more at the equator than at the poles. This means that a body at the equator is farther away from the earth.s center than a body at the poles. So, the gravitational force is maximum at the poles.

There are mainly three factors that contribute to the maximum gravity at pole and minimum at equator:

- The radius of the equator
- Centrifugal force
- Mass

Hence, the correct option is (D).

23. Newton's third law:

- This law states that for every action there is an equal and opposite reaction.
- Action and reaction forces act on two different bodies.
- Action and reaction forces are not balanced because they act on two different bodies.
- If a pair of equal and opposite forces act on the same body then it is not an action-reaction pair.

Hence, the correct option is (B).

24. Given,

Current, (I) = 0.5 Ampere

Time, (t) = 20 minutes

= 20 × 60 sec

= 1200 sec

We know that,

Electric Charge (Q) = Current × Time

Q = I × t

Q = 0.5 A × 1200 sec

Q = 600 Coulomb

Hence, the correct option is (B).

25. Heating effect of current:

- When the ends of a conductor are connected to a battery, then the free electrons move and the electric current flows through the wire.
- These electrons collide continuously with the positive ions of the wire and thus the energy taken from the battery gets dissipated in the form of heat.
- The effect of electric current due to which heat is produced in a wire when current is passed through it is called the heating effect of current.
- The heat produced in the wire is,

$\Rightarrow H \propto I^2$

$\Rightarrow H \propto R$

$\Rightarrow H \propto t$

$\Rightarrow H = \frac{I^2Rt}{J}$

Where $H =$ heat

$I =$ current

$R =$ resistance

$t =$ time and

$J =$ Joule's equivalent

Given:

$I_2 = I_1, R_1 = R_2 = R$ and $t_1 = t_2 = t$

When the current is I_1,

$\Rightarrow H_1 = \frac{I_1^2Rt}{J}$....(1)

When the current is doubled,

$\Rightarrow H_2 = \frac{I_2^2Rt}{J}$

$\Rightarrow H_2 = \frac{(2I_1)^2Rt}{J}$

$\Rightarrow H_2 = \frac{4I_1^2Rt}{J}$.....(2)

By equation (1) and equation (2),

$\Rightarrow H_2 = 4H$

So, if the current in the wire is doubled then the heat produce will become four times.

Hence, the correct option is (D).

26. Radioactive substances do not emit protons.

Radioactivity:

- Radioactive decay is the process by which an unstable atomic nucleus loses energy by radiation. A material containing unstable nuclei is considered radioactive.
- A radioactive nucleus consists of an unstable assembly of protons and neutrons which becomes more stable by emitting an alpha, a beta particle, or a gamma photon.
- Atoms are radioactive if their nuclei are unstable and spontaneously (and random) emit various particles α, β, and/or γ radiations.

Three crucial forms of Radioactivity:

- Gamma Decay-(Photons having high energy are throw down).
- Beta Decay-(Discharge consists of Electrons).
- Alpha Decay-(Discharge consists of a Helium nucleus).

Hence, the correct option is (A).

27. The earth, while rotating around the sun, always keeps its axis pointed towards the Pole Star. The Pole Star is a bright star that is always directly above the north pole and which remains in the same position round the clock and throughout the year in the sky. It is also known as 'North Star'.

Hence, the correct option is (C).

28. Elastic potential energy: It is the potential energy created when an object undergoes an elastic deformation due to a force applied to it.

This energy is stored in the object as long as the force is in action and the object goes back to its original shape when the force is removed.

A spring undergoes a similar situation when a force acting on it causes a displacement due to elastic deformation.

The potential energy (U) required to stretch a string by x distance is given by

$$\Rightarrow U = \frac{1}{2}kx^2$$

Where k is the spring constant.

Let the potential energies of the spring be U_1 and U_2 when they are stretched be x_1 and x_2 respectively.

Given that: $U_1 = U$

When $x_1 = 2$ cm

$$\Rightarrow U_1 = \frac{1}{2}kx_1^2 = \frac{1}{2}k(2)^2 \text{......(1)}$$

When $x_2 = 10$ cm

$$\Rightarrow U_2 = \frac{1}{2}kx_2^2 = \frac{1}{2}k(10)^2 \text{......(2)}$$

On dividing equation (1) and (2), we get

$$\Rightarrow \frac{U_1}{U_2} = \frac{\frac{1}{2}k(2)^2}{\frac{1}{2}k(10)^2} = \frac{2^2}{10^2} = \frac{1}{25}$$

$$\Rightarrow U_2 = 25U_1 = 25U$$

Hence, the correct option is (A).

29. Pitch is that characteristic of sound which distinguishes a sharp or shrill sound from a grave or dull sound. It depends upon frequency. Higher the frequency higher will be the pitch and shriller will be the sound and vice versa.

Hence, the correct option is (C).

30. The elements dissolved in sea water have been commercially extracted in many quantity. They are sodium and chlorine in the form of common salt, magnesium and some of its compounds, and bromine.

Hence, the correct option is (A).

31. Given:

V A R S T E

1 2 3 4 5 6

The correct order of the letters is STARVE ↔ (4, 5, 2, 3, 1, 6)

Hence, the correct option is (C).

32. The logic follows here is:

As "SORE" is coded as "2861" and "CHAIR" is coded as "37546".

Thus, the code for "SEARCH" will be 215637".

Hence, the correct option is (A).

33. 1) 3, 1, 4, 6, 2, 5

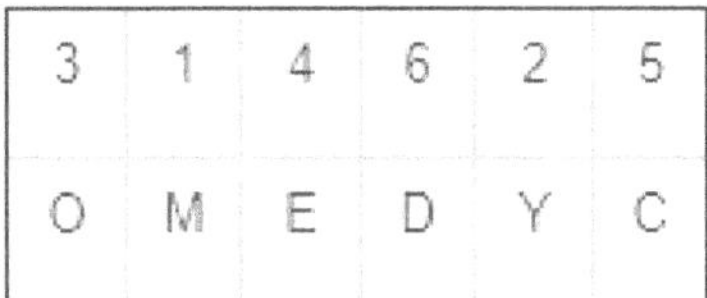

3	1	4	6	2	5
O	M	E	D	Y	C

2) 5, 3, 1, 4, 6, 2

5	3	1	4	6	2
C	O	M	E	D	Y

3) 5, 3, 2, 4, 1, 6

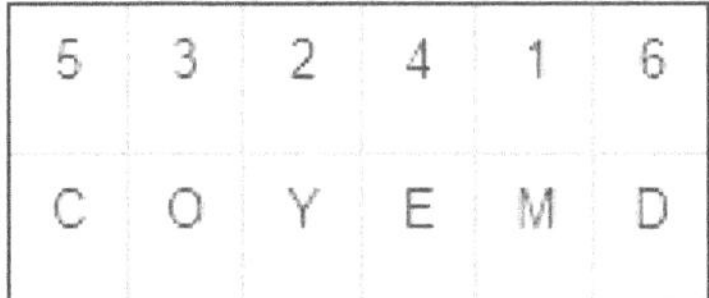

5	3	2	4	1	6
C	O	Y	E	M	D

4) 4, 3, 1, 6, 2, 5

4	3	1	6	2	5
E	O	M	D	Y	C

'COMEDY' is a meaningful English word.

Hence, the correct option is (B).

34. The correct order is:

5. Advertisement

6. Application

2. Interview

3. Selection

4. Appointment

1. Probation

Hence, the correct option is (C).

35. Given equation:

18 × 9 ÷ 3 + 8 - 4 = ?

Replace the signs in the equation with the above signs

18 - 9 + 3 × 8 ÷ 4 = ?

Using the BODMAS rule,

= 18 - 9 + 3 × 2

= 18 - 9 + 6

= 24 - 9

= 15

Hence, the correct option is (A).

36. The logical order of cooking potato fries are as follows:

2. Peel the potatoes.

5. Cut potatoes into thin straw-like pieces.

1. Add oil in the frying pan.

4. Add the sliced potatoes to the oil in the frying pan.

3. Remove and place the potato fries on a plate with paper towels to absorb the leftover cooking oil.

So, the meaningful order is 2, 5, 1, 4, 3

Hence, the correct option is (B).

37. We know that:

1 inch = 0.0254 meter

1 foot = 0.3048 meter

1 yard = 0.9144 meter

1 mile = 1609.34 meters

These units of length have been written in ascending order according to their value in meters.

3. Inch

1. Foot

2. Yard

5. Meter

4. Mile

So, the correct order is "3, 1, 2, 5, 4"

Hence, the correct option is (C).

38. The alternate position of faces becomes opposite to each other, as shown below:

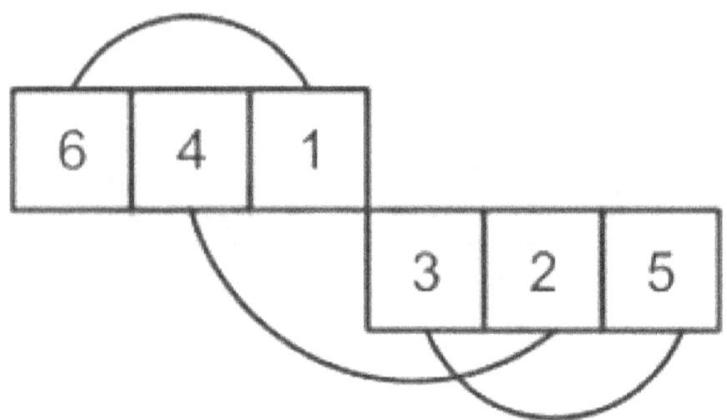

The opposite pairs are (6-1), (3-5), and (4-2).

The face opposite to the face having the number 6 is 1.

Hence, the correct option is (D).

39. The pattern follows here is:

One arrow is removed in each step.

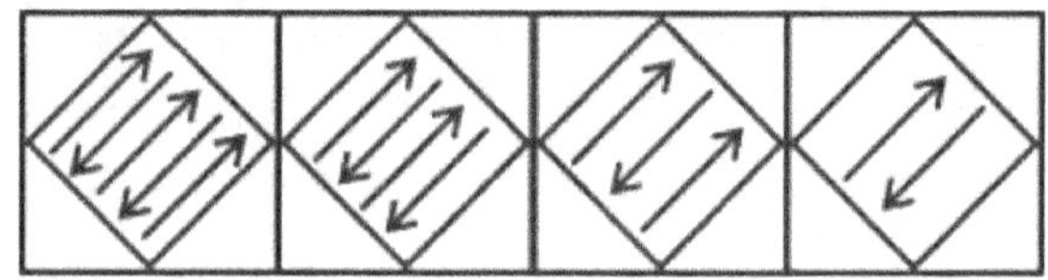

So the next term is:

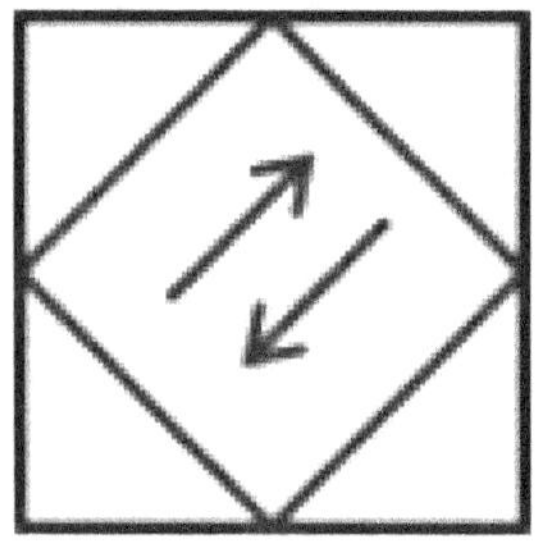

Hence, the correct option is (C).

40. The logic follows here is:

F I R E

-2 -2 -2 -2 -2

D G P C

Similarly,

S H O T

-2 -2 -2 -2

Q F M R

The coded word is QFMR.

The last letter of the coded word is R.

Hence, the correct option is (A).

41. Given:

Loss% if Selling Price is Rs. 540 = 20%

Profit at which Selling Price to be calculated = 40%

We know that,

$$SP = CP \times \left[\frac{100-\text{Loss\%}}{100}\right]$$

Where SP = Selling Price

CP = Cost Price

$\Rightarrow$ Rs. $540 = CP \times \left[\frac{100-20\%}{100}\right]$

$\Rightarrow CP = 540 \times \frac{100}{80}$

$\Rightarrow CP =$ Rs. 675

New SP = ?

Using Formula,

$SP = CP \times \left[\frac{100+\text{Gain}\%}{100}\right]$

$\Rightarrow SP = 675 \times \left[\frac{100+40\%}{100}\right]$

$\Rightarrow SP = 675 \times \frac{140}{100}$

$\Rightarrow SP =$ Rs. 945

$\therefore$ The Selling price is Rs. 945.

Hence, the correct option is (D).

42. Given:

30% of a number + 86 = $\frac{7}{9}$th of that number

Let, the total number $= x$

According to the question,

$\left(\frac{30}{100} \times x\right) + 86 = \frac{7}{9} \times x$

$\Rightarrow 86 = \frac{7x}{9} - \frac{3x}{10}$

$\Rightarrow \frac{43x}{90} = 86$

$\Rightarrow x = 180$

$\therefore$ Required number $= 180$

Hence, the correct option is (B).

43. Given,

Time $= 12$ years

The time is double at simple interest

Let,

Principal, $P =$ Rs. 100

Amount, $A =$ Rs. 200

Interest $=$ Rs. 100

Rate of interest $= \frac{\text{Total Interest}}{\text{Given Time}}$

$= \frac{100}{12}$

$= 8\frac{1}{3}\%$

Hence, the correct option is (A).

44. Given:

$\frac{\sqrt[5]{27 \times \sqrt[2]{81}}}{\sqrt[3]{125}} + \frac{\sqrt[2]{49}}{\sqrt[4]{256}}$

$\Rightarrow \frac{\sqrt[5]{27 \times 9}}{5} + \frac{7}{4}$

$\Rightarrow \frac{3}{5} + \frac{7}{4}$

$\Rightarrow \frac{12+35}{20}$

$\Rightarrow \frac{47}{20}$

Hence, the correct option is (C).

45. The given expression is,

$(\tan 45° \times \cot 30°)^2 + \sin 30° \times \tan 30° \times \cos 90°$

We know that,

$\tan 45° = 1$

$\cot 30° = \sqrt{3}$

$\sin 30° = \frac{1}{2}$

$\tan 30° = \frac{1}{\sqrt{3}}$

$\cos 90° = 0$

Putting the above values in the given expression,

$(\tan 45° \times \cot 30°)^2 + \sin 30° \times \tan 30° \times \cos 90°$

$= \left(1 \times \sqrt{3}\right)^2 + \frac{1}{2} \times \frac{1}{\sqrt{3}} \times 0$

$= \left(\sqrt{3}\right)^2 + 0$

$= 3$

Hence, the correct option is (D).

46. Given:

PQ = QR, ∠Q = x and ∠P = 3x − 15°

The Sum of all angles of a triangle is 180°.

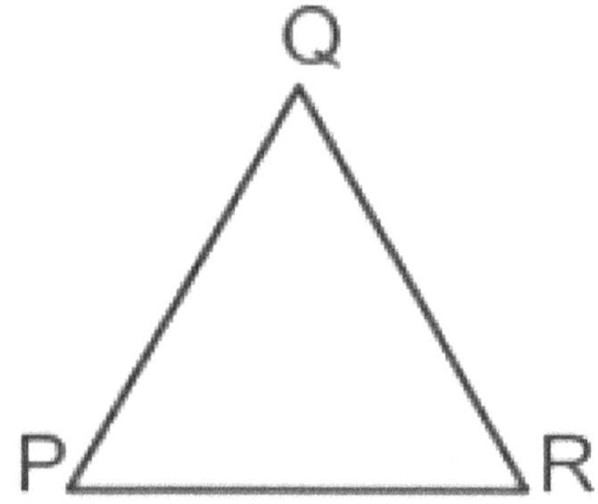

PQ = QR

⇒ ∠PRQ = ∠RPQ = 3x – 15°

⇒ ∠P + ∠Q + ∠R = 180°

⇒ (3x – 15°) + x + (3x – 15°) = 180°

⇒ 2(3x – 15°) + x = 180°

⇒ 6x – 30° + x = 180°

⇒ 7x = 210°

⇒ x = 30°

∴ ∠Q is 30°.

Hence, the correct option is (C).

47. Given:

The length of the cuboid = 12 cm

The breadth of the cuboid = 9 cm

The height of the cuboid = 8 cm

$D = \sqrt{l^2 + b^2 + h^2}$

where,

$D =$ The longest diagonal of a cuboid

$l =$ The length of a cuboid

$b =$ The breadth of a cuboid

$h =$ The height of a cuboid

According to the question,

$D = \sqrt{(12)^2 + (9)^2 + (8)^2}$

$\Rightarrow \sqrt{144 + 81 + 64}$

$\Rightarrow \sqrt{289}$

$\Rightarrow 17$ cm

∴ The longest diagonal of the cuboid is 17 cm.

Hence, the correct option is (C).

48. Given:

$f(x) = 4x^3 + 2x^2 + 5x - a$

and $x = 3$

When we put the value of root in the polynomial, then the value of the polynomial is equal to zero.

$F(3) = 4(3)^3 + 2(3)^2 + 5(3) - a$

$\Rightarrow 0 = 108 + 18 + 15 - a$

$\Rightarrow 0 = 141 - a$

$\Rightarrow a = 141$

∴ Value of a is 141.

Hence, the correct option is (B).

49. Given:

Data is $8,12,7,15,9,21,x$

Mean $= 13$

We know that,

Mean $= \frac{\text{Sum of all obsevations}}{\text{number of observation}}$

Mean $= \frac{8+12+7+15+9+21+x}{7}$

$\Rightarrow 13 = \frac{72+x}{7}$

$\Rightarrow 72 + x = 91$

$\Rightarrow x = 91 - 72$

$\Rightarrow x = 19$

∴ The required value of x is 19.

Hence, the correct option is (D).

50. Given:

Boy runs a distance of 20 km in 2.5 hrs.

We know that,

Speed $= \frac{\text{distance}}{\text{time}}$

Speed of boy $= \frac{20}{2.5}$

$= 8$ km/hr

If the speed is doubled the new speed will be $= 8 \times 2 = 16$ km/hr

Then the time taken by the boy to run 32 km

Time $= \frac{\text{distance}}{\text{speed}}$

Time $= \frac{32}{16}$

$= 2$ hours

∴ Required time to run 32 km is 2 hrs.

Hence, the correct option is (D).

51. Given:

A can do $\frac{2}{5}$ of the work in 24 days

B can do 60% work in 18 days

According to the question, we have

$$\Rightarrow \frac{2}{5} \times A = 24$$

$$\Rightarrow A = \frac{24 \times 5}{2}$$

$$\Rightarrow A = 60 \text{ days}$$

A can do the work in 60 days

A can do the work in 1 day is $\frac{1}{60}$ unit

Now, B can do 60% work in 18 days

$$\Rightarrow \frac{3}{5} \times B = 18$$

$$\Rightarrow B = \frac{18 \times 5}{3}$$

$$\Rightarrow B = 30 \text{ days}$$

So, B can do the same work in 30 days

B can do the work in 1 day is $\frac{1}{30}$ unit

Now, the number of days taken by A and B to do the same work together is,

Required number of days $= \frac{1}{A} + \frac{1}{B}$

$$= \frac{1}{60} + \frac{1}{30}$$

$$= \frac{1+2}{60}$$

$$= \frac{3}{60}$$

$$= \frac{1}{20}$$

So, A and B can do the work together in 20 days.

∴ Required number of days taken by A and B can do the work together In 20 days.

Hence, the correct option is (B).

52. Given:

A : B = 3 : 7.....(1)

B : C = 7 : 9....(2)

From equation (1) and (2), we get

A : B : C = 3 : 7 : 9

Required ratio = A : C = 3 : 9

= 1 : 3

∴ A : C is equal to 1 : 3.

Hence, the correct option is (D).

53. Given:

a + b = 13

ab = 42

We know that,

$$(a+b)^3 = a^3 + b^3 + 3ab(a+b)$$

We have,

$$(13)^3 = a^3 + b^3 + 3 \times 42 \times (13)$$

$$\Rightarrow a^3 + b^3 = (13)^3 - 3 \times 42 \times 13$$

$$\Rightarrow a^3 + b^3 = 2197 - 1638$$

$$\Rightarrow a^3 + b^3 = 2197 - 1638$$

$$\Rightarrow a^3 + b^3 = 559$$

∴ The value of $a^3 + b^3$ is 559.

Hence, the correct option is (C).

54. Given,

$$\sqrt[3]{138 - \sqrt[2]{181 - \sqrt[2]{324 - 180}}}$$

$$\Rightarrow \sqrt[3]{138 - \sqrt[2]{181 - \sqrt[2]{144}}}$$

$$\Rightarrow \sqrt[3]{138 - \sqrt[2]{181 - 12}}$$

$$\Rightarrow \sqrt[3]{138 - \sqrt[2]{169}}$$

$$\Rightarrow \sqrt[3]{138 - 13}$$

$$\Rightarrow \sqrt[3]{125}$$

$$\Rightarrow 5$$

$$\therefore \sqrt[3]{138 - \sqrt[2]{181 - \sqrt[2]{324 - 180}}} = 5$$

Hence, the correct option is (D).

55. Given:

Amount = 6P

Time = 10 years

We know that,

$$SI = \frac{PRT}{100}$$

Amount = SI + P

Where,

P = Principal

R = Rate of interest

T = Time duration

SI = Simple interest

Let the principal be P.

SI = 6P - P

= 5P

According to the question, we have,

$5P = \frac{P \times R \times 10}{100}$

$\Rightarrow 5 = \frac{R}{10}$

⇒ R = 50%

∴ The rate of interest is 50%.

Hence, the correct option is (D).

56. Given:

Total surface area of sphere $= 9\pi$ cm ^{2}

We know that,

Total surface area $= 4\pi r^2 = 9\pi$

$\Rightarrow r^2 = \frac{9}{4}$

$\Rightarrow r = \frac{3}{2}$

$\Rightarrow r = 1.5$ cm

And Volume of the sphere $= \frac{4}{3}\pi r^3 = \frac{4}{3} \times \pi \times \left(\frac{3}{2}\right)^3$

$\Rightarrow \frac{4}{3}\pi r^3 = \frac{9}{2}\pi$ cm ^{3}

∴ The volume of the sphere is $\frac{9}{2}\pi$ cm ^{3}.

Hence, the correct option is (B).

57. Given:

Numbers = {21, 22, 24, 25, 25, 18, 26}

We know that,

Mean = $\frac{\text{Sum of numbers}}{\text{Number of observations}}$

Sum of numbers = 21 + 22 + 24 + 25 + 25 + 18 + 26

Sum = 161

Mean = $\frac{161}{7}$

Mean = 23

Arranging the numbers in ascending order

18, 21, 22, 24, 25, 25, 26

Median = 24

∴ The mean is 23 and the median is 24.

Hence, the correct option is (A).

58. Given:

$$a^3 + b^3 + c^3 = 3abc$$

$$a^3 + b^3 + c^3 - 3abc = 0$$

We know that,

$$a^3 + b^3 + c^3 - 3abc = (a + b + c)$$
$$(a^2 + b^2 + c^2 - ab - bc - ca)$$

$$\Rightarrow (a + b + c)(a^2 + b^2 + c^2 - ab - bc - ca) = 0$$

So,

$$(a^2 + b^2 + c^2 - ab - bc - ca) = 0$$

And,

$$a + b + c = 0$$

∴ The value of $a + b + c$ is 0.

Hence, the correct option is (D).

59. Given:

$$(\cos A + \sin A)(\cot A + \tan A)$$

$$= (\cos A + \sin A)\left[\frac{(\cos A)}{(\sin A)} + \frac{(\sin A)}{(\cos A)}\right]$$

$$= (\cos A + \sin A)\left[\frac{(\cos^2 A) + (\sin^2 A)}{(\sin A)(\cos A)}\right]$$

$$= (\cos A + \sin A)\left[\frac{1}{(\sin A)(\cos A)}\right]$$

$$= \frac{1}{\sin A} + \frac{1}{\cos A}$$

$$= cosecA + \sec A$$

Hence, the correct option is (A).

60. Given:

Mean = 5

Median = 6

We know that,

Mode = 3Median − 2Mean

Mode = 3(6) - 2(5)

⇒ 18 - 10 = 8

Hence, the correct option is (C).

Mock Test 02

English

Ques (1-2):Direction: Read the following passages carefully and choose the best answer to questions.

Good health depends on several things. Fresh air and sunlight are very important for our health. Fresh air helps us to improve our immune system and overall health. So a morning walk is very useful for health. Sunlight helps our body to produce vitamin-D. A dirty and damp atmosphere causes lots of diseases. Fresh and pure drinking water is also necessary for good health. Impure drinking- water is the cause of several diseases. So, we must take care of these things. Food is another necessary thing for the body. Nutritious foods help us to maintain good health. Consumption of healthy foods helps us to minimize any health-related problems. We all should know, how, when and what to eat. We should always include a portion of green vegetables, fruits, or salads in our meals. Green vegetables are sources of vital nutrients. Our digestive system plays a key role in our overall health. Fiber-rich foods such as whole-grain wheat, bran rice, etc. help us improve our digestive system. A balanced and nutritious diet helps the proper growth of the body. But we must remember that we eat to live and not that we live to eat. In India, over-eating causes a large number of deaths. If we eat less, we may live more.

Cleanliness is essential for good health. Without cleanliness, it is very difficult to maintain proper health. We should clear our house and the surrounding areas every day. Every day, we should bathe twice, in the morning and in the evening. After eating food, we should clean our hands with soap.

Various types of diseases erupt from unclean surroundings. We should always throw the garbage in the dustbin. A disease-free body is a healthy body, and cleanliness is the key to health. We must know some simple rules of hygiene. Our house must be airy and sunny. Apart from all this, we must form good habits. We should keep ourselves free from care and anxieties. Early rising is equally necessary for good health. So we must try to keep fit. Health is the real wealth. Health is a great treasure. It is the highest blessing. It is the source of all happiness. Money can't buy happiness. Happiness is priceless and not dependent upon the wealth of a person. Good health, however, contributes to the emotional well-being and happiness of a person. Even with limited income, a person with sound health can lead a happy and enjoyable life.

Q.1 Consumption of water which is not clean and pure can lead to:

A. Several diseases **B.** Malnutrition
C. Indigestion **D.** None of these

Q.2 It is difficult to sustain proper health devoid of:

A. Wealth **B.** Cleanliness
C. Sunlight **D.** Anxieties

Ques (3-4):Direction: Select the most appropriate synonym of the given word.

Q.3 Novice

A. Beginner **B.** Trainer **C.** Virtuous **D.** Glory

Q.4 Diligent

A. Burn **B.** Control
C. Modest **D.** Industrious

Q.5 Direction: Select the most appropriate antonym of the given word.

Anxious

A. Carefree **B.** Active **C.** Taste **D.** Rise

Q.6 Which sentence makes most grammatical sense?

A. Despite the rush, Ali decided to go to the mall but purchase clothes.
B. Despite the rush, Ali decided to go to the mall and purchase clothes.
C. Despite the rush, Ali decided to go to the mall or purchase clothes.
D. Despite the rush, Ali decided to go to the mall though purchase clothes.

Q.7 Direction: Choose the option that is the active form of the given sentence.

The building was being designed by the architect.

A. The architect designed the building.
B. The architect had designed the building.
C. The architect has been designing the building.
D. The architect was designing the building.

Q.8 Direction: Choose the appropriate preposition for the given sentence.

He agreed _____ me.

A. upon **B.** to
C. with **D.** None of these

Q.9 Direction: Complete the following sentence choosing the most appropriate tense.

Recently, Tom Cruise as well as some other Hollywood stars __________ the Hollywood Foreign Press Association in protest for a lack of diversity within its membership.

A. have condemned **B.** has condemned
C. has lauded **D.** have lauded

Q.10 Direction: In the following question, a question is given in Direct speech. Out of the four alternatives, select the one which best expresses the sentence in Indirect speech.

The teacher said to the students, "You should get up early in the morning and spend some time with nature".

A. The teacher advised the students that they should get up early in the morning and spend some time with nature.
B. The teacher told the students that they should get up early

in the morning and spend sometime with nature.

C. The teacher told the students to get up early in the morning and spend some time with nature.

D. The teacher told the students that they should got up early in the morning and spent some time with nature.

Q.11 Direction: Choose the most appropriate meaning of the underlined phrase/idiom.

Engineering graduates are <u>dime a dozen today</u>. I want to employ an arts graduate.

A. Uncommon and worthy
B. Worthy but common
C. Common and worthless
D. Very rare

Q.12 Direction: Choose the correct part of speech for the underlined word.

The public's response to the crisis appeal was <u>**generous**</u> and compassionate.

A. Verb **B.** Noun
C. Adjective **D.** Preposition

Q.13 Direction: Choose the most appropriate meaning of the underlined phrase/idiom.

That was a really <u>**close call**</u>, but the politician managed to evade time in prison.

A. close enough
B. A narrow escape from disaster
C. A great chance
D. None of these

Q.14 Direction: Select the most appropriate verb's form to fill in the blank.

We are _____ to watch the reunion of the T.V. show "Friends" tomorrow.

A. plan **B.** planning **C.** planned **D.** to plan

Q.15 Direction: Complete the following sentence choosing the most appropriate pronoun.

Lata never likes ____ comparing her with her estranged father.

A. my **B.** me **C.** mine **D.** myself

General Knowledge

Q.16 The Ministry of Women and Child Development had extended the PM Cares for Children Scheme till 28th _________.

A. February 2022 **B.** March 2022
C. February 2022 **D.** December 2022

Q.17 Who is known as the Flying Sikh of India?

A. Mohinder Singh **B.** Joginder Singh
C. Ajit Pal Singh **D.** Milkha Singh

Q.18 When was the resolution of Purna Swaraj passed by Congress?

A. February 26, 1930, Karachi
B. January 26, 1930, Lahore
C. November 26, 1931, Calcutta
D. January 26, 1930, Bombay

Q.19 Which State in India has the longest coastline?

A. Kerala **B.** Tamil Nadu
C. Maharashtra **D.** Gujarat

Q.20 Arjuna Award is related to which field?

[UPSSSC Forest Guard, 2015]

A. Dance **B.** Cinema
C. Doordarshan **D.** Sports

Science

Q.21 A spacecraft takes off by expelling a large amount of gases at a very high speed produced as a result of the combustion of fuel. The fuel is expelled in the vertically downward direction and the spacecraft takes off in a vertically upward direction. Which Newton's laws of motion can be used to describe this process:

A. Newton's first law of motion
B. Newton's second law of motion
C. Newton's third law of motion
D. None of these

Q.22 Becquerel is the unit of measurement of ________.

A. Radioactivity **B.** Velocity
C. Conductivity **D.** Resistivity

Q.23 Physical quantity of _______ is measured in watts.

A. kinetic energy **B.** power
C. momentum **D.** impulse

Q.24 Which is the coldest planet in solar system?

A. Mercury **B.** Venus **C.** Earth **D.** Neptune

Q.25 Electrical conductance through metals is called electronic conductance and it _____________.

A. decreases with increase in temperature
B. increases with increase in temperature
C. decreases with decrease in temperature
D. does not depend on temperature

Q.26 A body falls freely from rest under gravity. If its speed is v when it has lost an amount V of gravitational potential energy, then its mass is (assume mechanical energy is conserved):

A. $\frac{vg}{V^2}$ **B.** $\frac{V^2}{g}$ **C.** $\frac{2V}{v^2}$ **D.** $\frac{Vg}{v^2}$

Q.27 If a_0 is the Bohr's radius, then the radius of Li^{++} ion in its ground state, on the basis of Bohr's model is:

A. $\frac{a_0}{2}$ **B.** $\frac{a_0}{4}$ **C.** $\frac{a_0}{3}$ **D.** a_0

Q.28 The radiative power of a black body at $500K$ is 1.0×10^5 Joule/sec/m^2. The temperature at which its radiative power will be 81×10^5 Joule/sec/m^2, is:

A. 2500 K **B.** 2000 K **C.** 1500 K **D.** 1000 K

Q.29 Which of the following non-metal is lustrous?

A. Sulfur **B.** Oxygen **C.** Nitrogen **D.** Iodine

Q.30 Bauxite is an ore of:

A. Hg **B.** Al **C.** Fe **D.** Cu

Reasoning

Q.31 Which option will replace the question mark and complete the given figure series?

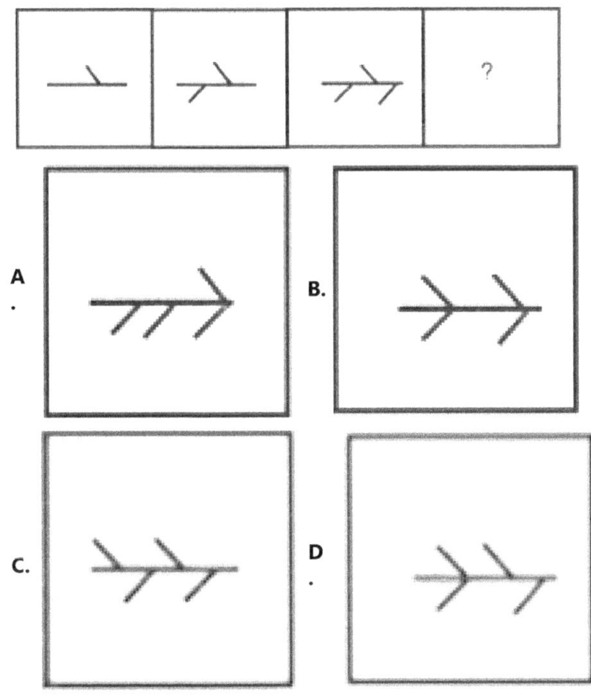

Q.32 Select the dice (from among the figures A, B, C, and D) that can be formed by folding the given sheet along the lines.

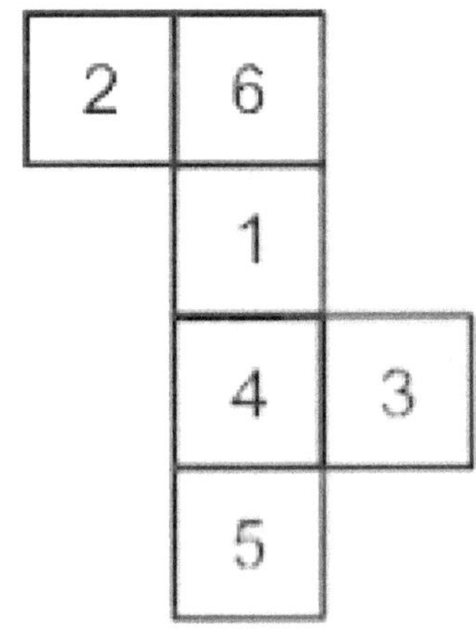

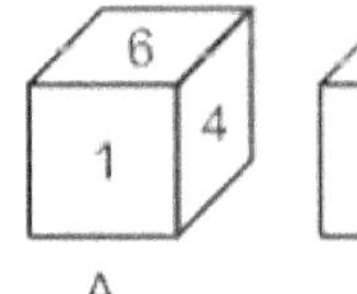
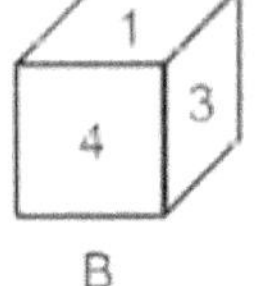
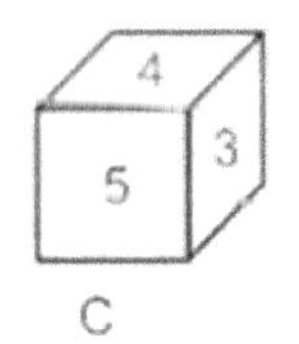
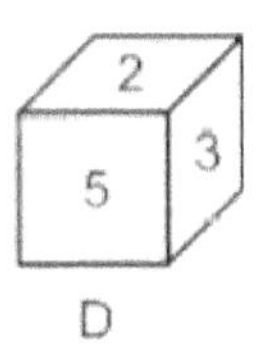

A B C D

A. Only A, B and C **B.** Only B, C and D
C. Only B and C **D.** Only B and C

Q.33 Direction: In the question, a few complete messages are given in a coded language. Based on It find the code for a particular word.

If HARD is coded as 1357 and SOFT as 2468, what will 21448 stand for?

A. SHAFT **B.** SHORT **C.** SHOOT **D.** SHART

Q.34 In a certain code language, "WEAPON" is written as "7#@893" and "HELMET" is written as "6#5$#4". How is "WALT" written in that code language?

A. 7#54 **B.** 7$#4 **C.** 7@54 **D.** 7@$5

Ques (35-36):Direction: From the given alternative words, select the word which cannot be formed using the letters of the given word:

Q.35 CHRONOLOGICAL

A. CALL **B.** LOGIC
C. CALICO **D.** ANALOGY

Q.36 PRONOUNCEMENT

A. PAVEMENT **B.** NOUN
C. CEMENT **D.** MOUNT

Q.37 Which two signs should be interchanged to make the given equation correct?

25 - 5 × 50 ÷ 10 + 35 = 155

A. + and - **B.** × and ÷ **C.** × and - **D.** × and +

Q.38 Select the correct combination of mathematical signs that can sequentially replace the * signs from left to right to balance the following equation.

32 * 2 * 60 * 30 * 15 * 51

A. ×, -, +, ÷, = **B.** ×, ÷, +, - , =
C. ×, +, ÷, -, = **D.** -, ÷, +, ×, =

Q.39 Rearrange the jumbled-up letters in a meaningful sequence and find the odd one out.

A. TGMAINSRA **B.** BILEMO
C. BKFOCEOA **D.** HTWSPAPA

Q.40 A word with letters jumbled has been given. Choose the correct order of letters which are required to form the correct word.

IMNFRO

A. 2, 5, 4, 1, 3, 6 **B.** 6, 1, 3, 2, 5, 4
C. 1, 3, 4, 6, 5, 2 **D.** 4, 3, 6, 2, 1, 5

Mathematics

Q.41 The score of 9 students are: 92, 84, 75, 115, 99, 129, 119, 72, 109. Find the median of the score.

A. 92 **B.** 75 **C.** 109 **D.** 99

Q.42 The Mean and Median of observation are 12 and 17 respectively. What is the Mode of this observation?

A. 27 **B.** 29 **C.** 5 **D.** 204

Q.43 The difference between simple and compound interests compounded annually on a certain sum of money for 2 years at 4% per annum is Re. 1. The sum (in Rs.) is:

A. 625 **B.** 630 **C.** 640 **D.** 650

Q.44 What is the value of the expression?

$(\sin 0^\circ \cdot \sin 1^\circ \cdot \sin 2^\circ \cdot \sin 3^\circ \cdot \sin 4^\circ \ldots\ldots \sin 89^\circ)$

A. 1 **B.** 0 **C.** $\frac{1}{2}$ **D.** Infinity

Q.45

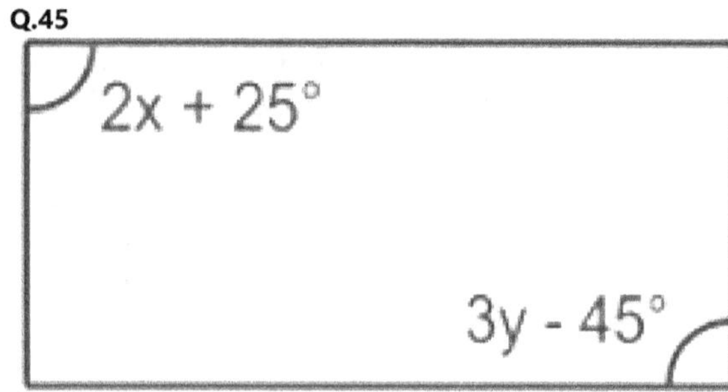

In this rectangle, the value of 2x + y is:

A. 95° **B.** 110° **C.** 30° **D.** 135°

Q.46 The ratio of the length and the breadth of a rectangle is 4 : 3 and the area of the rectangle is 6912 sq cm. Find the ratio of the breadth and the area of the rectangle?

A. 1 : 96 **B.** 1 : 48 **C.** 1 : 84 **D.** 1 : 68

Q.47 The breadth of a rectangular hall is two-fifth of its length. If the area of the floor is 1000 m^2. Then, the difference between the length and breadth of the hall is:

A. 15 m **B.** 30 m **C.** 6 m **D.** 18 m

Q.48 $\sqrt{1+\frac{27}{169}} = 1+\frac{x}{13}$, then find the value of x.

A. 1 **B.** 5 **C.** 6 **D.** 3

Q.49 Rajiv is a dishonest dealer who sells his goods at 16% loss on the cost price but uses 300 grams instead of 400 grams. Find his actual profit or loss percentage.

A. 15% **B.** 20% **C.** 12% **D.** 10%

Q.50 The cost price of 40 articles is the same as the selling price of x articles. If the profit is 25%, then what is the worth of x?

A. Rs. 25 **B.** Rs. 32 **C.** Rs. 42 **D.** Rs. 64

Q.51 Find the compound interest on a sum of Rs. 2000 at 10% per annum for 1 year, compounded half-yearly.

A. Rs. 200 **B.** Rs. 150 **C.** Rs. 205 **D.** Rs. 155

Q.52 The compound interest on Rs. 8,000 at the rate of 10% per annum for 1.5 years, if the interest is calculated half-yearly is:

A. Rs. 9,261 **B.** Rs. 860
C. Rs. 961 **D.** Rs. 1,261

Q.53 A and B are two alloys in which ratios of gold and copper are 5 : 3 and 5 : 11 respectively. If these equal amounts of two alloys are melted and made alloy C. What will be the ratio of gold and copper in alloy C?

A. 25 : 23 **B.** 33 : 25 **C.** 15 : 17 **D.** 17 : 15

Q.54

A can do certain work at the same time in which B and C together can do it. If A and B together could do it in 10 days and C alone in 50 days, then B alone could do it in:

A. 15 days **B.** 20 days **C.** 25 days **D.** 30 days

Q.55 If 2 men or 3 boys can complete a work in 48 hours, then 4 men and 2 boys will complete the same work in how many hours?

A. 16 **B.** 14 **C.** 18 **D.** 20

Q.56 If $4b^2+\frac{1}{b^2}=2$, then the value of $8b^3+\frac{1}{b^3}$ is:

A. 0 **B.** 1 **C.** 2 **D.** 5

Q.57 Find the minimum value of x which the expression $x^3-7x^2+11x-5 \geq 0$.

A. 0 **B.** 5 **C.** 1 **D.** -3

Q.58 Find the value of a and b if $(x-1)$ and $(x+1)$ are factors of $x^4+ax^3-3x^2+2x+b$.

A. 2, -1 **B.** -2, 1 **C.** -2, 2 **D.** 1, -1

Q.59

A man completes a journey in 10 hours. He travels the first half of the journey at the rate of 21 km/hr and the second half at the rate of 24 km/hr. Find the total journey in km.

A. 220 km **B.** 224 km **C.** 230 km **D.** 234 km

Q.60 If $x=a, y=b$ is the solution of the equations $x+y=5$ and $2x-3y=4$, then the value of a and b are respectively:

A. 6, -1 **B.** 2 ,3 **C.** 1, 4 **D.** $\frac{19}{5},\frac{6}{5}$

// Smart Answer Sheet //

Correct Percentage of students who answered correctly. **Skipped** Percentage of students who skipped.

Q.	Ans.	Correct	Skipped	Q.	Ans.	Correct	Skipped	Q.	Ans.	Correct	Skipped	Q.	Ans.	Correct	Skipped	Q.	Ans.	Correct	Skipped	Q.	Ans.	Correct	Skipped
1	A	54.01 %	1.89 %	11	C	56.15 %	1.57 %	21	C	61.97 %	1.46 %	31	C	82.98 %	0.0 %	41	D	88.56 %	0.0 %	51	C	31.51 %	4.3 %
2	B	44.84 %	1.74 %	12	C	57.06 %	1.14 %	22	A	77.32 %	0.0 %	32	C	31.13 %	4.17 %	42	A	53.92 %	1.04 %	52	D	40.39 %	1.08 %
3	A	12.38 %	4.71 %	13	B	56.6 %	1.86 %	23	B	85.23 %	0.0 %	33	C	56.37 %	1.1 %	43	A	20.26 %	3.66 %	53	C	56.96 %	1.59 %
4	D	49.17 %	1.82 %	14	B	86.69 %	0.0 %	24	D	79.81 %	0.0 %	34	C	43.0 %	1.94 %	44	B	55.46 %	1.27 %	54	C	65.26 %	1.52 %
5	A	82.73 %	0.0 %	15	A	56.7 %	1.07 %	25	A	67.34 %	1.73 %	35	D	85.7 %	0.0 %	45	B	14.45 %	3.61 %	55	C	40.26 %	1.2 %
6	B	82.53 %	0.0 %	16	A	41.36 %	1.65 %	26	D	28.5 %	4.63 %	36	A	84.61 %	0.0 %	46	A	79.22 %	0.0 %	56	A	18.63 %	4.88 %
7	D	21.35 %	3.19 %	17	D	58.51 %	1.48 %	27	C	43.81 %	1.3 %	37	C	48.98 %	1.93 %	47	B	40.42 %	1.93 %	57	C	52.48 %	1.02 %
8	C	89.96 %	0.0 %	18	B	65.0 %	1.56 %	28	C	21.1 %	3.01 %	38	C	18.21 %	3.24 %	48	A	49.7 %	1.82 %	58	C	20.39 %	4.71 %
9	B	48.49 %	1.12 %	19	D	85.67 %	0.0 %	29	D	43.07 %	1.29 %	39	B	64.83 %	1.4 %	49	C	51.13 %	1.89 %	59	B	43.51 %	1.02 %
10	A	18.24 %	4.0 %	20	D	85.41 %	0.0 %	30	B	40.96 %	1.41 %	40	C	55.22 %	1.37 %	50	B	82.53 %	0.0 %	60	D	55.97 %	1.43 %

//Hints and Solutions//

1. According to the line given in the passage, Fresh and pure drinking water is also necessary for good health. Impure drinking-water is the cause of several diseases.

Hence, the correct option is (A).

2. According to the line given in the passage, Cleanliness is essential for good health. Without cleanliness, it is very difficult to maintain proper health.

Hence, the correct option is (B).

3. Novice: a person who is not experienced in a job or situation

Beginner: a person who is starting to do something or learn something for the first time

Trainer: a person who teaches skills to people or animals and prepares them for a job, activity, or sport

Virtuous: having good moral qualities and behaviour

Glory: praise and thanks, especially as given to God

Hence, the correct option is (A).

4. Diligent: careful and using a lot of effort

Industrious: An industrious person works hard

Burn: to be hurt, damaged, or destroyed by fire or extreme heat, or to cause this to happen

Control: to order, limit, or rule something, or someone's actions or behaviour

Modest: not large in size or amount, or not expensive

Hence, the correct option is (D).

5. Anxious: worried and nervous

Carefree: having no problems or not being worried about anything

Active: busy with a particular activity

Taste: the flavor of something, or the ability of a person or animal to recognize different flavors

Rise: to move upwards

Hence, the correct option is (C).

6. The correct sentence is 'Despite the rush, Ali decided to go to the mall and purchase clothes.'

The conjunction 'and' is used to connect grammatically coordinate words, phrases, or clauses.

The usage of the conjunction 'but' is incorrect as it is used to introduce two contrasting sentences.

The usage of the conjunction 'or' is incorrect as it is used to link alternatives.

The usage of the conjunction 'though' is incorrect as it is also used to introduce two contradictory sentences.

Hence, the correct option is (B).

7. The instructions given below should be followed while changing an assertive sentence to an active voice.

Find the subject and object of the sentence and exchange their places; make changes in their cases as well if subject and object are pronouns.

If 'was being + V_3' is used in the passive form, 'was + V_1 + ing' will be used in the active form. (was designing)

At last line up the remaining part.

The correct sentence is: The architect was designing the building.

Hence, the correct option is (D).

8. He agreed **with** me.

'Upon' is incorrect because we use the phrase 'agreed upon' to express that something is noncontroversial.

'To' is incorrect because the phrase 'agree to' is followed by a thing/concept and not a person.

In this sentence, one person is agreeing or accepting someone else's idea or point of view.

Therefore, the word 'with' should be used to make the sentence grammatically correct.

Hence, the correct option is (C).

9. The complete sentence is: Recently, Tom Cruise as well as some other Hollywood stars has condemned the Hollywood Foreign Press Association in protest for a lack of diversity within its membership.

The verb 'condemn' means 'to criticize something or someone strongly, usually for moral reasons'.

The verb 'laud' means 'to praise'.

The sentence talks about some actors' protesting gesture against the Hollywood Foreign Press Association for a lack of diversity within its membership.

The Options having verb 'lauded' can't be the correct answers as they are not praising the association but protesting against it.

The prepositional phrase 'as well as' means 'in addition to; and also'.

When two subjects are connected using 'as well as', the verb agrees with the the first subject.

In the question sentence the first subject is 'Tom Cruise' which is a singular proper noun. Thus, the verb should be singular in form.

'have condemned' is plural.

'has condemned' is the right choice as it is singular in form.

Hence, the correct option is (B).

10. This is an assertive sentence.

It will be changed into Indirect speech as under:

- 'Said to' will be changed into told.
- Comma and inverted commas will be removed.

- The conjunction that will be used.
- 'You' will be changed according to 'students'.
- Should is not changed and it remains the same in Indirect speech as well.
- No change in verb will be done.

The correct answer is: The teacher advised the students that they should get up early in the morning and spend some time with nature.

Hence, the correct option is (A).

11. Dime a dozen: (phrase) very common and of no particular value or worthless

Example: Those toys are attractive but they are dime a dozen.

Hence, the correct option is (C).

12. Here, in the given sentence the underlined word is an 'adjective'.

An adjective is a word naming an attribute of a noun, such as sweet, red, or technical.

Example: His mother is one generous woman.

In the above example, the adjective 'generous' is an attribute of that woman.

Hence, the correct option is (C).

13. The idiom 'Close call' means a narrow escape from disaster; refers to narrowly avoiding a situation of events that are quite dangerous; being able to escape something bad and harmful that was just about to happen to you.

Example: It was quite a close call, but my father managed to avoid hitting the animal that ran across the highway.

Hence, the correct option is (B).

14. We are **planning** to watch the reunion of the T.V. show "Friends" tomorrow.

From the given sentence, one thing is clear that an action is going to take place soon or in the near future.

The planning is still in the process, which means that it is a continuation.

Hence, the correct option is (B).

15. Lata never likes **my** comparing her with her estranged father.

The possessive adjectives are my, your, his, her, its, our, their, and whose. A possessive adjective sits before a noun (or a pronoun) to show who or what owns it.

The sentence says that Lata don't like that I compare her with her father. In the sentence, 'comparing' is a gerund.

We use possessive form of a noun or pronoun before a gerund.

Hence, the correct option is (A).

16. The Ministry of Women and Child Development had extended the PM Cares for Children Scheme till 28th February 2022. Earlier the scheme was valid till 31st December 2021. The scheme covers all children who have lost both parents, surviving parents, or legal guardian/adoptive parents/single adoptive parent due to COVID 19 pandemic, starting from 11 March 2020.

Hence, the correct option is (A).

17. Milkha Singh, also known as The Flying Sikh, was an Indian track and field sprinter who was introduced to the sport while serving in the Indian Army. He is the only athlete to win gold at 400 metres at the Asian Games as well as the Commonwealth Games. He also won gold medals in the 1958 and 1962 Asian Games.

Hence, the correct option is (D).

18. The Indian National Congress issued the Purna Swaraj declaration on January 26, 1930, resolving the Congress and Indian nationalists to fight for Purna Swaraj or full independence from the British Empire. Jawaharlal Nehru raised the Indian flag on the banks of the Ravi River in Lahore, Pakistan, on December 31, 1929. The Congress had requested that India's people commemorate January 26 as Independence Day.

The Indian flag was raised in public around the country by Congress volunteers, nationalists, and the general public. The Congress designated January 26 as India's Independence Day, honoring those who fought for the country's independence. The British decided to hand over power and political clout to India in 1947, and 15 August was designated as India's official Independence Day. As drafted and approved by the Constituent Assembly, the new Constitution of India was to take effect on January 26, 1950, to commemorate the 1930 declaration. India became a republic on that day in 1950. Every year, January 26 is observed as India's Republic Day.

Hence, the correct option is (B).

19. Gujarat has the longest coastline in India with a total length of about 1600 Km. India has a land boundary of about 15,200 km. The total length of the coastline of the mainland, including Andaman and Nicobar, and Lakshadweep, is 7,516.6 km. The States/UTs having coastlines are Gujarat, Maharashtra, Goa, Daman and Diu, Karnataka, Kerala, Tamil Nadu, Puducherry, Andhra Pradesh, Odisha, and West Bengal. Island territories having coastlines are – Andaman & Nicobar Islands and Lakshadweep Islands.

Hence, the correct option is (D).

20. The Arjuna Awards were instituted in 1961 by the government of India to recognize outstanding achievements in National sports. The award carries a cash prize of Rs. 500,000, a bronze statuette of Arjuna, and a scroll. Over the years the scope of the award has been expanded and a large number of sportspersons who belonged to the pre-Arjun Award era were also included in the list.

The Government has recently revised the scheme for the Arjun Award. As per the revised guidelines, to be eligible for the Award, a sportsperson should not only have had good performance consistently for the previous three years at the international level with excellence for the year for which the Award is recommended, but should also have shown qualities of leadership, sportsmanship and a sense of discipline.

From the year 2001, the award is given only in disciplines falling under the following categories:

- Olympic Games/Asian Games/Commonwealth Games/World Cup/World Championship Disciplines and Cricket
- Indigenous Games
- Sports for the Physically Challenged

Hence, the correct option is (D).

21. Newton's third law of motion: To every action, there is an equal and opposite reaction.

Forces always exist in pairs and an action-reaction pair acts on two distinct objects.

Thrust: A force acting perpendicular to a surface is called thrust.

A jet of a large amount of high-speed gases produces a thrust in a downward direction which in turn generates an equal and opposite thrust on the spacecraft in an upward direction and thus the rocket takes off.

Hence, the correct option is (C).

22. Becquerel is the unit of measurement of Radioactivity. Radioactivity was discovered by A. H. Becquerel (1896). Radioactivity is defined as the spontaneous and continuous disintegration of a nucleus of a heavy element on its own with the emission of a certain type of radiation is known as natural radioactivity. One becquerel (1Bq) is equal to 1 disintegration per second.

Hence, the correct option is (A).

23. Physical quantity of power is measured in watts.

The rate of consumption of energy is called power.

$$P = \frac{\Delta E}{\Delta t}$$

ΔE = Change in energy

Δt = Change in time

Hence, the correct option is (B).

24. Neptune is the coldest planet and has 14 satellites. It is an ice giant. It is the eighth and farthest known planet from the Sun. It is the fourth-largest planet by diameter, the third-most-massive planet, and the densest giant planet in the Solar System.

Hence, the correct option is (D).

25. Electrical conductance through metals is called electronic conductance and it decreases with increase in temperature.

With metals, there are plenty of mobile carriers, and the motion of the lattice atoms due to thermal energy causes them to interfere with the transport of mobile carriers through the lattice.

Hence, the correct option is (A).

26. Potential Energy:

The energy of the object due to its position with respect to the ground is called Gravitational potential energy.

For a body at height h from the ground, and mass m is

P = m g h

g is the acceleration due to gravity.

While the body reaches the ground in free fall, the whole potential energy is converted into kinetic energy.

Kinetic Energy:

The energy of the body in motion by virtue of motion is called kinetic energy.

$$K = \frac{1}{2}mv^2$$

m is the mass of the body, v is the speed of the body.

Free Fall:

Freefall is the condition, in which the body falls from a height under influence of gravity with an initial velocity of zero.

The potential energy is getting converted into kinetic energy during the process.

So, in free fall, loss in Potential energy = Gain in Kinetic energy

$$V = \frac{1}{2}mv^2$$

$$\Rightarrow \frac{2V}{v^2} = m$$

Hence, the correct option is (D).

27. Bohr's model of a Hydrogen atom: Bohr proposed that atoms had a planetary model with electrons orbiting the nucleus of an atom in specific orbits with a fixed radius.

The radius of nth orbit of an atom according to Bohr's model is given as:

$$\Rightarrow r = a_0 \times \frac{n^2}{Z}$$

Where Z is the atomic number and a_0 is the smallest allowed radius for the hydrogen atom also known as the Bohr's radius with a value 0.529×10^{-10} m.

The atomic number of Li (Lithium) $(Z) = 3$

The ground state represents $n = 1$

The Bohr's radius of Li^{++} ion is

$$\Rightarrow r = a_0 \times \frac{n^2}{Z}$$

$$\Rightarrow r = a_0 \times \frac{1^2}{3}$$

$$\Rightarrow r = \frac{a_0}{3}$$

Hence, the correct option is (C).

28. A perfect black body absorbs all the electromagnetic radiation incident on it.

The black body radiation spectrum is the spectrum of radiation emitted by a black body when it is at a higher temperature than its surroundings.

Stefan-Boltzmann's law states that the total power radiated per unit surface area of a black body is proportional to the fourth power of the temperature of the black body.

$\Rightarrow P \propto T^4$

$\Rightarrow P = kT^4$

In the above equation, T is the temperature of the black body in Kelvin, k is the proportionality constant and P is the power radiated per unit surface area of a black body in Joule/sec/m^2.

Given:

$P_1 = 1.0 \times 10^5$ Joule/sec/m^2,

$P_2 = 81 \times 10^5$ Joule/sec/m^2,

and $T_1 = 500K$

Case 1:

$\Rightarrow P_1 = kT_1^4$

$\Rightarrow k = \frac{P}{T^4} = \frac{1.0\times10^5}{500^4} = 1.6 \times 10^{-6} \frac{J}{s.m^2.K^4}$

Case 2:

$\Rightarrow P_2 = kT_2^4$

$\Rightarrow T_2^4 = \frac{P_2}{k} = \frac{81.0\times10^5}{1.6\times10^{-6}} = 5.0625 \times 10^{12} K^4$

$\Rightarrow T_2 = 1500K$

Hence, the correct option is (C).

29. Non-metals do not have luster. They do not reflect light from their surface (exception diamond and iodine). Non-metals have a dull appearance.

Iodine is a non-metallic, dark gray/purple-black, lustrous, solid element. Iodine is the most electropositive halogen and the least reactive of the halogens even if it can still form compounds with many elements.

Hence, the correct option is (D).

30. Bauxite is the principal ore of aluminum which is one of the most important non ferrous metals used in modern industry. It is also an essential ore for the Refractory and Chemical industries. The country has 3,896 million tonnes of resources of bauxite which is sufficient to meet both domestic and export demands.

Hence, the correct option is (B).

31. The pattern followed is,

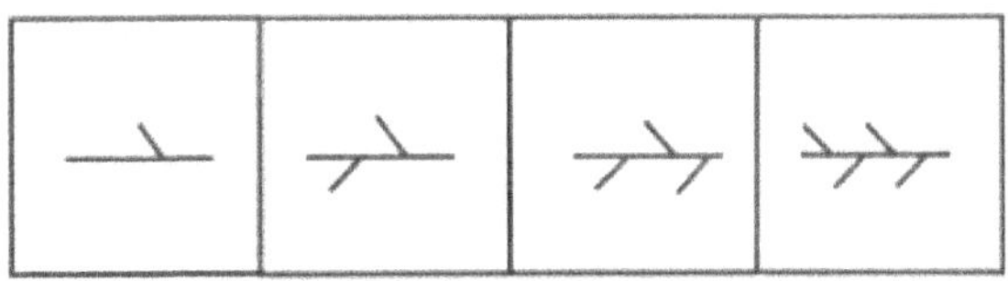

Hence, the correct option is (C).

32. When the unfolded dice is folded, the faces opposite to each other is:

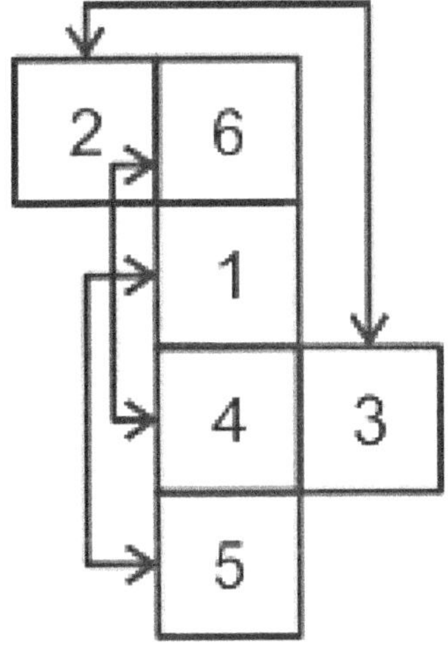

The Opposite of 2 is 3.

The Opposite of 6 is 4.

The Opposite of 1 is 5.

The dice A and D cannot be formed when the given sheet is folded because the opposite faces appear together in these dice.

Hence, the correct option is (C).

33. The logic is:

H	A	R	D
1	3	5	7

And,

S	O	F	T
2	4	6	8

Similarly,

2	1	4	4	8
S	H	O	O	T

Hence, 'SHOOT' is the correct answer.
Hence, the correct option is (C).

34. The logic follows here is:

Letter	**W**	E	**A**	P	O	N
Code	**7**	#	**@**	8	9	3

Letter	H	E	**L**	M	E	**T**
Code	6	#	**5**	$	#	**4**

Thus, using respective codes for the alphabets in the given word WALT:

Letter	W	A	L	T
Code	7	@	5	4

Hence, the correct option is (C).

35. The given word is CHRONOLOGICAL.

Checking the options:

(A) CALL → Can be formed

The letters of CALL are in the given word as shown:

CHRONO**L**OGIC**AL**

(B). LOGIC → Can be formed

The letters of LOGIC are in the given word as shown:

CHRONO**LOGIC**AL

(C) CALICO → Can be formed

The letters of CALICO are in the given word as shown:

CHR**O**NOLOG**ICAL**

4. ANALOGY → Cannot be formed

As seen Y which are in ANALOGY are not in the given word CHRONOLOGICAL.

Hence, the correct option is (D).

36. The given word is PRONOUNCEMENT.

Checking the given options:-

(A) PAVEMENT

It cannot be formed using the letters in the given word.

PAVEMENT has the letters A and V, which are not in PRONOUNCEMENT.

(B) NOUN

The letters of this word are is in the given word as shown:

PRO**NOUN**CEMENT

(C) CEMENT

The letters of this word are is in the given word as shown:

PRONOUN**CEMENT**

(D) MOUNT

The letters of this word are in the given word as shown:

PRON**OUN**CE**M**EN**T**

So, only PAVEMENT cannot be formed from PRONOUNCEMENT.

Hence, the correct option is (A).

37. Given equation:

25 - 5 × 50 ÷ 10 + 35 = 155

Let's check through options:

(A) + and -

25 + 5 × 50 ÷ 10 - 35 = 155

= 25 + 5 × 5 - 35

= 25 + 25 - 35

= 50 - 35

= 15 ≠ 155

(B) × and ÷

25 - 5 ÷ 50 × 10 + 35 = 155

$= 25 - \frac{1}{10} \times 10 + 35$

= 25 - 1 + 35

= 60 - 1

= 59 ≠ 155

(C) × and -

25 × 5 - 50 ÷ 10 + 35 = 155

= 25 × 5 - 5 + 35

= 125 - 5 + 35

= 160 - 5

= 155 = 155

(D) × and +

25 - 5 + 50 ÷ 10 × 35 = 155

= 25 - 5 + 5 ÷ 35

= 25 - 5 + 7

= 25 - 12

= 23 ≠ 155

Hence, × and - is correct.

Hence, the correct option is (C).

38. Given:

32 * 2 * 60 * 30 * 15 * 51

(A) ×, -, +, ÷, =

32 × 2 - 60 + 30 ÷ 15 = 51

= 32 × 2 - 60 + 2

= 64 - 60 + 2

= 66 - 60 = 6 ≠ 51

(B) ×, ÷, +, - , =

32 × 2 ÷ 60 + 30 - 15 = 51

$= 32 \times \frac{1}{30} + 30 - 15$

= 1.67 + 30 - 15

= 31.67 - 15 = 16.67 ≠ 51

(C) ×, +, ÷, -, =

32 × 2 + 60 ÷ 30 - 15 = 51

= 32 × 2 + 2 - 15

= 64 + 2 - 15

= 66 - 15 = 51

(D) -, ÷, +, ×, =

32 - 2 ÷ 60 + 30 × 15 = 51

= 32 - 0.0333 + 450

= 32 - 450.0333

= -420.0333 ≠ 51

Hence, ×, +, ÷, -, = is correct.

Hence, the correct option is (C).

39. Let's unjumbled the given options:

(A) TGMAINSRA = INSTAGRAM

(B) BILEMO = MOBILE

(C) BKFOCEOA = FACEBOOK

(D) HTWSPAPA = WHATSAPP

Thus, MOBILE is not an application but a device whereas INSTAGRAM, FACEBOOK, and WHATSAPP are social networking applications.

Hence, the correct option is (B).

40.

1	3	4	6	5	2
I	N	F	O	R	M

Hence, '1, 3, 4, 6, 5, 2' is the correct answer.

Hence, the correct option is (C).

41. Given:

The score of the students 92, 84, 75, 115, 99, 129, 119, 72, 109

Where N is a number of students

N=9 which is odd

Median = $\left[\frac{N+1}{2}\right]^{th}$ term

Arrange the score in ascending order,

72, 75, 84, 92, 99, 109, 115, 119, 129

Total number = 9

Then $\frac{9+1}{2}$

= $\frac{10}{2}$

= 5th number = 99

Median = 99

Hence, the correct option is (D).

42. Given:

Mean = 17

Median = 12

We know that,

Mode = 3 Median - 2 Mean

⇒ Mode = (3 × 17) - (2 × 12)

⇒ Mode = 51 - 24

⇒ Mode = 27

∴ The mode is 27.

Hence, the correct option is (A).

43. Given,

Time = 2 years

Let the sum be Rs. **X**.

Then,

C.I. $= \left[x\left(1+\frac{4}{100}\right)^2 - x\right]$

$= \left(\frac{676}{625}x - x\right)$

$= \frac{51}{625}x$

S.I. $= \left(\frac{x \times 4 \times 2}{100}\right)$

$= \frac{2x}{25}$

$\therefore \frac{51x}{625} - \frac{2x}{25} = 1$

$\Rightarrow x = 625$

Hence, the correct option is (A).

44. Given:

$(\sin 0^\circ \cdot \sin 1^\circ \cdot \sin 2^\circ \cdot \sin 3^\circ \cdot \sin 4^\circ \dots\dots \sin 89^\circ)$

$= \sin 0^\circ \times (\sin 1^\circ \cdot \sin 2^\circ \cdot \sin 3^\circ \cdot \sin 4^\circ \dots\dots \sin 89^\circ)$

$= 0 \times (\sin 1^\circ \cdot \sin 2^\circ \cdot \sin 3^\circ \cdot \sin 4^\circ \dots\dots \sin 89^\circ)$

$= 0$

Hence, the correct option is (B).

45. Given:

Measurement of each angle in a rectangle is 90°

So,

$\Rightarrow (2x + 25)^\circ = 90^\circ$

$\Rightarrow 2x = 90^\circ - 25^\circ$

$\Rightarrow x = \frac{65°}{2}$

$\Rightarrow x = 32.5°$

Same as

$\Rightarrow (3y - 45)° = 90°$

$\Rightarrow 3y = 90° + 45°$

$\Rightarrow y = \frac{135°}{3} = 45°$

According to question

$\Rightarrow 2x + y = 2 \times 32.5° + 45°$

$\Rightarrow 2x + y = 65° + 45°$

$\Rightarrow 2x + y = 110°$

Hence, the correct option is (B).

46. Given,

Area of the rectangle $= 6912\ cm^2$

Let the length and the breadth of the rectangle be $4x\ cm$ and $3x$ respectively.

$(4x)(3x) = 6912$

$\Rightarrow 12x^2 = 6912$

$\Rightarrow x^2 = 576 = 4 \times 144 = 2^2 \times 12^2 (x > 0)$

$\Rightarrow x = 2 \times 12 = 24$

Ratio of the breadth and the areas $= 3x : 12x^2$

$= 1 : 4x$

$= 1 : 96$

Hence, the correct option is (A).

47. Given:

The breadth of the rectangular hall is two-fifth of length.

Area of the floor = 1000 m^2

We know that,

Area of rectangle = Length × Breadth

Perimeter of rectangle = 2 × (Length + Breadth)

Let the length of the hall be 5x, then breadth be 2x

Now, Area of hall = 1000 m^2

⇒ 5x × 2x = 1000

⇒ $10x^2$ = 1000

⇒ x^2 = 100

⇒ x = 10

Length = 5x = 50 m and breadth = 2x = 20 m

Now, Difference of length and breadth = 50 m - 20 m = 30 m

∴ The difference between the length and breadth of the rectangular hall is 30 m.

Hence, the correct option is (B).

48. Given:

$\sqrt{1 + \frac{27}{169}} = 1 + \frac{x}{13}$

$\Rightarrow \sqrt{\frac{196}{169}} = 1 + \frac{x}{13}$

$\Rightarrow \frac{14}{13} - 1 = \frac{x}{13}$

$\Rightarrow \frac{1}{13} = \frac{x}{13}$

$\therefore x = 1$

Hence, the correct option is (A).

49. Given:

Rajiv uses 300 grams instead of 400 grams.

Rajiv sells at 16% loss

We know that,

Selling price = Cost price × $\frac{100 - loss\%}{100}$

Profit = Selling price - Cost price

Profit % = $\frac{Profit}{Cost\ price}$ × 100

Let the cost price of 400 grams be Rs. 100

Cost price of 300 grams = Rs. $\frac{300}{400}$ × 100

= Rs. 75

Rajiv sells his goods at a loss of 16%

Selling price = Cost price × $\frac{100 - loss\%}{100}$

= 100 × $\frac{100 - 16}{100}$

= Rs. 84

Profit = Selling price - Cost price

= 84 - 75

= Rs. 9

Profit % = $\frac{Profit}{Cost\ price}$ × 100

= $\frac{9}{75}$ × 100

= 12%

∴ Actual profit percentage of Rajiv is 12%.

Hence, the correct option is (C).

50. Given,

Articles = 40

The profit is 25%

Cost price of 40 articles = 40 CP

Selling price of 40 acticles = $x \times SP$

$40CP = x \times SP$

$\Rightarrow \frac{CP}{SP} = \frac{x}{40}$.......(i)

As the profit% is 25%

$\frac{CP}{SP} = \frac{100}{125} = \frac{4}{5}$.....(ii)

Equating (i) and (ii), we'll get

$\Rightarrow \frac{x}{40} = \frac{4}{5}$

$\Rightarrow x = \frac{4}{5} \times 40$

$\Rightarrow x = 32$

∴ The value of x is Rs. 32.

Hence, the correct option is (B).

51. Given:

Sum = Rs. 2000

Time = 1 year

Rate = 10%

$A = P\left(1 + \frac{R}{100}\right)^T$

$CI = A - P$

Where, $A =$ Amount,

$P =$ Principal,

$T =$ Time,

$CI =$ Compound interest and

$R =$ rate of interest

According to the question,

$R = \frac{10\%}{2} = 5\%$

$T = 2 \times 1 = 2$ years

$A = P\left(1 + \frac{R}{100}\right)^T$

$= 2000\left(1 + \frac{5}{100}\right)^2$

$= 2000\left(1 + \frac{1}{20}\right)^2$

$= 2000\left(\frac{21}{20}\right)^2$

$= 2000\left(\frac{441}{400}\right)$

$= 5 \times 441$

$= 2205$

$CI = 2205 - 2000$

$= 205$

∴ The compound interest is Rs. 205.

Hence, the correct option is (C).

52. Given:

Principal sum = Rs. 8000

Rate = 10%

Interest is calculated half-yearly,

So, Rate, $R = \frac{10}{2} = 5\%$

Time = 1.5 years = 3 half years,

So, n = 3

We know that,

Amount = Principal $\times \left(1 + \frac{r}{100}\right)^n$

Amount $= 8000 \times \left(1 + \frac{5}{100}\right)^3$

Amount $= 8000 \times \frac{21}{20} \times \frac{21}{20} \times \frac{21}{20}$

∴ Amount $=$ Rs. 9261

Compound interest = Amount - Principal

∴ Compound interest $= 9261 - 8000 =$ Rs. 1261

Hence, the correct option is (D).

53. Ratio of Gold and Copper In Alloy A $= 5:3$

Ratio of Gold and Copper in Alloy B $= 5:11$

Amount of Gold in Alloy A $= \frac{5}{8}$

Amount of Gold In Alloy B $= \frac{5}{16}$

Amount of Copper in A $= \frac{3}{8}$

Amount of Copper in B $= \frac{11}{16}$

Amount of Gold in C $=$ Amount of gold in A + Amount of gold in B

$= \frac{5}{8} + \frac{5}{16}$

$= \frac{10+5}{16} = \frac{15}{16}$

Amount of Copper in C $=$ Amount of Copper in A + Amount of Copper in B

$= \frac{3}{8} + \frac{11}{16}$

$= \frac{17}{16}$

So, Ratio of Gold and Copper in C,

$= \frac{15}{16} : \frac{17}{16}$

$= 15 : 17$

Hence, the correct option is (C).

54. (A + B)'s 1 day's work $= \frac{1}{10}$

C's 1 day's work $= \frac{1}{50}$

(A + B + C)'s 1 day's work $= \left(\frac{1}{10} + \frac{1}{50}\right) = \frac{6}{50} = \frac{3}{25}$.....(i)

A's 1 day's work = (B + C)'s 1 day's work .... (ii)

From (i) and (ii), we get:

$2 \times$ (A's 1 day's work) $= \frac{3}{25}$

A's 1 day's work $= \frac{3}{50}$

$\therefore$ B's 1 day's work $= \left(\frac{1}{10} - \frac{3}{50}\right) = \frac{2}{50} = \frac{1}{25}$

So, B alone could do the work in 25 days.

Hence, the correct option is (C).

55. Given:

2 men can complete the work in 48 hours

3 boys can complete the same work in 48 hours

We know that,

Work done $=$ Time $\times$ Efficiency

$M_1 \times T_1 = M_2 \times T_2$

Where M is the number of men

T is time

According to the question

$2M \times 48 = 3B \times 48$

$\Rightarrow \frac{M}{B} = \frac{3}{2}$

Total work $= 2 \times 3 \times 48 = 288$

The efficiency of 4 men and 2 boys

$= 4 \times 3 + 2 \times 2$

$= 12 + 4$

$= 16$

Time to complete the work $= \frac{288}{16}$

$= 18$ hours

$\therefore$ 4 men and 2 boys will complete the work in 18 hours.

Hence, the correct option is (C).

56. Given:

$4b^2 + \frac{1}{b^2} = 2$

$\Rightarrow (2b)^2 + \left(\frac{1}{b}\right)^2 + 4 - 4 = 2$

$\Rightarrow \left(2b + \frac{1}{b}\right)^2 - 4 = 2$

$\Rightarrow \left(2b + \frac{1}{b}\right)^2 = 6$

$\Rightarrow 2b + \frac{1}{b} = \sqrt{6}$

Take cube both sides

$\Rightarrow \left(2b + \frac{1}{b}\right)^3 = \left(\sqrt{6}\right)^3$

$\Rightarrow 8b^3 + \frac{1}{b^3} + 3 \times 2b \times \frac{1}{b}\left(2b + \frac{1}{b}\right) = 6\sqrt{6}$

$\Rightarrow 8b^3 + \frac{1}{b^3} + 6\sqrt{6} = 6\sqrt{6}$

$\Rightarrow 8b^3 + \frac{1}{b^3} = 6\sqrt{6} - 6\sqrt{6}$

$\Rightarrow 8b^3 + \frac{1}{b^3} = 0$

Hence, the correct option is (A).

57. $x^3 - 7x^2 + 11x - 5 \geq 0$

$\Rightarrow x^3 - 5x^2 - 2x^2 + 10x + x - 5 \geq 0$

$\Rightarrow x^2(x - 5) - 2x(x - 5) + 1(x - 5) \geq 0$

$\Rightarrow (x - 5)(x^2 - 2x + 1) \geq 0$

$\Rightarrow (x - 5)(x - 1)^2 \geq 0$

$\Rightarrow (x - 5)(x - 1)(x - 1) \geq 0$

So, $x = 1$ and 5

Equation satisfies at both the values, but the minimum value of these two $x = 1$

Hence, the correct option is (C).

58. If $(x-1)$ and $(x+1)$ are the factors y equation then,
$x-1=0$

$\Rightarrow x=1$

Put $x=1$, we get

$1+a-3+2+b=0$

$a+b=0$.....(i)

$\Rightarrow x+1=0$

$\Rightarrow x=-1$

Put $x=-1$, we get

$1-a-3-2+b=0$

$b-a=4$.......(ii)

After solving (i) and (ii), we get

$a=-2, b=2$

Hence, the correct option is (C).

59. Given:

Total time = 10 hours

Half journey at the rate of speed = 21 km/hr

and

Half journey at the rate of speed = 24 km/hr

We know that,

Time = $\frac{\text{Distance}}{\text{Speed}}$

Let distance = x

$\frac{\left(\frac{1}{2}\right)x}{21}+\frac{\left(\frac{1}{2}\right)x}{24}=10$

$\Rightarrow \frac{x}{21}+\frac{x}{24}=20$

$\Rightarrow 15x=168\times 20$

$\Rightarrow x=\left(\frac{160\times 20}{15}\right)=224$ km

Hence, the correct option is (B).

60. Given:

$x=a$ and $y=b$ is the solution of the equations $x+y=5$ and $2x-3y=4$

Then,

$a+b=5$.......(i)

$2a-3b=4$.......(ii)

Equation (i) multiplied by 3

$3a+3b=15$.....(iii)

Sum of equation (ii) and (iii)

$5a=19$

$\Rightarrow a=\frac{19}{5}$

Put $a=\frac{19}{5}$ in (i), we get

$\frac{19}{5}+b=5$

$\Rightarrow b=5-\frac{19}{5}$

$\Rightarrow b=\frac{25-19}{5}$

$\Rightarrow b=\frac{6}{5}$

$\therefore$ The value of $a=\frac{19}{5}$ and $b=\frac{6}{5}$.

Hence, the correct option is (D).

Mock Test 03

English

Q.1 Direction: A sentence is given in Active/Passive voice. Out of the four alternatives suggested, select the one which best expresses the same sentence in Active/Passive voice.

The gardener is watering the flowers.

A. The flowers is watered by the gardener
B. The flowers are watered by the gardener
C. The flowers are being watered by the gardener
D. The flowers were watered by the gardener

Q.2 Direction: A sentence is given in Active/Passive voice. Out of the four alternatives suggested, select the one which best expresses the same sentence in Active/Passive voice.

He had given her all the instructions.

A. She had been given all the instructions by him
B. She had been giving all the instructions by him
C. She has been given all the instructions by he
D. She had being given all the instructions by him

Q.3 Direction: Select the correct indirect form of the given sentence.

He said, "Please give me a glass of water".

A. He told to give a glass of water
B. He ordered to give him a glass of water
C. He requested to give him a glass of water
D. He requested to given him a glass of water

Q.4 Direction: Select the correct indirect form of the given sentence.

She said to me, "Will you buy the book?"

A. She asked me whether I will buy the book
B. She asked me whether I would buy the book
C. She asked me that I would buy the book
D. She asked me I would buy the book

Q.5 Direction: Complete the sentence by choosing the appropriate non-finite from the following.

"I wish ______ to your notice the faulty product you have recently launched."

A. bring **B.** to bringing
C. to brought **D.** to bring

Q.6 Direction: Fill in the blank to make the sentence in simple past tense.

There was a time when the national marriage rate was _______ too high.

A. fairly **B.** fair
C. rather **D.** None of the above

Q.7 Direction: Fill in the blank to make the sentence in simple past tense.

I expected to fail the exam, but I ______ after all.

A. passes **B.** passed
C. pass **D.** will be passing

Q.8 Choose the correctly punctuated sentence.

A. It is mentioned in the notice, all of us should read it
B. It is mentioned in the notice! all of us should read it
C. It is mentioned in the notice? all of us should read it
D. It is mentioned in the notice; all of us should read it

Q.9 Direction: Fill in the blanks with Interrogative Pronouns.

__________ did you finish the game?

A. where **B.** when
C. why **D.** None of the above

Q.10 Direction: In the following question, choose the word opposite in meaning to the given word.

Amicable

A. Hostile **B.** Friendly
C. Haughty **D.** Unpleasant

Q.11 Direction: In the following question, choose the word opposite in meaning to the given word.

Acrimonious

A. Devious **B.** Genial
C. Callous **D.** Benevolent

Q.12 Direction: Select the most appropriate antonym of the given word.

Eminent

A. Dishonesty **B.** Suspicious
C. Unknown **D.** Cleverness

Q.13 Direction: Fill in the blank with a correct preposition.

A prisoner was accused _______ murder.

[UPTET Paper - I, 2018]

A. of **B.** for **C.** to **D.** off

Ques (14-15):Direction: Read the following passage and answer the question that follows.

The world's oceans are warming at a rapidly increasing pace, new research shows, and the heat is having devastating effects on marine life and intensifying extreme weather. Last year, the oceans were warmer than any time since measurements began over 60 years ago, according to a study published Monday in the journal Advances in Atmospheric Sciences. While global surface temperature measurements go back farther in time, the measurement of ocean heat content is considered one of the most effective ways to show how fast Earth is warming because more than 90 percent of the heat trapped by greenhouse gases goes into the oceans. The warming of the oceans has widespread effects. It causes marine heat waves that kill fish and coral reefs, fuels hurricanes and coastal downpours, spawns harmful toxin-producing algal blooms and also contributes to heat waves on land, said study co-author Kevin Trenberth, with the National Center for Atmospheric Research.

In addition to increasing precipitation from tropical storms, rising ocean heat has consequences for sea level rise and for El Niño, Trenberth said. "In the Pacific, a consequence is El Niños being bigger, and with stronger droughts and floods around the world," he said. "Even more modest things in the tropical Indian Ocean, called the Indian Ocean Dipole, can lead to patterns of weather that contribute to the heat waves and bushfires in Australia." In late in 2019, these anomalies changed radically and it became very warm around Indonesia, creating major flooding in Jakarta and continuing the dry spell over Australia, he said. "This problem is not going to go away, it is getting worse. We are already seeing the impacts of warming on society, from rising sea levels to hotter waters to more intense storms and to more wild weather. "But this problem is solvable". "The first thing we need to do is use energy more wisely. Let's not waste energy for no reason. Let's make our cars, homes and workplaces more efficient. In the end, we will reduce greenhouse gas emissions and save money."

Q.14 The measurement of ocean heat content is considered one of the most effective ways to show how fast Earth is warming because:

A. It is easier to measure temperature of the oceans
B. More than 90 percent of the heat trapped by greenhouse gases goes into the oceans
C. It is causing a lot of change in weather pattern
D. It is a more refined science

Q.15 When did the study of measuring ocean temperature begin?

A. 60 years ago **B.** 60 years after
C. 61 years after **D.** 59 years ago

General Knowledge

Q.16 Who is the Chief Minister of Tamil Nadu?

A. Edappadi K. Palaniswami
B. Muthuvel Karunanidhi Stalin
C. O. Panneerselvam
D. K. Ponmudy

Q.17 Where is 'National Museum of India' located?

A. Chennai **B.** Bangalore
C. Patna **D.** Delhi

Q.18 What is the currency of Malaysia?

A. Malaysian Dinar **B.** Malaysian Dollars
C. Malaysian Euro **D.** Malaysian Ringgit

Q.19 Gazi Malik was the founder of which dynasty?

A. Tughlaq **B.** Khilji **C.** Sayyid **D.** Lodhi

Q.20 Fertile of soil can be improved by _______.

A. Adding living earthworms
B. Adding dead earthworms
C. Removing dead earthworms
D. Removing living earthworms and adding dead earthworms

Science

Q.21 A Person holds a bucket by applying a 10n force. He then moves a horizontal distance of 5m and climbs up a vertical distance of 10m. Find out the total work done by him?

A. 100 J **B.** 150 J **C.** 160 J **D.** 200 J

Q.22 What is the S.I. unit of Luminous Flux?

A. Lux **B.** Lumen
C. Candela **D.** None of the above

Q.23 Ethanoic Acid is commonly called _____ Acid.

A. Citric **B.** Hydrochloric
C. Acetic **D.** Nitric

Q.24 'Big-Bang theory' explains the origin of-

A. Mammals **B.** Ice-age
C. Universe **D.** Ocean

Q.25 Which of the following is an example of contact force?

A. Magnetic force **B.** Electrostatic force
C. Gravitational force **D.** Frictional force

Q.26 How low is the gravity on the Moon compared to Earth?

A. Eight times **B.** Four times
C. Six times **D.** Ten Times

Q.27 The bullet that has been fired from a gun can pierce a target due to its ________?

A. Heat energy **B.** Mechanical energy
C. Acceleration **D.** Kinetic energy

Q.28 The electric current flowing through a metallic wire is directly proportional to the potential difference V across its ends, provided its _________ remains the same.

A. voltage **B.** energy
C. charge **D.** temperature

Q.29 The Heisenberg Principle states that ___________.

A. no two electrons in the same atom can have the same set of four quantum numbers.
B. two atoms of the same element must have the same number of protons.
C. it is impossible to determine accurately both the position and momentum of an electron simultaneously.
D. electrons of atoms in their ground states enter energetically equivalent sets of orbitals singly before they pair up in any orbital of the set.

Q.30 A sound source is moving towards a stationary observer with $\frac{1}{10}$ of the speed of sound. The ratio of apparent to real frequency is:

A. $\frac{10}{9}$ **B.** $\frac{11}{10}$ **C.** $(\frac{11}{10})^2$ **D.** $(\frac{9}{10})^2$

Reasoning

Q.31 If in a certain code language,'HANGER' is written as 'MZGQDF', how 'ACTIVE' will be written in that language?

A. BZSUHD **B.** ZBSUDH
C. SBZDUH **D.** SUHBZD

Q.32 In a coded language "POWDER" is coded as "876214" and "CATCH" is coded as "50359", then what would be the code for "WATER"?

A. 60213 **B.** 60314 **C.** 60123 **D.** 60315

Q.33 Unscramble the word: OPSOESRCR

A. PRECOSSOR **B.** PROCESSOR
C. PROSSECOR **D.** PORCESSOR

Q.34 Unscramble the word: RAAEHWRD

A. DARHWARE **B.** HARDWARE
C. WARDHARE **D.** RADHWARE

Q.35 Arrange the words given below in a meaningful sequence.

1. Death
2. Marriage
3. Education
4. Birth
5. Funeral

A. 5, 1, 2, 3, 4 **B.** 4, 2, 3, 1, 5
C. 4, 3, 2, 5, 1 **D.** 4, 3, 2, 1, 5

Q.36 Arrange the words given below in a meaningful sequence.

1. Presentation
2. Recommendation
3. Arrival
4. Discussion
5. Introduction

A. 5, 3, 4, 1, 2 **B.** 3, 5, 4, 2, 1
C. 3, 5, 1, 4, 2 **D.** 5, 3, 1, 2, 4

Q.37 Direction: The sheet of paper shown in the figure (x) given on the left hand side, in each problem, is folded to form a box. Choose from amongst the alternatives (1), (2), (3) and (4), the boxes that are similar to the box that will be formed.

Choose the box that is similar to the box formed from the given sheet of paper (x).

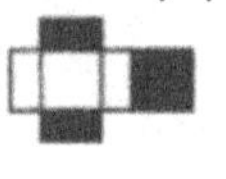

(x) (1) (2) (3) (4)

A. (1) and (3) only **B.** (2) and (4) only
C. (3) and (4) only **D.** (1) and (4) only

Q.38 Direction: The sheet of paper shown in the figure (x) given on the left hand side, in each problem, is folded to form a box. Choose from amongst the alternatives (1), (2), (3) and (4), the boxes that are similar to the box that will be formed.

Choose the box that is similar to the box formed from the given sheet of paper (x).

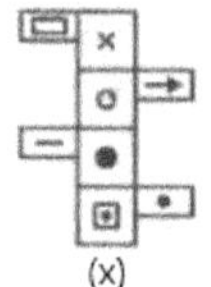

(x) (1) (2) (3) (4)

A. (1) and (2) only **B.** (1) and (3) only
C. (1), (3) and (4) only **D.** (1), (2), (3) and (4)

Q.39 Direction: Study the following graph and answer the question that follow.

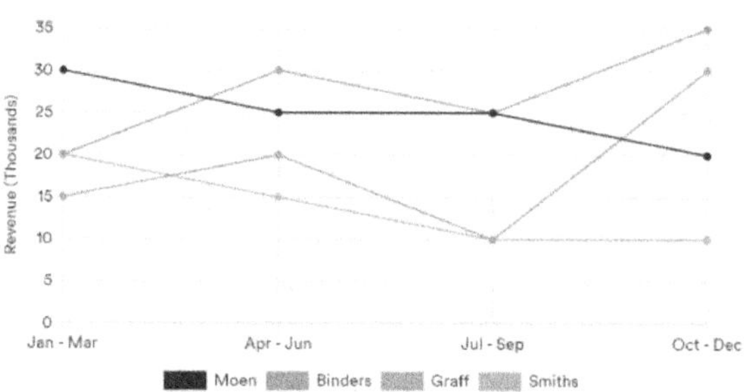

What was the percentage change in revenue for Graff from quarter 1 to quarter 4?

A. 25% **B.** 30% **C.** 50% **D.** 100%

Q.40 Direction: Study the following graph and answer the question that follow.

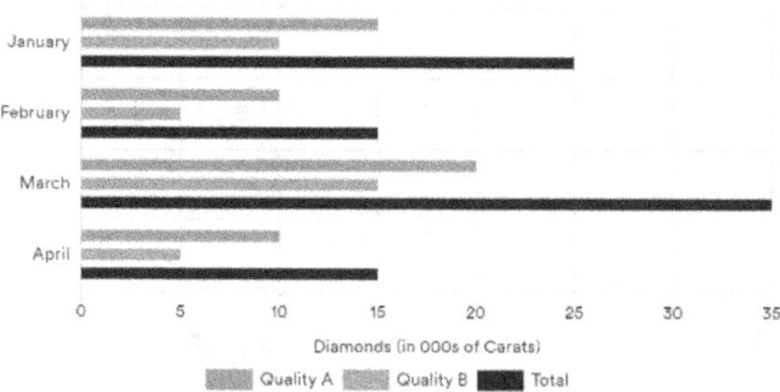

from April, the production of Quality A diamonds is expected to increase by 12% per month cumulatively. What is the predicted figure for June in carats.

A. 11, 200 carats **B.** 12, 544 carats
C. 12, 400 carats **D.** 14, 049 carats

Mathematics

Q.41 If some electric toy cars are bought at Rs. 650 and sold at Rs. 780 each, then what is the profit percentage?

A. 15% **B.** 25% **C.** 20% **D.** 22%

Q.42 If a person deposits Rs. 1,000 in the bank for 2 years at 10% compound interest rate, find the amount at the end of the year.

A. Rs. 1,200 **B.** Rs. 1,210
C. Rs. 1,100 **D.** Rs. 1,150

Q.43 Find the percentage change in area if the length of the rectangle is increased by 10% and breadth is decreased by 20%.

A. 12% decrease **B.** 12% increase
C. 8% decrease **D.** 8% increase

Q.44 A chord 10 cm long is drawn in a circle of diameter 26 cm. The perpendicular distance of the chord from center is:

A. 12 cm **B.** 5 cm **C.** 7 cm **D.** 8 cm

Q.45 If cosec A = sec(36° + 5A), find the value of cos(10A)?

A. -1 **B.** $\frac{1}{2}$ **C.** 0 **D.** 1

Q.46 Find the total surface area of a sphere whose radius is 1.4 cm.

A. 28.44 cm² **B.** 27.54 cm²
C. 26.32 cm² **D.** 24.64 cm²

Q.47 The ratio of a and b is 5 : 6, then find the value of $\frac{(6a+5b)}{(2a-b)}$.

A. 15 **B.** 20 **C.** 25 **D.** 12

Q.48 Find the value of the expression $x^4 - 3x^3 + 4x^2 - 3x + 5$ at x = 3.

A. 12 **B.** 34 **C.** 32 **D.** 48

Q.49 Find the mode of 3, 6, 5, 4, 3, 4, 3, 7, 3, 1, 3.

A. 3 **B.** 7 **C.** 5 **D.** 4

Q.50 A can complete $\frac{3}{7}$ work in 9 days and B can do $\frac{1}{3}$ of the same work in 14 days. In how many days they complete the work working together?

A. 14 days **B.** 11 days **C.** 10 days **D.** 9 days

Q.51 Which one is correct option:

$$(3x+2)^3 - (2x^2+3)$$

A. $27x^3 + 52x^2 + 36x + 5$
B. $27x^3 - 52x^2 + 36x - 5$
C. $2x^3 - 52x^2 + 63x - 5$
D. $7x^3 + 28x^2 - 36x - 5$

Q.52 What will come in place of the question mark?

$(1.44 \times 1.69)^{\frac{1}{2}} + (5.76 + 0.49)^{\frac{1}{2}} \times (0.125)^{\frac{-2}{3}} = ?$

A. 11.56 **B.** 22.96 **C.** 35.97 **D.** 46.66

Q.53 75% of x + 20% of 90 = x .Find the value of x.

A. 64 **B.** 72 **C.** 37 **D.** 48

Q.54 By selling an item for Rs. 25, shopkeeper losses as much percent as the cost price of the item. The cost price of the item is:

A. Rs. 60 **B.** Rs. 45 **C.** Rs. 55 **D.** Rs. 50

Q.55 If sinθ = $\frac{3}{5}$, then find the value of tanθ.

A. $\frac{4}{5}$ **B.** $\frac{3}{5}$ **C.** $\frac{3}{4}$ **D.** $\frac{4}{3}$

Q.56

A man completes a certain journey by a car. If he covered 30% of the distance at the speed of 20kmph, 60% of the distance at 40km/h and the remaining of the distance at 10 kmph, his average speed is:

A. 25 km/h **B.** 28 km/h **C.** 30 km/h **D.** 33 km/h

Q.57 Given that $x^8 - 47x^4 + 1 = 0$, x > 0. What is the value of $(x^3 - x^{-3})$?

A. $8\sqrt{5}$ **B.** $6\sqrt{5}$ **C.** $9\sqrt{5}$ **D.** $2\sqrt{5}$

Q.58 The factors of $x^{39} - x^{32} + x^{17} - 1$ is/are:

A. Only (x - 1) **B.** Only (x + 1)
C. (x - 1) and (x + 1) **D.** None of the above

Q.59 Solve: $\frac{7}{x} + \frac{8}{y} = 2, \frac{2}{x} + \frac{13}{y} = 22$

A. x = $\frac{-1}{2}$ and y = $\frac{1}{2}$ **B.** x = $\frac{-1}{2}$ and y = $\frac{-1}{2}$
C. x = $\frac{1}{2}$ and y = $\frac{1}{2}$ **D.** x = $\frac{1}{2}$ and y = $\frac{-1}{2}$

Q.60 In a class test, a student must secure 30% marks to pass. Amit gets 225 marks, but fails by 15 marks. What are the maximum marks for the test?

A. 650 **B.** 775 **C.** 600 **D.** 800

// Smart Answer Sheet //

Correct Percentage of students who answered correctly. Skipped Percentage of students who skipped.

Q.	Ans.	Correct	Skipped	Q.	Ans.	Correct	Skipped	Q.	Ans.	Correct	Skipped	Q.	Ans.	Correct	Skipped	Q.	Ans.	Correct	Skipped	Q.	Ans.	Correct	Skipped
1	C	24.56 %	7.02 %	11	B	7.02 %	59.65 %	21	A	10.53 %	54.38 %	31	C	12.28 %	52.63 %	41	C	26.32 %	54.38 %	51	A	14.04 %	54.38 %
2	A	28.07 %	59.65 %	12	C	15.79 %	59.65 %	22	B	21.05 %	56.14 %	32	B	38.6 %	54.38 %	42	B	24.56 %	54.39 %	52	A	15.79 %	54.39 %
3	C	26.32 %	59.64 %	13	A	12.28 %	59.65 %	23	C	26.32 %	56.14 %	33	B	36.84 %	54.39 %	43	A	17.54 %	54.39 %	53	B	19.3 %	54.38 %
4	B	29.82 %	59.65 %	14	B	19.3 %	57.89 %	24	C	33.33 %	56.14 %	34	B	42.11 %	54.38 %	44	A	14.04 %	54.38 %	54	D	15.79 %	54.39 %
5	D	15.79 %	59.65 %	15	A	35.09 %	59.65 %	25	D	29.82 %	56.14 %	35	D	28.07 %	54.39 %	45	C	17.54 %	54.39 %	55	C	22.81 %	54.38 %
6	C	10.53 %	59.65 %	16	B	24.56 %	56.14 %	26	C	24.56 %	56.14 %	36	C	22.81 %	54.38 %	46	D	15.79 %	54.39 %	56	A	15.79 %	54.39 %
7	B	28.07 %	59.65 %	17	D	29.82 %	57.9 %	27	D	29.82 %	56.14 %	37	A	12.28 %	54.39 %	47	A	28.07 %	54.39 %	57	A	17.54 %	54.39 %
8	D	17.54 %	59.65 %	18	D	8.77 %	57.9 %	28	D	10.53 %	56.14 %	38	B	15.79 %	54.39 %	48	C	24.56 %	54.39 %	58	A	21.05 %	54.39 %
9	B	29.82 %	59.65 %	19	A	12.28 %	57.9 %	29	C	17.54 %	56.14 %	39	D	1.75 %	54.39 %	49	A	29.82 %	54.39 %	59	A	14.04 %	52.63 %
10	A	17.54 %	59.65 %	20	A	28.07 %	57.89 %	30	A	5.26 %	56.14 %	40	B	15.79 %	54.39 %	50	A	14.04 %	54.38 %	60	D	15.79 %	54.39 %

//Hints and Solutions//

1. The above-given sentence is in active voice.

We need to change it into passive voice.

The following steps will be followed for converting the given active voice into passive voice:-

The subject 'The gardener' will become the object of the passive voice.

The object 'the flowers' will become the subject of the passive voice.

Hence, the correct option is (C).

2. The given sentence is in Past Perfect Tense and Active Voice.

The rule for changing a Past Perfect Tense from Active voice to Passive voice:

Interchange the object and subject with each other, i.e. object of the active sentence become the subject of the passive sentence.

Hence, the correct option is (A).

3. The given sentence is an example of an imperative sentence.

While changing the narration of an imperative sentence, we need to follow the given steps.

The conjunction 'to' should be used in place of a comma (,) and inverted commas (" ") 'said to' is changed into 'ordered/ requested/ advised/ urged/ forbade, etc.'

The notion of the given sentence is 'request'. Hence, 'reporting verb' 'said' will be changed into 'requested'.

Hence, the correct option is (C).

4. An interrogative sentence has a question.

The rule for changing Direct Speech to Indirect Speech:

Remove the commas and inverted commas.

Will Changes to would.

Do not use that in the sentence of indirect speech.

The reporting verb said/said to is changed in asked, demanded, ordered, enquired as per the nature of the sentence.

Remove the question mark in the sentence of Indirect speech.

If a direct speech sentence begins with an auxiliary verb/helping verb, the joining clause should be if or whether.

Hence, the correct option is (B).

5. The correct answer is to bring.

Remember, the non-finite infinitive is formed by placing 'to' before the base verb. In option (A) 'to' is missing. In options (B) and (C) the base verb changes form. Remember, an infinitive is the simplest form of the verb as it is exactly the same as the base verb and is usually preceded by 'to.' In a sentence, the infinitive always comes with a main verb.

Hence, the correct option is (D).

6. 'Rather' is used to a positive and comparative degree and it is followed by 'too'.

'Fairly' is used to a positive degree and it is not followed by 'too'.

'Fair' is an adjective.

Thus, the word 'rather' should be used to make the sentence grammatically correct.

Hence, the correct option is (C).

7. The given sentence is in simple past form. Simple past tense tells us about an action completed in the past time.

For writing sentence in simple past form, general rule that followed:

Subject + 2nd form of the verb + object. All other given options are inappropriate. So, the correct answer will be:

I expected to fail the exam, but I passed after all.

Hence, the correct option is (B).

8. A correct answer is an option (D), i.e. It is mentioned in the notice; all of us should read it.

The semicolon; is used to join two complete sentences or independent clauses.

Example: Your mother looks worried; she has checked your report card.

Hence, the correct option is (D).

9. The correct answer is:

When did you finish the game?

Hence, the correct option is (B).

10. Amicable: Characterized by friendliness and absence of discord.

Hostile: Showing or feeling opposition or dislike; unfriendly.

Friendly: Kind and pleasant.

Haughty: Arrogantly superior and disdainful.

Unpleasant: publicly display (a work of art or item of interest) in an art gallery or museum or at a trade fair.

Hence, the correct option is (A).

11. Acrimonious: (typically of speech or discussion) angry and bitter.

Genial: friendly and cheerful.

Devious: clever but not honest or direct.

Callous: showing or having an insensitive and cruel disregard for others.

Benevolent: well meaning and kindly.

Hence, the correct option is (B).

12. The most appropriate antonym of the given word 'Eminent' is 'Unknown'.

Unknown- Not known or familiar.

Dishonesty- Not honest.

Suspicious- Making you feel that something illegal is happening or that something is wrong.

Cleverness- Ability to understand and learn quickly and easily.

Hence, the correct option is (C).

13. 'of' is the correct preposition for the blank because it expresses the relationship between a part and a whole, here it forms a relationship between the prisoner and murder.

Look at the following points-

'for' is wrong because it means in support of or in favour of.

'to' means expressing motion in the direction of.

'off' means away from the place in question.

Hence, the correct option is (A).

14. The measurement of ocean heat content is considered one of the most effective ways to show how fast Earth is warming because more than 90 percent of the heat trapped by greenhouse gases goes into the oceans.

As stated in the passage that the measurement of ocean heat content is considered one of the most effective ways to show how fast Earth is warming because more than 90 percent of the heat trapped by greenhouse gases goes into the oceans.

Hence, the correct option is (B).

15. 60 years ago the study of measuring ocean temperature begins.

As stated in the passage that last year, the oceans were warmer than any time since measurements began over 60 years ago, according to a study published Monday in the journal Advances in Atmospheric Sciences.

Hence, the correct option is (A).

16. Muthuvel Karunanidhi Stalin is an Indian Tamil politician serving as the 8th and current Chief Minister of Tamil Nadu.

He has also served as president of the Dravida Munnetra Kazhagam party since 28 August 2018.

Dravida Munnetra Kazhagam is a political party from India, which has a major influence on the state of Tamil Nadu and the union territory of Puducherry.

Hence, the correct option is (B).

17. The National Museum of India is located in New Delhi. The National Museum was established in the Durbar Hall of Rashtrapati Bhavan on August 15, 1949. The museum was formally inaugurated in its present premises on 18 December 1960. Museums are the storehouses of our cultural heritage and their collections save historical, technical and other material things from being destroyed.

Hence, the correct option is (D).

18. The Malaysian Ringgit (formerly the Malaysian Dollar) is the currency of Malaysia. It is divided into 100 sen (cents). Its currency code is MYR. Ringgit is issued by Bank Negara Malaysia. Ringgit means 'toothed' in the Malay language, which was actually used for the silver-pointed (toothed) Spanish dollar widely prevalent during Portuguese colonization in the 16th and 17th centuries.

Hence, the correct option is (D).

19. Gazi Malik or Tughlaq was the founder of the Tughlaq dynasty who ascended the throne of Delhi on 8 September 1320 under the name Ghiyasuddin Tughlaq. He was the first Sultan of the Delhi Sultanate to add the word 'Ghazi' (slayer of infidels) to his name. It thwarted the Mongol invasion a total of 29 times and established a balance (Ram-e-Miyan) between restraint, strictness and softness in its policies.

Hence, the correct option is (A).

20. Fertility of soil can be improved by adding living earthworms. Worms help to increase the amount of air and water that gets into the soil. They break down organic matter, like leaves and grass into things that plants can use. When they eat, they leave behind castings that are a very valuable type of fertilizer. Earthworms are like free farm help.

Hence, the correct option is (A).

21. Given,

$s = 5m$, $F = 10N$, and $\theta = 90°$

Work done is given by, $W_1 = F s \cos\theta$

$= 10 \times 5 \times \cos 90°$

$= 0$

In the case of vertical motion, the angle between force and displacement is 0°

Here, $F = 10N$, $s = 10m$, and $\theta = 0°$

So, work done, $W_2 = 10 \times 10 \times \cos 0 = 100$ J

Therefore, the total work done = $W_1 + W_2$

= 100 J

Hence, the correct option is (A).

22. Luminous flux, in SI units, is measured in the lumen (lm).

It is a measurement of energy released in the form of visible light from a light-producing source.

Luminous flux is often a criterion of light bulb comparison. Luminous flux is also known as luminous power.

Hence, the correct option is (B).

23. Ethanoic Acid is commonly called Acetic Acid.

Ethanoic acid (CH_3COOH) belongs to the group of carboxylic acids and is commonly called acetic acid.

It is slightly heavier than water with a density of 1.05 g/cm^3.

Ethanoic acid is widely used in many industries.

Commercially it is used in the manufacturing of esters, vinegar, and many polymeric materials.

It is used as an anti-fungal agent.

Hence, the correct option is (C).

24. Big Bang Theory is about the origin of the Universe. It suggests that about 1370 crore (13.7 billion) years ago, all matter and energy in the universe was concentrated into an area smaller than an atom. At this instant, matter, energy, space and time were not existent.

Hence, the correct option is (C).

25. Friction is a force that opposes the relative tangential motion between two planes. The value of the force of friction depends on the force normal between the two planes. There are two types of friction: static friction and kinetic friction.

Hence, the correct option is (D).

26. Moon has six times low gravity as compared to the gravity on Earth.

As the mass of the moon is $\frac{1}{100}$ times the mass of Earth and radius of the moon is $\frac{1}{4}$ times the radius of the Earth.

As a result, the gravitational attraction on the moon is about one-sixth when compared to that of the Earth.

Hence, the correct option is (C).

27. The bullet that has been fired from a gun can pierce a target due to its kinetic energy.

The kinetic energy of a body by the virtue of its motion is known as kinetic energy. Any moving object can do work. Thus, a bullet that is fired from a gun can pierce a target due to its kinetic energy.

Hence, the correct option is (D).

28. The electric current flowing through a metallic wire is directly proportional to the potential difference V across its ends, provided its temperature remains the same.

$$V = IR$$

The law of Ohm has sometimes been described as, "for a conductor in a given state, the electromotive force is proportional to the generated current."

That is, "does not vary with the current strength." the resistance, the electromotive force (or voltage) ratio applied to the current.

The word "in a given state" is generally understood as meaning "at a constant temperature," because "in a given state" resistivity.

Since current conduction is related to the conducting body's Joule heating, the temperature of a conducting body can change when it carries a current, according to Joule's first law.

Hence, the correct option is (D).

29. Heisenberg's Uncertainty Principle states that there is inherent uncertainty in the act of measuring a variable of a particle. Commonly applied to the position and momentum of a particle, the principle states that the more precisely the position is known the more uncertain the momentum is and vice versa.

Hence, the correct option is (C).

30. Let the speed of sound in air be $\overline{v}$

i.e $v_{\text{sound}} = v$ Thus the velocity of source $v_{\text{source}} = \frac{v}{10}$

Let v and v' be the real frequency of the source and apparent frequency heard by the observer respectively.

Using Doppler effect when the source is moving towards the stationary observer:

$$v' = v\left[\frac{v}{v-\frac{v}{Tin}}\right]$$

$$= \frac{10}{9}v$$

$$= \frac{v'}{v}$$

$$= \frac{10}{9}$$

Hence, the correct option is (A).

31. The pattern for the code is as follows,

Here the letter at second and fifth position are decreased by one or we can say one step behind and placed at their respective same place, while the letter at first and third position are interchanged their place also the value will be decreased by one or we can say one step behind. same pattern will be for letter at fourth and sixth.

Same pattern will be follow in given word,

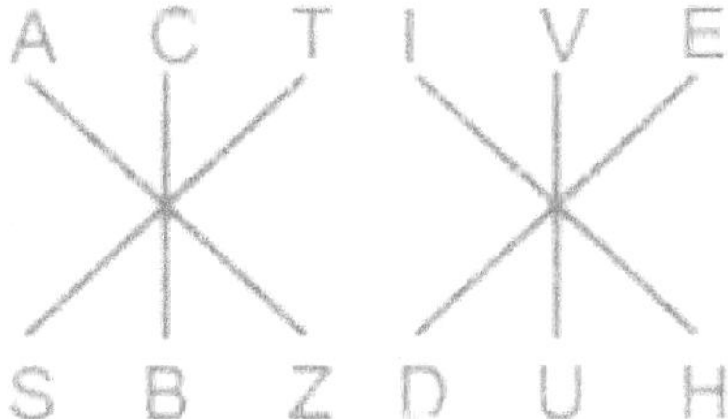

Hence, the correct option is (C).

32. Given:

Letters	P	O	W	D	E	R
Code	8	7	6	2	1	4

And,

Letters	C	A	T	C	H
Code	5	0	3	5	9

Similarly,

By following the coded logic:

Letters	W	A	T	E	R
Code	6	0	3	1	4

Hence, the correct option is (B).

33. The correct word is PROCESSOR.

A processor is an integrated electronic circuit that performs the calculations that run a computer. A processor performs arithmetical, logical, input/output (I/O) and other basic instructions that are passed from an operating system (OS). Most other processes are dependent on the operations of a processor.

Hence, the correct option is (B).

34. The correct word is HARDWARE.

Hardware is the physical components that a computer system requires to function. It encompasses everything with a circuit board that operates within a PC or laptop; including the motherboard, graphics card, CPU (Central Processing Unit), ventilation fans, webcam, power supply, and so on.

Hence, the correct option is (B).

35. First of all a man is born then he takes education; after this he is married. Then after sometimes he dies. After death the order is of Funeral. The correct order is-

4. Birth

3. Education

2. Marriage

1. Death

5. Funeral

Hence, the correct option is (D).

36. The correct order is:

3. Arrival

5. Introduction

1. Presentation

4. Discussion

2. Recommendation

Hence, the correct option is (C).

37. The figure (x) is similar to Figure (1). So, when the sheet shown in figure (x) is folded to form a box (cuboid), then the two rectangular-shaded faces lie opposite to each other, two rectangular white faces lie opposite to each other and the two square shaped faces (one shaded and one white) lie opposite to each other. Clearly, the cuboids shown in figures (2) and (4) cannot be formed as in each of the two cuboids the two shaded rectangular faces appear adjacent to each other. So, only the cuboids in figures (1) and (3) can be formed.

Hence, the correct option is (A).

38. The figure (x) is similar to the Figure (4). So, when a cube is formed by folding the sheet shown in figure (x), then and are the two faces and these two faces lie opposite to each other. Also, the face bearing the ('x') sign lies opposite to the face bearing the black circle and the face bearing the white circle lies opposite to the face bearing the square (having a dot inside it). Now, the cubes in figures (2) and (4) consist of faces which are not formed when the sheet in figure (x) is folded. Hence, these two cubes are not, formed. Therefore, only the cubes in figures (1) and (3) are formed.

Hence, the correct option is (B).

39. Step 1: Get Graff's revenue in the first quarter of the year: 15,000

Step 2: Get Graff's revenue in the fourth quarter of the year: 30,000

Step 3: Subtract the most recent quarter from the oldest:

30,000 - 15,000 = 15,000

Step 4: Divide this by the first quarter figure, the 'oldest' figure.

$\frac{15{,}000}{15{,}000} \times 100$ = 100%

Hence, the correct option is (D).

40. Step 1: April production = 10, 000 carats

Step 2: To calculate May production, you need to increase by 12%.

May production $= 10{,}000 \times 1.12$ (12% increase)

$= 11{,}200$ carats

Step 3: To calculate June production, you need to increase the May figure by 12%.

June production $= 11{,}200 \times 1.12$ (12% increase)

= 12,544 carats

Hence, the correct option is (B).

41. Given:

C.P = Rs. 650

S.P = Rs. 780

Profit percentage = $\frac{(Profit)}{(C.P)} \times 100$

C.P = Rs. 650

S.P = Rs. 780

Profit = S.P - C.P

Profit = Rs. (780 - 650)

= Rs. 130

Profit percentage = $\frac{130}{650} \times 100$

⇒ 20%

∴ The profit percentage is 20%.

Hence, the correct option is (C).

42. Given:

If a person deposits Rs. 1,000 in the bank for 2 years at 10% compound interest rate.

Amount = Principal(P)$(1 + \frac{R}{100})^T$

R = rate, T = time

According to the question,

Amount = $1000(1 + \frac{10}{100})^2$

⇒ 1210

∴ The amount at the end of the year Rs. 1210.

Hence, the correct option is (B).

43. Given:

Increase in length is 10%.

Decrease in breadth is 20%.

Formula used:

Area of rectangle = L × B

where,

L is Length of the rectangle and B is Breadth of the rectangle.

Let the length and breadth of the rectangle be L and B respectively.

Area of rectangle = LB

According to the question, we have

Increase in Length is

⇒ (100 + 10)% of L

⇒ $\frac{110L}{100}$

⇒ 1.1L

Decrease in Breadth is

⇒ (100 - 20)% of B

⇒ $\frac{80B}{100}$

⇒ 0.8B

Area of the new rectangle is

⇒ Area = 1.1L × 0.8B

⇒ Area = 0.88LB

Now, Percentage change is

⇒ Percentage change = $\{\frac{(0.88LB - LB)}{LB}\} \times 100$

⇒ Percentage change = $(\frac{-0.12LB}{LB}) \times 100$

⇒ Percentage change = -12%

⇒ Percentage change = 12% decrease

∴ The percentage change in area is 12% decrease.

Hence, the correct option is (A).

44. Given:

Diameter of circle = 26 cm

Radius OA = 13 cm

Length of chord AB = 10 cm

Perpendicular drawn from the center of the circle to the chord, bisects the chord.

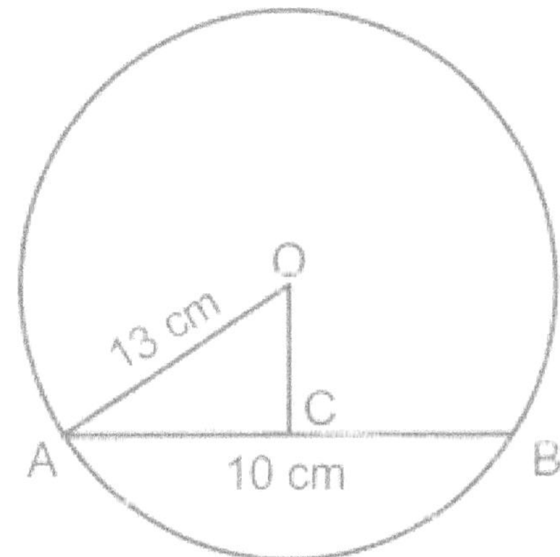

AC = $\frac{AB}{2}$

= $\frac{10}{2}$

= 5 cm ....(⊥ drawn from the center of the circle, bisects the chord)

Using Pythagorean Theorem,

$OA^2 = OC^2 + AC^2$

$\Rightarrow 13^2 = OC^2 + 5^2$

$\Rightarrow 169 = OC^2 + 25$

$\Rightarrow OC^2 = 144$

$\Rightarrow$ OC = 12 cm

∴ The perpendicular distance of the chord from center is 12 cm.

Hence, the correct option is (A).

45. Given:

cosec A = sec(36° + 5A)

sec(90° - θ) = cosec θ

cos 90° = 0

cosec A = sec (36° + 5 A)

⇒ cosec A = sec {90° – (54°- 5A)}

⇒ cosec A = cosec (54° – 5A)

⇒ A = 54° – 5A

⇒ 6A = 54°

⇒ A = 9°

⇒ cos (10A) = cos 90° = 0

∴ The value of cos(10A) is 0.

Hence, the correct option is (C).

46. Given:

Radius is 1.4 cm

Total surface area of sphere = $4\pi r^2$

where,

r is Radius of circle

According to the question, we have

The radius of the sphere is 1.4 cm

Total surface area of the sphere is

$\Rightarrow 4\pi r^2$

$\Rightarrow 4 \times (\frac{22}{7}) \times (1.4) \times (1.4)$

$\Rightarrow 4 \times 22 \times 0.2 \times 1.4$

$\Rightarrow 24.64\ cm^2$

∴ The surface area of the sphere is 24.64 cm^2.

Hence, the correct option is (D).

47. Given:

The ratio of a and b = 5 : 6

Let the ratio of a and b be 5x and 6x respectively.

According to the question,

$\frac{(6a+5b)}{(2a-b)}$

$\Rightarrow \frac{[(6\times 5x)+(5\times 6x)]}{[(2\times 5x)-(1\times 6x)]}$

$\Rightarrow \frac{(30x+30x)}{(10x-6x)}$

$\Rightarrow \frac{60x}{4x}$

⇒ 15

∴ The required value of $\frac{(6a+5b)}{(2a-b)}$ is 15.

Hence, the correct option is (A).

48. Given:

$x^4 - 3x^3 + 4x^2 - 3x + 5$ and x = 3

$(3)^4 - 3(3)^3 + 4(3)^2 - 3(3) + 5$

⇒ 81 - 81 + 36 - 9 + 5

⇒ 27 + 5

⇒ 32

Hence, the correct option is (C).

49. Given:

The given data = 3, 6, 5, 4, 3, 4, 3, 7, 3, 1, 3

Arrange the number in order. The number which appears most often is the mode.

Arrange the numbers 1, 3, 3, 3, 3, 3, 4, 4, 5, 6, 7

Here only 3 repeats

⇒ 3 is the number that appears most often (5 times)

∴ The mode is 3.

Hence, the correct option is (A).

50. Given:

Time taken by A to complete $\frac{3}{7}$ of the work = 9 days.

Time taken by B to complete $\frac{1}{3}$ of the work = 14 days.

A complete $\frac{3}{7}$ of the work in 9 days.

Time taken by A to complete the whole work = $\frac{9}{(\frac{3}{7})}$

= 21 days

B complete $\frac{1}{3}$ work in 14 days.

Time taken by B to complete the whole work = $\frac{14}{\left(\frac{1}{3}\right)}$

= 42 days

Total work = L.C.M. (21, 42)

= 42 units

Combined efficiency of A and B = $(\frac{42}{21}) + (\frac{42}{42})$

⇒ Combined efficiency of A and B = 2 + 1

= 3 units/day

Time taken by A and B to complete the whole work = $\frac{42}{3}$

⇒ Time taken by A and B to complete the whole work = 14 days

∴ The time taken by A and B to complete the work is 14 days.

Hence, the correct option is (A).

51. Given:

$$(3x+2)^3 - (2x^2+3)$$

Using formula,

$$(a+b)^3 = (a^3+b^3+3a^2b+3ab^2)$$

$$(3x+2)3 = [(3x)^3+(2)^3+3(3x)^2(2)+3(3x)(2)^2]$$

$$\Rightarrow (3x+2)^3 = [27x^3+8+54x^2+36x]$$

According to question:

$$(27x^3+8+54x^2+36x)-(2x^2+3)$$

$$\Rightarrow 27x^3+5+52x^2+36x$$

$$\Rightarrow (27x^3+8+54x^2+36x)-(2x^2+3)$$

$$= 27x^3+5+52x^2+36x$$

$$= 27x^3+52x^2+36x+5$$

Hence, the correct option is (A).

52. Given:

$(1.44 \times 1.69)^{\frac{1}{2}} + (5.76 + 0.49)^{\frac{1}{2}} \times (0.125)^{\frac{-2}{3}} = ?$

$\Rightarrow (1.2 \times 1.3) + (6.25)^{\frac{1}{2}} \times (\frac{1}{0.125})^{\frac{2}{3}} = ?$

$\Rightarrow (1.2 \times 1.3) + (2.5) \times (\frac{1}{0.125})^{\frac{2}{3}} = ?$

$\Rightarrow 1.56 + 2.5 \times (\frac{1}{0.5})^2 = ?$

⇒ 1.56 + 2.5 × 4 = ?

⇒ ? = 11.56

∴ The required value is 11.56.

Hence, the correct option is (A).

53. Given:

75% of x + 20% of 90 = x

$\Rightarrow x = (\frac{75}{100}) \times x + (\frac{20}{100}) \times 90 = (\frac{3}{4})x + 18$

$\Rightarrow x - (\frac{3}{4})x = 18$

$\Rightarrow \frac{x}{4} = 18$

⇒ x = 72

∴ The Value of x is 72.

Hence, the correct option is (B).

54. Given:

The shopkeeper sold item = Rs. 25

Formula used:

Selling Price = $\frac{CostPrice \times (100 - loss\%)}{100}$

Let the cost price be Rs. x

Loss percent $= x\%$

Now,

$$25 = \frac{x \times (100-x)}{100}$$

$$\Rightarrow 2500 = 100x - x^2$$

$$\Rightarrow x^2 - 100x + 2500 = 0$$

$$\Rightarrow x^2 - 50x - 50x + 2500 = 0$$

$$\Rightarrow x(x-50) - 50(x-50) = 0$$

$$\Rightarrow (x-50)(x-50) = 0$$

$$\Rightarrow x = Rs. 50$$

∴ The cost price is Rs. 50

Hence, the correct option is (D).

55. Given:

sinθ = $\frac{3}{5}$

In a right-angled triangle

sinθ = $\frac{Perpendicular}{hypotenuse}$

tanθ = $\frac{perpendicular}{base}$

Pythagoras theorem

$H^2 = P^2 + B^2$

⇒ $B^2 = 5^2 - 3^2$

⇒ $B^2 = 25 - 9$

⇒ $B^2 = 16$

⇒ B = 4

⇒ $\tan\theta = \frac{3}{4}$

∴ The value of $\tan\theta$ is $\frac{3}{4}$.

Hence, the correct option is (C).

56. Let the total distance be 100 km.

Average speed

$$= \frac{\text{Total distance covered}}{\text{Time taken}}$$

$$= \frac{100}{\frac{30}{20}+\frac{60}{40}+\frac{10}{10}}$$

$$= \frac{100}{\frac{3}{2}+\frac{3}{2}+1}$$

$$= \frac{100}{\frac{3+3+2}{2}}$$

$$= \frac{100\times2}{8}$$

$$= \frac{100 \times 2}{8}$$

= 25 km/h

Hence, the correct option is (A).

57. Given:

$x^8 - 47x^4 + 1 = 0$

⇒ $x^8 + 1 = 47x^4$

On dividing by x^4 and adding 2 on both sides:

$$\Rightarrow x^4 + \frac{1}{x^4} + 2 = 47 + 2$$

$$\Rightarrow \left(x^2 + \frac{1}{x^2}\right)^2 = 49$$

$$\Rightarrow \left(x^2 + \frac{1}{x^2}\right) = 7$$

On adding 2 on both sides:

$$\Rightarrow \left(x^2 + \frac{1}{x^2} - 2\right) = 7 - 2$$

$$\Rightarrow \left(x - \frac{1}{x}\right)^2 = 5$$

$$\Rightarrow \left(x - \frac{1}{x}\right) = \sqrt{5}$$

On cubing both sides:

$$\Rightarrow \left(x^3 - \frac{1}{x^3}\right) - 3 \times (x) \times \frac{1}{x}\left(x - \frac{1}{x}\right) = 5\sqrt{5}$$

$$\Rightarrow \left(x^3 - \frac{1}{x^3}\right) - 3 \times \sqrt{5} = 5\sqrt{5}$$

$$\Rightarrow \left(x^3 - \frac{1}{x^3}\right) = 5\sqrt{5} + 3\sqrt{5}$$

$$= 8\sqrt{5}$$

Hence, the correct option is (A).

58. At x = 1,

The given polynomial, $1^{39} - 1^{32} + 1^{17} - 1$

= 1 - 1 + 1 - 1

= 0

Therefore (x - 1) is a factor of $x^{39} - x^{32} + x^{17} - 1$.

At x = -1,

The given polynomial, $(-1)^{39} - (-1)^{32} + (-1)^{17} - 1$

= -1 -1 -1 -1

= -4

Thus, (x-1) is not a factor.

Hence, the correct option is (A).

59. Let $\frac{1}{x}$ = a and

$\frac{1}{y}$ = b

Now the equations become:

7a + 8b = 2 and

2a + 13b = 22

a = -2 and b = 2

Now putting the value of a and b in $\frac{1}{x}$ and $\frac{1}{y}$ we get,

x = $\frac{-1}{2}$ and y = $\frac{1}{2}$

Hence, the correct option is (A).

60. Given:

Passing marks percentage = 30%

Marks obtained by the student = 225

Fails by marks = 15

Maximum marks percentage = 100%

Amit gets 225 marks and fails by 15 marks

⇒ Pass marks = 225 + 15

⇒ 240 Marks

Now, according to question, percentage marks need to pass = 30%

⇒ 30% = 240 Marks

⇒ 100% = $\left(\frac{240}{30}\right)$ × 100 Marks

⇒ 800 Marks

∴ Required Maximum marks = 800.

Hence, the correct option is (D).

Mock Test 04

English

Ques (1-2):Direction: In the following question, a sentence has been given in Active/Passive Voice. Out of the four alternative suggested, select the one which best expresses the same sentence in Passive/Active Voice.

Q.1 The burglar destroyed several items in the room. Even the carpet has been torn.

A. Several items destroyed in the room by the burglar. Even the carpet he has torn.
B. Several items in the room were destroyed by the burglar. Even the carpet was torn.
C. Including the carpet, several items in the room have been torn by the burglar.
D. The burglar, being destroyed several items in the room, also carpet has torn.

Q.2 We must respect the elders.

A. The elders deserve respect from us.
B. The elders must be respected.
C. The elders must respected.
D. Respect the elders we must.

Ques (3-4):Direction: Change the Narration:

Q.3 Raja said to Mohan, "Are you going home today?"

A. Raja asked Mohan if he is being gone home that day.
B. Raja asked Mohan to he is going home that day.
C. Raja asked Mohan if he was going home that day.
D. Raja asked Mohan if he is going home that day.

Q.4 He says, "My friend came yesterday."

A. He says that his friend had came the day before.
B. He said that his friend had came the day before.
C. He says that his friend came the day before.
D. He said that his friend had come the day before.

Ques (5-6):Direction: Select the most appropriate word to fill in the blank.

Q.5 I have been waiting for you _____ seven o'clock.

A. at **B.** for **C.** on **D.** since

Q.6 In case of an emergency, the pilot will ______ the floor lighting on the plane.

A. deactivate **B.** actuate
C. halt **D.** stop

Q.7 Direction: Choose the word that can substitute the given sentence.

Not fit to eat

A. Inevitable **B.** Potable
C. Gourmet **D.** Inedible

Q.8 Direction: Select the meaning of the given idiom.

A red letter day

A. A sorrowful day
B. A day when one feels lazy
C. A day that is pleasantly noteworthy or memorable
D. Most dangerous day of one's life

Q.9 Direction: Which of phrases given below each sentence should replace the phrase printed in bold type to make the grammatically correct?

There are not many men who are so famous that they are frequently referred to by their **short names** only:

A. initials **B.** signatures
C. pictures **D.** middle names

Q.10 Which of the following sentences is correct?

A. Nothing happens ever by chance
B. Nothing ever happens by chance
C. Nothing happen by chance
D. Nothing happens never by chance

Ques (11-12):Direction: Select the most appropriate synonym of the given word.

Q.11 Determined

A. Willing **B.** Agreed
C. Resolved **D.** Ready

Q.12 Disrupt

A. Break **B.** End
C. Conclude **D.** Build

Q.13 Direction: Select the most appropriate antonym of the given word.

Expertise

A. Impatient **B.** Conscious
C. Polite **D.** Incompetence

Q.14 Choose the word that is opposite in meaning to the given word.

Enormous

A. Huge **B.** Uncover
C. Diminish **D.** Petite

Q.15 Complete the sentence by choosing the appropriate non-finite from the following.

"I watched the mild scolding with a ______ frown."

A. to worry **B.** worry **C.** worried **D.** worries

General Knowledge

Q.16 Who was the first Indian to become the Junior Wimbledon Champion?

A. Ramanathan Krishnan
B. Premjit Lal
C. Vijay Amritraj
D. Leander Paes

Q.17 Indian Army Day is celebrated on ______ of every year.

A. 15th January **B.** 11th January
C. 13th January **D.** 22th January

Q.18 Which Indian city, famous for its lagoons, is known as the Venice of the East?

A. Hyderabad **B.** Jaipur
C. Mumbai **D.** Alappuzha

Q.19 Who founded the Slave Dynasty?

[RRB (NTPC), 2020]

A. Iltutmish
B. Qutbuddin Aibak
C. Ghiyas ud din Balban
D. Razia Sultana

Q.20 Expand the term SWIFT.

A. Society for Worldwide International Financial Telecommunications
B. Society for Worldwide Interbank Financial Telecommunications
C. Society for Worldwide International Financial Transfers
D. Society for Worldwide Interbrain Fiscal Transactions

Science

Q.21 Newton's first law of motion is not valid for _____.

A. Inertial frame
B. Non-inertial frame
C. Both Inertial and non-Inertial frame
D. None of the above

Q.22 The earth is divided in to what number of time zones?

A. 20 **B.** 42 **C.** 90 **D.** 24

Q.23 The SI unit of 'g' is same as that of acceleration, that is ___.

A. ms^1 **B.** ms^{-2} **C.** ms^2 **D.** ms^{-1}

Q.24 A porter lifts a luggage of 15 kg from the ground and puts it on his head 1.5 m above the ground. Calculate the work done by him on the luggage. ($g = 10\ ms^{-2}$)

A. 200 J **B.** 225 J **C.** 275 J **D.** 250 J

Q.25 Which of the following is poor conductor of Electricity despite being a metal?

A. Lead **B.** Nickel **C.** Copper **D.** Tin

Q.26 Two particles of same mass having kinetic energies 400 J and 900 J, then ratio of their momentum will be:

A. 2 : 3 **B.** 2 : 4 **C.** 4 : 3 **D.** 4 : 9

Q.27 Which of the following compounds of carbon does not consist of ions?

A. $CHCl_3$ **B.** $CaCO_3$
C. $NaHCO_3$ **D.** Ca_2C

Q.28 The force of friction always ______ the applied forces.

A. Adds up to **B.** Opposes
C. Reflects **D.** Conducts

Q.29 Metals, except Al and Zn, react with oxygen to form ______ oxides.

A. acidic **B.** neutral
C. amphoteric **D.** basic

Q.30 What is the relationship between the frequency and the pitch of a sound wave?

A. Higher the frequency, higher the pitch
B. Lower the frequency, higher the pitch
C. Pitch is not dependent on the frequency
D. None of the above

Reasoning

Q.31 In a certain code language, "PANIC" is written as "71832" and "TRAIN" is written as "94138". How is "CAPTAIN" written in that code language?

A. 5432158 **B.** 2711938 **C.** 2179138 **D.** 1729388

Q.32 In a certain code language, CAD is coded as CZB and MAT is coded as SZL, which word would be coded as PET?

A. SOD **B.** DSO **C.** ODS **D.** SDO

Q.33 Direction: The sheet of paper shown in the figure (x) given on the left hand side, in each problem, is folded to form a box. Choose from amongst the alternatives (A), (B), (C) and (D), the boxes that are similar to the box that will be formed.

Select the dice that can be formed by folding the given sheet along the lines.

(x) (A) (B) (C) (D)

A. Only (A) **B.** Only (B) and (C)
C. Only (A) and (B) **D.** Only (C)

Q.34 Arrange the words given below in a meaningful sequence.

1. Elephant
2. Cat
3. Mosquito
4. Tiger
5. Whale

A. 5, 3, 1, 2, 4 **B.** 3, 2, 4, 1, 5
C. 1, 3, 5, 4, 2 **D.** 2, 5, 1, 4, 3

Q.35 Arrange the words given below in a meaningful sequence

1. Yarn
2. Plant
3. Saree
4. Cotton
5. Cloth

A. 2, 4, 5, 1, 3 **B.** 2, 4, 3, 5, 1
C. 2, 4, 1, 5, 3 **D.** 2, 4, 5, 3, 1

Q.36 Unscramble the word: SPGINLE

A. SGPINEL **B.** SPIGNEL
C. SIGPENL **D.** SGIPELN

Q.37 Unscramble the word: FAULOBUS

A. FABULOUS **B.** FBLUOUSA
C. FLABOUSU **D.** FLBAOUUS

Q.38 Direction: The sheet of paper shown in the figure (x) given on the left hand side, in each problem, is folded to form a box. Choose from amongst the alternatives (1), (2), (3) and (4), the boxes that are similar to the box that will be formed.

Choose the box that is similar to the box formed from the given sheet of paper (x).

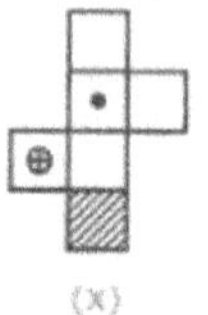

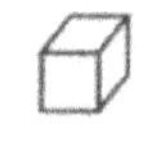

(X) (1) (2) (3) (4)

A. (1) only **B.** (1), (2) and (3) only
C. (2) and (3) only **D.** (1), (2), (3) and (4)

Q.39 Direction: Study the following table and answer the question that follow.

Drink	Price	Primary School	Secondary School
Juice	£1.50	21	45
Water	£0.80	12	115
Coca-Cola	£1.20	33	51
Sprite	£1.20	45	45
Milk	£1.40	9	12
Chocolate Milk	£1.90	30	32

What was the daily turnover for the drink vender in the Secondary School?

A. £352.30 **B.** £247.05 **C.** £452.90 **D.** £345.50

Q.40 Direction: Study the following table and answer the question that follow.

	Year 1($000s)	Year 2($000s)	Year 3($000s)
Turnover	1,345	1,547	1,701
Cost of Sale	847	932	1,055
Gross Profit	498	615	647
Administration Expenses	149	138	97
Distribution Costs	235	201	194
Net Profit	114	276	356
Tax 20%	23	55	71
Profit after Tax	91	221	284

If the company had wanted to increase its turnover by 45% from Year 1 to Year 3, by what percentage did it miss that target?

A. 12.8% **B.** 14.8% **C.** 13.8% **D.** 15.8%

Mathematics

Q.41 Rate of petrol first decreased by 20% and in next month increased by 45%. Find the net % change in the price of petrol.

A. 18% **B.** 24% **C.** 16% **D.** 32%

Q.42 A car covers a distance of 4 km in 6 minutes. If it's speed is decreased by 2 km/hr, then find the time taken by the car to cover same distance.

A. $\frac{120}{19}$ min **B.** $\frac{2}{19}$ min **C.** 45 min **D.** $\frac{60}{19}$ min

Q.43 Find the value of x, if x = $\frac{(Tan^2 30° + Cosec^2 45° + Sin^2 90°)}{(1 + Sin^2 45° + Sec^2 30°)}$.

A. $\frac{17}{20}$ **B.** $\frac{20}{17}$ **C.** $\frac{15}{17}$ **D.** $\frac{13}{20}$

Q.44 Solve: 345678 × 999999?

A. 345677653422 **B.** 354677654322
C. 345677654322 **D.** 346577564322

Q.45 If $x^2 - 2x + 1 = 0$, find the value of $x^3 + (\frac{1}{x^3})$.

A. 2 **B.** −2 **C.** −3 **D.** 3

Q.46 A and B undertook to do a piece of work for Rs. 4,500. A alone could do it in 8 days and B alone in 12 days. With the assistance of C they finished the work in 4 days. Then C's share of money is (in rupees).

A. 2,250 **B.** 1,500 **C.** 750 **D.** 375

Q.47 The angles of a quadrilateral are in the ratio 4 : 7 : 6 : 13. What is the difference between the smallest and the greatest angles of the quadrilateral?

A. 102° **B.** 108° **C.** 117° **D.** 156°

Q.48 What will be the compound interest on a principal of Rs. 8000 at the rate of 5% per annum compounded annually for three years?

A. Rs. 331 **B.** Rs. 1200 **C.** Rs. 1225 **D.** Rs. 1261

Q.49 Sum of mode and median of the data 12, 15, 11, 13, 18, 11, 13, 12, 13 is:

A. 25 **B.** 26 **C.** 31 **D.** 36

Q.50 A, B and C invested some money for an year. If their profit is divided in the ratio 4 : 11 : 7 and half the difference of shares of A and C is Rs. 2100, then find the total profit they made?

A. Rs. 30,200 **B.** Rs. 30,800
C. Rs. 37,500 **D.** Rs. 31,800

Q.51 Two numbers are in ratio 7 : 5. If 1 is subtracted from the first number and 3 is subtracted from the second number, their ratio becomes 3 : 2. What is the second number?

A. 35 **B.** 25 **C.** 45 **D.** 55

Q.52 Find the value of x if $\tan 3x = \sin 45^\circ \cos 45^\circ + \sin 30^\circ$

A. 20° **B.** 15° **C.** 12° **D.** 30°

Q.53 If the circumradius of an equilateral triangle ABC be 8 cm, then the height of the triangle is:

A. 12 cm **B.** 16 cm **C.** 8 cm **D.** 7 cm

Q.54 The angle between the two sides of the triangle having length 6 cm and 8 cm is 60°, find the third side of the triangle.

A. $\sqrt{52}$ cm **B.** $\sqrt{26}$ cm **C.** 12 cm **D.** 13 cm

Q.55 If two factors of $x^4 - x^3 - 19x^2 - 11x + 30$ is x+2 and x-1, then find out another two factors of this polynomial.

A. (x – 4) and (x + 3) **B.** (x – 3) and (x + 5)
C. (x + 4) and (x – 3) **D.** (x + 3) and (x – 5)

Q.56 Solve for x and y in

$5y + 2x = 9$ (1)

$2y + 2x = 6$ (2)

A. y = 1, x = 2 **B.** y = 2, x = 1
C. y = -2, x = +1 **D.** None of the above

Q.57 The value of $\omega^{15} + \omega^{20} + \omega^{25}$ is:

A. 1 **B.** 0 **C.** 2 **D.** 3

Q.58 Wages of 20 boys for 15 days is Rs 9000. If the daily wage of man is one and half times that of a boy, how many men must work for 30 days to earn Rs 13500.

A. 10 men **B.** 2 men **C.** 6 men **D.** 8 men

Q.59 If factors of polynomial $5x^3 + 4x^2 - 60x + k = 0$ is $2 < x < 5$, then which of the option is true.

A. $-144 < k < 9$ **B.** $-5 < k < 5$
C. $-3 < k < 7$ **D.** $-5 < k < 6$

Q.60 The diameter of the base of a cone-shaped tent is 24 meters and its height is 16 meters. What is the area of the canvas required to erect it?

A. $\frac{5180}{7}$ m^2 **B.** $\frac{5280}{7}$ m^2 **C.** $\frac{4180}{7}$ m^2 **D.** $\frac{4380}{7}$ m^2

// Smart Answer Sheet //

Correct Percentage of students who answered correctly. Skipped Percentage of students who skipped.

Q.	Ans.	Correct	Skipped	Q.	Ans.	Correct	Skipped	Q.	Ans.	Correct	Skipped	Q.	Ans.	Correct	Skipped	Q.	Ans.	Correct	Skipped	Q.	Ans.	Correct	Skipped
1	B	51.15 %	1.69 %	11	C	47.96 %	1.44 %	21	B	46.27 %	1.04 %	31	C	50.19 %	1.84 %	41	C	82.96 %	0.0 %	51	A	62.77 %	1.43 %
2	B	49.98 %	1.75 %	12	A	65.34 %	1.38 %	22	D	67.27 %	1.69 %	32	D	50.69 %	1.01 %	42	A	45.43 %	1.63 %	52	B	43.57 %	1.16 %
3	C	45.52 %	1.19 %	13	D	55.79 %	1.12 %	23	B	66.28 %	1.76 %	33	C	10.56 %	3.55 %	43	B	76.99 %	0.0 %	53	A	30.72 %	3.24 %
4	C	49.1 %	1.58 %	14	D	66.55 %	1.16 %	24	B	16.57 %	3.88 %	34	B	85.1 %	0.0 %	44	C	57.08 %	1.55 %	54	A	65.25 %	1.53 %
5	D	48.88 %	1.7 %	15	C	41.96 %	1.24 %	25	A	81.72 %	0.0 %	35	C	76.68 %	0.0 %	45	A	50.19 %	1.31 %	55	D	67.97 %	1.84 %
6	B	65.97 %	1.1 %	16	A	19.2 %	4.12 %	26	A	49.16 %	1.73 %	36	B	64.92 %	1.12 %	46	C	14.87 %	3.89 %	56	A	50.18 %	1.25 %
7	D	43.93 %	1.15 %	17	A	86.41 %	0.0 %	27	A	12.15 %	4.53 %	37	A	88.94 %	0.0 %	47	B	63.04 %	1.41 %	57	B	48.88 %	1.97 %
8	C	18.79 %	3.81 %	18	D	50.17 %	1.92 %	28	B	83.97 %	0.0 %	38	D	16.89 %	4.31 %	48	D	57.39 %	1.05 %	58	A	61.41 %	1.08 %
9	A	82.1 %	0.0 %	19	B	32.36 %	4.42 %	29	D	40.58 %	1.74 %	39	A	65.33 %	1.32 %	49	B	62.17 %	1.05 %	59	A	51.03 %	1.09 %
10	B	46.94 %	1.93 %	20	B	81.35 %	0.0 %	30	A	53.16 %	1.13 %	40	A	65.56 %	1.04 %	50	B	13.65 %	4.94 %	60	B	57.66 %	1.33 %

//Hints and Solutions//

1. Several items in the room were destroyed by the burglar. Even the carpet was torn.

Above it contains two sentence one is in Past Simple sentence (Active Voice) and Second sentence is in Present Perfect tense (Passive Voice). We change First sentence according to voice rule and second sentence also be change according to same rule but tense of both sentence become same.

Hence, the correct option is (B).

2. The elders must be respected by us.

The given sentence contains one of Model verb (Model Verb = will, shall, can, may, might, could, might, must, would). It is in active voice.

Hence, the correct option is (B).

3. Raja asked Mohan if he was going home that day.

An interrogative sentence has a question.

The rule for changing Direct Speech to Indirect Speech:

- The given sentence is in Present Continuous Tense.
- Present Continuous Tense changes to Past Continuous tense.
- Remove the commas and inverted commas.
- Are Changes to is (according to the subject 'he').
- Do not use that in the sentence of indirect speech.
- The reporting verb said/said to is changed in asked, demanded, ordered, enquired as per the nature of the sentence.
- Remove the question mark in the sentence of Indirect speech.
- 'Today' changes to 'that day.'
- If a direct speech sentence begins with an auxiliary verb/helping verb, the joining clause should be if or whether.

Hence, the correct option is (C).

4. He says that his friend came the day before.

The given sentence is in Simple Past Tense.

The rule for changing Direct Speech to Indirect Speech:

- The time expression does not change if the reporting verb is in the present tense or future tense.
- Simple Past Tense Changes to Past Perfect Tense.
- 'Yesterday' in the Direct Speech changes to 'the day before' in the indirect speech.
- Remove the inverted comma's from the direct speech and replace them with an appropriate conjunction.
- The second person of direct speech changes as per the object of reporting speech.

Hence, the correct option is (C).

5. I have been waiting for you since seven o'clock.

Let us see the usage of given prepositions:

- Here, 'since' is correct because it is used to refer to a specific point in time.
- 'At' is incorrect because it is used to say where something/somebody is or where something happens.
- 'For' is incorrect because it is used for a period of time.
- Use 'on' when something is touching the surface of something.

Hence, the correct option is (D).

6. In case of an emergency, the pilot will actuate the floor lighting on the plane.

The given sentence is talking about doing something with floor lighting in an emergency.

The use of the word 'emergency' in the sentence indicates a serious, unexpected, and often dangerous situation requiring immediate action.

Therefore, the most appropriate word to be filled in the blank is 'actuate.'

'Actuate' means to cause a machine or device to operate.

Hence, the correct option is (B).

7. Let us explore the given options:

'Inedible' means not fit or suitable for eating.

'Inevitable' means certain to happen, unavoidable.

'Potable' means safe to drink.

'Gourmet' is a person with refined tastes in food and wine.

Hence, the correct option is (D).

8. The most appropriate meaning of the given idiom 'A red letter day' is "A day that is pleasantly noteworthy or memorable".

A red-letter day: a special, happy, and important day that you will always remember

- Example: The day I first set foot in America was a red-letter day for me.

Hence, the correct option is (C).

9. There are not many men who are so famous that they are frequently referred to by their initials only.

Initials are the capital letters that begin each word of a name.

Hence, the correct option is (A).

10. Nothing ever happens by chance.

- In a sentence, the verb is used according to person and number.
- In the case of the following words, the verbs used will be singular.

- Each, every/everyone, someone/somebody, none/nobody/nothing, one, any, many a, more than one, etc.

Hence, the correct option is (B).

11. Determined: wanting to do something very much and not allowing anyone or any difficulties to stop you.

Resolved: to find an answer to a problem.

Willing: to be happy to do something if it is needed.

Agreed: to have the same opinion as somebody/something.

Ready: prepared and suitable for fast activity.

Hence, the correct option is (C).

12. Disrupt: to stop something happening as or when it should.

Break: to separate, or make something separate, into two or more pieces.

End: termination of a state or situation.

Conclude: bring or come to an end.

Build: become stronger or more intense.

Hence, the correct option is (A).

13. Expertise: a high level of knowledge or skill.

Incompetence: lack of ability to do something successfully or as it should be done.

Impatient: easily annoyed by someone's mistakes or because you have to wait.

Conscious: to notice that a particular thing or person exists or is present.

Polite: behaving in a way that is socially correct and shows an understanding of and care for other people's feelings.

Hence, the correct option is (D).

14. Enormous that is opposite in meaning to the given is petite.

Enormous: very big in size or in amount.

Petite: a woman who is petite is short and attractively thin.

Hence, the correct option is (D).

15. Remember, the non-finite participle is formed by adding '-ing', '-d, '-ed, '-en, '-t or '-n' to the base verb (worry-worried). In the other options, the verbs are the wrong form for a participle.

Hence, the correct option is (C).

16. In 1954, Young Ramanathan Krishnan became the first Junior Wimbledon Champion. He was also the first Asian to do so.

- Winner of the Wimbledon Junior Championship in 1979 and French Open Junior title in 1979. Ranked World number 1 among juniors in 1979.
- Won the Grand Prix Tournament in 1984 at France.
- Received the Arjuna award in 1978-79 and Padma Shri in 1998

Hence, the correct option is (A).

17. Indian Army Day is celebrated on15th January of every year.

Indian Army Day is celebrated in recognition of Field Marshal Kodandera M. Cariappa's taking over as the first Commander-in-Chief of the Indian. Field Marshal K. M. Cariappa took over from General Francis Bucher, the last British Commander-in-Chief of India, on 15 January 1949. Army Day is a grand celebration of India's military might and its unsung personnel. The Army Day parade is typically held at Parade Ground, Delhi Cantonment.

Hence, the correct option is (A).

18. Alappuzha is famous for its lagoons and is known as the Venice of the East. Allapuzha is located in Kerala. The city is locally known as Alleppey. It is known for its serene backwaters and the scenic beauty of backwater.

Hence, the correct option is (D).

19. Qutbuddin Aibak was slave of Muhammad Ghori.

When Ghori was assassinated, Aibak declared himself Sultan of Delhi in 1206 and his dynasty was recognized as Slave Dynasty. Slave dynasty rule from 1206-90 and became the first Muslim dynasty ruled over India. Qutbuddin Aibak, Iltutmish, Razia Sultan, Balban were eminent kings of this dynasty. He began the construction of Qutb Minar in Delhi. He reigned till his death in 1210.

Dynasty ended when Jalaluddin Firuz Khilji overthrew the last Mamluk ruler Muizuddin Qaiqabad in 1290.

Hence, the correct option is (B).

20. Society for Worldwide Interbank Financial Telecommunications is the full form of SWIFT. Society for Worldwide Interbank Financial Telecommunications (SWIFT) is a member-owned cooperative that provides safe and secure financial transactions for its members. Established in 1973, SWIFT uses a standardized proprietary communications platform to facilitate the transmission of information about financial transactions.

Hence, the correct option is (B).

21. Newton's First Law: It states that a body continues in its state of rest or uniform motion in a straight line until and unless an unbalanced force acts on it.

It is valid only in an inertial frame of reference.

Newton's First Law is also known as the law of inertia.

Inertia is the property of the inability of a body to change its position of rest or uniform motion in a straight line.

Mass is the measure of the inertia of a body.

Inertial Frame: A frame of rest or uniform motion. Ex- A bus moving with constant acceleration.

Non-inertial frame: A-frame which is accelerating either in a linear fashion or rotating around its axis. Ex- A car turning with constant speed at corners.

Newton's First law of motion says about the state of rest or uniform motion and is valid on only Inertial Frame.

Thus newton's laws are not valid in a non-inertial frame.

Hence, the correct option is (B).

22. Time zones Coordinated Universal Time or UTC is the primary time standard by which the world regulates clocks and time. It is within about 1 second of mean solar time at 0° longitude and is not adjusted for daylight saving time. It is effectively a successor to Greenwich Mean Time (GMT). There are countries having their separate time zones. Based o the UTC time zone the world is divided into 24 time zones.

Hence, the correct option is (D).

23. Whenever an object falls towards the earth, it gains an acceleration. This is called acceleration due to gravity (g). Thus its Si unit is similar to acceleration, i.e, ms^{-2}.

Hence, the correct option is (B).

24. Work done by a force is equal to the scalar or dot product of the force and the displacement of the body.

Given,

Mass of luggage (m) = 15 kg and displacement (s) = 1.5 m

Work done can be calculated as,

$\Rightarrow W = F \times s = mg \times s$

$\Rightarrow W = 15\ kg \times 10\ ms^{-2} \times 1.5\ m$

$\Rightarrow W = 225\ J$

Hence, the correct option is (B).

25. Lead is a chemical element with the symbol Pb (from the Latin plumbum) and atomic number 82.

It is a heavy metal that is denser than most common materials.

Lead is soft and malleable, and also has a relatively low melting point.

Lead is a poor conductor of electricity.

Hence, the correct option is (A).

26. Given:

$K.E_1 = 400\ J$, $K.E_2 = 900\ J$

$m_1 = m_2 = m$

The relation between the momentum and the kinetic energy is given by:

$$p = \sqrt{2mK \cdot E}$$

$$\therefore p \propto \sqrt{K.E}$$

Or, $\frac{P_1}{P_2} = \sqrt{\frac{KE_1}{KE_2}}$

$$= \sqrt{\frac{400}{900}}$$

$$= \frac{2}{3}$$

Thus, ratio = 2 : 3

Hence, the correct option is (A).

27. Carbon always forms covalent compounds by sharing its electrons with other atoms. Now, in covalent bonding, the two electrons shared by the atoms are attracted to the nucleus of both atoms and neither atom completely loses or gains electrons as in ionic bonding. So the compounds in which all the atoms are directly attached to C-atom, contain covalent bonding and no ionic bond.

In $CHCl_3$, all the three chlorine atoms are bonded covalently to the carbon atom, not to the hydrogen atom. So $CHCl_3$ is a covalent compound and does not consist of ions.

Hence, the correct option is (A).

28. The force of friction always opposes the applied force.

The Force that opposes the motion of an object is called frictional force.

Friction is caused by the irregularities on the two surfaces in contact.

Friction depends on the nature of surfaces in contact.

The Force of friction is greater if a rough surface is involved.

Hence, the correct option is (B).

29. Most of the metals react with oxygen to form metal oxides.

For example: magnesium reacts with oxygen to form magnesium oxide. The reaction involved is:

$2Mg(s) + O_2(g) \rightarrow 2MgO(s)$

The metal oxide form alkali solution when dissolved in water. This solution turns red litmus paper to blue. Hence, these metal oxides are basic in nature.

Hence, the correct option is (D).

30. A high pitch sound corresponds to a high frequency sound wave and a low pitch sound corresponds to a low frequency sound wave.

Hence, the correct option is (A).

31. The logic is:

P	A	N	I	C
7	1	8	3	2

and,

T	R	A	I	N
9	4	1	3	8

Similarly,

C	A	P	T	A	I	N
2	1	7	9	1	3	8

Hence, the correct option is (C).

32. The pattern for the code is as follows,

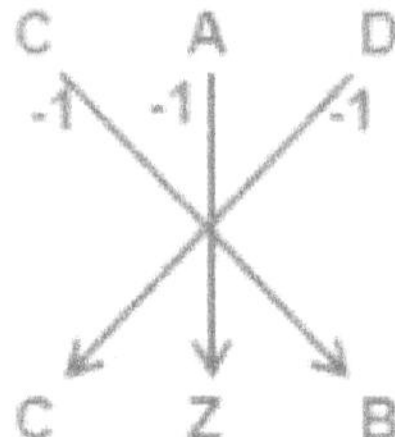

And,

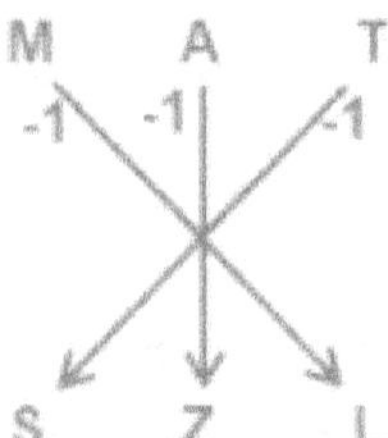

Similarly,

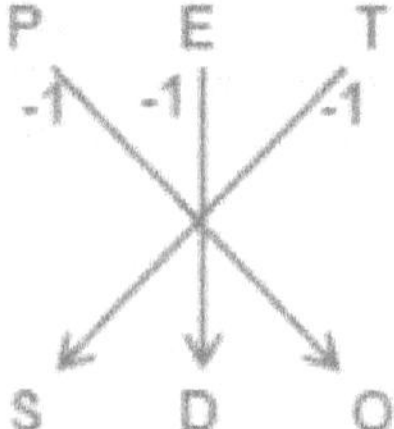

Hence, the correct option is (D).

33. When the dice that can be formed by folding the given sheet along the lines, the following numbers will be opposite to each other is shown below:

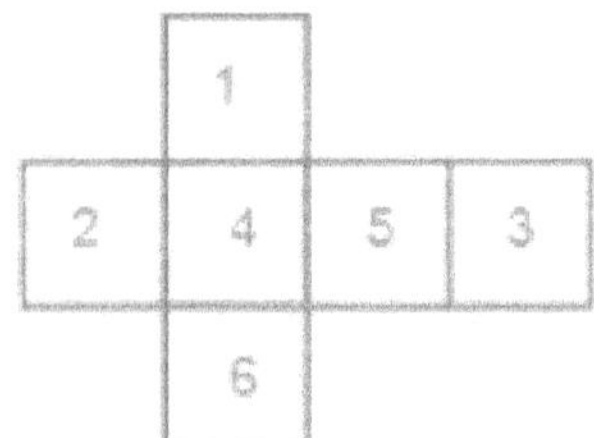

1 is opposite to 6.

2 is opposite to 5.

3 is opposite to 4.

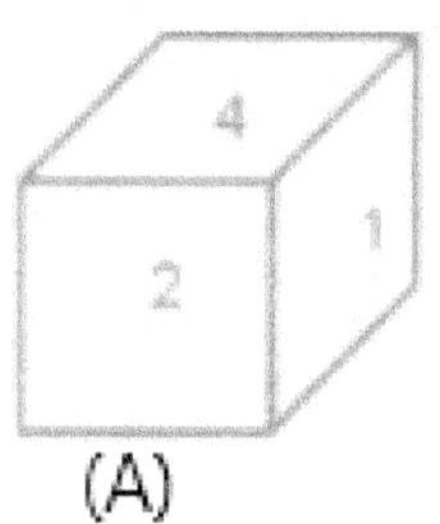

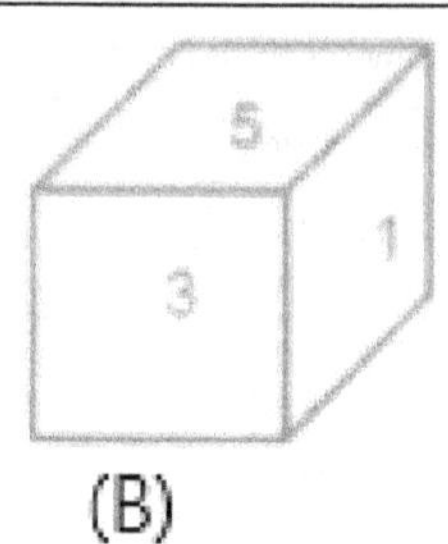

So, the dice (A) and (B) are the only possible dice formed after folding.

Hence, the correct option is (C).

34. The correct order is:

3. Mosquito

2. Cat

4. Tiger

1. Elephant

5. Whale

Hence, the correct option is (B).

35. The correct order is:

2. Plant

4. Cotton

1. Yarn

5. Cloth

3. Saree

Hence, the correct option is (C).

36. The correct word is SPIGNEL.

SPIGNEL: An aromatic plant of the parsley family with white flowers, found on mountains in Europe.

Hence, the correct option is (B).

37. The correct word is FABULOUS.

FABULOUS: the meaning of fabulous is someone or something that is imaginary, hard to believe, or very good.

Hence, the correct option is (A).

38. The figure (x) is similar to the Form (5). So, when the sheet in figure (x) is folded to form a cube, then the face bearing a dot appears opposite to a blank face, the face bearing a '+' sign appears opposite to another blank face and the face bearing a circle appears opposite to the third blank face. Clearly, all the four cubes shown in figures (1), (2), (3) and (4) can be formed.

Hence, the correct option is (D).

39. Step 1: This is a simple multiplication question. We start by calculating the turnover:

Turnover = number of people x price of drink

Juice: $45 \times £1.50 = £67.50$

Water: $115 \times £0.80 = £92$

Coca-Cola: $51 \times \varepsilon 1.20 = £61.20$

Sprite: $45 \times \varepsilon 1.20 = £54$

Milk: $12 \times £1.40 = £16.80$

Chocolate Milk: $32x£1.90 = £60.80$

Step 2: Calculate total turnover by adding these all together which equals £352.30.

Hence, the correct option is (A).

40. Step 1: Calculate the turnover in Year 3 would have been

$$1{,}345 \times 1.45 = 1{,}950.25$$

Step 2: Calculate the nominal difference between the forecast and the actual

$$1{,}950.25 - 1{,}701 = 249.25$$

Step 3: Convert the nominal difference into the percentage change

$\frac{249.25}{1950.25} \times 100$ = 12.8%

Hence, the correct option is (A).

41. Given:

Decrement in the rate of petrol = 20%.

Increment in the rate of petrol = 45%.

Convert the percent into fractions

⇒ 20% = $\frac{1}{5}$

⇒ 45% = $\frac{9}{20}$

Let the price of Petrol be Rs. 100

According to the question,

⇒ Final price of petrol = 100 × $\frac{4}{5} \times \frac{29}{20}$

⇒ Final price of petrol = 116

⇒ Per cent change in the rate of petrol = $\frac{(116 - 100)}{100} \times 100$

⇒ Per cent change in the rate of petrol = 16%

∴ The net % change in the price of petrol is 16%

Hence, the correct option is (C).

42. Given:

Distance = 4 km

Time = 6 minutes

Distance = Speed × Time

Speed = $\frac{Distance}{Time}$

Time = 6 minutes

⇒ Time = $(\frac{6}{60})$ hr = $(\frac{1}{10})$ hr

⇒ Speed = $\frac{Distance}{Time} = \frac{4}{\left(\frac{1}{10}\right)}$

⇒ Speed = 40 km/hr

According to the question,

If its speed is decreased by 2 km/hr

⇒ New speed = (40 - 2) km/hr = 38 km/hr

Time taken by the car to cover same distance,

Time = $\frac{Distance}{Speed}$

⇒ Time = $(\frac{4}{38})$ hr = $(\frac{4}{38}) \times 60 = \frac{120}{19}$ minutes

∴ The time taken by the car to cover same distance is $\frac{120}{19}$ minutes.

Hence, the correct option is (A).

43. Given:

x = $\frac{(Tan^2 30° + Cosec^2 45° + Sin^2 90°)}{(1 + Sin^2 45° + Sec^2 30°)}$

⇒ x = $\left(\frac{\frac{1}{3}+2+1}{1+\frac{1}{2}+\frac{4}{3}}\right)$

⇒ x = $\left(\frac{\frac{1+6+3}{3}}{\frac{6+3+8}{6}}\right)$

⇒ x = $\left(\frac{\frac{10}{3}}{\frac{17}{6}}\right)$

⇒ x = $(\frac{10}{3}) \times (\frac{6}{17})$

⇒ x = $\frac{20}{17}$

∴ The value of x is $\frac{20}{17}$.

Hence, the correct option is (B).

44. Given,

345678 × 999999

Here, we can write 999999 as = 1000000 - 1

Now, solving by taking above representation

=345678 × (1000000 - 1)

= 345678000000 - 345678

= 345677654322

Hence, the correct option is (C).

45. Given equation is $x^2 - 2x + 1 = 0$

$$(a+b)^3 = a^3 + b^3 + 3ab(a+b)$$

According to the question, we have

$$x^2 - 2x + 1 = 0$$

After dividing equation by x, we get

$$\Rightarrow x - 2 + \left(\frac{1}{x}\right) = 0$$

$$\Rightarrow x + \left(\frac{1}{x}\right) = 2$$

After cubing both sides, we get

$$\Rightarrow \left\{x + \left(\frac{1}{x}\right)\right\}^3 = (2)^3$$

$$\Rightarrow x^3 + \left(\frac{1}{x^3}\right) + 3x\left(\frac{1}{x}\right)\left\{x + \left(\frac{1}{x}\right)\right\} = 8$$

$$\Rightarrow x^3 + \left(\frac{1}{x^3}\right) + 3\left\{x + \left(\frac{1}{x}\right)\right\} = 8$$

$$\Rightarrow x^3 + \left(\frac{1}{x^3}\right) + 3(2) = 8$$

$$\Rightarrow x^3 + \left(\frac{1}{x^3}\right) = 8 - 6$$

$$\Rightarrow x^3 + \left(\frac{1}{x^3}\right) = 2$$

∴ The value of $x^3 + \left(\frac{1}{x^3}\right)$ is 2.

Hence, the correct option is (A).

46. Given:

Time taken by A to do the work = 8 days

Time taken by B to do the work = 12 days

Time taken by A, B and C together to do the work = 4 days

Let the total work be LCM (8, 12, 4).

LCM (8, 12, 4) = 24 unit

In one day A do = $\frac{24}{8}$ unit

= 3 unit

In one day B do = $\frac{24}{12}$ unit

= 2 unit

In one day A, B and C do = $\frac{24}{4}$ unit

= 6 unit

In one day only C do = 6 - (3 + 2)

= 1 unit

The proportion of their shares = A's 1-day work : B's 1-day work : C's 1-day work

= 3: 2: 1

According to the question,

Total share = 4500

⇒ 6 unit = 4500

⇒ 1 unit = 750

So, C's share = Rs. 750

∴ The C's share of the money is Rs. 750.

Hence, the correct option is (C).

47. Given:

Ratio of angles of quadrilateral = 4 : 7 : 6 : 13

Sum of all the angles in quadrilateral is 360°

Let the angles of the quadrilateral be 4x, 7x, 6x, and 13x

⇒ 4x + 7x + 6x + 13x = 360°

⇒ 30x = 360°

⇒ x = 12°

Greatest angle = 13 × 12 = 156°

Smallest angle = 4 × 12 = 48°

Difference between the greatest and the smallest angle = 156°- 48°

⇒ 108°

∴ The difference between the greatest and the smallest angle is 108°.

Hence, the correct option is (B).

48. Given:

Principal = Rs. 8000

Rate of interest = 5% per annum

Time = 3 years

A = P(1 + $\frac{r}{100}$)^n

Compound interest = A - P

Where, A = Amount

P = Principal

r = Rate of interest

n = Time in years

A = 8000(1 + $\frac{5}{100}$)^3

⇒ A = 8000 × $\frac{21}{20} \times \frac{21}{20} \times \frac{21}{20}$

⇒ A = 9261

Compound interest = 9261 - 8000

⇒ Compound interest = Rs. 1261

∴ Compound interest is Rs. 1261.

Hence, the correct option is (D).

49. Given:

Data $= \{12,15,11,13,18,11,13,12,13\}$

Arranging the values in ascending order,

$11,11,12,12,13,13,13,15,18$

Most repeated term in the given data $= 13$ (3 times)

Number of terms $= 9$

Median $= \frac{(9+1)}{2}^{th}$ term

$= 5^{th}$ term

$= 13$

Sum of mode and median of the given data $= 13 + 13$

$= 26$

∴ The sum of mode and median of the given data is 26.

Hence, the correct option is (B).

50. Given:

Ratio of profit = 4 : 11 : 7

Difference of share of A and C = 2 × Rs. 2100

= Rs. 4200

Let, the share of A, B and C = 4a, 11a and 7a.

∵ Share of C - A = 4200

∴ 7a - 4a = 4200

⇒ 3a = 4200

⇒ a = $\frac{4200}{3}$

⇒ a = Rs. 1400

∴ Total Profit of A, B and C = 4a + 11a + 7a

= 22a

= 22 × 1400

= Rs. 30,800

Hence, the correct option is (B)

51. Given:

The ratio of two numbers = 7 : 5

Let first number = 7x

Second number = 5x

If 1 is subtracted from first number and 3 is subtracted from second number, then ratio = $\frac{(7x-1)}{(5x-3)}$

$\Rightarrow \frac{(7x-1)}{(5x-3)} = \frac{3}{2}$

⇒ 3(5x - 3) = 2(7x - 1)

⇒ 15x – 9 = 14x – 2

⇒ 15x – 14x = 9 – 2

⇒ x = 7

First number = 7x

= 7 × 7 = 49

Second number = 5x

= 5 × 7 = 35

∴ Second number is 35.

Hence, the correct option is (A).

52. We have, $\tan 3x = \sin 45^\circ \cos 45^\circ + \sin 30^\circ$

$\Rightarrow \tan 3x = \frac{1}{\sqrt{2}} \times \frac{1}{\sqrt{2}} + \frac{1}{2}$

$\Rightarrow \tan 3x = \frac{1}{2} + \frac{1}{2}$

$\Rightarrow \tan 3x = 1$

$\Rightarrow \tan 3x = \tan 45^\circ$

$\Rightarrow 3x = 45^\circ$

$\Rightarrow x = 15^\circ$

Hence, the correct option is (B).

53.

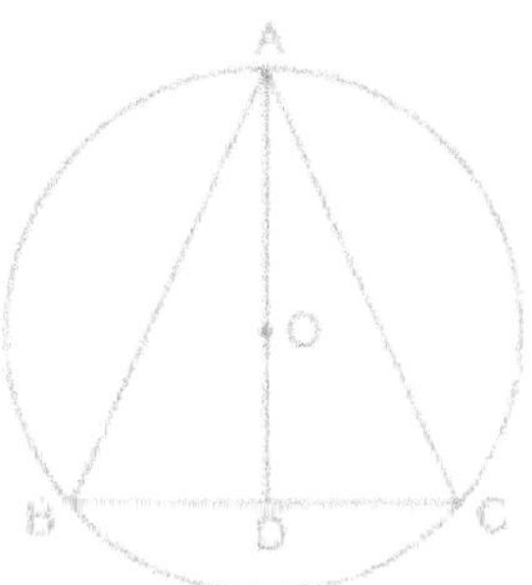

Circumcenter is the point of intersection of the perpendicular bisectors of a triangle.

From the diagram,

O be the Circumcenter of the triangle and AD is the perpendicular bisector.

∵ In case of equilateral triangle Circumcenter and Orthocenter are same.

∴ O is the orthocenter of the triangle.

∵ In case of equilateral triangle Perpendicular bisector and Median are same.

∴ AD is the median of the triangle.

∵ Orthocenter intersects the median in a ratio 2 : 1 and the longer part is nearer to the vertex.

∴ AO = $\left(\frac{2}{3}\right)$ × AD

Given,

Circumradius = AO

= 8 cm

⇒ 8 = $\left(\frac{2}{3}\right)$ × AD

⇒ AD = 12 cm

∴ Height of the triangle is 12 cm.

Hence, the correct option is (A).

54. Given:

a = 6, b = 8 and $\theta = 60°$

So according to the cosine rule,

$\cos(C) = \frac{a^2+b^2-c^2}{2ab}$

$\Rightarrow \cos 60 = \frac{6^2+8^2-c^2}{2(6)(8)}$

$\Rightarrow \frac{1}{2} = \frac{36+64-c^2}{96}$

$\Rightarrow 48 = 100 - c^2$

$\Rightarrow c^2 = 52$

$\therefore c = \sqrt{52}$ cm

Hence, the correct option is (A).

55. Given:

Two factors of $x^4 - x^3 - 19x^2 - 11x + 30$ is x + 2 and x – 1.

Here a = -2, b = 1

abcd = 30

⇒ we can get this from only option 1 and 2.

$(a + b + c + d)x^3 = x^3$

⇒ -2 + 1 + c + d = 1

⇒ c + d = 2

By taking option (A), c = -3 and d = 5

∴ another two factors of the polynomial $x^4 - x^3 - 19x^2 - 11x + 30$ is (x + 3) and (x – 5).

Hence, the correct option is (D).

56. If we subtract one equation from the other, we can eliminate the unknown, x.

$5y + 2x = 9$ Equation (1)

$2y + 2x = 6$ Equation (2)

$3y = 3$ from equation (1) $-$ equation (2)

$y = 1$

To obtain the value of x, we substitute the known value of y in any of the above equations. If we choose equation (2), then we would obtain, $2(1) + 2x = 6$

$\Rightarrow 2x = 6 - 2$

$\Rightarrow 2x = 4$

$x = 2$

Hence $y = 1$ and $x = 2$

Hence, the correct option is (A).

57. $\omega^{15} + \omega^{20} + \omega^{25}$

$= \omega^{15}(1 + \omega^5 + \omega^{10})$

$= \omega^{15} \times (1 + \omega^3 \cdot \omega^2 + \omega^9 \cdot \omega)$

$= (\omega^3)^5 \times (1 + \omega^2 + \omega)$

$= 1 \times (1 + \omega + \omega^2)$

$= 1 \times 0$

$= 0$

Hence, the correct option is (B).

58. Given,

Wage of 20 boys for 15 days = Rs. 9000

Wage of 20 boys per day = 600

Wage of 1 boy per day = Rs. 30

Daily wage of 1 man = Rs. 45

Required number of men = Rs. $\frac{13500}{45 \times 30}$

= 10 men

Hence, the correct option is (A).

59. Given,

$5x^3 + 4x^2 - 60x + k = 0$

If 2 < x < 5 it means x can take 3 and 4

Now,

$5x^3 + 4x^2 - 60x + k = 0$ when x = 3

⇒ $5 \times 3^3 + 4 \times 3^2 - 60 \times 3 + k = 0$

⇒ 135 + 36 – 180 + k = 0

$\Rightarrow -9 + k = 0$

$\Rightarrow k = 9$

$5x^3 + 4x^2 - 60x + k = 0$ when $x = 4$

$\Rightarrow 5 \times 4^3 + 4 \times 4^2 - 60 \times 4 + k = 0$

$\Rightarrow 320 + 64 - 240 + k = 0$

$\Rightarrow 144 + k = 0$

$\Rightarrow k = -144$

$\therefore -144 < k < 9$

Hence, the correct option is (A).

60. Given:

Diameter = 24 m

Radius, R = $\frac{24}{2}$

= 12 m

Height = 16 m

Slant height $L = \sqrt{R^2 + H^2}$

$= \sqrt{12^2 + 16^2}$

= 20 m

The area of the canvas required to erect a tent is equal to the lateral surface area of the cone. So,

Canvas required = Curved surface area of cone

$= \pi rl$

$= \frac{22}{7} \times 12 \times 20$

$= \frac{5280}{7}$ m^2

Hence, the correct option is (B).

Mock Test 05

English

Q.1 Direction: Select the correct passive form of the given sentence.

I am learning a new language this year.

A. A new language is being learnt by me this year.
B. A new language has been learnt by me this year.
C. A new language was being learnt by me this year.
D. A new language is going to be learnt by me this year.

Ques (2-3):Direction: Select the most appropriate synonym of the given word.

Q.2 Creeping

A. Spicy **B.** Speck **C.** Plethora **D.** Crawl

Q.3 Demolish

A. Destroy **B.** Strengthen
C. Built **D.** Construct

Q.4 Direction: Fill in the blank with the appropriate form of the verb.

Each one of them _______ a face mask for protection.

A. were wearing **B.** was wearing
C. have worn **D.** were worn

Q.5 Direction: Select the most appropriate meaning of the underlined phrase in the given sentence.

The news of a leopard in the city **spread like wildfire**.

A. caused fear **B.** spread slowly
C. caused damage **D.** spread rapidly

Q.6 Direction: Select the option that is the direct form of the given sentence.

Explaining her work she said that she made films for posterity to remember.

A. Explaining her work, she said, "She makes films for posterity to remember."
B. Explaining her work, she said, "I will make the films that will remember posterity."
C. Explaining her work, she said, "She made films for posterity to remember."
D. Explaining her work, she said, "I make films for posterity to remember."

Ques (7-8):Direction: Find the correct antonym of the following word.

Q.7 Plausible

A. Fabulous **B.** Reasonable
C. Incredible **D.** Unlimited

Q.8 Immigrant

A. Expat **B.** Expatriate
C. Alien **D.** Native

Q.9 Direction: Select the most appropriate preposition to fill in the blank.

The Indian law prohibits the employment _____ children in factories but the law is violated several times.

A. by **B.** from **C.** of **D.** at

Q.10 Direction: Fill in the blank with a suitable pronoun.

My son and my daughter are very fond of _______.

A. herself **B.** each other
C. themselves **D.** himself

Q.11 Direction: Choose the correct form of the tense.

The Headmaster _________ to speak to you.

[KVS PRT, 2018]

A. wants **B.** wants **C.** wants **D.** wants

Q.12 Direction: Select the most appropriate option to improve the underlined segment in the given sentence. If there is no need to improve it, select 'No improvement'.

My friend was a very lazy person and **hate doing** any kind of work.

A. Hated doing **B.** Hates doing
C. Hates do **D.** No improvement

Ques (13-14):Direction: Read the following passage carefully and choose the most appropriate answer to the questions out of the four alternatives.

Most economists in the United States seem captivated by the spell of the free market. Consequently, nothing seems good or normal that does not accord with the requirements of the free market. A price that is determined by the seller or, for that matter (for that matter: so far as that is concerned), established by anyone other than the aggregate of consumers seems pernicious. Accordingly, it requires a major act of will to think of price-fixing (the determination of prices by the seller) as both "normal" and having a valuable economic function. In fact, price-fixing is normal in all industrialized societies because the industrial system itself provides, as an effortless consequence of its own development, the price-fixing that it requires. Modern industrial planning requires and rewards great size. Hence, a comparatively small number of large firms will be competing for the same group of consumers. That each large firm will act with consideration of its own needs and thus avoid selling its products for more than its competitors charge is commonly recognized by advocates of free-market economic theories. But each large firm will also act with full consideration of the needs that it has in common with the other large firms competing for the same customers.

Q.13 A major act of will will bring about price-fixing that will be seen as:

A. effective and productive
B. constructive and practical

C. normal and having valuable economic function

D. systematic and relevant

Q.14 Large firms selling a commodity at a price that is not more than that charged by competitors is:

A. rejected by the free market system

B. opposed by the advocates of the free market theories

C. considered suspicious by the free market theorists

D. recognized by the advocates of the free market theories

Q.15 Direction: Fill in the blank with the appropriate adjective.

We saw _______ animals at the zoo.

A. much **B.** many

C. so many **D.** None of the above

General Knowledge

Q.16 In which of the following countries did Prime Minister Narendra Modi start 'Ramayana Circuit' on May 11, 2018?

[Super TET Paper - I, 2019]

A. Nepal **B.** Indonesia

C. Sri Lanka **D.** Myanmar

Q.17 Which of the following competitions is not associated with Indian football?

A. Ranji Trophy **B.** Federation Cup

C. Santosh Trophy **D.** Durand Cup

Q.18 Chandi Padvo festival is primarily celebrated in:

A. Maharashtra **B.** Gujarat

C. Punjab **D.** Kerala

Q.19 The book 'Mein Kampf' was written by:

A. Stalin **B.** Hitler

C. Lenin **D.** Mussolini

Q.20 What is the full form of ICAR?

A. International Committee of Agriculture Research

B. Indian Council of Agricultural Research

C. Indian Cooperation of Aeronautical Research

D. None of the above

Science

Q.21 Which physical quantity has kWh as its unit?

A. Force **B.** Momentum

C. Energy **D.** Power

Q.22 Which of the following physical quantity measures the rate of work done?

A. Force **B.** Energy

C. Power **D.** Momentum

Q.23 The height at which the weight of a body becomes $\frac{1}{16}$th of its weight on the surface of the earth (radius R) is:

A. 4 R **B.** 5 R **C.** 15 R **D.** 3 R

Q.24 Which of the following involves Newton's second law of motion?

A. When two bodies of unequal masses are acted upon by the same force for the same time, the momentum gained by both the bodies is the same.

B. A body at rest moves in the same direction as that of the applied force.

C. A boy hitting a wall with his hand using muscular force experiences pain.

D. Both (A) and (B)

Q.25 What happens to the weight of a person when lift goes down with some acceleration?

A. Increases **B.** Decreases

C. Zero **D.** Remain same

Q.26 How much time will be needed by a 30 W bulb to perform 540 J of work?

A. 27 sec **B.** 54 sec **C.** 18 sec **D.** 37 sec

Q.27 Which method is used for the purification of Bauxite ore?

A. Magnetic separation **B.** Electrolysis

C. Leaching **D.** Levigation

Q.28 For a sound wave, frequency is 8800 Hz and speed is 352 m/s in a given medium. The wavelength of the wave is:

A. 0.4 m **B.** 0.03 m **C.** 0.25 m **D.** 0.04 m

Q.29 The direction of heat flow between two bodies depends on which of the following?

A. Their specific heat

B. Their latent heat

C. Their temperatures

D. Their area of contact

Q.30 Four resistances of 1 ohm, 2 ohms, 3 ohms, and 6 ohms are connected in series. The total resistance of the combination is:

A. 12 ohms **B.** 1 ohm **C.** 36 ohms **D.** 3 ohms

Reasoning

Q.31 In a certain code language, 'BOTANY' is written as 'CQWESE '. How will 'CAMERA' be written as in that language?

A. DPCWGI **B.** WIDPGC

C. DCPIWG **D.** GWPCGI

Q.32 In a certain code language, "You are Gorgeous" means "pek din pew", "Boys are Handsome" means "pek bek hek", "Gorgeous likes Handsome" means "bek din meo". Which is the code for "likes" in that code language?

A. bek **B.** meo **C.** hek **D.** din

Q.33 If a mirror is placed on the line HN, then which of the answer figures is the right image of the given figure?

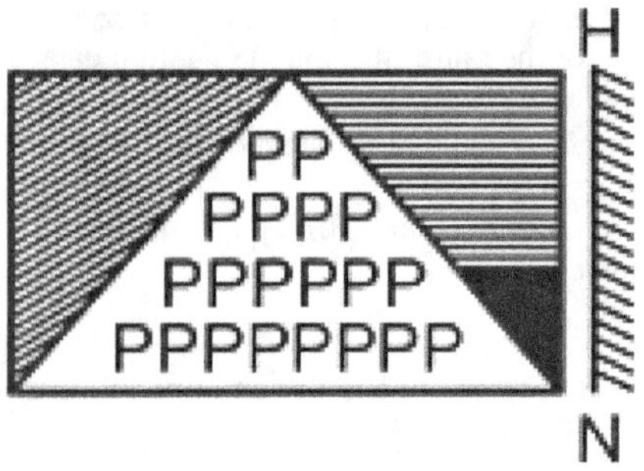

A. 

B. 

C. 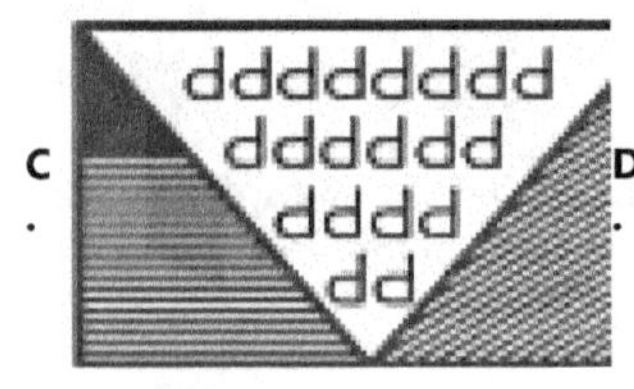

D. 

Q.34 Which answer figure will complete the pattern in the question figure?

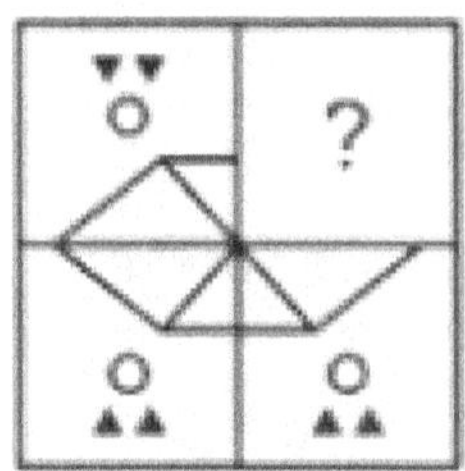

[UP Police Constable, 2019]

A. 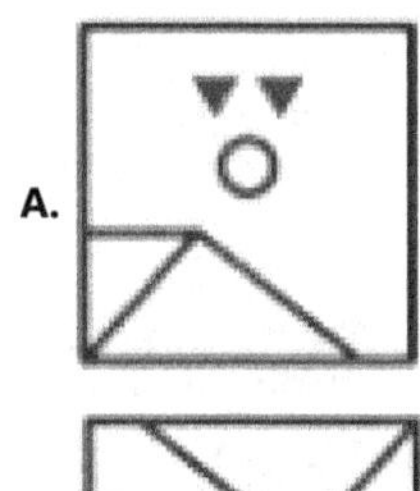

B. 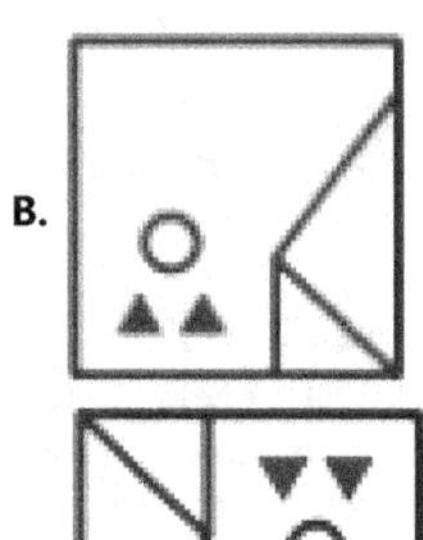

C. 

D.

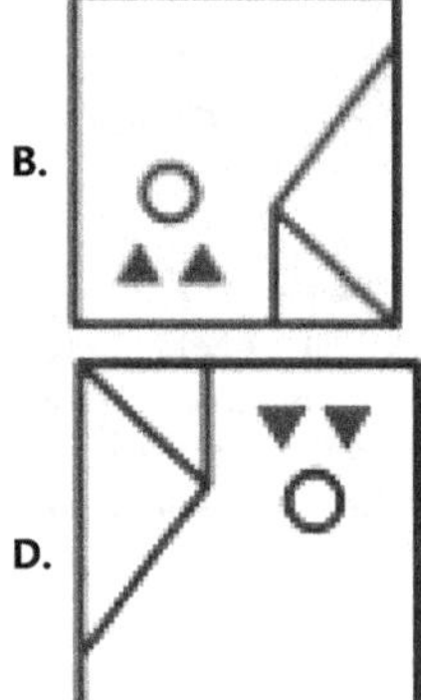

Q.35 Which of the following interchanges of signs would make the given equation correct?

6 + 7 ÷ 2 – 8 × 4 = 18

A. ÷ and × **B.** + and × **C.** + and ÷ **D.** + and –

Ques (36-37):Direction: A word with letters jumbled has been given. Choose the correct order of letters that are required to form the correct word.

Q.36 RINDAOYR

A. 7, 4, 2, 1, 6, 8, 3, 5 **B.** 4, 7, 2, 1, 6, 3, 8, 5
C. 6, 8, 4, 2, 3, 5, 1, 7 **D.** 5, 8, 2, 1, 7, 3, 6, 4

Q.37 MYOECD

A. 3, 1, 4, 6, 2, 5 **B.** 5, 3, 1, 4, 6, 2
C. 5, 3, 2, 4, 1, 6 **D.** 4, 3, 1, 6, 2, 5

Q.38 Which two signs to be interchanged to make the following equation correct?

135 - 5 + 21 × 8 ÷ 112 = 83

A. × and - **B.** – and ÷ **C.** + and ÷ **D.** × and ÷

Ques (39-40):Direction: Arrange the words given below in a meaningful sequence.

Q.39

1. Heel
2. Shoulder
3. Skull
4. Neck
5. Knee
6. Chest
7. Thigh
8. Stomach
9. Face
10. Hand

A. 3, 4, 7, 9, 2, 5, 8, 10, 6, 1
B. 3, 9, 4, 2, 10, 6, 8, 7, 5, 1
C. 2, 4, 7, 10, 1, 5, 8, 9, 6, 3
D. 4, 7, 10, 1, 9, 6, 2, 5, 8, 3

Q.40

1. Rainbow
2. Rain
3. Sun
4. Happy
5. Child

A. 4, 2, 3, 5, 1 **B.** 2, 3, 1, 5, 4
C. 4, 5, 1, 2, 3 **D.** 2, 1, 4, 5, 3

Mathematics

Q.41 Find the value of x:

$$3^x - 3^{x-1} = 486$$

A. 7 **B.** 9 **C.** 5 **D.** 6

Q.42 Out of three numbers, the first is twice the second and is half of the third. If the average of the three numbers is 63, then the difference between the first and third numbers is:

A. 27 **B.** 50 **C.** 54 **D.** 48

Q.43 If the mode of the data 8, 6, 6, x, 5, 5, 6, 8, 8, 10, 5 is 6, then what is the value of x?

A. 10 **B.** 6 **C.** 7 **D.** 5

Q.44 A sum of money at simple interest amounts of Rs. 1012 in 2.5 yrs and to Rs. 1067.20 in 4 yrs; Find the rate of interest per annum.

A. 2% **B.** 4% **C.** 5% **D.** 3%

Q.45 A dealer claims that he sold his goods at cost price, but he uses a false weight of 750 g instead of 1000 g. Find his profit%.

A. 33.33% **B.** 83.33% **C.** 22.22% **D.** 66.66%

Q.46 If X and Y can complete a piece of work in 15 days, and X alone can do the same work in 30 days, find how many days will Y alone take to complete the same work?

A. 60 days **B.** 45 days **C.** 30 days **D.** 15 days

Q.47 The distance between two points A and B is 600 km. When they start moving towards each other they meet in 12 hours. If A started moving 5 hours after B, then they meet in 10 hours. Taking these into account find the speed of B.

A. 20 km/hr **B.** 25 km/hr **C.** 30 km/hr **D.** 15 km/hr

Q.48 In a class there are total 550 students. Ratio of boys and girls is 6 : 5. How many girls should join the class so that ratio becomes 5 : 6.

A. 60 **B.** 80 **C.** 90 **D.** 110

Q.49 The value of $(\cos^2 1° + \cos^2 3° + \cos^2 5° + \cdots ... + \cos^2 89°)$ is:

A. 0 **B.** 22.5 **C.** 22 **D.** 23

Q.50 Find the value of $\left(\frac{\tan x+1-\sec x}{\cot x+1-cosec x}\right)\cos x$.

A. $\cos x$ **B.** $\sin x$ **C.** $\sec x$ **D.** $\tan x$

Q.51 Find the value of x in the given figure.

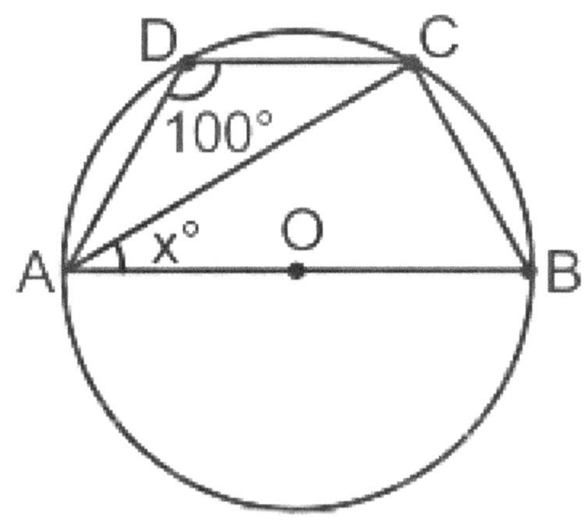

A. 20° **B.** 10° **C.** 7° **D.** 30°

Q.52 AB is a chord of a circle and PQ is a tangent of that circle. AB is produced to meet the tangent at a point Q. The length of tangent PQ is 15 cm and the length of BQ is 5 cm. Find the length of the chord.

A. 44 cm **B.** 40 cm **C.** 35 cm **D.** 45 cm

Q.53 Find the remainder when $f(x) = 4x^5 + 3x^4 + 2x^3 + 5x^2 + x - 3$ is divided by $(x + 1)$.

A. 0/ **B.** -1 **C.** -2 **D.** -3

Q.54 If $p \times 2^2 = 8^2$, then find the value of p^3.

A. 16 **B.** 256 **C.** 4096 **D.** 65536

Q.55 The curved surface area of two cylinders are in the ratio 2 : 3, while their heights are in the ratio 2 : 1. What is the ratio of their volumes?

A. 2 : 3 **B.** 4 : 3 **C.** 2 : 9 **D.** 4 : 9

Q.56 How many bullets can be made from a sphere of 9 cm radius, if it is required that the radius of each new bullet be 0.3 cm?

A. 12000 **B.** 20000 **C.** 27000 **D.** 7500

Q.57 If $x = 2015, y = 2014$ and $z = 2013$, then value of $x^2 + y^2 + z^2 - xy - yz - zx$ is:

A. 3 **B.** 4 **C.** 6 **D.** 2

Q.58 What is the value of $x + y$ in the solution of the equations $\frac{x}{4} + \frac{y}{3} = \frac{5}{12}$ and $\frac{x}{2} + y = 1$?

A. $\frac{1}{3}$ **B.** $\frac{3}{2}$ **C.** 2 **D.** $\frac{5}{2}$

Q.59 Solve this:

30% of 1225 - 64% of 555 = ?

A. 10.7 **B.** 12.3

C. 13.4 **D.** None of these

Q.60 Two candidates fought in an election one get 65% of the votes and won by 300 votes. The total number of votes polled is:

A. 700 **B.** 950 **C.** 1000 **D.** 900

// Smart Answer Sheet //

Correct: Percentage of students who answered correctly. Skipped: Percentage of students who skipped.

Q.	Ans.	Correct	Skipped	Q.	Ans.	Correct	Skipped	Q.	Ans.	Correct	Skipped	Q.	Ans.	Correct	Skipped	Q.	Ans.	Correct	Skipped	Q.	Ans.	Correct	Skipped
1	A	61.1 %	1.57 %	11	A	89.88 %	0.0 %	21	C	88.08 %	0.0 %	31	C	53.2 %	1.16 %	41	D	58.08 %	1.14 %	51	B	16.79 %	3.22 %
2	D	69.72 %	1.65 %	12	A	13.51 %	4.79 %	22	C	59.67 %	1.76 %	32	B	24.28 %	3.44 %	42	C	67.04 %	1.4 %	52	B	62.41 %	1.4 %
3	A	76.43 %	0.0 %	13	C	66.13 %	1.23 %	23	D	16.07 %	4.55 %	33	D	81.63 %	0.0 %	43	B	88.47 %	0.0 %	53	C	81.66 %	0.0 %
4	B	64.18 %	1.75 %	14	D	64.91 %	1.82 %	24	A	58.78 %	1.91 %	34	A	28.35 %	3.56 %	44	B	52.67 %	1.77 %	54	C	67.73 %	1.54 %
5	D	52.62 %	1.44 %	15	B	86.81 %	0.0 %	25	B	89.49 %	0.0 %	35	A	29.55 %	4.92 %	45	A	77.24 %	0.0 %	55	C	31.58 %	3.31 %
6	D	58.06 %	1.25 %	16	A	41.95 %	1.49 %	26	C	67.42 %	1.52 %	36	C	50.67 %	1.0 %	46	C	48.28 %	1.75 %	56	C	50.92 %	1.82 %
7	C	18.95 %	3.79 %	17	A	46.98 %	1.96 %	27	C	43.51 %	1.97 %	37	B	44.47 %	1.6 %	47	A	67.19 %	1.53 %	57	A	28.79 %	3.53 %
8	D	77.89 %	0.0 %	18	B	54.02 %	1.44 %	28	D	15.53 %	4.87 %	38	B	30.21 %	4.26 %	48	D	66.97 %	1.83 %	58	B	54.77 %	1.42 %
9	C	62.94 %	1.35 %	19	B	54.3 %	1.42 %	29	C	65.37 %	1.97 %	39	B	61.41 %	1.24 %	49	B	43.16 %	1.05 %	59	B	86.03 %	0.0 %
10	B	47.8 %	1.45 %	20	B	12.97 %	4.77 %	30	A	77.66 %	0.0 %	40	B	80.02 %	0.0 %	50	B	78.59 %	0.0 %	60	C	56.13 %	1.57 %

//Hints and Solutions//

1. In Passive Voice, a sentence emphasizes the action or the object of the sentence.

The given sentence is in the active voice and 'I' is the subject and 'a new language' is the object.

When we convert this sentence into passive voice, the subject 'I' of the active voice becomes the object 'me', the object 'a new language' becomes the subject.

The passive format "'is + being + V_3 (learnt)" should be used.

This is the active and passive voice rule for the present continuous tense.

The correct answer is 'A new language is being learnt by me this year'.

Hence, the correct option is (A).

2. Creeping: happening, developing, or moving slowly or gradually

Crawl: move at an unusually slow pace

Spicy: containing strong flavors from spices

Speck: a very small mark, piece, or amount

Plethora: a very large amount of something, especially a larger amount than you need, want, or can deal with

Hence, the correct option is (D).

3. Demolish: pull or knock down (a building)

Destroy: end the existence of (something) by damaging or attacking it

Strengthen: make or become stronger

Built: construct (something) by putting parts or material together

Construct: build or make (something, typically a building, road, or machine)

Hence, the correct option is (A).

4. Each one of them **was wearing** a face mask for protection.

We know that after 'Each of, Every of, One of, Each one of' plural Noun/Pronoun and Singular Verb/Adjective/Pronoun is used.

In the given sentence 'was wearing' will be used because as per the rule given above we should use a singular helping verb.

Hence, the correct option is (B).

5. Given phrase: Spread like wildfire means to spread, circulate, or propagate very quickly and widely.

From the given options, option (D) is the most appropriate meaning of the given idiom.

Hence, the correct option is (D).

6. The given sentence is an indirect speech.

The basic rules for changing or converting indirect speech into direct speech:

The commas and inverted commas are added and 'that' is removed.

The third person pronoun 'she' will be changed into the first person pronoun 'I'.

The past simple tense format 'Subject + V_2 (made) + Object' will be changed into the present simple tense format 'Subject + V_1 (make) + Object'.

Correct sentence: Explaining her work, she said, "I make films for posterity to remember".

Hence, the correct option is (D).

7. Plausible: seeming likely to be true, or able to be believed

Incredible: Beyond belief or understanding

Fabulous: Extremely pleasing

Reasonable: Showing reason or sound judgment

Unlimited: Having no limits in range or scope

Hence, the correct option is (C).

8. Immigrant: a person who comes to live permanently in a foreign country

Native: a person born in a specified place or associated with a place by birth, whether subsequently resident there or not

Expat: a person who lives outside their native country

Expatriate: a person who lives outside their native country

Alien: belonging to a foreign country

Hence, the correct option is (D).

9. The Indian law prohibits the employment **of** children in factories but the law is violated several times.

'of' is used to tell the belongingness

'by' is used as an agent

'from' is used for the beginning point

'at' is used to express small places or fixes time

Hence, the correct option is (C).

10. My son and my daughter are very fond of **each other**.

The pronoun 'each other' is used for two people whereas 'themselves' is used for more than two people.

Hence, the correct option is (B).

11. The Headmaster **wants** to speak to you.

The simple present tense is used when an action is happening right now, or when it happens regularly or unceasingly.

The structure is given below:

Subject + V_1 + object.

The verb will take 's/es' if the given noun/pronoun (3rd person) is singular.

Certain verbs used only in the simple present tense are given below:

see, think, know, possess, like, want, desire, hate, seem, imagine, etc.

Hence, the correct option is (A).

12. The use of the phrase 'Hate doing' is incorrect in the given sentence.

The given sentence is in the past tense form, therefore the verb hate should be in the past tense form.

Hence, the underlined part of the sentence should be replaced by Hated doing.

Correct sentence: My friend was a very lazy person and hated doing any kind of work.

Hence, the correct option is (A).

13. The passage is about the price-fixing and how, in one form or another, it is an inevitable part of and benefit to the economy of any industrialized society.

The following is stated in the passage: "...it requires a major act of will to think of price-fixing (the determination of prices by the seller) as both "normal" and having a valuable economic function."

Hence, the correct option is (C).

14. The passage is about the price-fixing and how, in one form or another, it is an inevitable part of and benefit to the economy of any industrialized society.

The following is stated in the passage: "That each large firm will act with consideration of its own needs and thus avoid selling its products for more than its competitors charge is commonly recognized by advocates of free-market economic theories."

Hence, the correct option is (D).

15. The correct sentence is: We saw many animals at the zoo.

'Many' is used when we are speaking about a plural noun. When we speak about 'many' and 'much', it's worth mentioning countable and uncountable nouns. Countable nouns can be used with a number and have singular and plural forms.

Hence, the correct option is (B).

16. On May 11, 2018, Prime Minister Narendra Modi and Nepalese Prime Minister KP Sharma Oli jointly flagged-off a direct bus service between the two sacred cities Janakpur and Ayodhya, as part of the Ramayana Circuit.

The bus service seeks to promote religious tourism and built a strong foundation for people-to-people contact between the two countries. As per the mythological story 'Ramayana', Ayodhya is Lord Rama's birthplace, while, Janakpur is the birthplace of goddess Sita.

Hence, the correct option is (A).

17. Among the options, only Ranji Trophy is not associated with Indian football.

Ranji Trophy is associated with cricket. The Ranji Trophy is a domestic first-class cricket tournament played between multiple teams from state cricket associations in India. The tournament is named after former India cricketer Ranjitsinhji. The first edition of the Ranji Trophy tournament was held in 1934–35. Mumbai is the most successful team in the Ranji Trophy tournament history with 41 titles.

Important competitions associated with Indian football are:

- Federation cup
- Santosh trophy
- Durand cup
- Subroto Mukherjee cup
- Sanjay gold cup
- Nizam gold cup

Hence, the correct option is (A).

18. The Chandi Padvo festival, which falls a day after Sharad Poornima, is widely celebrated by Surtis, or the people native to Surat (Gujarat) across the country and abroad, by consuming Ghari (Sweet) and Bhusu (namkeen) sitting in the open to celebrate the full moon.

Hence, the correct option is (B).

19. Mein Kampf was a political manifesto written by Adolf Hitler. It was his only complete book, and the work became the bible of National Nazism in Germany's Third Reich.

It was published in two volumes in 1925 and 1927, and an abridged edition appeared in 1930.

Hence, the correct option is (B).

20. The Indian Council of Agricultural Research (ICAR) is an autonomous body responsible for coordinating agricultural education and research in India. It reports to the Department of Agricultural Research and Education, Ministry of Agriculture. It is the largest network of agricultural research and education institutes in the world. The Indian Council of Agricultural Research is headquartered in New Delhi. In 2019, ICAR has published an Integrated Mobile App called KISAAN.

Hence, the correct option is (B).

21. kWh is a unit of electrical energy.

Power: The rate of work done by the electric energy is called power. It is denoted by P.

The SI unit of power is the watt (W).

Watt is a small unit that's why kilowatt-hour is used as the unit for electrical energy.

1 unit of electric energy: When one-kilowatt load works for 1 hour then the energy consumed is called 1 unit of electricity.

1 Unit of electricity $= 1KWh = 1000$ Watt-hour $= 3.6 \times 10^6 J$

1 Kilo-watt $= 1000$ Watt

Hence, the correct option is (C).

22. Power (P): Measures of the rate of work done is called power.

Work done is measured as the force on a body times the distance through which that force is applied.

Work done $(W)=$ Force $(F)\times$ Distance (s)

Power $(P)=\frac{\text{work done (W)}}{\text{Time taken}}$

Energy $(E)=$ power $(P)\times$ time (t)

Momentum $(p)=$ mass $(m)\times$ velocity (v)

Hence, the correct option is (C).

23. Acceleration Due to Gravity:

The force of attraction exerted by the earth on a body is called gravitational pull or gravity.

We know that when a force acts on a body, it produces acceleration. Therefore, a body under the effect of gravitational pull must accelerate.

The acceleration produced in the motion of a body under the effect of gravity is called acceleration due to gravity, it is denoted by g.

If g is the acceleration due to gravity, then

$$g=\frac{GM}{R^2}$$

Where G = universal gravitational constant, M = mass of the earth, and R = radius of the earth

Weight:

The weight of an object is defined as the force of gravity on the object and may be calculated as the mass times the acceleration of gravity, i.e.,

W = mg

Where m = mass of the object and g = acceleration due to gravity

Given:

Weight of body at height (W') = mg', the weight of the body on the surface of earth (W) = mg and

Acceleration due to gravity at height h from the surface of the earth

$$\Rightarrow g'=\frac{g}{\left(1+\frac{h}{R}\right)^2} \text{.....(1)}$$

Multiply both sides by m, then we get

$$\Rightarrow mg'=\frac{mg}{\left(1+\frac{h}{R}\right)^2}$$

$$\Rightarrow W'=\frac{W}{\left(1+\frac{h}{R}\right)^2}$$

According to question,

$$W=\frac{W}{16}$$

$$\Rightarrow \frac{W}{16}=\frac{W}{\left(1+\frac{h}{R}\right)^2}$$

$$\Rightarrow \frac{1}{16}=\frac{1}{\left(1+\frac{h}{R}\right)^2}$$

$$\Rightarrow \left(1+\frac{h}{R}\right)^2=16$$

$$\Rightarrow \left(1+\frac{h}{R}\right)=4$$

$$\Rightarrow \frac{h}{R}=3$$

$$\Rightarrow h=3R$$

Hence, the correct option is (D).

24. Newton's Second Law of Motion:

The rate of change of linear momentum of a body is directly proportional to the external force applied on the body and this change takes place always in the direction of the applied force.

According to the second law of motion, force

Force $\propto \frac{\text{change in momentum}}{\text{time}}$

$$\Rightarrow F=K\frac{p_2-p_1}{t}=K\frac{m(v-u)}{t}=Kma \quad \left[\because \frac{v-u}{t}=a\right]$$

Where, K = constant of proportionality,

p = momentum of the body,

m = mass of the body,

u = initial velocity of the body,

v = final velocity of the body, and

a = acceleration of the body

$$\Rightarrow F=\frac{dp}{dt}$$

$$\Rightarrow dp=F\times dt$$

Here, two bodies of unequal masses are acted upon by the same force for the same time, therefore from the above equation, it is clear that the momentum gained by both the bodies is the same.

According to Newton's First Law, a body continues to be in its state of rest or of uniform motion along a straight line unless it is acted upon by some external force to change the state.

Hence, the correct option is (A).

25. When the lift goes down the weight of the body decreases because when the lift goes down there is a force called pseudo force which pushes lift upward and results in a decrease in weight.

When the lift moves downwards with acceleration a. Then the net downward force on the person is:

Mg - R = ma

∴ Apparent weight, R = mg - ma = m (g - a)

So, when a lift accelerates downwards, the apparent weight of the person inside it decreases.

Hence, the correct option is (B).

26. Given that:

Power of the bulb (P) = 30 W

Work done (W) = 540 J

We know that power is the work done per unit time (t), that is,

$P = \frac{W}{t}$

or, $t = \frac{W}{P}$

$= \frac{540}{30}$

= 18 sec

Hence, the correct option is (C).

27. Leaching is used for the purification of Bauxite ore. Leaching is a process that is used in extractive metallurgy. In this process, the ore is treated with chemicals to convert the valuable metals into soluble salts while impurity remains insoluble.

Hence, the correct option is (C).

28. Velocity $=$ Frequency $\times$ Wavelength

Velocity $= 352$ m/s

Frequency $= 8800Hz$

∴ Wavelength $= \frac{\text{Velocity}}{\text{Frequency}}$

$= \frac{352}{8800}$

$= 0.04$ m

So, wavelength is 0.04 m.

Hence, the correct option is (D).

29. The direction of heat flow between two bodies depends on their temperatures. Heat always flows from a body at a higher temperature to a body at a lower temperature. Temperature is the measure of the amount of internal energy of particles.

Hence, the correct option is (C).

30. Given that

$R_1 = 1$ ohm

$R_2 = 2$ ohms

$R_3 = 3$ ohms

$R_4 = 6$ ohms

All resistance are connected in series combination.

$R_{eq} = R_1 + R_2 + R_3 + R_4$

$\Rightarrow R_{eq} = 1 + 2 + 3 + 6$

$\Rightarrow R_{eq} = 12$ ohms

Hence, the correct option is (A).

31. The logic is:

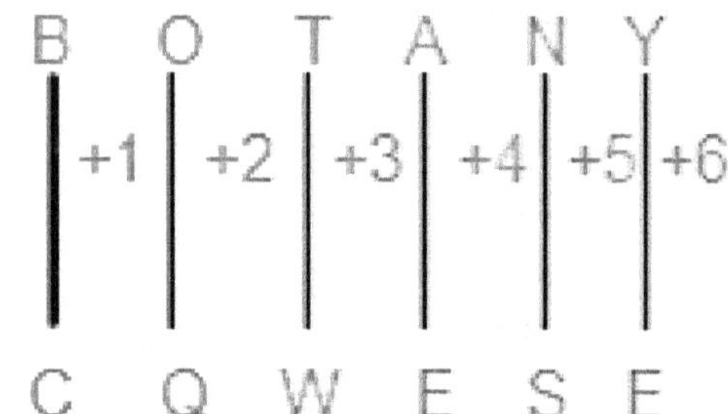

Similarly,

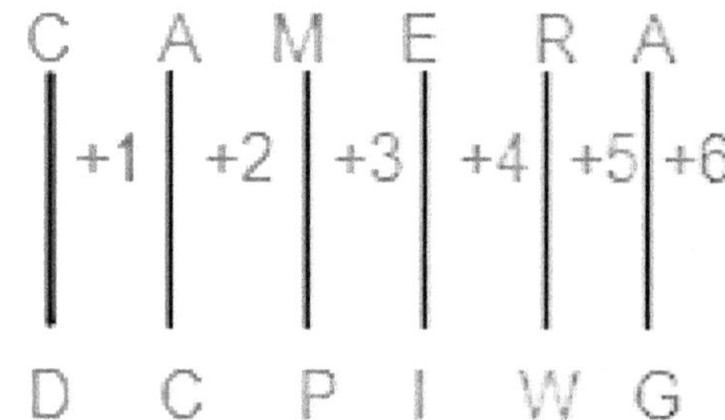

Hence, the correct option is (C).

32. The logic follows here is:

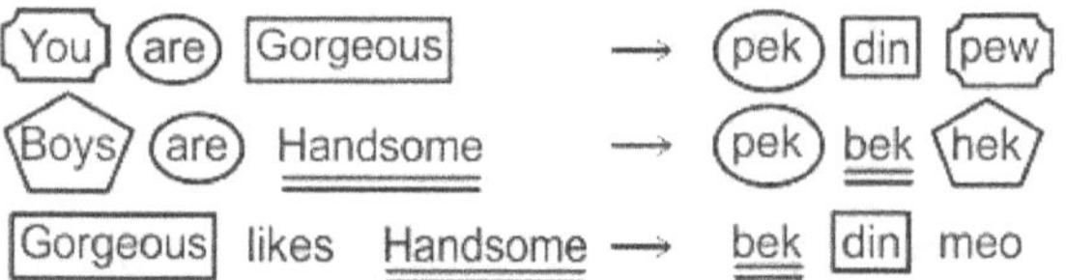

Code for likes is meo.

Hence, the correct option is (B).

33.

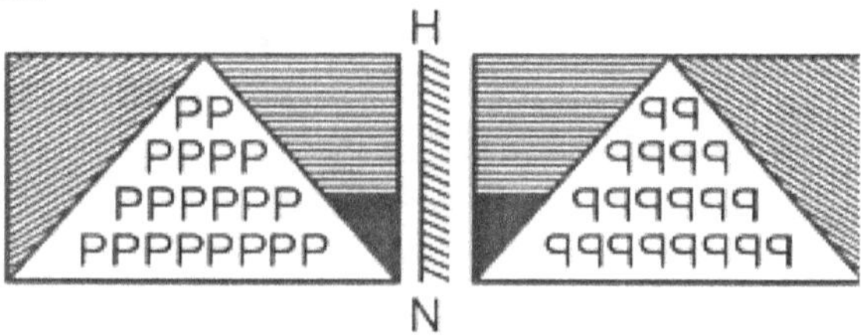

Hence, the correct option is (D).

34.

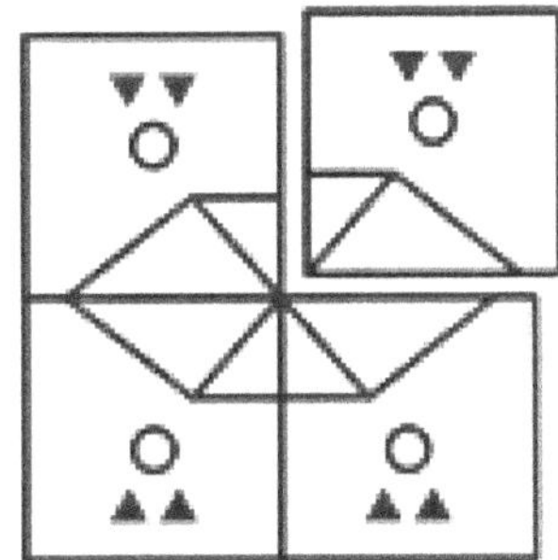

Hence, the correct option is (A).

35. Given equation:

6 + 7 ÷ 2 – 8 × 4 = 18

Let's check each option,

(A) Interchanging ÷ and ×

Equation will become 6 + 7 × 2 - 8 ÷ 4

= 6 + 7 × 2 - 2

= 6 + 14 - 2

= 20 - 2

= 18 = 18

(B) Interchanging + and ×

Equation will become 6 × 7 ÷ 2 - 8 + 4

= 6 × 3.5 - 8 + 4

= 21 - 8 + 4

= 25 - 8

= 17 ≠ 18

(C) Interchanging + and ÷

Equation will become 6 ÷ 7 + 2 – 8 × 4

= 0.8571 + 2 - 8 × 4

= 0.8571 + 2 - 32

= 2.8571 - 24

= - 21.1429 ≠ 18

(D) Interchanging + and -

Equation will become 6 - 7 ÷ 2 + 8 × 4

= 6 - 3.5 + 8 × 4

= 6 - 3.5 + 32

= 38 - 3.5

= 34.5 ≠ 18

Hence, the correct option is (A).

36.

6	8	4	2	3	5	1	7
O	R	D	I	N	A	R	Y

'ORDINARY' is a meaningful English word.
Hence, the correct option is (C).

37.

5	3	1	4	6	2
C	O	M	E	D	Y

'COMEDY' is a meaningful English word.
Hence, the correct option is (B).

38. Given expression:

135 - 5 + 21 × 8 ÷ 112 = 83

(A) × and -

After interchanging the symbols, we get:

L.H.S = 135 × 5 + 21 - 8 ÷ 112

= 675 + 21 – 0.071

= 696 – 0.071

= 695.92 ≠ R.H.S

(B) – and ÷

After interchanging the symbols, we get:

L.H.S = 135 ÷ 5 + 21 × 8 - 112

= 27 + 168 - 112

= 195 - 112

= 83 = R.H.S

(C) + and ÷

After interchanging the symbols, we get:

L.H.S = 135 - 5 ÷ 21 × 8 +112 = 83

= 135 - 0.23 × 8 + 112

= 135 - 1.90 + 112

= 245.1 ≠ R.H.S

(D) × and ÷

After interchanging the symbols, we get:

L.H.S = 135 - 5 + 21 ÷ 8 × 112

= 135 - 5 + 2.625 × 112

= 135 - 5 + 294

= 424 ≠ R.H.S

Hence, the correct option is (B).

39. The correct order is:

3. Skull

9. Face

4. Neck

2. Shoulder

10. Hand

6. Chest

8. Stomach

7. Thigh

5. Knee

1. Heel

Hence, the correct option is (B).

40. The correct order is:

2. Rain

3. Sun

1. Rainbow

5. Child

4. Happy

Hence, the correct option is (B).

41. Given expression is:

$\Rightarrow 3^x - 3^{x-1} = 486$

$\Rightarrow 3^x - 3^x \times 3^{(-1)} = 486$

$\Rightarrow 3^x(1 - 3^{(-1)}) = 486$

$\Rightarrow 3^x\left(1 - \frac{1}{3}\right) = 486$

$\Rightarrow 3^x\left(\frac{3-1}{3}\right) = 486$

$\Rightarrow 3^x\left(\frac{2}{3}\right) = 486$

$\Rightarrow 3^x = 486 \times \frac{3}{2}$

$\Rightarrow 3^x = 729$

$\Rightarrow 3^x = 3^6$

Comparing powers on both the sides

$\Rightarrow x = 6$

Hence, the correct option is (D).

42. Let the second number be x

∵ The first number is twice the second, the first number = 2x

Also, since the first number is half of the third, the third number = 4x

Now, the average of the 3 numbers is 63.

We know that,

Average = $\frac{Sum\ of\ all\ quantities}{Number\ of\ quantities}$

∴ $\frac{2x+x+4x}{3} = 63$

⇒ 7x =189

⇒ x = 27

Thus, the numbers are 54, 27 and 108

The difference between first and third number = 108 – 54 = 54

Hence, the correct option is (C).

43. Given data is 8, 6, 6, x, 5, 5, 6, 8, 8, 10, 5

Mode = 6

If we put x = 6, then the number of 6 appears most often than any other i.e., 4 times, so the value of x will be 6.

Hence, the correct option is (B).

44. Given:

Amount in 2.5 years = 1012

Amount in 4 years = 1067.20

Simple Interest for 1.5 years

= 1067.20 – 1012 = 55.20

Simple Interest for 1 year = $\frac{55.20}{1.5}$ = 36.8

Simple Interest for 2.5 years = 36.8 × 2.5 = 92

Principal = Amount – Simple Interest

⇒ 1012 – 92 = 920

Rate = $\frac{100 \times Simple\ Interest}{P \times t}$

Where P = Principal

t = time

R = Rate of Interest

⇒ $\frac{100 \times 92}{920 \times \frac{5}{2}}$ = 4%

∴ The rate of interest is 4%.

Hence, the correct option is (B).

45. Given:

Cost price = selling price

Let cost price of 1000 g = Rs. 1000

Selling price of 1000 g = Rs. 1000

Due to false weight,

Selling price of 750 g = Rs. 1000

And Cost price of 750 g = Rs 750

Profit% = $\frac{Selling\ price - Cost\ price}{Cost\ price} \times 100$

$= \frac{1000-750}{750} \times 100$

= 33.33%

Hence, the correct option is (A).

46. Given:

X and Y can complete a piece of work in 15 days,

∴ One day work of X and Y combined = $\frac{1}{15}$ unit

and X alone can do the same work in 30 days

∴ One day work of X = $\frac{1}{30}$ unit

One day work of Y,

$\Rightarrow \frac{1}{15} = \frac{1}{30} + \frac{1}{Y}$

$\Rightarrow \frac{1}{Y} = \frac{1}{15} - \frac{1}{30}$

$\Rightarrow \frac{1}{Y} = \frac{2-1}{30}$

$\Rightarrow \frac{1}{Y} = \frac{1}{30}$

⇒ Y = 30

∴ Y alone takes 30 days to complete the same work.

Hence, the correct option is (C).

47. Given:

Distance between A and B = 600 km

Time taken to meet each other (when they start together) = 12 hours

Distance = Speed × Time

Relative speed of two bodies when they travel towards each other = Sum of their speed

When they start moving towards each other, they meet in 12 hours,

Let the speed of A be 'A' km/hr and the speed of B be 'B' km/hr

$\Rightarrow \frac{600}{(A+B)} = 12$

⇒ A + B = 50......(1)

If A started moving 5 hours after B, then they meet in 10 hours,

Distance covered by A and B in 10 hours = 50 × 10 = 500

Remaining distance (600 - 500 = 100 km) was already covered by B in 5 hours

Speed of B = $\frac{100}{5}$ = 20 km/hr

∴ The speed of B is 20 km/hr

Hence, the correct option is (A).

48. Given

Total students = 550

Ratio of boys and girls = 6 : 5

Number of boys $= 550 \times \frac{6}{11} = 300$

Number of girls $= 550 \times \frac{5}{11} = 250$

Let the number of girls joining the class be x.

Now,

$\frac{300}{250+x} = 5:6$

$\Rightarrow 250 + x = 300 \times \frac{6}{5}$

$\Rightarrow 250 + x = 360$

$\Rightarrow x = 360 - 250 = 110$

∴ The required girls is 110.

Hence, the correct option is (D).

49. We know that,

$\cos(90-\theta)^\circ = \sin\theta^\circ$

$\sin^2\theta + \cos^2\theta = 1$

Given:

$\cos^2 1^\circ + \cos^2 3^\circ + \cos^2 5^\circ + \cdots .. + \cos^2 89^\circ$

$\Rightarrow (\cos^2 1^\circ + \cos^2 89^\circ) + (\cos^2 3^\circ + \cos^2 87^\circ) + \ldots . + (\cos^2 43^\circ + \cos^2 47^\circ) + \cos^2 45^\circ$

$\Rightarrow (\cos^2 1^\circ + \cos^2(90-1)^\circ) + (\cos^2 3^\circ + \cos^2(90-3)^\circ) + \ldots\ldots + (\cos^2 43^\circ + \cos^2(90-43)^\circ) + \cos^2 45^\circ$

$\Rightarrow (\cos^2 1^\circ + \sin^2 1^\circ) + (\cos^2 3^\circ + \sin^2 3^\circ) + \ldots\ldots + (\cos^2 43^\circ + \sin^2 43^\circ) + \cos^2 45^\circ$

$\Rightarrow 1 + 1 + \cdots \ldots + \left(\frac{1}{\sqrt{2}}\right)^2 = 22 + \frac{1}{2} = 22.5$

$\therefore \cos^2 1^\circ + \cos^2 3^\circ + \cos^2 5^\circ + \ldots\ldots + \cos^2 89^\circ = 22.5$

Hence, the correct option is (B).

50. Given:

$\left(\frac{\tan x+1-\sec x}{\cot x+1-\operatorname{cosec} x}\right)\cos x$

$= \left(\frac{\frac{\sin x}{\cos x}+1-\frac{1}{\cos z}}{\frac{\cos x}{\sin x}+1-\frac{1}{\sin x}}\right)\cos x$

$= \frac{(\cos x+\sin x-1)\times\sin x}{(\sin x+\cos x-1)\times\cos x} \times \cos x$

$= \sin x$

Hence, the correct option is (B).

51. Given:

∠ADC = 100°

The angle made by the diameter at the circumference in a semicircle is 90°.

If ABCD is a cyclic quadrilateral, so the sum of a pair of two opposite angles will be 180°.

∠A + ∠C = 180°

∠B + ∠D = 180°

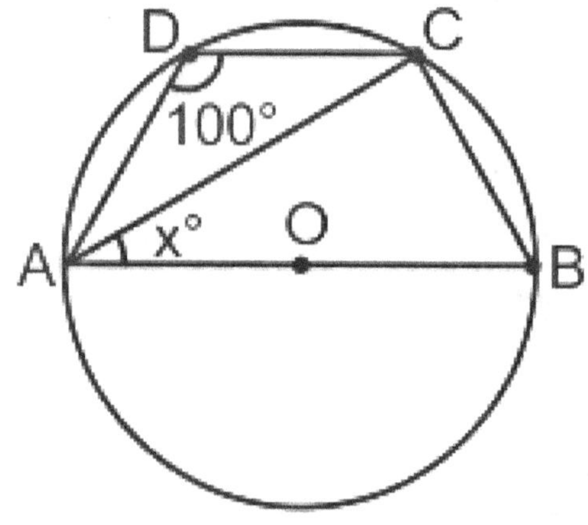

In ΔACB,

⇒ ∠ACB = 90°

⇒ ∠ADC + ∠ABC = 180°

⇒ 100° + ∠ABC = 180°

⇒ ∠ABC = 80°

In ΔABC,

∠ACB + ∠CAB + ∠ABC = 180°

⇒ x° + 90° + 80° = 180°

⇒ x° = 180° – 170°

⇒ x° = 10°

∴ The value of x is 10°.

Hence, the correct option is (B).

52. Given:

PQ = 15 cm

BQ = 5 cm

If AQ is a secant and PQ is a tangent, then

$(PQ)^2 = AQ \times BQ$

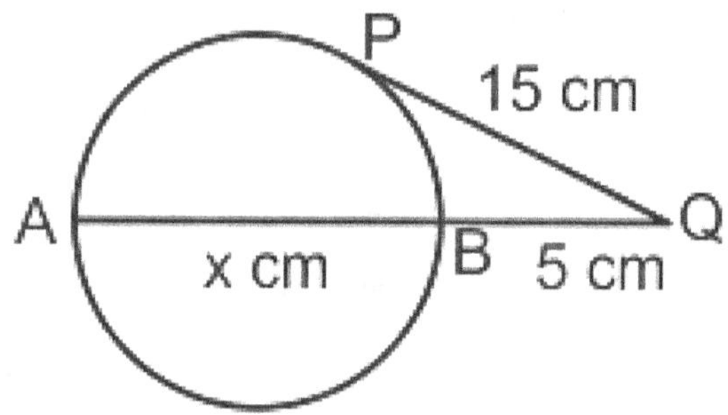

Let the length of the chord be x.

$\Rightarrow (15)^2 = (x+5) \times 5$

$\Rightarrow \frac{(15)^2}{5} = x+5$

$\Rightarrow x+5 = 45$

$\Rightarrow x = 45 - 5$

$\Rightarrow x = 40$

∴ The length of the chord is 40 cm.

Hence, the correct option is (B).

53. When a polynomial $f(x)$ is divided by $(x-a)$, the remainder $= f(a)$.

⇒ Remainder $= f(-1)$

$\Rightarrow 4(-1)^5 + 3(-1)^4 + 2(-1)^3 + 5(-1)^2 + (-1) - 3$

$\Rightarrow -4 + 3 - 2 + 5 - 1 - 3$

∴ Remainder is -2

Hence, the correct option is (C).

54. Given:

$p \times 2^2 = 8^2$

$\Rightarrow p \times 2 \times 2 = 8 \times 8$

$\Rightarrow p = \frac{8\times8}{2\times2}$

$\Rightarrow p = 4 \times 4$

$\Rightarrow p = 16$

$\Rightarrow p^3 = (16)^3$

$\Rightarrow p^3 = 4096$

Hence, the correct option is (C).

55. Let the radii of the two cylinders be 'r_1' and 'r_2' units and their respective heights be 'h_1' and 'h_2' units respectively

$\Rightarrow \frac{h_1}{h_2} = 2$.....(1)

$\because$ Curved surface area of a cylinder $= 2\pi \times$ radius $\times$ height

Ratio of curved surface areas $= \frac{2\pi r_1 h_1}{2\pi r_2 h_2} = \frac{2}{3}$

Substituting from (1),

$\Rightarrow \frac{r_1}{r_2} = \frac{2}{3} \times \frac{1}{2} = \frac{1}{3}$......(2)

Now,

Volume of a cylinder $= \pi \times (\text{radius})^2 \times$ height

Ratio of volumes of cylinders $= \frac{\pi r_1^2 h_1}{\pi r_2^2 h_2}$

Substituting from (1) and (2),

$\therefore$ Ratio of volumes of cylinders $= \frac{1}{9} \times 2 = \frac{2}{9} = 2:9$

Hence, the correct option is (C).

56. Given;

Radius of sphere = 9cm and radius of bullet = 0.3 cm

Let n be the number of bullets that can be made out of the sphere.

Volume of sphere $= \frac{4}{3}\pi r^3$

$= \frac{4}{3} \times \pi \times (9)^3$

Volume of each bullet $= \frac{4}{3} \times \pi \times (0.3)^3$

Now,

Number of bullets $= \frac{\text{Volume of the sphere}}{\text{Volume of each bullet}}$

$\Rightarrow n = \frac{\frac{4}{3}\times\pi\times(9)^3}{\frac{4}{3}\times\pi\times(0.3)^3}$

$\Rightarrow n = \frac{(9)^3}{(0.3)^3}$

$\Rightarrow n = 27000$

Hence, the correct option is (C).

57. $x - y = 2015 - 2014 = 1$

$y - z = 2014 - 2013 = 1$

$z - x = 2013 - 2015 = -2$

$\therefore x^2 + y^2 + z^2 - xy - yz - zx$

Numerator and denominator multiplied by 2

$= \frac{1}{2}(2x^2 + 2y^2 + 2z^2 - 2xy - 2yz - 2zx)$

$= \frac{1}{2}(x^2 + y^2 - 2xy + y^2 + z^2 - 2yz + z^2 + x^2 - 2zx)$

$= \frac{1}{2}[(x-y)^2 + (y-z)^2 + (z-x)^2]$

$= \frac{1}{2}[1 + 1 + 4]$

$= \frac{1}{2} \times 6$

$= 3$

Hence, the correct option is (A).

58. Given equations,

$\frac{x}{4} + \frac{y}{3} = \frac{5}{12}$

$\Rightarrow \frac{3x+4y}{12} = \frac{5}{12}$

$\Rightarrow 3x + 4y = 5$....(i)

$\frac{x}{2} + y = 1$

$\Rightarrow \frac{x+2y}{2} = 1$

$\Rightarrow x + 2y = 1 \times 2$

$\Rightarrow x + 2y = 2$....(ii)

Solving (i) and (ii), we get

$y = \frac{1}{2}$ and $x = 1$

So, $x + y = \frac{3}{2}$

Hence, the correct option is (B).

59. Given,

30% of $1225 - 64\%$ of $555 = (?)$

$= \left(\frac{30}{100} \times 1225\right) - \left(\frac{64}{100} \times 555\right)$

$= (367.5 - 355.2)$

$= 12.3$

Hence, the correct option is (B).

60. Given:

Two candidates fought an election one get 65% of the votes and won by 300 votes.

Let the total number of votes be x

According to the question,

$\Rightarrow 65\%$ of $x - 35\%$ of $x = 300$

$\Rightarrow 30\%$ of $x = 300$

$\Rightarrow \frac{30}{100}x = 300$

$\Rightarrow x = \frac{30000}{30}$

$\Rightarrow x = 1000$

∴ The total number of votes polled is 1000.

Hence, the correct option is (C).

Mock Test 06

English

Q.1 Direction: In the following question, a sentence has been given in Active voice. Change the sentence to Passive voice.

Someone has lit the fire.

A. The fire was lit by someone.
B. You are requested to light the fire by someone.
C. The fire has been lit by someone.
D. The fire had been lit by someone.

Q.2 Direction: In the question below the sentence has been given in Direct speech. From the given alternatives, choose the one which best expresses the given sentence in Indirect/Direct speech.

"If you don't keep quiet I shall shoot you", he said to her in a calm voice.

A. He warned her to shoot if she didn't keep quiet calmly.
B. He said calmly that I shall shoot you if you don't be quiet.
C. He warned her calmly that he would shoot her if she didn't keep quiet.
D. Calmly he warned her that be quiet or else he will have to shoot her.

Ques (3-5):Direction: Read the passage carefully and answer the question that follow.

It is notable that power major NTPC has joined hands with oil giant IOC to set up a series of electric vehicle (EV) charging stations in cities and along highways. There is much potential for India to emerge as a leader in small and public EVs, given high latent demand. The benefits in reducing demand for imported crude oil can be huge, apart from reducing carbon emissions and other air pollutants.

The most effective way to bring down carbon emissions and pollution from transport is to vastly expand and improve public transport — buses are just 2% of the vehicles on the road. That said, there is much scope to replace India's giant fleet of two-wheelers with electric bikes. India has over 170 million two-wheelers, and sales data from the last six years show that 79% of on-road vehicles here are two-wheelers. It would make perfect sense to boost supply of EVs, especially two-wheelers, e-rickshaws, tempos and small cars, so as to **complement** and supplement public transport going forward.

Estimates suggest that by meeting a rising part of the incremental demand for mobility, EVs can lead to macroeconomic benefits, and sooner rather than later.

Assuming only about half a litre of petrol consumption per two-wheeler daily, or about 200 litres annually, the volumes would add up to over 30 billion litres. And the bill for which, at current prices, would amount to well over Rs 2 lakh crore.

In tandem, we need power reforms to rev up utility realisations and strengthen the grid. India also has an opportunity in supplying on-board electric batteries. Swapping services to provide charged batteries on lease would step-up diffusion of EVs. A power-electronics industry ecosystem would raise production and provide high-efficiency subsystems for EVs. India must not miss the bus on EVs.

Q.3 "There is much potential for India to emerge as a leader in small and public EVs, given high latent demand." What can be logically deducted from the given sentence?

I. Electric vehicles are less in developed countries as compared to India.

II. India has not yet adopted electric vehicles fully.

III. Indians are already demanding a huge number of electric vehicles.

A. Only III **B.** Only II
C. Only I and III **D.** All of I, II and III

Q.4 Which of the following is/are true with respect to the two wheelers in India?

I. India has over 160 million two-wheelers.

II. 79% of on-road vehicles in India are two-wheelers.

III. People prefer two wheelers to four wheelers due to ease of use.

A. Only I **B.** Only II
C. Only I and II **D.** Only I and III

Q.5 What is the tone of the passage?

A. Sarcastic **B.** Caustic
C. Cynical **D.** Laudatory

Q.6 Direction: In the question choose the word which best expresses the meaning of the given word.

Stalemate

A. Degeneration **B.** Deadlock
C. Exhaustion **D.** Settlement

Q.7 Direction: In the question choose the word which is the exact OPPOSITE of the given words.

Gravitate

A. Meditate **B.** Become serious
C. Deteriorate **D.** Retreat

Q.8 Fill in the blank with proper preposition

Many species of insects were wiped ______ when the jungle was cleared.

A. of **B.** away **C.** off **D.** out

Q.9 Direction: In below compare the bold part of the sentence with alternatives A, B, C and D. Choose the correct expression which is an improvement upon the bold part.

The small child does whatever his father **was done.**

A. has done **B.** did **C.** does **D.** had done

Q.10 Choose the present indefinite tense.

A. I write articles on different topics.

B. She watched television.
C. They were all shocked at his failure in the competition.
D. She had met him before the party.

Q.11 Direction: Fill in the blank with a proper adjective.
What about this? Isn't it ______?
A. Beautiful **B.** Beauteous
C. Beauty **D.** Beauties

Q.12 Fill in the blank with proper pronoun.
If you can't find your book, you can borrow _____.
A. me **B.** mine **C.** myself **D.** my

Ques (13-14):Direction: In the question given below out of four alternatives, choose the one which can be substituted for the given phrase.

Q.13 One who studies the evolution of mankind
A. Anthropologist **B.** Astronaut
C. Calligraphist **D.** Compere

Q.14 A person, who travels in spacecraft
A. Curator **B.** Laxicographer
C. Astronaut **D.** Psephologist

Q.15 What is the meaning of Anachronistic?
A. Misplaced chronologically
B. Eagerness
C. Enhance power, wealth or status
D. Renouncing a belief or doctrine

General Knowledge

Q.16 Ustad Ali Ahmed Hussain Khan, who passed away recently was a famous:

[RRB (NTPC), 2017]

A. Santoor Player **B.** Tabla Player
C. Sarod Player **D.** Shehnai Player

Q.17 Rasleela is the folk dance of which of the following states?
A. Gujarat **B.** Himachal Pradesh
C. Bihar **D.** Uttar Pradesh

Q.18 Which is the highest gallantry award in India?
A. Param Vishishtat Seva Medal
B. Param Vir Chakra
C. Kirti Chakra
D. Vir Chakra

Q.19 Where is Lake Superior, the largest fresh water lake in the world located?
A. USA **B.** Brazil **C.** Canada **D.** Russia

Q.20 When did Subhash Chandra Bose set up the Interim Government?
A. 1941 **B.** 1942 **C.** 1943 **D.** 1945

Science

Q.21 What is the ability of an object to do work due to its motion called?
A. Kinetic energy **B.** Potential energy
C. Chemical energy **D.** Electrical energy

Q.22 Horsepower is equal to how many watts?
A. 746 watts **B.** 846 watts
C. 946 watts **D.** 796 watts

Q.23 Which of the following is the fastest method of heat transfer?
A. Convection **B.** Conduction
C. Radiation **D.** Insolation

Q.24 The nucleus of an atom consists of the following particles:
A. Protons and neutrons
B. Electron and proton
C. Only protons
D. Electron and neutron

Q.25 The value of the time period of a sound wave is 0.01s. The frequency of sound is:
A. 10 Hz **B.** 100 Hz **C.** 1000 Hz **D.** 1 Hz

Q.26 The molecular formula of ethane is C_2H_6 in:
A. 6 Covalent bonds **B.** 7 Covalent bonds
C. 8 Covalent bonds **D.** 9 Covalent bonds

Q.27 Which of the following metals are kept immersed in kerosene?
A. Magnesium **B.** Sodium
C. Mercury **D.** Tungsten

Q.28 On what principle does a rocket work?
A. Law of conservation of energy
B. Law of conservation of mass
C. Law of conservation of momentum
D. Newton's third law of motion

Q.29 An object falling on the earth is attracted towards the earth. According to the third law of motion, an object also attracts the earth. But we cannot see the earth moving towards the object. Which of the following can explain this?
A. The first law of motion
B. The second law of motion
C. The third law of motion
D. None of these

Q.30 Which of the following will happen when a sheet of paper and a stone are dropped simultaneously from the same height (on the earth)?
A. Due to the less mass of the paper it will reach the ground after the stone.
B. Due to the friction on the paper, it will reach the ground after the stone.
C. Both will reach the ground together.
D. Due to the greater gravity acting on the stone, it will reach the bottom before the paper.

Reasoning

Q.31 If LOSE is coded as 1357 and GAIN is coded as 2468, what do the figures 84615 stand for?

A. NAILS **B.** SNAIL **C.** LANES **D.** SLAIN

Q.32 If in a sign language CHILD is written as IMOQJ, then how will BABE be written in that language?

A. HFHJ **B.** FGFK **C.** FFGJ **D.** HFGJ

Q.33 What should come next in the following number sequence?

$$1,3,8,19,42,89,?$$

A. 108 **B.** 184 **C.** 167 **D.** 97

Q.34 What should come next in the following number sequence?

$$5,16,51,158,?$$

A. 1452 **B.** 483 **C.** 481 **D.** 1454

Q.35 I, K, M, N, P, P, U are the letters of the name of a vegetable. If the letters are arranged correctly, then what is the last letter of that word?

A. M **B.** N **C.** K **D.** P

Q.36 How many independent complete words can be formed from the letters of the word 'HEARTLESS' using each letter only once and without changing the order of the letters?

A. Two **B.** Three **C.** Four **D.** Five

Q.37 If '*' means ' ×', '$' means '+', '#' means ' ÷' and '@' means '-' ; Then what will be the value of the following expression?

360 # 24 $ 56 * 5 @ 48

A. 253 **B.** 242 **C.** 247 **D.** 285

Q.38 If ' ×' means '+', '+' means ' ÷', ' ÷' means '-' and '-' means ' ×'; Then what will be the value of the following expression?

$$5-7\times9+3=2$$

A. 36 **B.** 315 **C.** 48 **D.** 44

Q.39 When put together properly, the top three puzzle pieces will create one of the following shapes (a-d).

Note that a side marked x has to touch x and a side marked y has to touch y.

Choose the correct answer.

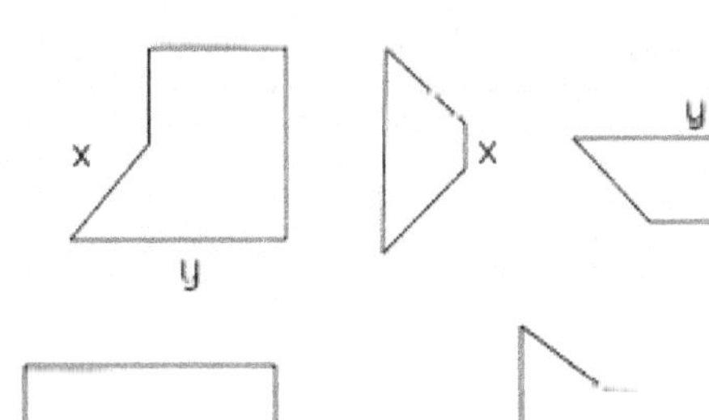

A.

B.

C.

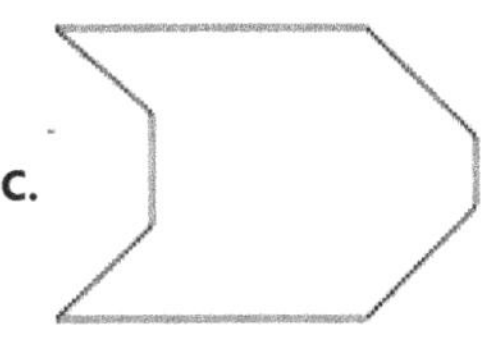

D.

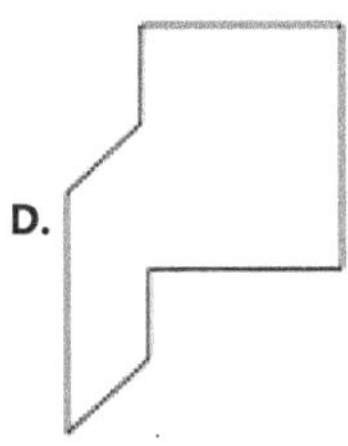

Q.40 When put together properly, the top three puzzle pieces will create one of the following shapes (a-d).

Note that a side marked x has to touch x and a side marked y has to touch y.

Choose the correct answer.

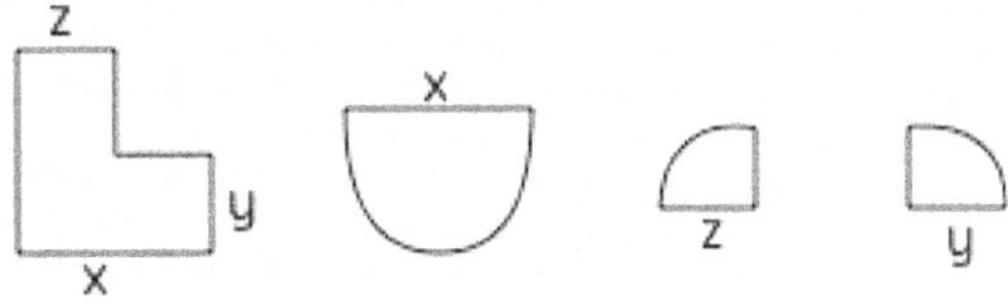

A.

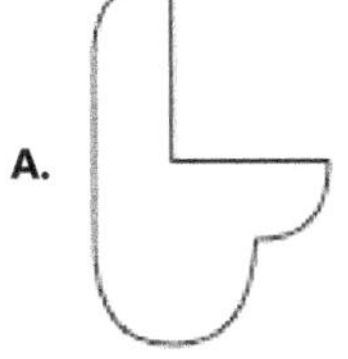

B.

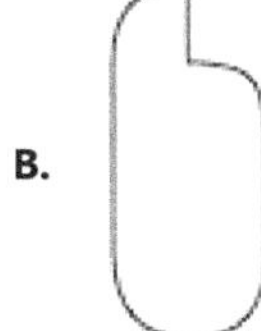

C.

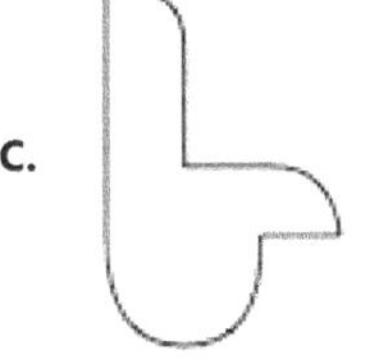

D.

Mathematics

Ques (41-42):Direction: What will come in place of question mark(?) in the following question?

Q.41 $3\frac{18}{57}\times48\frac{54}{63}\times6\frac{1}{9}+2\frac{1}{2}=?$

A. 792.5 **B.** 852.5 **C.** 1092.5 **D.** 992.5

Q.42 $4\frac{3}{10}+2\frac{5}{3}-5\frac{7}{8}=?$

A. $2\frac{111}{120}$ **B.** $2\frac{133}{115}$ **C.** $1\frac{119}{120}$ **D.** $2\frac{11}{120}$

Q.43 Solve: $\frac{6}{x}+\frac{3}{v}=7,\frac{3}{x}+\frac{9}{u}=11$

A. $x=\frac{3}{2},y=1$ **B.** $x-3,y=1$

C. $x=2,y=1$ **D.** $x=1,y=3$

Q.44 The wheel of a motor cycle is of radius 35 cm. The number of revolutions per minute must the wheel make so as to keep a speed of 66 km/h is:

A. 1100 **B.** 600 **C.** 500 **D.** 44

Q.45 Find the radius of a circle whose circumference is equal to the sum of the circumferences of two circles of radii 15 cm and 18 cm.

A. 44 cm **B.** 22 cm **C.** 33 cm **D.** 66 cm

Q.46 Five tables and eight chairs cost Rs. 7,350; three tables and five chairs cost Rs. 4,475. The price of a table is:

A. 950 **B.** 325 **C.** 925 **D.** 350

Q.47 If $x + \left(\frac{1}{x}\right) = 3$, then the value of $\frac{(3x^2-4x+3)}{(x^2-x+1)}$ is:

A. $\frac{4}{3}$ **B.** $\frac{3}{2}$ **C.** $\frac{5}{2}$ **D.** $\frac{5}{3}$

Q.48 The sum of all interior angles of a regular polygon is twice the sum of all its exterior angles. The number of sides of the polygon is:

A. 10 **B.** 8 **C.** 12 **D.** 6

Q.49 There are two regular polygons with a number of sides equal to (n – 1) and (n + 2). Their exterior angles differ by 6°. The value of n is:

A. 14 **B.** 12 **C.** 13 **D.** 11

Q.50 If sin 3A = cos (A – 26°), where 3A is an acute angle then the value of A is:

A. 29° **B.** 26° **C.** 23° **D.** 28°

Q.51 The average of a non-zero number and its square is 7 times the number. The number is:

A. 13 **B.** 17 **C.** 29 **D.** 28

Q.52 A sum of Rs, 800 amounts to Rs. 920 in 3 years at simple interest. If the interest rate is increased by 3%, it would amount to how much?

A. Rs. 652 **B.** Rs. 752 **C.** Rs. 992 **D.** Rs. 562

Q.53 A certain sum of money amounts to Rs. 1008 in 2 years and to Rs. 1164 in $\frac{7}{2}$ years. Find the sum and the rate of interest.

A. 10% **B.** 11% **C.** 12% **D.** 13%

Q.54 The total number of students in a school is 2140. If the number of girls in the school is 1200, then what is the respective ratio of the total number of boys to the total number of girls in the school?

A. 26 : 25 **B.** 47 : 60 **C.** 18 : 13 **D.** 31 : 79

Q.55 The income of A is 150% of the income of B and the income of C is 120% of the income of A. If the total income of A, B and C together is Rs. 86000, what is C's income?

A. Rs. 30000 **B.** Rs. 32000
C. Rs. 20000 **D.** Rs. 36000

Q.56 The price of an article is first increased by 20% and later decreased by 25% due to decrease in sales. Find the net percentage change in the final price of the article.

A. 20% **B.** 18% **C.** 38% **D.** 10%

Q.57 In an examination it is required to get 290 of the aggregate marks to pass. A student gets 203 marks and is declared failed by 12% of total marks, what are the maximum aggregate marks a student can get?

A. 775 **B.** 750 **C.** 725 **D.** 730

Q.58 A and B together can complete a piece of work in 12 days, B and C can do it in 20 days and C and A can do it in 15 days. A, B and C together can complete it in:

A. 12 days **B.** 6 days **C.** 8 days **D.** 10 days

Q.59 'A' can do a piece of work in 20 days and 'B' can do the same work in 15 days. How long will they take to finish the work, if both work together?

A. 15 days **B.** 10 days **C.** $8\frac{4}{7}$ days **D.** 20 days

Q.60 Raj and Prem walk in opposite direction at the rate of 3 km and 2 km per hour respectively. How far will they be from each other after 2 hours?

A. 6 km **B.** 8 km **C.** 10 km **D.** 2 km

// Smart Answer Sheet //

Correct Percentage of students who answered correctly. **Skipped** Percentage of students who skipped.

Q.	Ans.	Correct	Skipped	Q.	Ans.	Correct	Skipped	Q.	Ans.	Correct	Skipped	Q.	Ans.	Correct	Skipped	Q.	Ans.	Correct	Skipped	Q.	Ans.	Correct	Skipped
1	C	84.93 %	0.0 %	11	A	57.92 %	1.13 %	21	A	45.34 %	1.12 %	31	A	89.94 %	0.0 %	41	D	40.74 %	1.69 %	51	A	63.21 %	1.56 %
2	C	50.52 %	1.96 %	12	B	77.75 %	0.0 %	22	A	86.91 %	0.0 %	32	A	54.15 %	1.59 %	42	D	58.64 %	1.67 %	52	C	40.36 %	1.91 %
3	B	18.86 %	3.85 %	13	A	52.32 %	1.19 %	23	C	63.11 %	1.54 %	33	B	58.13 %	1.1 %	43	A	54.31 %	1.17 %	53	D	57.59 %	1.13 %
4	C	31.98 %	4.48 %	14	C	47.69 %	1.63 %	24	A	83.59 %	0.0 %	34	C	67.06 %	1.14 %	44	C	51.19 %	1.49 %	54	B	43.35 %	1.34 %
5	D	65.22 %	1.62 %	15	A	42.07 %	1.89 %	25	B	51.08 %	1.07 %	35	B	84.01 %	0.0 %	45	C	43.94 %	1.97 %	55	D	57.01 %	1.22 %
6	B	52.16 %	1.7 %	16	D	25.88 %	3.47 %	26	B	50.9 %	1.81 %	36	B	54.14 %	1.68 %	46	A	56.18 %	1.08 %	56	D	52.92 %	1.85 %
7	D	61.88 %	1.03 %	17	D	56.68 %	1.77 %	27	B	26.74 %	4.23 %	37	C	42.29 %	1.55 %	47	C	66.46 %	1.42 %	57	C	57.26 %	1.45 %
8	D	81.41 %	0.0 %	18	B	66.11 %	1.31 %	28	D	46.33 %	1.65 %	38	A	28.55 %	3.31 %	48	D	43.91 %	1.41 %	58	D	15.53 %	4.92 %
9	C	64.76 %	1.67 %	19	A	45.15 %	1.78 %	29	B	19.91 %	4.32 %	39	B	86.02 %	0.0 %	49	C	12.24 %	3.06 %	59	C	42.03 %	1.89 %
10	A	76.05 %	0.0 %	20	C	49.85 %	1.6 %	30	B	47.86 %	1.53 %	40	A	20.76 %	3.55 %	50	A	83.35 %	0.0 %	60	C	40.99 %	1.56 %

//Hints and Solutions//

1. The given sentence is in active voice and it is in Present Perfect Tense. In the passive form conversion take place like this,

Subject + (has /have) + been + V^3 + Other agents

The sentence is, "The fire has been lit by someone."

Hence, the correct option is (C).

2. In the given sentence, there are two sentences, have been added by two type of tenses. First one is Present indefinite tense and the second one is Future indefinite tense.

So, for the indirect speech we will convert Present indefinite tense into Past indefinite tense and in Future indefinite tense, "will" converts into "would" and "shall" converts into "should". Therefore,

The sentence in the indirect speech is, "He warned her calmly that he would shoot her if she didn't keep quiet."

Hence, the correct option is (C).

3. Statement II: India has not yet adopted electric vehicles fully.

This is correct. Since there is scope for adoption of a huge number of EVs, India has the potential to emerge as a global leader in this sector but it has not yet achieved so. Thus, statement II is valid.

Statement I: Electric vehicles are less in developed countries as compared to India.

Nothing has been indicated regarding the number of electric vehicles in developed countries. This makes statement I an invalid one.

Statement III: Indians are already demanding a huge number of electric vehicles.

The demand for electric vehicles in India is still latent, i.e., existing but not yet developed or manifested. This, thus, makes statement III invalid.

Hence, the correct option is (B).

4. According to the question, that said, there is much scope to replace India's giant fleet of two-wheelers with electric bikes. India has over 170 million two-wheelers, and sales data from the last six years show that 79% of on-road vehicles here are two-wheelers.

Statement I: India has over 160 million two-wheelers.

If the number is over 170 million, it would also be over 160 million.

Thus, statement I is valid.

Statement II: 79% of on-road vehicles in India are two-wheelers.

This fact is given in the passage. Thus, statement II is valid.

Statement III: People prefer two wheelers to four wheelers due to ease of use.

Nothing regarding the preference of Indians for two wheelers has been mentioned in the passage. This, thus, makes statement III invalid.

Hence, the correct option is (C).

5. Sarcastic, caustic, and cynical are tones that correspond to negative passages. However, the given passage is not negative in nature. Thus, options (A), (B), and (C) are eliminated.

The tone of this passage is positive and optimistic. The author supports as well as justifies the subject.

Hence, the correct option is (D).

6. Stalemate: A situation in an argument in which neither side can win or make any progress

Deadlock: A situation in which two sides cannot reach an agreement

Degeneration: Declension

Exhaustion: The state of being extremely tired

Settlement: The act of reaching an agreement

Hence, the correct option is (B).

7. Gravitate: Move towards or be attracted to a person or thing

Retreat: To move backwards

Meditate: To think carefully and deeply

Become serious: To begin to seriously focus on something

Deteriorate: To become worse

Hence, the correct option is (D).

8. We use 'out' as a preposition to talk about movement from within somewhere or something, usually with a verb that expresses movement (e.g. go, come). It shows where something is or was going. So, here we will use 'out'.

Then the sentence is, "Many species of insects were wiped **out** when the jungle was cleared."

Hence, the correct option is (D).

9. In the given sentence, 'was done' is replaced by 'does'.

Then, the correct sentence is, "The small child does whatever his father does."

Hence, the correct option is (C).

10. In the simple present tense when an action is happening right now, or when it happens regularly (or unceasingly, which is why it's sometimes called present indefinite). Depending on the person, the simple present tense is formed by using the root form or by adding -s or -es to the end.

Then, "I write articles on different topics." is a sentence of present indefinite tense.

Hence, the correct option is (A).

11. A proper adjective is a word that modifies nouns and pronouns and is formed from a proper noun.

What about this? Isn't it **Beautiful?**

Hence, the correct option is (A).

12. A pronoun is a word that takes the place of a noun. Pronouns can be subjects of the sentence (I, he, she, it, you, we).

Then the sentence is, "If you can't find your book, you can borrow **mine**."

Hence, the correct option is (B).

13. Anthropologist: A person engaged in the study of aspects of humans within past and present societies.

Astronaut: A person who is trained to travel in a spacecraft.

Calligraphist: Someone skilled in penmanship.

Compere: A person who introduces the performers or contestants in a variety show.

Hence, the correct option is (A).

14. Astronaut: A person who is trained to travel in a spacecraft.

Curator: One in charge of a museum, zoo, or other places of the exhibit.

Lexicographer: A person who compiles dictionaries.

Psephologist: Someone who studies elections.

Hence, the correct option is (C).

15. The meaning of Anachronistic is 'Misplaced chronologically'.

Renouncing a belief or doctrine: Abnegation

Eagerness: Alacrity

Enhance power, wealth or status: Aggrandize

Hence, the correct option is (A).

16. Ustad Ali Ahmed Hussain Khan, who passed away recently was a famous Shehnai Player.

The renowned Shehnai exponent Ustad Ali Ahmad Hussain Khan (77) passed away on 16 March 2016, in Kolkata, West Bengal. He was known for his innovative style and mastery over the classical, semi-classical, and folk music repertoire.

Hence, the correct option is (D).

17. Rasleela is a folk dance of Uttar Pradesh. Rasleela or Krishnalila consists of the activities of young and child Krishna. Rasleela is staged from place to place, in which the decorated Shri Krishna is shown expressing his love for Radha in different forms. Seeing this rasleela the audience feels as if they have actually reached the era of Shri Krishna.

Hence, the correct option is (D).

18. The Param Vir Chakra is India's highest gallantry award, awarded for gallantry and sacrifice of a high order in the presence of enemies. In most cases this honor is given posthumously. The award was instituted on 26 January 1950 when the Republic of India was declared.

Hence, the correct option is (B).

19. Lake Superior is a lake located in America. It is one of the largest lakes. To the north of Lake Superior are the Canadian provinces of Ontario and the US states of Minnesota, and to the south are the states of Wisconsin and Michigan. It is the largest lake in both the area and volume of the giant lakes. It is the third largest fresh water lake in the world in terms of size.

Hence, the correct option is (A).

20. In 1943, Subhash Chandra Bose established an interim government named Arzi Hukumat-e-Azad Hind in Singapore. It was supported by Axis powers of imperial Japan, Nazi Germany, Italian Social republic and their allies under provincial government Bose was PM and minister of war and foreign affairs Rash Behari Bose was designated as supreme advisor Capital Laxmi headed Women's organization.

Hence, the correct option is (C).

21. The ability of an object to do work due to its motion is called kinetic energy. Kinetic energy is the excess energy of a body due to its linear velocity or angular velocity or both. Its value is equal to the work done in accelerating that body from rest to that velocity. Like in running water, in an arrow released from a bow, the ball thrown by the player has kinetic energy.

Hence, the correct option is (A).

22. Horsepower is the unit of measurement of power. It is a non-SI unit. There are many standards for horsepower and there are many types. One horsepower is equal to 746 watts.

Hence, the correct option is (A).

23. Heat transfer occurs in three ways:

1. Conduction
2. Convection
3. Radiation

Radiation is the fastest method of heat transfer. Radiation is a form of energy that is emitted in the form of waves. Under this definition, the radiation includes ordinary visible light rays, infrared light rays, ultraviolet rays, X rays, etc.

Hence, the correct option is (C).

24. The nucleus is made up of the nuclear particles protons and neutrons. These particles are called nucleons. Both protons and neutrons have almost equal mass and both have an intrinsic angular momentum (spin) $\frac{1}{2}$. The proton unit is electrically charged while the neutron is uncharged.

Hence, the correct option is (A).

25. Given,

The value of the time period of a sound wave is 0.01s.

As we know,

Frequency of sound = $\frac{1}{Time\ period}$

$= \frac{1}{0.01}$

$= 100$ Hz

Hence, the correct option is (B).

26. The bond formed between two atoms by sharing one electron pair is called a covalent bond.

The structure of the molecular formula of ethane is as follows:

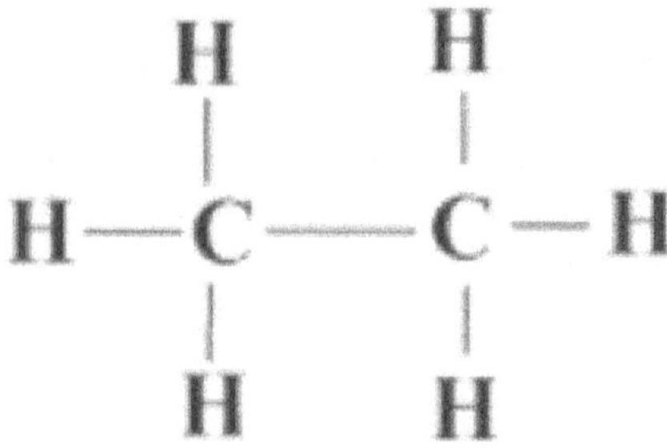

It is clear from the structure that one covalent bond is between carbon-carbon and 6 covalent bond is between carbon-hydrogen. So ethane has total 7 covalent bonds.

Hence, the correct option is (B).

27. Sodium is kept immersed in kerosene because sodium is an active metal that reacts with oxygen present in the air to form sodium oxide. It reacts with water to produce sodium hydroxide and hydrogen. If left open in the air, it catches fire. Therefore, being a very active metal, it is preserved by immersing it in kerosene.

Hence, the correct option is (B).

28. A rocket is a type of vehicle whose flying principle is based on Newton's third law of motion, action, and equal and opposite reaction. When hot air is thrown backward at high speed, the rocket receives a force of equal proportion in the forward direction.

Hence, the correct option is (D).

29. According to the third law of motion, the object also attracts the earth, but according to the second law of motion, the acceleration for a given force is inversely proportional to the mass of the object. $[F = ma]$ means the greater the mass, the greater the force. And the mass of the object is negligible compared to the Earth. That's why we don't see the earth moving towards the object.

Hence, the correct option is (B).

30. On dropping a sheet of paper and a stone from the same height on the earth together, the paper will reach the ground after the stone. This is due to the resistance of the air. Air exerts resistance on falling moving objects due to friction. The resistance of air on paper is greater than that on stone.

Hence, the correct option is (B).

31.

$$\begin{matrix} L & O & S & E \\ \downarrow & \downarrow & \downarrow & \downarrow \\ 1 & 3 & 5 & 7 \end{matrix}$$

And

$$\begin{matrix} G & A & I & N \\ \downarrow & \downarrow & \downarrow & \downarrow \\ 2 & 4 & 6 & 8 \end{matrix}$$

Similarly,

$$\begin{matrix} 8 & 4 & 6 & 1 & 5 \\ \downarrow & \downarrow & \downarrow & \downarrow & \downarrow \\ N & A & I & L & S \end{matrix}$$

Hence, the correct option is (A).

32.

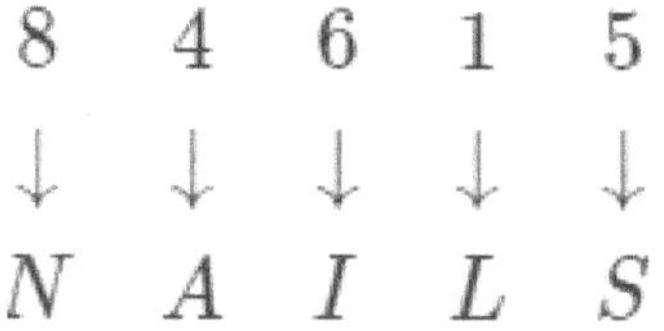

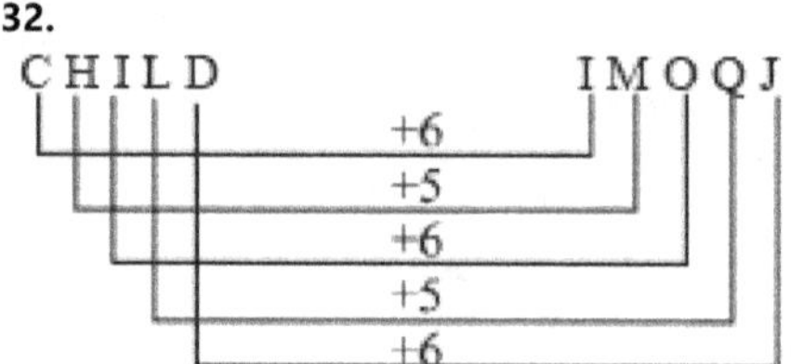

Similarly,

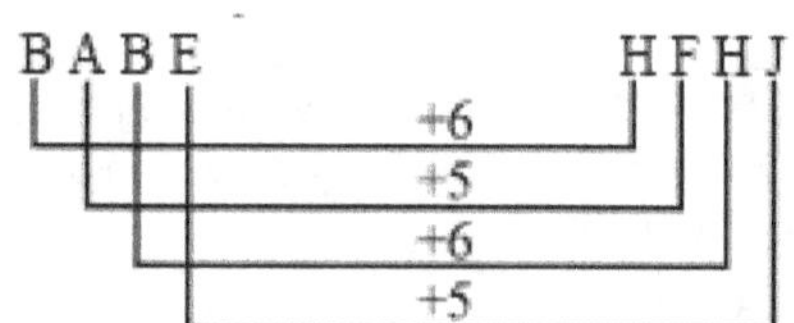

Hence, the correct option is (A).

33. The pattern is as follows:

1 × 2 + 1 = 3

3 × 2 + 2 = 8

8 × 2 + 3 = 19

19 × 2 + 4 = 42

42 × 2 + 5 = 89

89 × 2 + 6 = 184

Hence, the correct option is (B).

34. The pattern is as follows:

$5 \times 3 + 1 = 16$

$16 \times 3 + 3 = 51$

$51 \times 3 + 5 = 158$

$158 \times 3 + 7 = 481$

Hence, the correct option is (C).

35. I, K, M, N, P, P, U are the letters of "PUMPKIN" vegetable name. If the letters are arranged correctly, the last letter of that word will be N.

Hence, the correct option is (B).

36. Three independent complete words can be formed from the letters of the word 'HEARTLESS' using each letter only once and without changing the order of the letters.

So, the words are HE, ART, LESS.

Hence, the correct option is (B).

37. Given,

360 # 24 $ 56 * 5 @ 48

After change the symbol in expression, we get

$? = 360 \div 24 + 56 \times 5 - 48$

or $? = 15 + 280 - 48 = 247$

Hence, the correct option is (C).

38. Given,

' $\times$' means '+', '+' means ' $\div$',' $\div$' means '-' and '-' means ' $\times$'.

Then,

$5 - 7 \times 9 + 3 \div 2 = ?$

or $? = 5 \times 7 + 9 \div 3 - 2$

or $? = 5 \times 7 + 3 - 2$

or $? = 35 + 3 - 2 = 36$

Hence, the correct option is (A).

39.

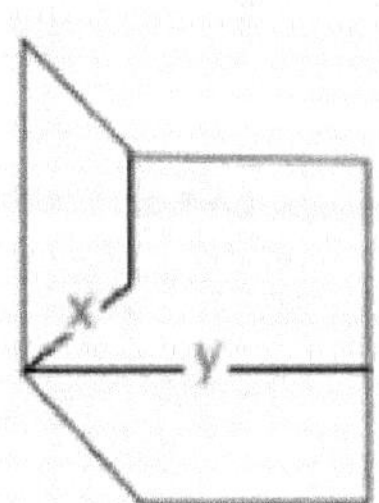

Hence, the correct option is (B).

40.

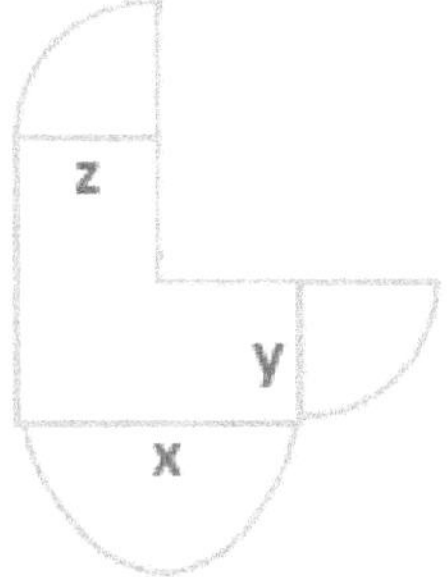

Hence, the correct option is (A).

41. Given,

$3\frac{18}{57} \times 48\frac{54}{63} \times 6\frac{1}{9} + 2\frac{1}{2} = ?$

$\Rightarrow \frac{189}{57} \times \frac{3078}{63} \times \frac{55}{9} + \frac{5}{2} = ?$

$\Rightarrow 18 \times 55 + 2.5 = ?$

$\Rightarrow ? = 990 + 2.5$

$\Rightarrow ? = 992.5$

Hence, the correct option is (D).

42. Given,

$4\frac{3}{10} + 2\frac{5}{3} - 5\frac{7}{8} = ?$

$\Rightarrow ? = (4 + 2 - 5) + \left(\frac{3}{10} + \frac{5}{3} - \frac{7}{8}\right)$

$\Rightarrow ? = 1 + \left(\frac{36+200-105}{120}\right)$

$\Rightarrow ? = 1 + \left(\frac{131}{120}\right)$

$\Rightarrow ? = \frac{120+131}{120}$

$\Rightarrow ? = \frac{251}{120}$

$\Rightarrow ? = 2\frac{11}{120}$

Hence, the correct option is (D).

43. Given,

$\frac{6}{x} + \frac{3}{y} = 7$

$\frac{3}{x} + \frac{9}{y} = 11$

Putting, $\frac{1}{x} = u$ and $\frac{1}{y} = v$

Then the given equation is as follows,

$\Rightarrow 6u + 3v = 7$ and

$\Rightarrow 3u + 9v = 11$

On solving these equations, we get:

$u = \frac{2}{3}$ and $v = 1$

$\therefore \frac{1}{x} = \frac{2}{3}$

$\Rightarrow \frac{1}{y} = 1$

So,

$x = \frac{3}{2}$ and $y = 1$

Hence, the correct option is (A).

44. Given,

The radius of a wheel $= r = 35$ cm $= 0.35$ cm

The speed it must keep $= s = 66$ km/h

$= \frac{66 \times 1000}{60}$ m/min $= 1100$ m/min

Let the number of revolution $= n$

The circumference of the wheel $C = 2\pi r$

$= 2 \times \frac{22}{7} \times 0.35$

$= 2.2$ m

The distance the wheel covers in 1 min $= d = 1100$ m

Now the distance covered by a wheel in one revolution $= d =$ the circumference of the wheel

$\therefore$ Here, the number of revolution $= n = \frac{d}{C}$

$= \frac{1100}{2.2} = 500$

Hence, the correct option is (C).

45. Given,

The radii of two circles are,

$r_1 = 15$ cm

$r_2 = 18$ cm

Circumference of the new circle,

$C = C_1 + C_2$

Where, $C_1 = 2\pi r_1$

$C_2 = 2\pi r_2$

$\therefore$ Circumference of the new circle $C = 2\pi(r_1 + r_2)$

$= 2\pi(15 + 18)$

$= 66\pi$ cm

$\therefore 2\pi r = 66\pi$

$r = \frac{66}{2}$ cm

$r = 33$ cm

Hence, the correct option is (C).

46. Let the cost of the table be Rs. x and the cost of the chair be Rs. y

According to the question,

$5x + 8y = 7350 \cdots$ (i)

and $3x + 5y = 4475 \cdots$ (ii)

On multiplying by 5 in equation (i), we get

$\Rightarrow 25x + 40y = 36750 \cdots$ (iii)

On multiplying by 8 in equation (ii), we get

$\Rightarrow 24x + 40y = 35800 \cdots$ (iv)

On subtracting equation (iv) from equation (iii), we get

$x = 36750 - 35800$

$\Rightarrow x = 950$

Thus, the cost of the table is Rs. 950.

Hence, the correct option is (A).

47. Given,

$x + \left(\frac{1}{x}\right) = 3$

So, $\frac{(3x^2-4x+3)}{(x^2-x+1)}$

$\Rightarrow \frac{3x\{x-\left(\frac{4}{3}\right)+\left(\frac{1}{x}\right)\}}{x\{x-1+\left(\frac{1}{x}\right)\}}$

$= \frac{3[\{x+\left(\frac{1}{x}\right)\}-\left(\frac{4}{3}\right)]}{\{x+\left(\frac{1}{x}\right)\}-1}$

From equation (i),

$= \frac{3\{3-\left(\frac{4}{3}\right)\}}{3-1} = \frac{3\left(\frac{5}{3}\right)}{2}$

$= \frac{5}{2}$

Hence, the correct option is (C).

48. Let the number of sides of a polygon be n. Then,

Sum of interior angles = (2n – 4) × 90°

Sum of exterior angles = 360°

∴ (2n – 4) × 90° = 2 × 360°

2n – 4 = 8

2n = 12

n = 6

Hence, the correct option is (D).

49. Given,

There are two regular polygons with a number of sides equal to (n – 1) and (n + 2). Their exterior angles differ by 6°.

According to the question,

$\{\frac{360°}{(n-1)}\} - \{\frac{360°}{(n+2)}\} = 6°$

$\Rightarrow 360°[\frac{(n+2-n+1)}{\{(n-1)(n+2)\}}] = 6°$

$\Rightarrow (n-1)(n+2) = 180$

$\Rightarrow n^2 + n - 2 = 180$

$\Rightarrow n^2 + n - 182 = 0$

$\Rightarrow n^2 + 14n - 13n - 182 = 0$

$\Rightarrow n(n+14) - 13(n+14) = 0$

$\Rightarrow (n-13)(n+14) = 0$

$\Rightarrow n = 13, -14$

$[\because n \neq -14]$

So, n = 13

Hence, the correct option is (C).

50. Given,

$\sin 3A = \cos(A - 26°)$

$\Rightarrow \cos(90° - 3A) = \cos(A - 26°)$

$[\because \cos(90° - \theta) = \sin\theta]$

$\Rightarrow 90° - 3A = A - 26°$

$\Rightarrow 4A = 116°$

$\Rightarrow A = 29°$

Hence, the correct option is (A).

51. Let the number be x.

According to the question,

$\frac{x+x^2}{2} = 7x$

$\Rightarrow x^2 + x = 14x$

$\Rightarrow x^2 - 13x = 0$

$\Rightarrow x[x - 13] = 0$

$\Rightarrow x = 0,13$

Hence, the correct option is (A).

52. Given,

Principal $=$ Rs. 800

Time $= 3$ years

Amount = Rs. 920

Simple Interest $=$ Amount - Principal

$=$ Rs. $(920 - 800) =$ Rs. 120

Simple Interest = $\frac{(Principal \times Rate \times Time)}{100}$

So, Rate $= \left(\frac{100 \times 120}{800 \times 3}\right)\% = 5\%$

If the rate of interest is increased by 3%, then

New Rate $(5+3)\% = 8\%$

New Simple Interest $= \left(\frac{800 \times 8 \times 3}{100}\right) = 192$

So, New amount $= (800 + 192)$

$=$ Rs. 992

Hence, the correct option is (C).

53. Simple Interest for $1\frac{1}{2}$ years $=$ Simple Interest for $3\frac{1}{2}$ years $-$ Simple Interest for 2 years

$= (1164 - 1008)$

$= 156$

Simple Interest for 1 years $= \left(156 \times \frac{2}{3}\right) =$ Rs. 208

Simple Interest for 2 years $= \left(156 \times \frac{2}{3} \times 2\right) =$ Rs. 208

So, principal $=$ (Amount of 2 yrs $-$ Simple Interes of 2 years

$= (1008 - 208)$

$= 800$

Now Principal $= 800$

Time $= 2$ years

Simple Interest $=$ Rs. 208

So, Rate $= \left(\frac{100 \times 208}{800 \times 2}\right)\%$

$= 13\%$

Hence, the correct option is (D).

54. Given,

The total number of students in a school is 2140.

The total number of girls in the school is 1200.

Total Number of boys = 2140 – 1200

= 940

Respective ratio = 940 : 1200

= 47 : 60

Hence, the correct option is (B).

55. Let's take B's income as Rs. 100.

According to the question,

$A:B:C = 150:100:\frac{120\times150}{100}$

$= 15:10:18$

∴ C's share $= \frac{18}{(15+10+18)} \times 86000$

$= \frac{18}{43} \times 86000$

$=$ Rs. 36000

Hence, the correct option is (D).

56. Given,

The price of an article is first increased by 20% and later decreased by 25% due to a decrease in sales.

Net percentage change $= x - y - \frac{x\times y}{100}$

$= 20 - 25 - \frac{25\times20}{100}$

$= 20 - 25 - 5$

$= -10\%$

Hence, the correct option is (D).

57. Given,

In an examination it is required to get 290 of the aggregate marks to pass. A student gets 203 marks and is declared failed by 12% of total marks.

Let's maximum aggregate marks $= x$

12% of $203 + x = 290$

12% of $x = 290 - 203$

$\Rightarrow x = \frac{87\times100}{12}$

$= 725$

Hence, the correct option is (C).

58. If A and B can do a piece of work in x days, B and C in y days, C and A in z days, then $(A + B + C)$ working together will do the same work in $\left[\frac{2xyz}{xy+yz+zx}\right]$ days.

A and B together finish a piece work $= x = 12$ days

Band C together finish a piece work $= y = 20$ days

C and A together finish a piece work $= z = 15$ days

A, B and C can do the work $= \frac{2\times12\times20\times15}{12\times20+20\times15+15\times12}$ days

After taking 20 as a common term we get,

$= \frac{2\times12\times15}{12+15+9}$ days

After taking 3 as a common term we get,

$= \frac{2\times4\times15}{4+5+3}$ days

$= \frac{120}{12} = 10$ days

Hence, the correct option is (D).

59. If A can do a piece of work in x days and B can do it in y days then A and B working together will do the same work in work in $\left(\frac{xy}{x+y}\right)$ days.

A's time $= x = 20$ days

B's time $= y = 15$ days

$A + B$ can do the work $= \frac{20\times15}{20+15}$ days

$= \frac{300}{35}$

$= \frac{60}{7}$

$= 8\frac{4}{7}$ days

Hence, the correct option is (C).

60. Given,

Raj and Prem walk in opposite direction at the rate of 3 km and 2 km per hour respectively.

Distance covered per hour = Relative speed × Time

= (3 + 2) × 1 = 5 km [opposite direction]

∴ Distance covered in 2 hours = 5 × 2 = 10 km

Hence, the correct option is (C).

Mock Test 07

English

Q.1 Direction: In the following question, a sentence has been given in Active voice. Change the sentence to Passive voice.

The boy killed the snake with a stick.

A. The snake was killed by the boy with a stick.
B. A stick was killed by the boys with a snake.
C. A snake with a stick was killed by the boy.
D. A snake is killed by the boy with a stick.

Q.2 Direction: In the question below the sentence has been given in Direct speech. From the given alternatives, choose the one which best expresses the given sentence in Indirect speech.

He said to his father, "Please increase my pocket money."

A. He told his father please increase the pocket money.
B. He pleaded his father to please increase my pocket money.
C. He requested his father to increase his pocket money.
D. He asked his father to increase his pocket money.

Ques (3-5):Direction: Read the following passage carefully and answer the question that follows.

The Madras High Court on Friday granted 30 days of ordinary leave to S. Nalini, 52, a life convict in the former Prime Minister Rajiv Gandhi's assassination case. The order was passed after she argued her case in person and made a **fervent** plea to the judges in a choked voice that she may be allowed to step out of prison for some days to make arrangements for the marriage of her daughter, who is residing in London.

Nalini had many years ago come out on short paroles of a day each to attend her brother Bhagyanathan's wedding and her father's last rites.

Justices M.M. Sundresh and M. Nirmal Kumar took judicial notice that the State Cabinet itself had on September 9 last year made a recommendation to the Governor to release all seven convicts in the Rajiv Gandhi assassination case. "If, in the view of the government, the petitioner can be allowed to lead a normal life and she would not be a hindrance to the society, the request for leave can never be objected to," they said.

The judges also directed the State government to bear the expenses of providing escort to her during the period of leave since she expressed difficulty in paying the charges.

"There is no material to hold that she is a woman of means. Admittedly, she and her husband are in incarceration for decades. Asking the petitioner to pay the cost would in a way take away the very order passed by us when it is impossible of compliance," they said.

Q.3 Why was S. Nalini sentenced to lifetime imprisonment by the judiciary of the country?

A. She murdered a lot of people during her school days and that came out in the open later.
B. She murdered her family out of mercy though her husband had left her for another woman before that.
C. She did not do anything but the court was of the view that she could do something if left to fend for himself within the society.
D. She was involved in the assassination of the former Prime Minister of India.

Q.4 Which among the following is correct regarding the attitude of the State Government towards the sentence of life imprisonment given to S Nalini?

A. The state government has nothing to say in the whole issue since the case was dealt with by the central government.
B. The state government could not understand the fact that there was nothing wrong done by S Nalini many years ago.
C. The State government is of the opinion that the sentence given to S Nalini can be remitted at once.
D. The state government wants the convict to continue with the given sentence by the court for the crime committed by her.

Q.5 Which among the following are not correct, as per the given passage?

I. This is the first time that S. Nalini has been given permission to come out on parole.

II. S. Nalini has been granted the right to come out on parole to perform the last rites of her husband.

III. S. Nalini has no child and that is why she is not at all happy with the sentence.

A. Both I and II **B.** Both II and III
C. Both I and III **D.** All I, II and III

Q.6 Direction: In the question choose the word which best expresses the meaning of the given word.

Squander

A. Expensive **B.** Waste
C. Litter **D.** Economical

Q.7 Direction: In the question choose the word which is the exact OPPOSITE of the given words.

Hideous

A. Abominable **B.** Grotesque
C. Alluring **D.** Macabre

Q.8 Fill in the blank with proper preposition.

You can obtain the answer _____ adding the date of birth to this figure.

A. to **B.** by **C.** on **D.** in

Q.9 Direction: Fill in the blank with a proper adjective.

He is the _______ boy in his class.

A. oldest **B.** older
C. old **D.** None of these

Q.10 Direction: In below compare the bold part of the sentence with alternatives (A), (B), (C), (D). Choose the correct alternative which is a correction upon the bold part.

There are not many men who are so famous that they are frequently referred to by their **short names** only.

A. initials **B.** signatures
C. pictures **D.** middle names

Q.11 Fill in the blank with a proper pronoun.

The little boy tied his shoelaces _____.

A. himself **B.** him **C.** his **D.** he

Ques (12-13):Direction: In the question given below out of four alternatives, choose the one which can be substituted for the given phrase.

Q.12 A person who writes beautiful writing

A. Cartographer **B.** Calligraphist
C. Compere **D.** Psephologist

Q.13 One who draws maps

A. Anthropologist **B.** Calligraphist
C. Chauffeur **D.** Cartographer

Q.14 What is the meaning of Blandishment?

A. Intentional flattery for persuasion
B. Persuade by flattery or coaxing
C. Proclaim something noisily
D. Enjoyable atmosphere or jovial company

Q.15 Identify the tense used in the given sentence. "You are always working on your laptop."

A. Present indefinite tense
B. Present perfect tense
C. Present continuous tense
D. Present perfect continuous tense

General Knowledge

Q.16 Who launched a grand challenge programme called "जनCARE" on September 28, 2021?

[Haryana Police Constable Commando Wing, 2021]

A. Dr. Jitendra Singh **B.** Jyotiraditya Scindia
C. Nirmala Sitharaman **D.** Smriti Irani

Q.17 Bharatnatyam is a famous classical dance of:

A. Telangana **B.** Assam
C. Tamil Nadu **D.** Haryana

Q.18 Suez Canal connects:

A. The Mediterranean and the Red Sea
B. Baltic and the Caspian Sea
C. The Mediterranean and the North Sea
D. Red and the Caspian Sea

Q.19 The Sepoy Mutiny of 1857 took place during the Governor Generalship of:

A. Lord Dalhousie
B. Lord Lytton
C. Lord William Bentinck
D. Lord canning

Q.20 Ugadi is the most distinctive festival of which of the following state?

A. Karnataka **B.** Tamil Nadu
C. Kerala **D.** Andra Pradesh

Science

Q.21 Longitudinal waves can be generated by:

A. Only in solid
B. In liquid only
C. Only in solid
D. Solid, liquid and gas

Q.22 The allotrope of carbon in which free electrons are found is:

A. Diamond **B.** Coal
C. Graphite **D.** Coke

Q.23 The major component of CNG is –

A. Carbon dioxide **B.** Methane
C. Aethen **D.** Oxygen

Q.24 The metal reacts with oxygen to form a compound with a high melting point. This compound is soluble in water. Then, tell the name of the metal:

A. Calcium **B.** Carbon **C.** Silicon **D.** Iron

Q.25 The weight of an object on the Moon in comparison to the weight on the Earth will be-

A. 6 times more **B.** $\frac{1}{6}$th part
C. $\frac{1}{66}$th part **D.** 66 times more

Q.26 The device to convert electrical energy into mechanical energy is:

A. Dynamo **B.** Transformer
C. Electric motor **D.** Inductor

Q.27 Which of the following is not a unit of heat?

A. Centigrade **B.** Calories
C. Erg **D.** Joule

Q.28 The energy of a particle moving at the rate of 5 m/s is 125 joules, then the mass of the particle will be:

A. 4 kg **B.** 6 kg **C.** 10 kg **D.** 15 kg

Q.29 The substance formed by the combination of two or more elements in a fixed ratio is called:

A. Element **B.** Compound
C. Mixture **D.** Solid

Q.30 What will be the thermal resistance of an ideal conductor?

A. Zero **B.** One **C.** Infinite **D.** Ten

Reasoning

Q.31 In a certain code, '37' means 'which class' and '583' means 'caste class'. What is the code for 'caste':

A. 3 **B.** 7
C. 8 **D.** Either 5 or 8

Q.32 If the word GBOQX stands for HAPPY, then the word CROSS stands for?

A. BSPTR **B.** BSNTR **C.** BNSTR **D.** BSNRT

Ques (33-34):निर्देश: दिए गए प्रश्न में कौन-सी आकृति प्रश्न आकृति के प्रतिरूप को पूरा करेगी?

Q.33 Question Figure

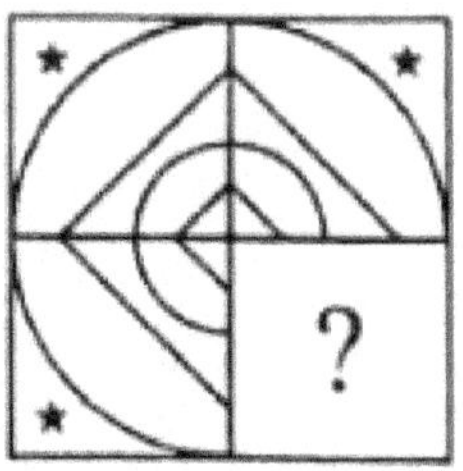

Answer Figure

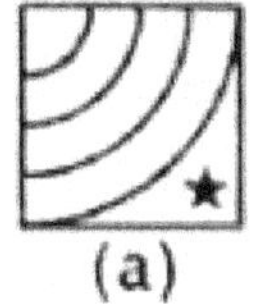
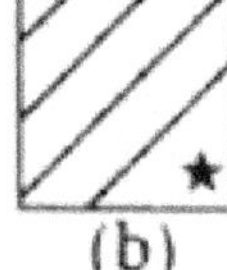
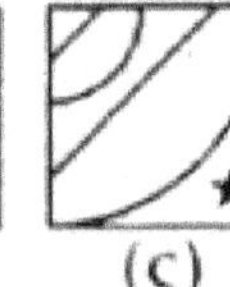

(a) (b) (c) (d)

A. (a) **B.** (b) **C.** (c) **D.** (d)

Q.34 Question Figure

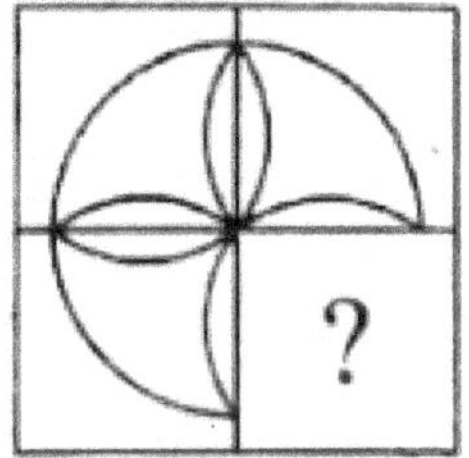

Answer Figure

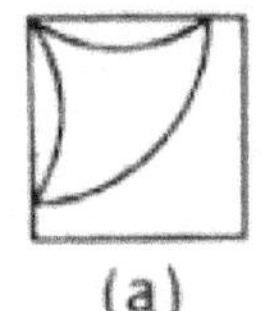
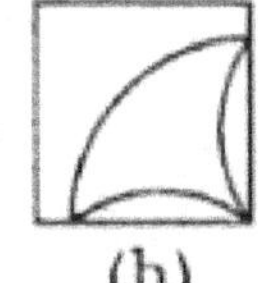
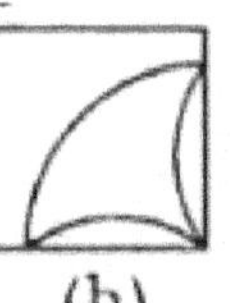

(a) (b) (c) (d)

A. (a) **B.** (b) **C.** (c) **D.** (d)

Ques (35-36): Arrange the words given below in a meaningful sequence.

Q.35 1. Income
2. Status
3. Education
4. Well-being
5. Job

A. 3, 1, 5, 2, 4 **B.** 1, 3, 2, 5, 4
C. 1, 2, 5, 3, 4 **D.** 3, 5, 1, 2, 4

Q.36 1. Heel
2. Shoulder
3. Skull
4. Neck
5. Knee
6. Chest
7. Thigh
8. Stomach
9. Face

A. 3, 4, 7, 9, 2, 5, 8, 6, 1
B. 3, 9, 4, 2, 6, 8, 7, 5, 1
C. 2, 4, 7, 1, 5, 8, 9, 6, 3
D. 4, 7, 1, 9, 6, 2, 5, 8, 3

Q.37 If means ×, × means +, + means – and – means, then find the value of 19 × 3 + 7 – 2 6.

A. 1 **B.** 21 **C.** 23 **D.** 0

Q.38 If + means, means –, – means × and × means +, then 16 + 8 4 – 3 × 10 = ?

A. 0 **B.** 2 **C.** 14 **D.** 25

Q.39 How many meaningful words can be formed by arranging the first four letters of the word DECISION in any number of ways?

A. One **B.** Two
C. Three **D.** More than three

Q.40 If in the word MEAT only the consonants are replaced by the letter immediately following it in the English alphabet and the rest of the letters remain unchanged, then how many meaningful words can be formed using the new set of letters only once?

A. Two **B.** Three **C.** One **D.** Zero

Mathematics

Ques (41-42): What will come in the place of question mark (?).

Q.41 $\left(\frac{18}{396}\right) \times \left(\frac{33}{288}\right) \times ? = 42$

A. 8126 **B.** 8238 **C.** 8028 **D.** 8064

Q.42 $\sqrt{(1686 - 317)} + \sqrt{(3441 - 525)} = ?$

A. 92 **B.** 95 **C.** 91 **D.** 99

Q.43 If one-third of a two-digit number exceeds its one-fourth by 8, then what is the sum of the digits of the number?

A. 6 **B.** 13 **C.** 15 **D.** 17

Q.44 If $x = 2016, y = 2015$ and $z = 2013$, then value of $x^2 + y^2 + z^2 - xy - yz - zx$ is:

A. 7 **B.** 4 **C.** 6 **D.** 2

Q.45 The measure of each interior angle of a regular polygon can never be:

A. 150° **B.** 105° **C.** 108° **D.** 144°

Q.46 The ratio between the number of sides of two regular polygons is 1 : 2 and the ratio between their interior angles is 2 : 3. The number of sides of these polygons is respectively.

A. 6, 12 **B.** 5, 10 **C.** 4, 8 **D.** 7, 14

Q.47 The value of $\sec^2\theta - \frac{(\sin^2\theta - 2\sin^4\theta)}{(2\cos^4\theta - \cos^2\theta)}$ is:

A. 1 **B.** 2 **C.** -1 **D.** 0

Q.48 The average of seven consecutive even numbers is 36. What is the difference between the highest and lowest numbers?

A. 2 **B.** 5 **C.** 12 **D.** 15

Q.49 What is the present worth of Rs. 132 due in 2 years at 5% simple interest per annum?

A. Rs. 123 **B.** Rs. 132 **C.** Rs. 120 **D.** Rs. 119

Q.50 In how many years will a sum of money triple itself in 24% per annum ?

A. 6 years 9 months **B.** 7 years 9 months
C. 8 years 3 months **D.** 8 years 4 months

Q.51 48% of the first number is 60% of the second number. What is the ratio of the first number to the second number?

A. 4 : 7 **B.** 3 : 4
C. 5 : 4 **D.** None of these

Q.52 Shreya, Nikita and Kamini share the profit in the ratio of 7 : 8 : 9. They has partnered for 12 months, 9 months and 6 months respectively. What was the ratio of their investments?

A. 21 : 32 : 54 **B.** 54 : 32 : 21
C. 21 : 54 : 32 **D.** 32 : 54 : 21

Q.53 In an examination, a student must get 36% marks to pass. A student who gets 190 marks failed by 35 marks. The total marks in that examination is:

[SBI Clerk, 2021]

A. 450 **B.** 550 **C.** 625 **D.** 810

Q.54 A person spends 30% of monthly salary on rent, 25% on food, 20% on children's education and 12% on electricity and the balance of Rs. 1040 on the remaining items. What is the monthly salary of the person?

A. Rs. 8000 **B.** Rs.9000
C. Rs. 9600 **D.** Rs. 10600

Q.55 If $\sin A = \frac{3}{5}$ and A is an acute angle, then $\tan A + \sec A$ is equal to:

A. 0 **B.** 1 **C.** 2 **D.** -1

Q.56 A completes a piece of work in 4 days and B completes it in 6 days. If they both work on it together, then the number of days required to complete the same work is:

A. $3\frac{5}{2}$ days **B.** $2\frac{3}{5}$ days **C.** $2\frac{2}{5}$ days **D.** $3\frac{2}{5}$ days

Q.57 Two buses start at the same time from Delhi and Agra, which are 300 km. apart, towards each other. After what time will they cross each other if their speeds are 38 km per hour and 37 km per hour?

A. 4 hours **B.** 3 hours **C.** 5 hours **D.** 6 hours

Q.58 With a uniform speed, a car covers a distance in 8 hours. Had the speed been increased by 4 km/hr, the same distance could have been covered in 7 hours and 30 minutes. What is the distance covered?

A. 420 km **B.** 480 km **C.** 520 km **D.** 640 km

Q.59 Find the area of a square whose one diagonal is 3.8 m long.

A. 7.22 m^2 **B.** 2.33 m^2 **C.** 4.77 m^2 **D.** 8.44 m^2

Q.60 One side of a rectangular field is 15m and one of its diagonals is 17m, find the area of the field?

A. 75 m^2 **B.** 120 m^2 **C.** 240 m^2 **D.** 350 m^2

// Smart Answer Sheet //

Correct Percentage of students who answered correctly. **Skipped** Percentage of students who skipped.

Q.	Ans.	Correct	Skipped	Q.	Ans.	Correct	Skipped	Q.	Ans.	Correct	Skipped	Q.	Ans.	Correct	Skipped	Q.	Ans.	Correct	Skipped	Q.	Ans.	Correct	Skipped
1	A	54.45 %	1.77 %	11	A	46.76 %	1.23 %	21	D	46.83 %	1.83 %	31	D	51.68 %	1.43 %	41	D	69.12 %	1.23 %	51	C	66.51 %	1.55 %
2	C	41.95 %	1.74 %	12	B	46.59 %	1.63 %	22	C	42.17 %	1.44 %	32	B	64.89 %	1.24 %	42	C	84.59 %	0.0 %	52	A	84.56 %	0.0 %
3	D	84.33 %	0.0 %	13	D	10.72 %	4.55 %	23	B	48.57 %	1.59 %	33	C	69.64 %	1.57 %	43	C	49.86 %	1.54 %	53	C	50.77 %	1.24 %
4	C	64.65 %	1.02 %	14	A	57.45 %	1.2 %	24	A	63.36 %	1.79 %	34	A	56.96 %	1.76 %	44	A	42.87 %	1.85 %	54	A	50.67 %	1.6 %
5	D	27.44 %	4.23 %	15	C	83.99 %	0.0 %	25	B	54.2 %	1.7 %	35	D	66.93 %	1.5 %	45	B	58.63 %	1.85 %	55	C	48.49 %	1.57 %
6	B	42.08 %	1.11 %	16	A	41.34 %	1.2 %	26	C	48.54 %	1.91 %	36	B	10.25 %	3.53 %	46	C	57.69 %	1.99 %	56	C	57.8 %	1.75 %
7	C	58.01 %	1.11 %	17	C	76.13 %	0.0 %	27	A	66.45 %	1.07 %	37	A	43.78 %	1.46 %	47	A	65.64 %	1.97 %	57	A	60.31 %	1.45 %
8	B	68.56 %	1.1 %	18	A	52.06 %	1.91 %	28	C	87.73 %	0.0 %	38	A	62.38 %	1.81 %	48	C	77.4 %	0.0 %	58	B	44.59 %	1.56 %
9	A	67.22 %	1.63 %	19	D	55.15 %	1.02 %	29	B	42.08 %	1.14 %	39	A	86.25 %	0.0 %	49	C	29.45 %	4.98 %	59	A	67.5 %	1.24 %
10	A	40.85 %	1.46 %	20	D	42.97 %	1.11 %	30	A	42.11 %	1.8 %	40	D	65.39 %	1.86 %	50	D	66.12 %	1.81 %	60	B	59.47 %	1.61 %

//Hints and Solutions//

1. The given sentence is in active voice and it is in Past simple tense. In the passive form conversion take place like this,

Subject + (was /were) + V^3+ Other agents.

Then the sentence is, 'The snake was killed by the boy with a stick.'

Hence, the correct option is (A).

2. "Please increase my pocket money." is an imperative sentence. Imperative sentences have a command (or an order), a request, an advice, or a suggestion. Therefore, to change them into Indirect Speech, some specific verbs (i.e. requested, order, advised, forbade, suggested) replace the verbs (e.g. said, told) of reporting verb. When the imperative sentence begins with "please", then we convert 'said to' into 'requested'.

The sentence in the indirect speech is, "He requested his father to increase his pocket-money."

Hence, the correct option is (C).

3. According to the question, "The Madras High Court on Friday granted 30 days of ordinary leave to S. Nalini, 52, a life convict in the former Prime Minister Rajiv Gandhi's assassination case."

Among the given options, we can see that our answer is described in Option (D) whereas all the other options are incorrect as per the given information in the passage.

Hence, the correct option is (D).

4. According to the question, "Justices M.M. Sundresh and M. Nirmal Kumar took judicial notice that the State Cabinet itself had on September 9 last year made a recommendation to the Governor to release all seven convicts in the Rajiv Gandhi assassination case."

It is the case that the state government already moved a petition to free all the seven prisoners in the Rajiv Gandhi assassination case implying that they have no issue with the rest of the sentence getting remitted by the competent authority. Among the given options, we can see that Option (C) is our pick whereas others are not correct as per the given information given in the passage.

Hence, the correct option is (C).

5. Statement I is not correct for the fact that S. Nalini has been given permission to come out on parole for the third time as she was given the permission twice before also. Refer to, "S. Nalini had many years ago come out on short paroles of a day each to attend her brother Bhagyanathan's wedding and her father's last rites."

Statement II is also not correct for the fact that S. Nalini has been released on parole in order to attend her daughter's wedding and to make arrangements for the marriage. Her daughter is staying in London. Refer to, "The order was passed after she argued her case in person and made a fervent plea to the judges in a choked voice that she may be allowed to step out of prison for some days to make arrangements for the marriage of her daughter, who is residing in London."

Statement III is also not correct for the fact that it is already said that S. Nalini has a daughter and that easily makes this particular statement incorrect.

Hence, the correct option is (D).

6. Squander: To waste time, money, etc

Waste: To give something to somebody who does not value it

Expensive: Costing a lot of money

Litter: Pieces of pape

Economical: That costs or uses less time

Hence, the correct option is (B).

7. Hideous: Very ugly or unpleasant

Abominable: Very bad or shocking

Grotesque: Strange or ugly in a way that is not natural

Alluring: Attractive and exciting in a way that is not easy to understand or explain

Macabre: Unpleasant and frightening because it is connected with death

Hence, the correct option is (C).

8. The word "by" is very common in English. It can be used in lots of different situations and contexts. It is mostly used as a preposition but it can also in fact be used as an adverb. In this article, I explain the common uses of "by" as a preposition.

Then the sentence is, "You can obtain the answer **by** adding the date of birth to this figure."

Hence, the correct option is (B).

9. A proper adjective is a word that modifies nouns and pronouns and is formed from a proper noun.

Then the sentence is, "He is the **oldest** boy in his class."

Hence, the correct option is (A).

10. In the given sentence, 'short names' is replaced by 'initials'.

Then the correct sentence is, "There are not many men who are so famous that they are frequently referred to by their initials only."

Hence, the correct option is (A).

11. A pronoun is a word that takes the place of a noun. Pronouns can be subjects of the sentence (I, he, she, it, you, we).

Then the sentence is, "The little boy tied his shoelaces **himself**."

Hence, the correct option is (A).

12. Calligraphist: Someone skilled in penmanship.

Cartographer: A person who draws or produces maps.

Compere: A person who introduces the performers or contestants in a variety show.

Psephologist: Someone who studies elections.

Hence, the correct option is (B).

13. Cartographer: A person who draws or produces maps.

Anthropologist: A person engaged in the study of aspects of humans within past and present societies.

Calligraphist: Someone skilled in penmanship.

Chauffeur: A person employed to drive a private or hired car.

Hence, the correct option is (D).

14. The meaning of Blandishment is 'Intentional flattery for persuasion'.

Persuade by flattery or coaxing: Cajole

Proclaim something noisily: Clamor

Enjoyable atmosphere or jovial company: Convivial

Hence, the correct option is (A).

15. The present continuous tense is formed with the subject plus the present particle form (-ing) of the main verb and the present continuous tense of the verb to be: am, is, are. One simple example of this tense is: He is swimming.

Then, the given sentence is of present continuous tense.

Hence, the correct option is (C).

16. Dr. Jitendra Singh launched a grand challenge programme called "जनCARE" on September 28, 2021.

Celebrating the Azadi Ka Amrit Mahotsav, Union Minister of State (Independent Charge) Science and Technology, Dr Jitendra Singh, launched the 'Amrit Grand Challenge Program' titled 'जनCARE' on 28 September 2021. The 'Amrit Grand Challenge Program' was launched under the umbrella of the Azadi Ka Amrit Mahotsav. It has become most important for new growing start-up ventures and entrepreneurs to come out with innovative Ideas and solutions for healthcare challenges faced by India. Biotechnology Industry Research Assistance Council (BIRAC), NASSCOM and NASSCOM Foundation jointly launched the 'Amrit Grand Challenge Program'. It is a nationwide 'Discover - Design - Scale' program and the challenge will end on 31 December 2021.

Hence, the correct option is (A).

17. Bharatanatyam is a major form of Indian classical dance that originated in Tamil Nadu. It is a solo dance performed exclusively by women and expresses religious themes and spiritual thoughts.

Hence, the correct option is (C).

18. The Suez Canal is an artificial sea-level waterway in Egypt that connects the Mediterranean Sea to the Red Sea via the Isthmus of Suez. It separates the continent of Africa from Asia. After 10 years of construction, it was officially opened on 10 November 1869.

Hence, the correct option is (A).

19. The Sepoy Mutiny started on 10 May 1857 and continued till 1858. Lord Canning (28 February 1856 – 1 November 1958) was then Governor-General. Lord Canning is also known as Charles John Canning. He was the first Viceroy of India and his tenure as governor lasted from 1856 to 1862.

Hence, the correct option is (D).

20. Ugadi is the most distinctive festival of Andhra Pradesh. Being the harbingers of a new year, people reconcile the Panchanga lessons by the process of Panchanga Sravanam. This festival inculcates a special sense of unity for all the residents of the state.

Hence, the correct option is (D).

21. Longitudinal waves are those waves in which the particles of the medium move in the same direction or opposite to the direction of motion of the wave. In longitudinal waves, the direction of vibration of the particles is parallel to the direction of propagation of the wave. Longitudinal waves can be produced in solid, liquid, and gas.

Hence, the correct option is (D).

22. Graphite molecules are arranged in a hexagonal structure. In a graphite molecule, one carbon atom binds to the other three carbon atoms to form a hexagonal array. Here one carbon atom is attached to three other carbon atoms due to which one electron remains free, due to this free electron graphite is a good conductor of electricity.

Hence, the correct option is (C).

23. Methane is the major component of CNG, its chemical formula is CH_4. The full name of CNG is Compressed Natural Gas. It adds liquid made keeping in excessive pressure to the flammable gas found naturally.

Hence, the correct option is (B).

24. Calcium metal reacts with oxygen to form a compound with a high melting point, which is calcium oxide (CaO). This compound is soluble in water. CaO is also called non-slaked lime.

$$2Ca + O_2 \rightarrow 2CaO$$

Hence, the correct option is (A).

25. The weight of an object does not remain the same everywhere, its value depends on the acceleration due to gravity (g). The value of acceleration due to gravity on Earth is considered to be 9.8 m/s^2. The value of g on the Moon is $\frac{1}{6}$ times the value of g on Earth. This is the reason why the weight on the Moon is very less compared to the Earth. The value of g on the Sun is about 27 times the value of g on Earth. The mass of the Moon is less than that of the Earth, due to which the Moon exerts less force of attraction on the objects. The weight of the object on the Moon is $\frac{1}{6}$ only one-thousandth of the weight of the Earth. For example, if the weight of a person is 60 kg on the earth, then the weight of that person on the moon will be $60 \times \frac{1}{6}$ =10 kg.

Hence, the correct option is (B).

26. An electric motor is an electro-mechanical device, which converts electrical energy into mechanical energy, that is, when it is connected to a suitable power source, it starts rotating, due to which the machine or machine connected to it also starts rotating. That is, it works in reverse of an electric generator which takes mechanical energy to produce electrical energy.

Hence, the correct option is (C).

27. Centigrade is a unit of temperature, not of heat. The units of heat are calorie, erg, joule. Heat is a form of energy, which is transferred from one substance to another due to temperature difference. The unit of heat in MKS and SI system is joule. And in CGS system the unit of heat is erg.

Hence, the correct option is (A).

28. Given,

The velocity of particle = 5 m/s

The energy of particle = 125 joules

As we know,

Kinetic energy $= \frac{1}{2} \times$ Mass $\times$ Velocity^2

$\Rightarrow 125 = \frac{1}{2} \times$ Mass $\times 5^2$

$\Rightarrow$ Mass $= \frac{250}{25}$

$\Rightarrow$ Mass $= 10$ kg

Hence, the correct option is (C).

29. A substance made by combining two or more elements in a fixed ratio is called a compound. In this way, the substance which is formed by the combination of two elements, that is, the compound is formed, that substance or compound is found in a stable state, but the properties of this compound are found to be different from the properties of its elements.

Example: Sulfuric acid, Common salt, etc.

Hence, the correct option is (B).

30. The substances in which heat is transmitted easily and rapidly through the conduction method are called good conductors. The thermal conductivity of an ideal conductor is infinite and the thermal resistance is zero. For example, gold, silver, copper, aluminum, etc. Silver has the highest thermal conductivity.

Hence, the correct option is (A).

31. Given,

'37' is coded as 'which class'.

'583' is coded as 'caste class'.

Then

The code of class is 3.

The code for caste is either 5 or 8.

Hence, the correct option is (D).

32. Given

GBOQX = HAPPY

The first letter of the word HAPPY is the next letter of the first letter of the word GBOQX and the second letter of the word HAPPY is the previous letter of the second letter of the word GBOQX. This pattern is repeated further.

So,

CROSS = BSNTR

Hence, the correct option is (B).

33.

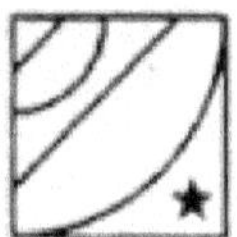

Hence, the correct option is (C).

34.

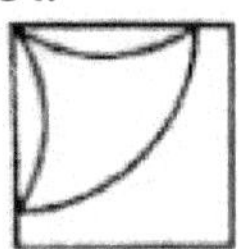

Hence, the correct option is (A).

35. The correct order is:

3. Education

5. Job

1. Income

2. Status

4. Well-being

Hence, the correct option is (D).

36. The correct order is :

3. Skull

8.Face

4. Neck

2. Shoulder

6. Chest

8. Stomach

7. Thigh

5. Knee

1. Heel

Hence, the correct option is (B).

37. According to the question,

$$19 + 3 - 7 \div 2 \times 6$$

$$\Rightarrow 19 + 3 - \frac{7}{2} \times 6$$

$$\Rightarrow 22 - 21$$

$\Rightarrow 1$

Hence, the correct option is (A).

38. According to the question,

16 ÷ 8 - 4 × 3 + 10 = ?

⇒ 2 - 12 + 10 = ?

⇒ 12 - 12 = ?

⇒ ? = 0

Hence, the correct option is (A).

39. Given word : DECISION

The first four letters are D, E, C, I. And only the word DICE can be made up.

Hence, the correct option is (A).

40. Given word: MEAT

According to the question,

The new set of letters are: N, E, A, U

No meaningful word can be made from these letters.

Hence, the correct option is (D).

41. Given,

$$\left(\frac{18}{396}\right) \times \left(\frac{33}{288}\right) \times ? = 42$$

$$\Rightarrow ? = \frac{42 \times 396 \times 288}{18 \times 33}$$

$$\Rightarrow ? = 42 \times 12 \times 16$$

$$\Rightarrow ? = 8064$$

Hence, the correct option is (D).

42. Given,

$$\sqrt{(1686 - 317)} + \sqrt{(3441 - 525)} = ?$$

$$\Rightarrow \sqrt{1369} + \sqrt{2916} = ?$$

$$\Rightarrow ? = 37 + 54$$

$$\Rightarrow ? = 91$$

Hence, the correct option is (C).

43. Let the number be y.

According to the question,

$$\frac{y}{3} = \frac{y}{4} + 8$$

$$\Rightarrow \frac{(4y - 3y)}{12} = 8$$

$$\Rightarrow y = 12 \times 8$$

$$\Rightarrow y = 96$$

∴ Sum of digits = 9 + 6

= 15

Hence, the correct option is (C).

44. Given,

$x = 2016, y = 2015$ and $z = 2013$

Then,

$$x - y = 2016 - 2015 = 1$$

$$y - z = 2015 - 2013 = 2$$

$$z - x = 2013 - 2016 = -3$$

$$\therefore x^2 + y^2 + z^2 - xy - yz - zx$$

As we know,

$$(a - b)^2 = a^2 - 2ab + b^2$$

Now, in the given equation, numerator & denominator multiplied by 2, we get

$$= \frac{1}{2}(2x^2 + 2y^2 + 2z^2 - 2xy - 2yz - 2zx)$$

$$= \frac{1}{2}(x^2 + y^2 - 2xy + y^2 + z^2 - 2yz + z^2 + x^2 - 2zx)$$

$$= \frac{1}{2} - [(x - y)^2 + (y - z)^2 + (z - x)^2]$$

$$= \frac{1}{2}[1 + 4 + 9]$$

$$= \frac{1}{2} \times 14 = 7$$

Hence, the correct option is (A).

45. Given,

Interior angles of a Regular Polygon $= [180° - \frac{360°}{n}]$

(A) $150° = 180° - \frac{360°}{n}$

$$\Rightarrow \frac{360°}{n} = 30°$$

$$\Rightarrow n = 12$$

(B) $105° = 180° - \frac{360°}{n}$

$$\Rightarrow \frac{360°}{n} = 75°$$

$$\Rightarrow n = \frac{24}{5}$$

(C) $180° = 180° - \frac{360°}{n}$

$$\Rightarrow \frac{360°}{n} = 72°$$

$$\Rightarrow n = 5$$

(D) $144^\circ = 180^\circ - \frac{360^\circ}{n}$

$\Rightarrow \frac{360^\circ}{n} = 36^\circ$

$\Rightarrow n = 10$

So, the measure of each interior angle of a regular polygon can never be 105°.

Hence, the correct option is (B).

46. Let the number of sides of two regular polygons be x and $2x$ respectively.

Interior angles of a Regular Polygon $= [180^\circ - \frac{360^\circ}{n}]$

According to the question,

$\Rightarrow \left\{180^\circ - \left(\frac{360^\circ}{x}\right)\right\} : \left\{180^\circ - \left(\frac{360^\circ}{2x}\right)\right\} = 2:3$

$\Rightarrow \left\{180^\circ \frac{(x-2)}{x}\right\} \times \left\{\frac{x}{180^\circ(x-1)}\right\} = \frac{2}{3}$

$\Rightarrow 3x - 6 = 2x - 2$

$\Rightarrow x = 4$

$\therefore$ Number of sides $= x = 4$ and

$2x = 2 \times 4 = 8$

Hence, the correct option is (C).

47. Given,

$\sec^2\theta - \frac{(\sin^2\theta - 2\sin^4\theta)}{(2\cos^4\theta - \cos^2\theta)}$

$= \sec^2\theta - \frac{\sin^2\theta(1-2\sin^2\theta)}{\cos^2\theta(2\cos^2\theta - 1)}$

$= \sec^2\theta - \frac{(\sin^2\theta\cos 2\theta)}{(\cos^2\theta\cos 2\theta)}$

$[\because \cos 2\theta = 1 - 2\sin^2\theta = 2\cos^2\theta - 1]$

$= \sec^2\theta - \frac{(\sin^2\theta)}{(\cos^2\theta)}$

$[\because \left(\frac{\sin\theta}{\cos\theta}\right) = \tan\theta]$

$= \sec^2\theta - \tan^2\theta$

$[\because \sec^2\theta - \tan^2\theta = 1]$

$= 1$

Hence, the correct option is (A).

48. Let the smallest even number be x.

So, according to the question the consecutive number are

$x, x+2, x+4, x+6, x+8, x+10, x+12$

So the diffrence is $x + 12 - x = 12$

Hence, the correct option is (C).

49. Let the present worth be Rs. x.

Then, Simple Interest $=$ Rs. $(132 - x)$

Applying a formula,

Simple Interest $= \frac{Principal \times Rate \times Time}{100}$

$\therefore \left(\frac{x \times 5 \times 2}{100}\right) = 132 - x$

$\Rightarrow 10x = 13200 - 100x$

$\Rightarrow 110x = 13200$

$\Rightarrow 120$

Hence, the correct option is (C).

50. Let the principal be x.

Amount $= 3x$

Then,

Simple Interest = Amount - Principal

$= 3x - x = 2x$

Time $= \frac{\text{Simple Interest} \times 100}{\text{Principal} \times \text{Rate}}$

$= \frac{2x \times 100}{x \times 24}$

$= \frac{100}{12}$

$= \frac{25}{3}$

$= 8$ years 4 months

Hence, the correct option is (D).

51. Let the first number be x and the second number be y.

Then, 48% of $x = 60\%$ of y

$\frac{x}{y} = \frac{60\%}{48\%}$

$\frac{x}{y} = \frac{\frac{60}{100}}{\frac{48}{100}}$

$\frac{x}{y} = \frac{5}{4}$

$\therefore$ Required ratio $= 5:4$

Hence, the correct option is (C).

52. Let the investment of Shreya be Rs. x.

That of Nikita be Rs. y and that of Kamini be Rs. z respectively.

Then, $12x:9y:6z = 7:8:9$

or, $\frac{12x}{9y} = \frac{7}{8}$

$\therefore 32x = 21y$

$x = \frac{21}{32}y$

And, $\frac{9y}{6z} = \frac{8}{9}$

$\therefore 27y = 16z$

$z = \frac{27}{16}y$

So, $x:y:z = \frac{21}{32}y:y:\frac{27}{16}y$

$= 21:32:54$

Hence, the correct option is (A).

53. Given,

Passing marks = 36%

A student gets = 190 marks

And he failed by 35 marks.

So, the total passing marks = 190 + 35

= 225

Let the total marks be x.

According to the question,

36% of x = 225

$\frac{36}{100} \times x = 225$

$x = \frac{225 \times 100}{36}$

$x = 300$

Hence, the correct option is (C).

54. Given,

A person spends 30% of monthly salary on rent, 25% on food, 20% on children's education and 12% on electricity and the balance of Rs. 1040 on the remaining items.

Let the monthly salary of the person be x.

Total spends of a person $= (30 + 25 + 20 + 12) = 87\%$

Remaining $\% = 100 - 87 = 13\%$

According to the question,

13% of $x = 1040$

$\frac{13}{100} \times x = 1040$

$x = \frac{1040 \times 100}{13}$

$x = 80 \times 100$

$x =$ Rs. 8000

Hence, the correct option is (A).

55. Given,

$\sin A = \frac{3}{5}$

We know that,

$\cos^2 A = 1 - \sin^2 A$

$\therefore \cos A = \sqrt{\{1 - \left(\frac{9}{25}\right)\}} = \sqrt{\left(\frac{16}{25}\right)} = \frac{4}{5}$

$\therefore \tan A + \sec A = \left(\frac{\sin A}{\cos A}\right) + \frac{1}{\cos A}$

$= \frac{(\sin A + 1)}{\cos A}$

$= \frac{\left(\frac{3}{5}\right)+1}{\left(\frac{4}{5}\right)}$

$= \left(\frac{8}{5}\right) \times \left(\frac{5}{4}\right) = 2$

Hence, the correct option is (C).

56. Given,

A completes a work = in 4 days

Work done by A in 1 day = $\frac{1}{4}$

B completes a work = in 6 days

Work done by B in 1 day = $\frac{1}{6}$

If they both work on it together, then the work done by them in 1 day = $\frac{1}{4} + \frac{1}{6}$

$= \frac{4+6}{4 \times 6}$

$= \frac{10}{24}$

Then, by unitary rule,

$\therefore$ Both (A+B) together do $\frac{10}{24}$ work = in 1 day

$\because$ Both (A+B) together do 1 work = in $\frac{24}{10}$ days

$=$ in $2\frac{2}{5}$ days

Hence, the correct option is (C).

57. Given,

Two buses start at the same time from Delhi and Agra, which are 300 km.

Distance between Agra and Delhi $= 300$ km

Relative speed $= 38 + 37 = 75$ km/hr

Time taken to cross each other $= \frac{\text{Distance}}{\text{speed}}$

$= \frac{300}{75} = 4$ hours

Hence, the correct option is (A).

58. Let the distance be x km.

As we know,

Speed = $\frac{\text{Distance}}{\text{Times}}$

The speed of the car $= \frac{x}{8}$

7 hours 30 minutes = $7 + \frac{1}{2}$ hours

= $\frac{15}{2}$ hours

If the speed was increased by 4 km/h, then the speed of the car $= \frac{x}{\frac{15}{2}}$

According to the question,

$\frac{x}{\frac{15}{2}} - \frac{x}{8} = 4$

$\Rightarrow \frac{16x - 15x}{120} = 4$

$\Rightarrow x = 480$ km

Hence, the correct option is (B).

59. As given,

A square, one of its diagonals is 3.8 m long.

Area of the square $= \frac{1}{2} \times$ diagonal^2

$= \left(\frac{1}{2} \times 3.8 \times 3.8\right)$ m^2

$= 7.22$ m^2

Hence, the correct option is (A).

60. Given,

One side of a rectangular field is 15 m and one of its diagonals is 17 m.

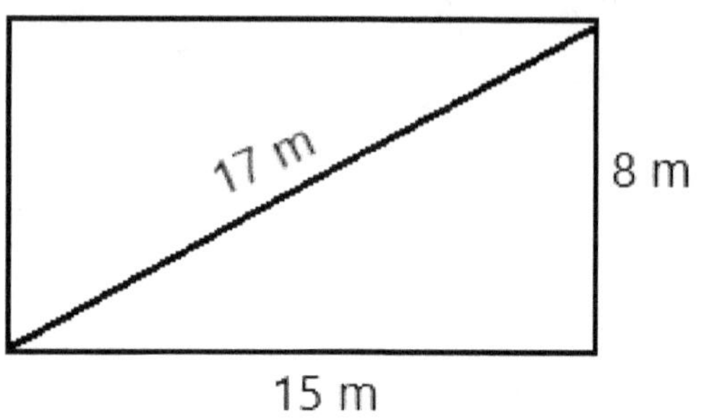

From the Pythagoras theorem,

Other side $= \sqrt{(17)^2 - (15)^2}$

$= \sqrt{289 - 225}$

$= \sqrt{64} = 8$ m

So,

Area of field = Length of field $\times$ Width of field

$= (15 \times 8)$ m^2

$= 120$ m^2

Hence, the correct option is (B).

Mock Test 08

English

Ques (1-2):Direction: Read the passage given below and answer the following questions.

India is home to immeasurable Ayurveda remedies from ancient times. In Ayurveda remedies, 'Kadha' is commonly proposed as a cure for fighting flu, cold, cough, and infections. Kadha refers to a medicinal drink, prepared from mixing different edible herbs and spices that are readily available in most Indian households. Ayurvedic kadha can not only protect you from seasonal infections triggered by changing weather conditions but may also work wonders for building your immunity.

Kadha can be made ready in several ways. It is an amalgamation of many ingredients. In fact, every family may have a unique kadha recipe of their own. It is usually prepared by boiling various whole spices and herbs in water to release their medicinal qualities and benefits. Natural immunity boosters like honey, tulsi, and ginger are frequently blended with the spice mixture to make the decoction more powerful.

Q.1 According to the passage, what is "kadha"?

A. A medicinal drink
B. A drink prepared from mixing different herbs and spices
C. None of the above
D. Both (A) and (B)

Q.2 What are the things blended with spice mixture to make the decoction more powerful?

A. honey, ginger and mint
B. honey, salt snd tulsi
C. honey, ginger and tulsi
D. sugar, salt and ginger

Ques (3-4):Direction: Choose an appropriate synonym for the given word.

Q.3 Pathos

A. Hesitant **B.** Sorrow **C.** Robuke **D.** Clumsy

Q.4 Relinquish

A. Continue **B.** Surrender
C. Hold **D.** Occupy

Ques (5-6):Direction: Select the most appropriate Antonym of the given word.

Q.5 Prudent

A. Perspicacious **B.** Polarize
C. Indiscreet **D.** Canny

Q.6 Apprise

A. Inform **B.** Acquaint
C. Deceive **D.** Enlighten

Q.7 Direction: Choose the appropriate preposition for the given sentence.

The child fell _____ from a great height.

A. under **B.** over **C.** up **D.** down

Q.8 Which of the followings would be the correct adjective of 'Benefit'?

A. Beneficence **B.** Beneficent
C. Beneficently **D.** None of these

Q.9 The adjective form of 'critic' is:

A. Criticise **B.** Criticised
C. Criticism **D.** Critical

Q.10 Direction: Select the correct direct form of the given sentence.

The boy asked his mother why she hadn't woken him up.

A. The boy said, "Why don't you wake me up, mother?"
B. The boy said, "Why you didn't wake me up, mother?"
C. The boy said, "Why didn't you wake me up, mother?"
D. The boy said, "Why didn't I wake you up, mother?"

Q.11 Direction: Select the correct passive form of the given sentence.

Whom did you laugh at?

A. By whom was you laughed at?
B. Who was laughed at by you?
C. You were laughed at by whom?
D. Did you laugh at who?

Q.12 Direction: Select the most appropriate meaning of the underlined idiom/phrase in the given sentence.

These days a team can not expect to win any match **<u>hands down</u>**.

A. Complicated **B.** Burdensome
C. Exhausting **D.** No sweat

Q.13 Direction: A part of the sentence is underlined. Four alternatives are given to the underlined part which will improve the sentence. Choose the correct alternative.

After a **<u>hard days work</u>**, I just want to go home.

A. Hard day's wor **B.** Hard days' work
C. Hard day work **D.** No improvement

Q.14 Direction: Fill in the blank with an appropriate tense.

He _______ from fever for a week.

A. is suffering **B.** was suffering
C. had suffering **D.** has been suffering

Q.15 Directions: Select the correct direct form of the given sentence.

The policeman warned us not to block the traffic.

A. The policeman said to us, "We should not block the

traffic."

B. The policeman said to us, "Do not block the traffic."

C. The policeman said to us, "Let us not block the traffic."

D. The policeman said to us, "You did not block the traffic."

General Knowledge

Q.16 Who has been elected as the new President of Israel (11th) in June 2021?

A. Reuven Rivlin

B. Isaac Herzog

C. Benjamin Netanyahu

D. Peter Szijjarto

Q.17 What is the chemical name for Vitamin B7?

A. Panotothenic Acid **B.** Cobalamin

C. Biotin **D.** Folic Acid

Q.18 In which of the following states is the Bihula festival very popular?

A. Bihar **B.** Madhya Pradesh

C. Odisha **D.** Gujarat

Q.19 The book Kitab- Ul-Hind was written by:

A. Ibn Battuta

B. Al-Biruni

C. Ibn Khaldun

D. Muhammad Al-Idrisi

Q.20 Jerusalem is the capital of which of the following countries?

A. Israel **B.** Austria **C.** Syria **D.** Ethiopia

Science

Q.21 200° Celsius = _____ Fahrenheit

A. -73° **B.** -328° **C.** 392° **D.** 73°

Q.22 Rate of doing work or rate of transfer of energy is called _______.

A. Joule **B.** Power **C.** Force **D.** Speed

Q.23 Light year is a unit of:

[Rajasthan Police Constable, 2020], [Bihar PSC, 2020]

A. Distance **B.** Time

C. Mass **D.** Intensity of light

Q.24 After completing the gold foil experiment, Rutherford concluded that the size of the nucleus is very small compared to the size of the atom because:

A. One out of every 12000 alpha particles deflected back after hitting the gold foil

B. Most of the alpha particles deflected back after hitting the gold foil

C. Some alpha particles were deflected by small angles

D. Very few of the alpha particles passed through the gold foil

Q.25 The number of protons present in the nucleus of an atom is called:

A. Atomic number of the element

B. Atomic weight of the element

C. Valency of the element

D. Mass number of the element

Q.26 What is the mass of an object whose weight is 49 N?

A. 49 kg **B.** 5 kg **C.** 5 g **D.** 49 g

Q.27 A bottle is filled with water at 30°C. When it is taken on the moon then:

A. Water will freeze

B. Water will boil

C. Water will decompose in hydrogen and oxygen

D. Nothing will happen to water

Q.28 Which of the following is thermodynamically most stable allotrope of carbon?

A. Graphite **B.** Diamond

C. Fullerene **D.** Carbon-black

Q.29 Brass is an alloy of copper and _____.

A. zinc **B.** tin **C.** iron **D.** silver

Q.30 Electric current is considered to be the flow of ________.

A. Negative charges **B.** Dielectric

C. Magnet pieces **D.** Positive charges

Reasoning

Q.31 Select the answer figure in which the question figure is embedded/hidden.

A. 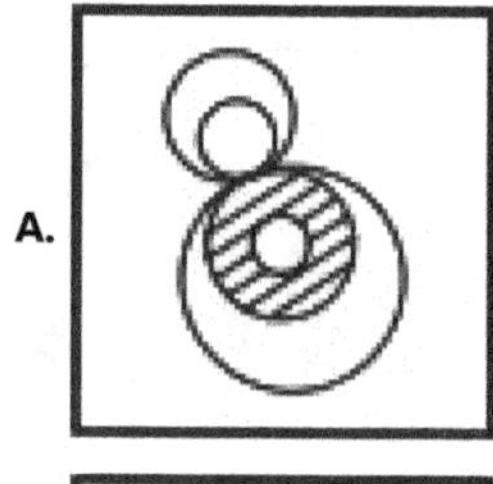

B. 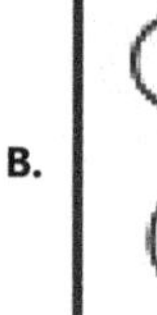

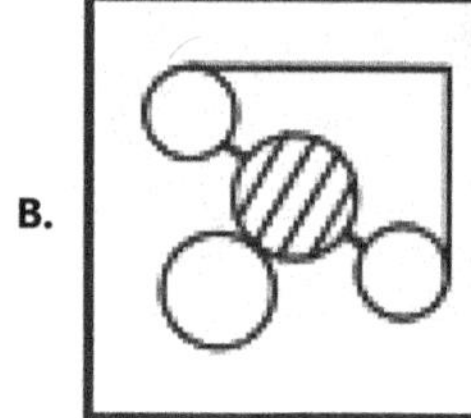

C. 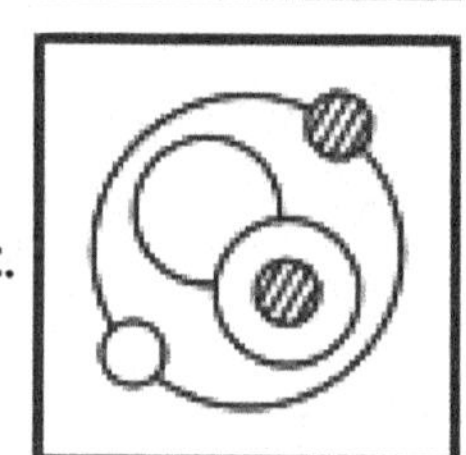

D. 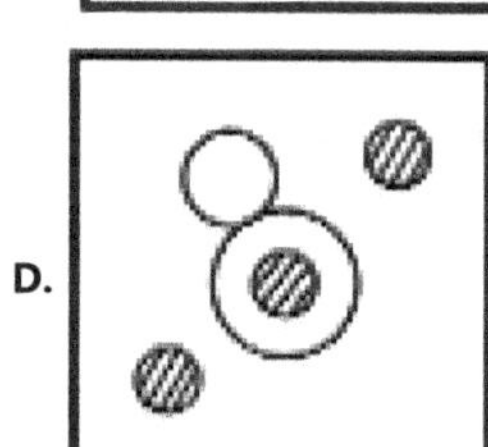

Q.32 In a certain code language, 'AGENT' is written as 'UOFHB', then how will 'EXILE' be written in that code language?

A. BMAYB **B.** FMJYE **C.** FMJYF **D.** QMSYQ

Q.33 If AMERICA = 1734651, INDIA = 68961, how will you write CANADA?

A. 719181 **B.** 518191 **C.** 519581 **D.** 715148

Q.34 To balance the given equation, select the correct mathematical combination replacing the * sign (symbol) sequentially.

2 * 2 * 312 * 12 * 54 = 0

A. +, ÷, ×, − **B.** +, ×, ÷, −
C. −, ×, ÷, + **D.** −, ×, +, ÷

Q.35 Find the next figure in the series.

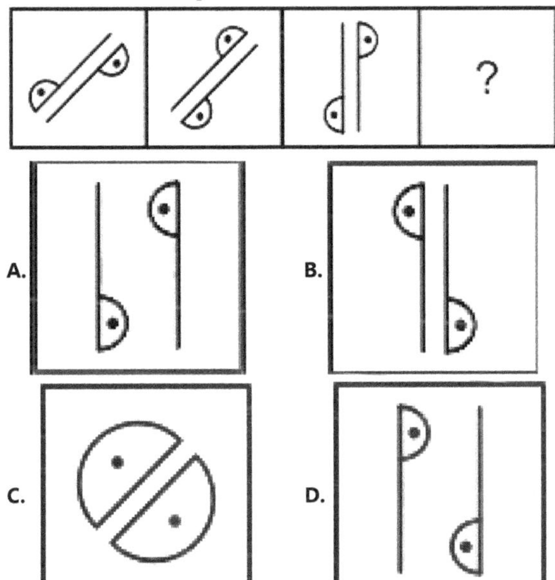

Q.36 In a certain code language, '×' represents '+', '÷' represents '×', '-' represents '÷' and '+' represents '-'. Find out the answer to the following question.

42 + 36 − 6 ÷ 15 × 8 ÷ 20 + 20 − 5 = ?

A. 100 **B.** 108 **C.** 105 **D.** 101

Q.37 Select the correct alternative to indicate the arrangement of the following words in a logical and meaningful order.

1. Credit decision
2. Loan application
3. Application processing
4. Underwriting process
5. Loan funding

A. 5, 4, 1, 3, 2 **B.** 2, 3, 4, 1, 5
C. 5, 2, 4, 1, 3 **D.** 2, 3, 1, 4, 5

Ques (38-39):Direction: From the given alternatives, select the word which CANNOT be formed using the letters of the given word.

Q.38 TRAVELLING

A. RING **B.** VASE
C. RATE **D.** GRAVEL

Q.39 PURIFICATION

A. FICTION **B.** RUST
C. CAUTION **D.** CATION

Q.40 Arrange the words given below in a meaningful sequence.

1. Puberty
2. Adulthood
3. Childhood
4. Infancy
5. Senescence
6. Adolescence

A. 2, 4, 6, 3, 1, 5 **B.** 4, 3, 1, 6, 2, 5
C. 4, 3, 6, 2, 1, 5 **D.** 5, 6, 2, 3, 4, 1

Mathematics

Q.41 A circle is inscribed in a triangle ΔPQR. It touches sides PQ, QR, and RS at points A, B, and C respectively. If AQ = 8.2 cm, PC = 6.4 cm and BR = 3.4 cm, then the perimeter (in cm) of the triangle ΔPQR is:

A. 36 **B.** 38 **C.** 35 **D.** 32

Q.42 Aman borrowed Rs. 12000 from a bank at the rate of 6% per annum at simple interest for 3 years and he lent it to Saurabh for the same time at the rate of 9% per annum for the same period of time. Find the profit gained by Aman at the end of 3 years.

A. Rs. 2160 **B.** Rs. 2400 **C.** Rs. 1080 **D.** Rs. 1620

Q.43 If $\sin(\alpha + \beta) = 6\sin(\alpha - \beta)$ and $k = \frac{\tan\alpha}{\tan\beta}$, then, what is the value of k?

A. $\frac{3}{5}$ **B.** $\frac{7}{5}$ **C.** $\frac{6}{5}$ **D.** $\frac{4}{5}$

Q.44 A hemisphere is put above an inverted cone of height 9 cm and radius 6 cm such that the base of the hemisphere and cone match. Find the volume of shape?

A. 120π cm ^{3} **B.** 360π cm ^{3}
C. 240π cm ^{3} **D.** 252π cm ^{3}

Q.45 The ratio of the monthly incomes of Radha and Rani is 3 : 2 and their expenditure ratio is 8 : 5 if each of them is saving Rs. 9000 per month, then find the sum of the monthly incomes of Radha and Rani?

A. Rs. 132000 **B.** Rs. 145000
C. Rs. 135000 **D.** Rs. 119000

Q.46 Both X and Y together can complete a work in 12 days and Y alone can complete the same work in 30 days. In how many days will X alone complete the work?

A. 15 **B.** 20 **C.** 18 **D.** 16

Q.47 In an election contested between two candidates, one candidate got 30% of total votes and still lost by 500 votes. What is the total number of votes casted?

A. 1250 **B.** 1380 **C.** 1470 **D.** 1500

Q.48 Sachin went to his office at a speed of 50 km/h and returned home from office at a speed of 30 km/h. Find the average speed of Sachin in whole journey.

A. 15 km/h **B.** 37.5 km/h
C. 30 km/h **D.** 40 km/h

Q.49 There is 100% increase to an amount in 8 years, at simple interest. Find the compound interest of Rs. 8000 after 2 years at the same rate of interest.

A. Rs. 2500 **B.** Rs. 2000 **C.** Rs. 2250 **D.** Rs. 2125

Q.50 The difference between simple interest and compound interest for 2 years on the sum Rs. 2900 at a certain rate is Rs. 14.21. What is the annual rate of interest?

A. 9% **B.** 5% **C.** 7% **D.** 8%

Q.51 $\frac{(100)^2+(46)^2}{(73)^2+(27)^2}$ is equal to:

A. 2 **B.** 3 **C.** 1 **D.** 0

Q.52 The value of $\frac{\frac{1}{5}\div\frac{1}{6}\text{of}\frac{1}{5}}{\frac{1}{5}+\frac{1}{6}\text{of}\frac{1}{5}}$ is:

A. $\frac{150}{21}$ **B.** 1 **C.** $\frac{180}{7}$ **D.** 30

Q.53 If $x+y=9$ and $x^2+y^2=45$, then find the value of $x^4+y^4+x^2y^2$.

A. 1600 **B.** 1657 **C.** 1701 **D.** 1890

Q.54 Find the mode from the following table.

Class	Frequency
0-10	15
10-20	25
20-30	30
30-40	20

A. 22.44 **B.** 23.33 **C.** 25.55 **D.** 26.66

Q.55 Find the value of k, for which the system of equations $kx+3y=26$ and $21x+(k+2)y=71+k$ has infinitely many solutions.

[MP Jail Prahari, 2018]

A. $k=9$ **B.** $k=7$ **C.** $k=6$ **D.** $k=0$

Q.56 On his first 5 biology tests, Bob received the following scores: 72, 86, 92, 63, and 77. What test score must Bob earn on his sixth test so that his average (mean score) for all six tests will be 80?

A. 90 **B.** 86 **C.** 95 **D.** 80

Q.57 If $(x+1)$ and $(x-2)$ are the factor of polynomial $p(x)=x^3-ax^2-bx+6$ find the quadratic polynomial $q(x)$, whose factors are $(x-a)$ and $(x-b)$.

A. $q(x)=x^2+3x+4$
B. $q(x)=x^2+3x-4$
C. $q(x)=x^2-3x-4$
D. $q(x)=x^2-3x+4$

Q.58 In an examination, a student secured 24% marks and he failed by 16 marks Another student secured 26% marks and he got failed by 6 marks, then find the minimum passing marks.

A. 120 **B.** 124 **C.** 136 **D.** 130

Q.59 Two numbers are respectively 14% and 23% less than a third number. The second number is approximately what percentage of the first number?

A. 61 **B.** 75 **C.** 80 **D.** 90

Q.60 Volume of a cube is 2744 cm ^{3}. Find total surface area of cube.

A. 1167 cm ^{2} **B.** 1176 cm ^{2}
C. 1276 cm ^{2} **D.** 1762 cm ^{2}

// Smart Answer Sheet //

Correct Percentage of students who answered correctly. **Skipped** Percentage of students who skipped.

Q.	Ans.	Correct	Skipped	Q.	Ans.	Correct	Skipped	Q.	Ans.	Correct	Skipped	Q.	Ans.	Correct	Skipped	Q.	Ans.	Correct	Skipped	Q.	Ans.	Correct	Skipped
1	D	67.91 %	1.77 %	11	B	68.36 %	1.24 %	21	C	61.19 %	1.69 %	31	C	43.51 %	1.69 %	41	A	29.51 %	3.16 %	51	A	69.47 %	1.5 %
2	C	59.97 %	1.38 %	12	D	58.51 %	1.99 %	22	B	78.26 %	0.0 %	32	C	11.93 %	3.31 %	42	C	47.36 %	1.55 %	52	C	54.16 %	1.07 %
3	B	40.93 %	1.95 %	13	A	85.68 %	0.0 %	23	A	51.37 %	1.93 %	33	B	63.49 %	1.19 %	43	B	20.91 %	3.52 %	53	C	29.15 %	3.56 %
4	B	13.58 %	4.56 %	14	D	65.13 %	1.89 %	24	A	63.25 %	1.14 %	34	B	25.23 %	3.52 %	44	D	45.97 %	1.62 %	54	B	42.86 %	1.1 %
5	C	15.23 %	4.95 %	15	B	50.09 %	1.56 %	25	A	49.96 %	1.73 %	35	B	79.2 %	0.0 %	45	C	52.66 %	1.46 %	55	B	31.55 %	4.23 %
6	C	55.9 %	1.89 %	16	B	56.88 %	1.81 %	26	B	56.03 %	1.89 %	36	B	49.74 %	1.19 %	46	B	59.0 %	1.57 %	56	A	79.27 %	0.0 %
7	D	84.85 %	0.0 %	17	C	32.63 %	4.49 %	27	B	69.23 %	1.0 %	37	B	17.94 %	4.9 %	47	A	63.78 %	1.23 %	57	C	14.2 %	4.38 %
8	B	81.96 %	0.0 %	18	A	61.4 %	1.89 %	28	A	51.35 %	1.03 %	38	B	79.58 %	0.0 %	48	B	77.71 %	0.0 %	58	C	54.44 %	1.28 %
9	D	58.45 %	1.04 %	19	B	60.7 %	1.0 %	29	A	86.51 %	0.0 %	39	B	82.15 %	0.0 %	49	D	26.07 %	4.26 %	59	D	82.2 %	0.0 %
10	C	51.68 %	1.77 %	20	A	67.21 %	1.38 %	30	A	43.43 %	1.64 %	40	B	52.67 %	1.47 %	50	C	67.84 %	1.71 %	60	B	53.77 %	1.23 %

//Hints and Solutions//

1. Let's refer to the third line of the passage:

Kadha refers to a medicinal drink, prepared from mixing different edible herbs and spices that are readily available in most Indian households.

From the above line, we can say that "kadha" is a medicinal drink that is prepared by mixing different herbs and spices.

Hence, the correct option is (D).

2. Let's refer to the last line of the passage:

Natural immunity boosters like honey, tulsi, and ginger are frequently blended with the spice mixture to make the decoction more powerful.

It is clearly mentioned in the passage that honey, tulsi, and ginger are blended with the spice mixture to make the decoction more powerful.

Hence, the correct option is (C).

3. Pathos: a quality in life or art that causes feelings of sadness or sympathy

Sorrow: a feeling of great sadness

Hesitant: to hold back

Rebuke: to speak angrily or scold someone

Clumsy: careless

Hence, the correct option is (B).

4. Relinquish: to give up (as a position of authority) formally

Surrender: to give up or hand over (a person, right, or possession), typically on compulsion or demand

Continue: to remain in existence or operation

Hold: keep or sustain in a specified position

Occupy: be situated in or at (a position in a system or hierarchy

Hence, the correct option is (B).

5. Prudent: careful and sensible; marked by sound judgment

Indiscreet: lacking discretion; injudicious

Perspicacious: acutely insightful and wise

Polarize: to cause to vibrate in a definite pattern

Canny: showing self-interest and shrewdness in dealing with others

Hence, the correct option is (C).

6. Apprise: to give information to someone

Deceive: deliberately cause someone to believe something that is not true, especially for personal gain

Inform: give someone facts or information; tell

Acquaint: make someone aware of or familiar with

Enlighten: give someone greater knowledge and understanding about a subject or situation

Hence, the correct option is (C).

7. The child fell **down** from a great height.

The preposition 'down' means to or at a lower level or place; from the top towards the bottom of something.

Hence, the correct option is (D).

8. Beneficent is an adjective form of verb "benefit".

Beneficent means doing or producing good.

Adding the following suffixes turns a verb into an adjective-

SUFFIX -able, -ible, -ant, -ent, -ive, -ing,

Hence, the correct option is (B).

9. The adjective form of 'critic' is **critical**.

'Critic' is a noun.

Some nouns are changed into adjectives by adding the suffix 'al'.

Hence, the correct option is (D).

10. The tense of direct speech is changed only when the reporting verb is in the past tense.

When the indirect speech is in an assertive form, we follow the steps given below:

The reporting verb asked will be replaced by 'said'.

Connectors 'whether/why' or 'if' are replaced by the comma and inverted commas.

The tense of reported speech is changed only when the reporting verb is in the past tense.

Change the reported speech from assertive to interrogative.

The personal pronouns will be changed according to the subject and object of the reporting verb.

Here the 3rd person 'she' will change into the 2nd person 'you' as per the object.

Similarly, 'him' will be replaced by 'me'.

Past perfect tense (hadn't woken him up) in indirect speech changes to Past simple in direct speech (didn't wake me up).

Correct sentence is: The boy said, "Why didn't you wake me up, mother?"

Hence, the correct option is (C).

11. The given sentence is in Active Voice. As per the given question we have to change it into Passive Voice.

Here, in the given sentence the direct object 'whom' in the active sentence will become the subject in the passive sentence, and its form is 'who'.

Hence, 'whom' will be changed into 'who'.

'did laugh' will be changed into 'was laughed'.

Lastly, the 'by' preposition will be added.

The correct Sentence is Who was laughed at by you?

Hence, the correct option is (B).

12. Context of the sentence: The given sentence talks about the condition of the match-winning.

'Hands down' means 'involving minimal difficulty or effort'

Hence, the correct option is (D).

13. In the given sentence, 'hard day's work' will be used.

It is so because "hard day's work" with an apostrophe 's' after 'day' is the correct phrase as it shows the singular possessive noun correctly.

"A hard day's" work will mean 'a hard day of work'.

We do not say 'days' as it is plural and incorrect to use after the article 'a'.

Hence, the correct option is (A).

14. He **has been suffering** from fever for a week.

It is so because since the line speaks of fever that started some time back and is still going on, the verb required here is a present perfect continuous tense.

Present perfect continuous tense is used to express those actions that had begun in the past and are still in progress.

Hence, the correct option is (D).

15. The given sentence is an indirect speech.

The basic rules for changing or converting indirect speech into direct speech:

The commas and inverted commas are added and 'that' is removed.

The reporting verb 'warned' is used in 'direct' speech, therefore, "do not" is used as a command or entreaty not to do something.

The correct answer is 'The policeman said to us, "Do not block the traffic." '

Hence, the correct option is (B)

16. Veteran politician Isaac Herzog has been elected Israel's (11th) President in a secret ballot in the Knesset (Parliament).

He replaced President Reuven Rivlin who was elected in 2014 to the largely ceremonial position. He will be the first President of Israel to be the son of a past President. His father, Chaim Herzog, served as President of Israel from 1983 until 1993. He is currently the head of the Jewish Agency, a nonprofit organization that works with the government to promote immigration to Israel. Between 2003 and 2018, he served in the Israeli Knesset as a legislator and minister with several positions.

Hence, the correct option is (B).

17. Biotin, also called Vitamin B7, is one of the B vitamins.

It is involved in a wide range of metabolic processes, both in humans and in other organisms, primarily related to the utilization of fats, carbohydrates, and amino acids. The name biotin derives from the Greek word "bios" (to live) and the suffix "-in" (a general chemical suffix used in organic chemistry). Biotin deficiency can be caused by inadequate dietary intake (rare) or the inheritance of one or more inborn genetic disorders that affect biotin metabolism.

The most common among these is biotinidase deficiency. The low activity of this enzyme causes a failure to recycle biotin from biocytin.

Hence, the correct option is (C).

18. Bihula festival:

It is a well-known festival in eastern Bihar, especially in the Bhagalpur district of Bihar. Devotees pray to Goddess Mansa for the well-being of their families during the festival, which takes place every August. The festival promotes the brilliant Manjusha art, which is on par with other well-known Bihar folk arts such as Jadopetiya of Santhal Parganas and Madhubani paintings of Mithilanchal.

This festival is held during the month of August each year.

Hence, the correct option is (A).

19.

- Kitab-ul-Hind was written by Al-Biruni.
- It is a famous Arabic text wherein he comments on Indian Sciences, Hindu religious beliefs, customs, and Social organization.
- Al-Biruni was the First Muslim Scholar to study India and its Brahmanical tradition.
- He is called the father of Indology and the first anthropologist.
- He is called one of the earliest and greatest polymaths of the Islamic World.
- Alberuni in his book Kitab-ul-Hind appreciated a very high degree of proficiency of Indians in the construction of Tanks and reservoirs at holy places.

Hence, the correct option is (B).

20. In July 1980, the Knesset passed the Jerusalem Law as part of the country's Basic Law, which declared Jerusalem the unified capital of Israel.

Hence, the correct option is (A).

21. Temperature: It is the measure of the degree of hotness and coldness of a body.

The various temperature scales commonly used are Celsius (C), Kelvin (K), Fahrenheit (F), and Rankine (Ra).

Given that:

Temperature $(T) = 200°C$

$$°F = \frac{9°}{5}C + 32$$

$$= \frac{9}{5} \times 200 + 32$$

$= 360 + 32$

$= 392°F$

Hence, the correct option is (C).

22. Power: The rate of doing work or the rate of transfer of energy is called Power.

P = $\frac{W}{t}$ or $\frac{H}{t}$

Where W is work done, t is time and H is energy transfer.

Hence, the correct option is (B).

23. Light year: It is the distance travelled by light in one year.

- A light-year is a convenient unit of measurement of large distances.
- Generally, a light-year is used to represent astronomical distances.
- One light-year is approximately 9 trillion (9×10^{12}) km.

Hence, the correct option is (A).

24. After completing the gold foil experiment, Rutherford concluded that the size of the nucleus is very small compared to the size of the atom because one out of every 12000 alpha particles deflected back after hitting the gold foil.

Rutherford's model says that an atom has a positively charged nucleus. So, the sub-atomic particle present in the nucleus of an atom is a proton (which carries a positive charge).

Conclusion of Rutherford Model

Most of the space inside the atom is empty because most of the α-particles passed through the gold foil without getting deflected.

Very few particles were deflected from their path, indicating that the positive charge of the atom occupies very little space.

A very small fraction of α-particles were deflected by 180°, indicating that all the positive charge and mass of the gold atom were concentrated in a very small volume within the atom.

Hence, the correct option is (A).

25. The number of protons in the nucleus of an atom is its atomic number, which is unique to each element. The number of protons identifies an element and determines its chemical properties.

The number of protons = Atomic number of an element

Nuclei = neutron + proton

Hence, the correct option is (A).

26. Weight:

The force applied by the earth on anybody having mass is called the weight of that body.

It is denoted by W.

Mathematically it is can be written as

W = mg

Where m = mass of the body and g = acceleration due to gravity

$\Rightarrow m = \frac{W}{g}$

$\Rightarrow m = \frac{49}{9.8}$

$\Rightarrow m = 5$ kg

Hence, the correct option is (B).

27. Any liquid will start to boil if the vapour pressure of the liquid is greater than the external pressure.

Since the pressure in a vacuum is zero, also any liquid will instantaneously boil when left open.

Water at 30° C will have some vapour pressure, hence will boil.

Hence, the correct option is (B).

28. The change in enthalpy of carbon in diamond to graphite form is negative. It shows that graphite should be more stable than diamond. The melting point of graphite is more than diamond which implies that it is a thermodynamically most stable allotrope of carbon.

Hence, the correct option is (A).

29. Brass is an alloy of copper and zinc. In proportions, it can be varied to achieve varying mechanical and electrical properties. An alloy is a metallic intimately mixed solid mixture of two or more different elements. An alloy in which one of the components is mercury is known as amalgam.

Hence, the correct option is (A).

30. As we know, some electrons are the free particles in the atoms. When we apply the electric potential across the conductor then these free electrons move and we call it electric current.

The charge on the electron is Negative.

So, we can say that Electric current is considered to be the flow of Negative Charge.

Hence, the correct option is (A).

31. The embedded part of this image is:

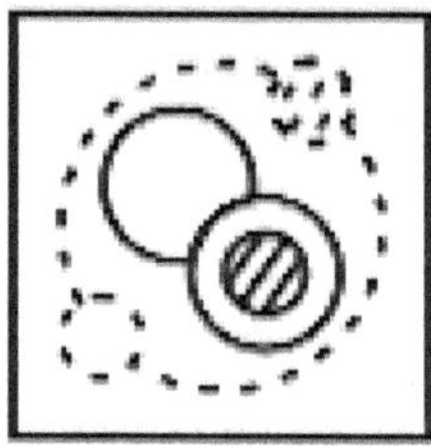

Hence, the correct option is (C).

32. The logic here is as follows:

'AGENT' is written as 'UOFHB'

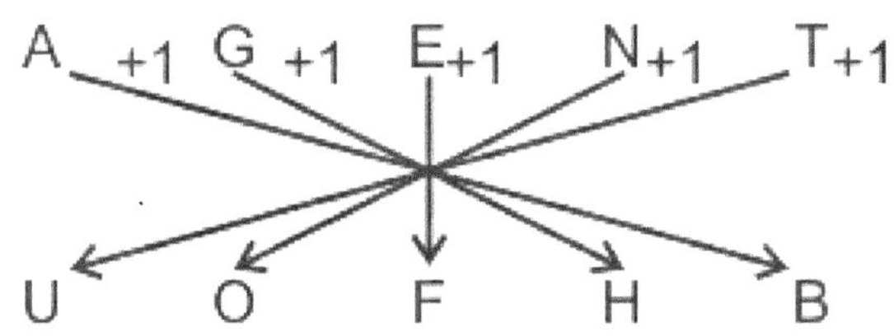

Similarly,

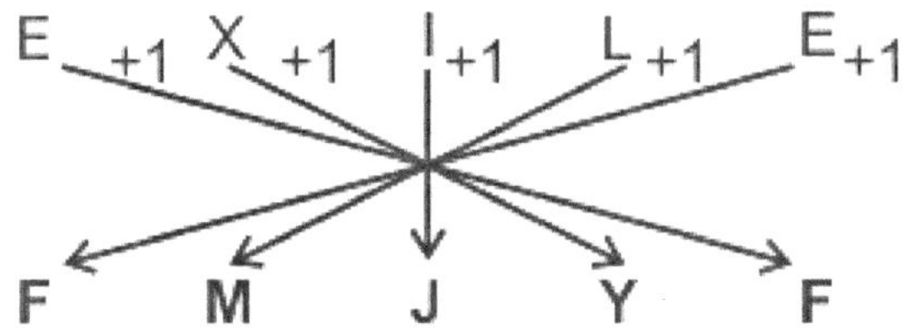

Hence, the correct answer is "FMJYF".

Hence, the correct option is (C).

33. Given,

A	M	E	R	I	C	A
1	7	3	4	6	5	1

I	N	D	I	A
6	8	9	6	1

So, CANADA is coded as:

C	A	N	A	D	A
5	1	8	1	9	1

Hence, the correct option is (B).

34. Given equation:

2 * 2 * 312 * 12 * 54 = 0

(A) +, ÷, ×, −

2 * 2 * 312 * 12 * 54

= 2 + 2 ÷ 312 × 12 - 54

= 2 + 0.076 - 54

= - 51.92 ≠ 0

(B) +, ×, ÷, −

2 + 2 × 312 ÷ 12 - 54

= 2 + 2 × 26 - 54

= 2 + 52 - 54

= 54 - 54

= 0

(C) −, ×, ÷, +

2 - 2 × 312 ÷ 12 + 54

= 2 - 2 × 26 + 54

= 2 - 52 + 54

= 56 - 52

= 4 ≠ 0

(D) −, ×, +, ÷

2 - 2 × 312 + 12 ÷ 54

= 2 - 2 × 312 + 0.22

= 2 - 624 + 0.22

= -621.78 ≠ 0

Hence, the correct option is (B).

35. The logic followed is:

In Figures 1st and 3rd, the figure is rotating by 45° in an anticlockwise direction.

Similarly,

In figures 2 and 3rd, the figure will be rotating by 45° in an anticlockwise direction.

Thus there is only option (B) which is satisfying the following pattern.

The completed series will be:

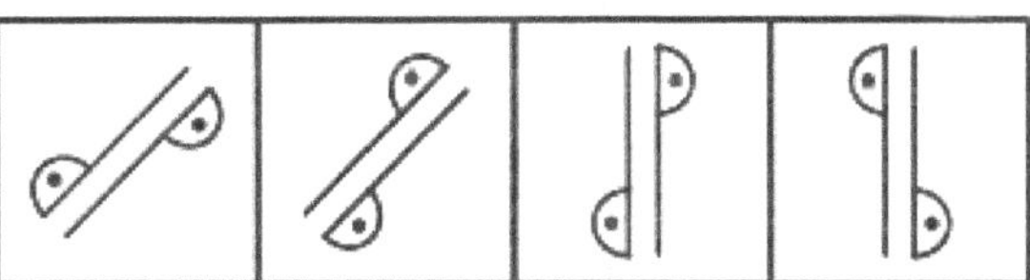

Hence, the correct option is B).

36. Given expression:

42 + 36 – 6 ÷ 15 × 8 ÷ 20 + 20 – 5 = ?

After changing the symbols:

42 – 36 ÷ 6 × 15 + 8 × 20 – 20 ÷ 5

= 42 – 6 × 15 + 160 – 4

= 42 – 90 + 160 – 4

= 108

Hence, the correct option is (B).

37. The theme is regarding loan approval by bank.

The correct order of arrangement is:

2. Loan application

3. Application processing

4. Underwriting process

1. Credit decision

5. Loan funding

Hence, the correct option is (B).

38. (A) RING - T**R**AVELL**ING** (Can be formed)

(B) VASE - TR**AV**E**L**LING (Cannot be formed because S is missing)

(C) RATE - **TRA**V**E**LLING (Can be formed)

(D) GRAVEL - T**RAVEL**LIN**G** (Can be formed)

Hence, the correct option is (B).

39. (A) FICTION - PURI**FICATION** (Can be formed)

(B) RUST - P**UR**IFICA**T**ION (Cannot be formed because S is missing)

(C) CAUTION - P**U**RIFI**CATION** (Can be formed)

(D) CATION- PURIFI**CATION** (Can be formed)

Hence, the correct option is (B).

40. The correct order is:

4. Infancy

3. Childhood

1. Puberty

6. Adolescence

2. Adulthood

5. Senescence

Hence, the correct option is (B).

41. Given:

AQ = 8.2 cm, PC = 6.4 cm, BR = 3.4 cm

The length of the tangents drawn to a circle from the same external point are equal.

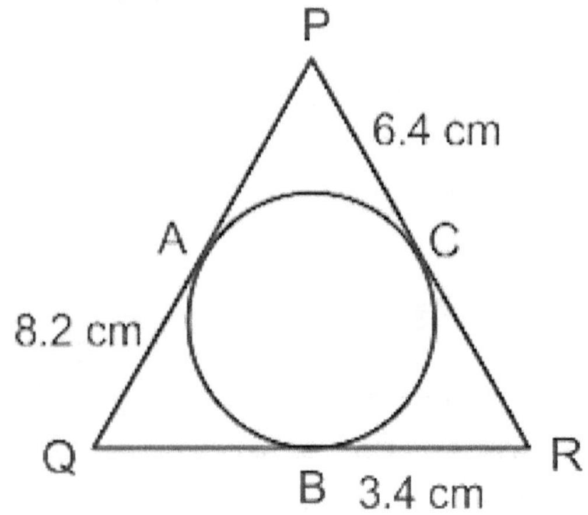

AQ = 8.2 cm

∴ BQ = 8.2 cm

PC = 6.4 cm

∴ PA = 6.4 cm

BR = 3.4 cm

∴ CR = 3.4 cm

Therefore, PQ = PA + AQ

= 6.4 cm + 8.2 cm

= 14.6 cm

We can write

PR = PC + CR

= 6.4 cm + 3.4 cm

= 9.8 cm

We can write

RQ = QB + BR

= 8.2 cm + 3.4 cm

= 11.6 cm

∴ Perimeter of ΔPQR = 14.6 + 9.8 + 11.6

= 36 cm

Hence, the correct option is (A).

42. Given:

The sum which was borrowed by Aman = Rs. 12000

Rate of interest of the bank = 6% per annum

Rate of interest on which Aman lent the amount = 9% per annum

Time = 3 years

We know that,

Interest = $\frac{P \times R \times T}{100}$

Amount = (P + Interest)

Where P = Principal

R = Rate of interest

T = Time

Interest paid by Aman to the Bank = $\frac{12000 \times 6 \times 3}{100}$

Interest = Rs. 2160

Amount paid to the bank = 12000 + 2160

Amount paid to the bank = Rs. 14160

Interest paid by Saurabh to Aman = $\frac{12000 \times 9 \times 3}{100}$

Interest = Rs. 3240

Amount paid by Saurabh to Aman = 12000 + 3240

Amount paid by Saurabh to Aman = Rs. 15240

Profit = (Amount received from Saurabh - Amount paid to the bank)

Profit = 15240 - 14160

Profit = Rs. 1080

∴ Profit gained by Aman is Rs. 1080.

Hence, the correct option is (C).

43. Given:

$\sin(\alpha+\beta) = 6\sin(\alpha-\beta)$ and $k = \frac{\tan\alpha}{\tan\beta}$

We know that,

$\sin(A+B) = \sin A\cos B + \sin B\cos A$

$\sin(A-B) = \sin A\cos B - \sin B\cos A$

$\sin(\alpha+\beta) = 6\sin(\alpha-\beta)$

$\Rightarrow \sin\alpha\cos\beta + \cos\alpha\sin\beta = 6\sin\alpha\cos\beta - 6\cos\alpha\sin\beta$

$\Rightarrow \cos\alpha\sin\beta + 6\cos\alpha\sin\beta = 6\sin\alpha\cos\beta - \sin\alpha\cos\beta$

$\Rightarrow 7\cos\alpha\sin\beta = 5\sin\alpha\cos\beta$

$\Rightarrow \frac{\sin\alpha}{\cos\alpha} = \frac{7}{5} \times \frac{\sin\beta}{\cos\beta}$

$\Rightarrow \tan\alpha = \frac{7}{5} \times \tan\beta$

$\Rightarrow k = \frac{\tan\alpha}{\tan\beta} = \frac{7}{5}$

Hence, the correct option is (B).

44. Given:

Radius of cone = 6 cm

Radius of hemisphere = 6 cm

Height of cone = 9 cm

Total volume of shape = Volume of cone + volume of hemisphere

Volume of cone $= \frac{1}{3} \times \pi r^2 h$

Volume of hemisphere $= \frac{2}{3} \times \pi r^3$

Total volume of shape $= \frac{1}{3} \times \pi \times 6^2 \times 9 + \frac{2}{3} \times \pi \times 6^3$

$= \frac{1}{3} \times \pi \times 36 \times (9+12)$

$= 12\pi \times 21$

$= 252\pi$ cm ^{3}

Hence, the correct option is (D).

45. Given:

The ratio of monthly incomes of Radha and Rani is 3 : 2 and that their expenditure is 8 : 5 if each of them saves Rs. 9,000 per month

Let Income of Radha and Rani be 3x and 2x and Expenditure be 8y and 5y

Saving = 3x – 8y = 2x – 5y

⇒ x = 3y....(1)

Saving = 9000

According to the question,

therefore

3x – 8y = 9000

⇒ 3(3y) – 8y = 9000

⇒ 9y – 8y = 9000

⇒ y = 9000

from the equation(1)

Then, total incomes of Radha and Rani = 5x = 5 × 3 × 9000

= Rs. 135000

Hence, the correct option is (C).

46. X and Y together can complete a work $= 12$ days

Y alone can complete the same work $= 30$ days

Let X alone can complete the same work $= x$ days

$\Rightarrow \frac{1}{x} + \frac{1}{30} = \frac{1}{12}$

$\Rightarrow \frac{1}{x} = \frac{1}{12} - \frac{1}{30}$

$\Rightarrow \frac{1}{x} = \frac{30-12}{30\times12}$

$\Rightarrow \frac{1}{x} = \frac{18}{360}$

$\Rightarrow \frac{1}{x} = \frac{1}{20}$

$\therefore x = 20$ days

In 20 days X alone will complete the work.

Hence, the correct option is (B).

47. Let the total number of votes casted be x, then,

According to the question,

Number of votes got by first candidate $= x \times \frac{30}{100}$

Number of votes got by second candidate $= x \times \frac{70}{100}$

Given that,

Difference in votes $= 500$

$\Rightarrow \frac{70x}{100} - \frac{30x}{100} = 500$

$\Rightarrow \frac{40x}{100} = 500$

$\Rightarrow x = \frac{500\times100}{40}$

$\Rightarrow x = 1250$

∴ The total number of votes casted is 1250.

Hence, the correct option is (A).

48. Let x be the distance of one side

Time taken by Sachin to reach his office $= \frac{x}{50}$ hours

Time taken by Sachin to return to his home $= \frac{x}{30}$ hours

Total distance travelled in whole journey $= 2x$ km

Total Time taken $= \frac{x}{50} + \frac{x}{30}$

$= \frac{8x}{150}$

Average speed $= \frac{\text{total distance}}{\text{total time}}$

$= \frac{2x}{\frac{8x}{150}}$ km/h

$= \frac{150}{4}$ km/h

$= 37.5$ km/h

Hence, the correct option is (B).

49. We know that,

Simple Interest (SI) $= \frac{P \times r \times t}{100}$

For Compound Interest (CI):

$A = P\left(1 + \frac{r}{100}\right)^t$

A is the amount at the end of time t

P is the principal

t is time

r is rate

For Simple Interest (SI), there is 100% increase to amount, thus A = 2P

⇒ Simple Interest (SI) = p

Time is 8 years.

$\therefore p = \frac{p \times r \times t}{100}$

$\Rightarrow r = \frac{100}{8}$

$\Rightarrow r = 12.5\%$

Now, $P =$ Rs. $8000, t = 2$ years and $r = 12.5\%$

$A = 8000\left(1 + \frac{12.5}{100}\right)^2$

$\Rightarrow A = 8000 \times \left(\frac{100+12.5}{100}\right)^2$

$\Rightarrow A = 8000 \times (1.125)^2$

$\Rightarrow A =$ Rs. 10125

$CI = A - P$

Where CI = Compound Interest

A = Amount

P = Principal

$\Rightarrow CI = 10125 - 8000 =$ Rs. 2125

Hence, the correct option is (D).

50. We know that the difference between the simple interest (SI_2) and compound interest (CI_2) for 2 years [compounded annually] on a sum of Rs. P at a rate R is,

$CI_2 - SI_2 = \frac{P \times R^2}{100^2}$

Now the given information,

$P =$ Rs. $2900,$

$CI_2 - SI_2 =$ Rs. 14.21

Putting the values we get,

$\Rightarrow 14.21 = \frac{2900 \times R^2}{100 \times 100}$

$\Rightarrow R = 7$

The annual rate of interest is 7%.

Hence, the correct option is (C).

51. Simplify the problem,

$100 = 73 + 27$

$46 = 73 - 27$

So,

$(100)^2 = (73 + 27)^2$

$(46)^2 = (73 - 27)^2$

$(100^2 + 46^2) = (73 + 27)^2 + (73 - 27)^2$

Using equations,

$(a + b)^2 = a^2 + 2ab + b^2$ and $(a - b)^2 = a^2 - 2ab + b^2$

$\Rightarrow [(100)^2 + (46)^2] = [(73)^2 + 2 \times 73 \times 27 + (27)^2 + (73)^2 - 2 \times 73 \times 27 + (27)^2]$

$\Rightarrow [(100)^2 + (46)^2] = 2(73^2 + 27^2)$

$\therefore \frac{(100)^2+(46)^2}{(73)^2+(27)^2} = 2$

Hence, the correct option is (A).

52. Given:

$\frac{\frac{1}{5}\div\frac{1}{6}of\frac{1}{5}}{\frac{1}{5}+\frac{1}{6}of\frac{1}{5}}$

$=\frac{\frac{1}{5}\div\frac{1}{30}}{\frac{1}{5}+\frac{1}{30}}$

$=\frac{6}{\frac{6+1}{30}}$

$=\frac{6\times30}{7}$

$=\frac{180}{7}$

Hence, the correct option is (C).

53. Given:

$x+y=9$ and $x^2+y^2=45$

We know that,

$(a+b)^2=a^2+b^2+2ab$

$x+y=9$

Squaring both sides

$\Rightarrow x^2+y^2+2xy=81$

$\Rightarrow 45+2xy=81$ $[\because x^2+y^2=45]$

$\Rightarrow 2xy=36$

$\Rightarrow xy=18$

Now for x^4+y^4 we should square x^2+y^2

$\Rightarrow (x^2+y^2)^2=(45)^2$

$\Rightarrow x^4+y^4+2x^2y^2=2025$

$\Rightarrow x^4+y^4=2025-648$

$\Rightarrow x^4+y^4=1377$

So,

$x^4+y^4+x^2y^2=1377+324$

$=1701$

$\therefore$ The correct answer will be 1701.

Hence, the correct option is (C).

54. We know that,

Mode $=L+\left[\frac{f_1-f_0}{2f_1-f_0-f_2}\right]\times i$

$i=$ class interval or class size

$f_1=$ frequency of modal class

$f_0=$ frequency of pre modal class

$f_2=$ frequency of success modal class

$L=$ lower limit of modal class

Here maximum frequency is 30, the class corresponding to this $20-30$

So modal class is $20-30$

Now lower limit of modal class $(L)=20$

Frequency (f_1) of modal class $=30$

Frequency (f_0) of preceding the modal class $=25$

Frequency (f_2) of the class succeeding the modal class $=20$

Class size $=10$

Using formula,

Mode $=L+\left[\frac{f_1-f_0}{2f_1-f_0-f_2}\right]\times i$

$\Rightarrow$ Mode $=20+\left[\frac{30-25}{2\times30-25-20}\right]\times10$

$\Rightarrow$ Mode $=20+\frac{10}{3}$

$\therefore$ Mode is 23.33.

Hence, the correct option is (B).

55. Given:

The given equation are $kx+3y=26$ and $21x+(k+2)y=71+k$

The equations $a_1x+b_1y+c=0$ and $a_2x+b_2y+c=0$ has many solution

If $\frac{a_1}{a_2}=\frac{b_1}{b_2}=\frac{c_1}{c_2}$

According to the question

$\frac{k}{21}=\frac{3}{k+2}=\frac{26}{71+k}$

Taking,

$\frac{3}{k+2}=\frac{26}{71+k}$

$\Rightarrow 3(71+k)=26(k+2)$

$\Rightarrow 213+3k=26k+52$

$\Rightarrow 26k-3k=213-52$

$\Rightarrow 23k=161$

$\therefore k=7$

Hence, the correct option is (B).

56. N= 5,

Values of all observations = 72 + 86 + 92 + 63 + 77

= 390

i.e., 90 (6 × 80) number less all the observations of Bob's score.

Bob needs to score in 6th Test = 90

So, that his Sum of the values of all 6 test = 480

Hence, the correct option is (A).

57. Given that,

$$p(x) = x^3 - ax^2 - bx + 6$$

According to the question, if $(x+1)$ and $(x-2)$ are the factor of a polynomial, therefore

$$p(-1) = (-1)^3 - a(-1)^2 - b(-1) + 6 = 0$$

$$\Rightarrow -1 - a + b + 6 = 0$$

$\Rightarrow a = b + 5$.....(1)

$$p(2) = (2)^3 - a(2)^2 - b(2) + 6 = 0$$

$$\Rightarrow 8 - 4a - 2b + 6 = 0$$

$$\Rightarrow 2a + b = 7$$

From equation (1)

$$2(b+5) + b = 7$$

$$\Rightarrow 3b = -3$$

$$\Rightarrow b = -1$$

Therefore from equation (1),

$$a = 4$$

Hence, quadratic polynomial $q(x)$, whose factors are $(x-a)$ and $(x-b)$

$$q(x) = (x-4)(x+1)$$

$$\Rightarrow q(x) = x^2 - 3x - 4$$

Hence, the correct option is (C).

58. Given:

The first student secured = 24% marks and failed by 16 marks

The second student secured = 26% marks and failed by 6 marks

Let the total number be x.

Passing marks for the first student $= (24\% \text{ of } x) + 16$

Passing marks for second student $= (26\% \text{ of } x) + 6$

According to the question,

Passing marks for the first student = Passing marks for second student

$$\Rightarrow (24\% \text{ of } x) + 16 = (26\% \text{ of } x) + 6$$

$$\Rightarrow \frac{24x}{100} + 16 = \frac{26x}{100} + 6$$

$$\Rightarrow 10 = \frac{2x}{100}$$

$$\Rightarrow \frac{2x}{100} = 10$$

$$\Rightarrow x = \frac{10 \times 100}{2}$$

$$\Rightarrow x = \frac{1000}{2}$$

$$\Rightarrow x = 500$$

Passing marks $= (24\% \text{ of } x) + 16$

Passing marks $= \left\{500 \times \frac{24x}{100}\right\} + 16$

Passing marks $= 136$

Hence, the correct option is (C).

59. Given:

Two numbers are respectively 14% and 23% less than a third number.

Let, the third number is x

The first number $= \frac{(100-14)x}{100}$

$$= \frac{86x}{100}$$

and the second number $= \frac{(100-23)x}{100}$

$$= \frac{77x}{100}$$

Thus, the percentage of second number to the first number

$$\frac{\frac{86x}{100}}{\frac{77x}{100}} \times 100 = 89.53 \approx 90\%$$

∴ The second number is approximately 90% of the first number.

Hence, the correct option is (D).

60. Given:

The volume of a cube $= 2744$ cm ^{3}

The volume of a cube $= (\text{Side})^3$

$$\Rightarrow 2744 = (\text{Side})^3$$

$\Rightarrow$ Side $= \sqrt[3]{2744}$

$\Rightarrow$ Side $= 14cm$

The total surface area of a cube $= 6 \times (\text{Side})^2$

$\Rightarrow$ The total surface area of a cube $= 6 \times (14)^2$

$\Rightarrow$ The total surface area of a cube $= 1176 \text{ cm}^2$

$\therefore$ Total surface area of a cube is 1176 cm^2.

Hence, the correct option is (B).

Mock Test 09

English

Ques (1-2):Direction: Read the following passage and answer the questions that follow it.

Dreams are both internal and external. Since the ego or the director is absent during sleep the neural pathways have a run of their own. Thus the day-long experiences or the existing memories are the driving force for the internal dreams. However, when there is tremendous thinking activity or Sanyam on a particular thought during waking time, it leads sometimes to solution dreams. Various great inventions and discoveries of the world have come through such a dreaming process. Why we do not remember dreams have been researched by lots of brain scientists and there are many reasons - part of it is to do with creating long-term memory. Never the less it is the dreams that we remember that make life interesting. There are many theories of dreams but we still do not know why we dream and why most of the time we have random and strange dreams. A possible answer may lie in how synapses behave during sleep. The more we dream during the night the less restful is the sleep. Really restful sleep is a deep sleep without dreams. This helps in the flushing out of the toxic material from the major part of the brain. Besides removing the toxins from the brain the increase of synaptic cleft may also help in explaining the dreaming process.

Q.1 When do neural pathways have a run of their own?

A. During Sanyam
B. During sleep
C. During intervals
D. During the process of waking up

Q.2 What is a really restful sleep?

A. A really restful sleep is deep sleep without dreams.
B. A really restful sleep is the one in which all the toxins of our brains are increase flushed out.
C. A really restful sleep is the one in which synaptic cleft is increased.
D. A really restful sleep is the one in which we dream of our past life.

Q.3 Direction: Choose the option that is the passive form of the given sentence.

The thief was caught red-handed by the police.

A. The police was caught red-handed by the thief.
B. The police caught the thief red-handed.
C. The police catches the thief red-handed.
D. The thief got caught red-handed.

Q.4 Direction: Select the most appropriate Tense to fill in the blank in the given sentence.

The jury ______ its verdict in favor of the victim.

A. has given **B.** have given
C. gives **D.** are given

Ques (5-6):Direction: In the following question, out of the four alternatives, select the word Similiar in meaning to the given word.

Q.5 Lethal

A. Fatal **B.** Curious **C.** Smooth **D.** Kind

Q.6 Clinch

A. Lose **B.** Clasp **C.** Seal **D.** Deal

Q.7 Direction: In the question below the sentence has been given in Direct/Indirect speech. From the given alternatives, choose the one which best expresses the given sentence in Indirect/Direct speech.

She told her mother that she was doing her work.

A. She said to her mother, "I do my work
B. She said to her mother, "I was doing my work"
C. She said to her mother, "I'm doing my work"
D. She said to her mother, "I have done my work"

Q.8 Direction: Spot the erroneous parts, if any, in the following sentences.

She says she's already paid me back, but I can't remember, so I'll have to take her word.

A. to take her word true
B. to take her at her word
C. to take her word for it
D. No improvement

Q.9 Direction: Choose the most appropriate preposition and fill in the blank.

If you go to Kashmir, you have to go to Dal Lake and try the local food ______ this area.

A. for **B.** around **C.** besides **D.** between

Q.10 Direction: Select the most appropriate pronoun to fill in the blank in the given sentence.

The server with _____ I was talking is my good friend.

A. who **B.** her **C.** whom **D.** which

Q.11 Direction: Fill in the blank with the most appropriate phrasal verb.

He asked him to _____ some documents.

A. set out **B.** go through
C. lookup **D.** imagine

Q.12 Direction: Choose the most appropriate preposition and fill in the blank.

It is not easy to distinguish a loyal friend _____ a flatterer.

A. from **B.** among **C.** between **D.** and

Q.13 Choose the correctly punctuated sentence.

A. He said, I do not like video games.
B. He said, I do not like video games?
C. He said, I do not like video games!

D. He said, "I do not like video games."

Q.14 Direction: Choose the correct adjective for the following sentence.

I think that childhood is a time when there are ______ ways to make life enjoyable.

A. many **B.** less **C.** little **D.** more

Q.15 Direction: Fill in the blank with the most appropriate verb.

Around 2000 people ________ under the debris in recent earthquake.

A. buried **B.** bury

C. have been buried **D.** are buried

General Knowledge

Q.16 Financial Assistance to Non-School Going Disabled Children (less than 18 years) is the Financial Assistance Scheme of which Department of State Government of Haryana?

[Haryana Police Constable Commando Wing, 2021]

A. Finance

B. Women and Child Development

C. Social Justice and Empowerment

D. Health and Family Welfare

Q.17 Dhauladhar Range forms part of which Himalayas?

[SSC MTS, 2019]

A. Lesser Himalayas **B.** Shivalik

C. Purvanchals **D.** Greater Himalayas

Q.18 Quit India movement was launched in response to which of the following events?

A. Simon Commission

B. Cabinet Mission Plan

C. Cripps Mission

D. Wavell Plan

Q.19

What J. B. Dunlop invented?

A. Pneumatic rubber tyre

B. Automobile wheel rim

C. Rubber boot

D. Model airplanes

Q.20 Deodhar Trophy is related to which sport?

A. Cricket **B.** Volleyball

C. Football **D.** Tennis

Science

Q.21 Which one of the following is not a characteristic of a compound?

A. Composition is variable

B. All particles of the compound are of only one type

C. Particles of the compound have two or more elements

D. Its constituents cannot be separated by simple physical methods

Q.22 Work done on the object does not depend on:

A. Displacement

B. Force applied

C. The angle between force and displacement

D. The initial velocity of an object

Q.23 Pitch of sound depends upon it:

A. Wavelength

B. Frequency

C. Amplitude

D. Periodicity and regularity

Q.24 The atomic number of Ni and Cu are 28 and 29 respectively. The electronic configuration $1s^2, 2s^2, 2p^6, 3s^2, 3p^6, 3d^{10}$ represents:

A. Cu^+ **B.** Cu^{2+} **C.** Ni^{2+} **D.** Ni

Q.25 Which of the following is responsible for hardness of water?

A. $CaHCO_3$ **B.** $CaCl_2$

C. Both (A) and (B) **D.** None of these

Q.26 Celsius is a unit of:

A. Temperature **B.** Heat

C. Specific heat **D.** Latent heat

Q.27 Galvanization is a method of protecting iron from rusting, by coating with a thin layer of:

A. Gallium **B.** Aluminium

C. Zinc **D.** Silver

Q.28 Find the power consumed by an electric iron having 110Ω resistance when feed from a $220\ V$ supply?

A. $4.4\ kW$ **B.** $220\ W$ **C.** $440\ W$ **D.** $2.2\ kW$

Q.29 Which one of the following thermometers are known as pyrometer?

A. Thermo-electric thermometers

B. Radiation thermometers

C. Gas thermometers

D. Liquid thermometers

Q.30 The passenger tends to lean forward when a running metro stops suddenly. It is because of:

A. Centripetal Force **B.** Inertia of Rest

C. Inertia of Motion **D.** Inertia of direction

Reasoning

Q.31 In a certain code, MONK is written as 53. How will TUTOR be written in that code?

A. 94 **B.** 96 **C.** 91 **D.** 77

Q.32 Arrange the words given below in a meaningful sequence.

1. Cut
2. Put on
3. Mark
4. Measure
5. Tailor

A. 3, 1, 5, 4, 2 **B.** 2, 4, 3, 1, 5
C. 1, 3, 2, 4, 5 **D.** 4, 3, 1, 5, 2

Q.33 If A = 4, K = 3, N = 2, P = 1, then the sum of which set of the letters makes the highest number?

A. KANPK **B.** NPAKN **C.** PKANA **D.** NAKNA

Q.34 Choose the meaningful words from the given jumbled word:

ETTLOB

A. BOTLTE **B.** BOTTEL
C. BETOTL **D.** BOTTLE

Q.35 Rearrange the jumbled letters to make meaningful words and then select the one which is different.

[AFCAT, 2021]

A. THLAAPS **B.** THANAPH
C. LESIED **D.** ENAHTME

Q.36 If COMMANDER is coded as 513368947 , then CONDEMN can be coded as:

A. 5159633 **B.** 5144789 **C.** 5183794 **D.** 5189438

Q.37 If " + " denotes " – ", " – " denotes " × ", " × " denotes " ÷ " and " ÷ " denotes " + ", then what is the value of 24 – 16 + 8 ÷ 4 × 2?

A. 94 **B.** 188 **C.** 378 **D.** 464

Q.38 Direction: In the question below, which one of the given responses would be a meaningful order of the following words? (Depending upon their value in descending order in terms of a litre)

1. 1 Cubic Metre
2. 1 Litre
3. 1 Millilitre
4. 1 Pint
5. 1 Gallon

A. 1, 3, 5, 4, 2 **B.** 4, 2, 5, 3, 1
C. 4, 5, 1, 2, 3 **D.** 1, 5, 2, 4, 3

Q.39 The given Problem Figure is embedded in one of the given Answer Figures. Which is that Answer Figure?

A.

B.

C.

D.

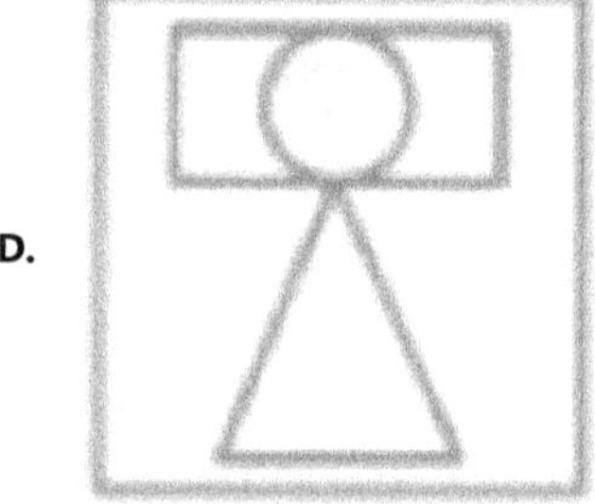

Q.40 Three different positions of the same dice are shown, the six faces of which are shown in dots numbered 1 to 6. How many dots will be on the opposite face of the face showing '3 dots'?

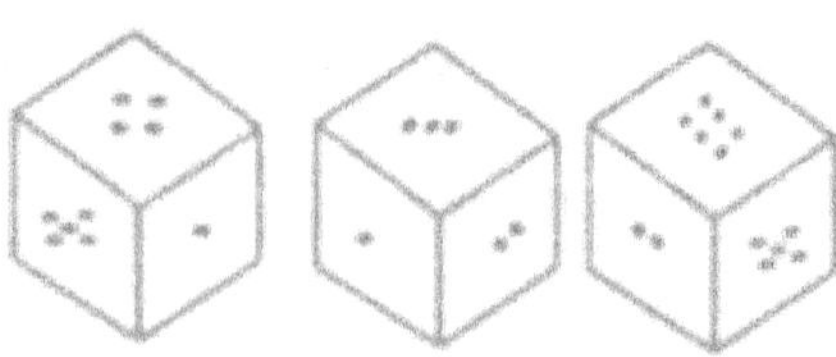

A. 4 **B.** 5 **C.** 6 **D.** 1

Mathematics

Q.41 Solve:

$$(25)^{7.5} \times (5)^{2.5} \div (125)^{1.5} = 5^{?}$$

A. 8.5 **B.** 13 **C.** 16 **D.** 17.5

Q.42 Solve:

$$\frac{(243)^{\frac{n}{5}}\times 3^{2n+1}}{9^n\times 3^{n-1}}$$

A. 1 **B.** 8 **C.** 9 **D.** 3^n

Q.43

Seats for Mathematics, Physics, and Biology in a school are in the ratio 5 : 7 : 8. There is a proposal to increase these seats by 40%, 50% and 75% respectively. What will be the ratio of increased seats?

A. 2 : 3 : 4 **B.** 6 : 7 : 8

C. 6 : 8 : 9 **D.** None of these

Q.44

$$\sqrt{(11x^3+6x^2+5x+62)}+\sqrt{(11x^3+6x^2+5x+42)}=10$$

then find the value of

$$\sqrt{(11x^3+6x^2+5x+62)}-\sqrt{(11x^3+6x^2+5x+42)}$$

A. -2 **B.** 0 **C.** 1 **D.** 2

Q.45 If $x+y+xy=1, y+z+yz=7$ and $x+z+xz=8$ then find the value of $18xyz$:

A. 15 **B.** 18 **C.** 31 **D.** 24

Q.46 $\left(x+\frac{1}{x}\right)\left(x-\frac{1}{x}\right)\left(x^2+\frac{1}{x^2}-1\right)\left(x^2+\frac{1}{x^2}+1\right)$ is equal to:

A. $x^6+\frac{1}{x^6}$ **B.** $x^8+\frac{1}{x^8}$ **C.** $x^8-\frac{1}{x^8}$ **D.** $x^6-\frac{1}{x^6}$

Q.47 5x − y = 5 and 3x + 2y = 29, find the value of x and y:

A. x = 5, y = -10 **B.** x = -5, y = 10

C. x = -5, y = 24 **D.** x = 3, y = 10

Q.48 The equation $\cos^2\theta=\frac{(x+y)^2}{4xy}$ is only possible when?

A. x = -y **B.** x > y **C.** x = y **D.** x < y

Q.49 The curved surface area of a cylindrical pillar is 264 m^2 and its volume is 924 m^3 The ratio of its diameter to height is:

A. 3 : 7 **B.** 7 : 3 **C.** 6 : 7 **D.** 7 : 6

Q.50 For the data $3,5,1,6,5,9,5,2,8,6$ the mean, median and mode are x, y and z respectively. Which one of the following is correct?

A. $x=y\neq z$ **B.** $x\neq y=z$

C. $x\neq y\neq z$ **D.** $x=y=z$

Q.51 The price of oil has increased by 25%. Ram has decided to spend only 10% more than what he initially did on buying oil. What is the percentage decrease in Ram's oil consumption?

A. 21% **B.** 20% **C.** 12% **D.** 15%

Q.52 Find the sum of $\angle CHI$ and supplementary of $\angle ABP$. If $B'G' \parallel C'H'$.

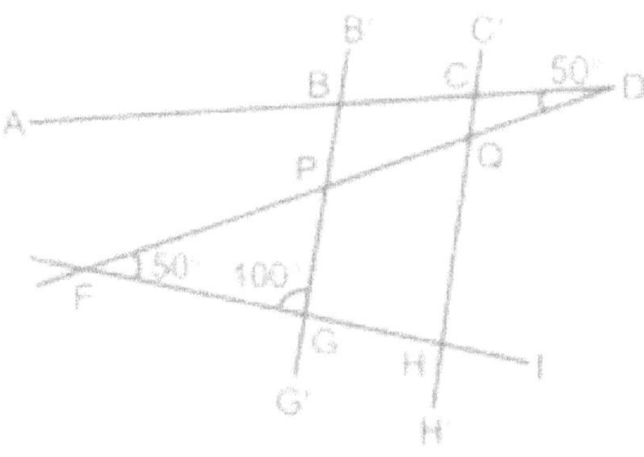

A. 180° **B.** 200° **C.** 230° **D.** 260°

Q.53 If A and B together can complete a piece of work in 15 days and B alone in 20 days, in how many days can A alone complete the work?

A. 60 **B.** 45 **C.** 40 **D.** 30

Q.54 Robert is travelling on his cycle and has calculated to reach point A at 2 P.M. if he travels at 10 kmph, he will reach there at 12 noon if he travels at 15 kmph. At what speed must he travel to reach A at 1 P.M.?

A. 8 kmph **B.** 11 kmph **C.** 12 kmph **D.** 14 kmph

Q.55 The compound interest on a sum of Rs. 20000 at 15% p.a. for 2 years, when interest compounded yearly is:

A. Rs. 6540 **B.** Rs. 6450 **C.** Rs. 6908 **D.** Rs. 6896

Q.56 The value of $\frac{(\cos 12^\circ+\sin 78^\circ)(\sec 12^\circ+cosec 78^\circ)}{\sin 64^\circ \sec 26^\circ+\cos 35^\circ cosec 55^\circ}$ is:

A. $\frac{1}{2}$ **B.** 4 **C.** 2 **D.** 1

Q.57 A trader sold two bullocks for Rs. 8400 each, neither losing nor gaining in total. If he sold one of the bullocks at a gain of 20%, then the other is sold at a loss of:

A. 20% **B.** $18\frac{2}{9}\%$ **C.** $14\frac{2}{7}\%$ **D.** 21%

Q.58 If $0\leq\theta\leq 90^\circ$, and $\sin(6\theta+16^\circ)=\cos(2\theta+10^\circ)$, then what is the value of θ (in degrees)?

A. 4° **B.** 16° **C.** 8° **D.** 12°

Q.59 In a triangle PQR, the side QR of a triangle is extended to M. If $\angle PRM=108^\circ$ and $\angle Q=\frac{4}{5}\angle P$, then find $\angle Q$?

A. 32° **B.** 36° **C.** 42° **D.** 48°

Q.60 On a certain principal if the simple interest for two years is Rs. 3200 and compound interest for the two years is Rs. 3472, what is the rate of interest?

A. 8.50% **B.** 30% **C.** 17% **D.** 22.50%

// Smart Answer Sheet //

Correct — Percentage of students who answered correctly. Skipped — Percentage of students who skipped.

Q.	Ans.	Correct	Skipped	Q.	Ans.	Correct	Skipped	Q.	Ans.	Correct	Skipped	Q.	Ans.	Correct	Skipped	Q.	Ans.	Correct	Skipped	Q.	Ans.	Correct	Skipped
1	B	68.87 %	1.61 %	11	B	42.53 %	1.66 %	21	B	82.84 %	0.0 %	31	A	82.43 %	0.0 %	41	B	40.19 %	1.43 %	51	C	67.8 %	1.15 %
2	A	50.48 %	1.79 %	12	A	22.42 %	4.58 %	22	D	56.65 %	1.47 %	32	D	85.9 %	0.0 %	42	C	62.5 %	1.29 %	52	A	31.17 %	3.68 %
3	B	63.46 %	1.05 %	13	D	88.54 %	0.0 %	23	B	85.98 %	0.0 %	33	D	81.42 %	0.0 %	43	A	57.83 %	1.58 %	53	A	82.22 %	0.0 %
4	A	78.9 %	0.0 %	14	A	65.49 %	1.2 %	24	A	12.56 %	3.58 %	34	D	57.22 %	1.71 %	44	D	43.4 %	1.44 %	54	C	51.19 %	1.23 %
5	A	84.47 %	0.0 %	15	C	54.9 %	1.1 %	25	C	67.78 %	1.01 %	35	D	55.66 %	1.87 %	45	A	12.65 %	3.31 %	55	B	55.4 %	1.49 %
6	A	60.35 %	1.25 %	16	C	62.98 %	1.67 %	26	A	85.45 %	0.0 %	36	D	51.13 %	1.36 %	46	D	50.59 %	1.02 %	56	C	40.5 %	1.74 %
7	C	30.49 %	3.21 %	17	A	88.15 %	0.0 %	27	C	41.88 %	1.91 %	37	C	50.38 %	1.36 %	47	D	51.22 %	1.63 %	57	C	69.17 %	1.81 %
8	C	66.32 %	1.58 %	18	C	58.25 %	1.62 %	28	C	81.37 %	0.0 %	38	D	13.58 %	3.51 %	48	C	77.37 %	0.0 %	58	C	89.68 %	0.0 %
9	B	82.18 %	0.0 %	19	A	79.32 %	0.0 %	29	B	58.1 %	1.2 %	39	A	42.47 %	1.51 %	49	B	60.21 %	1.06 %	59	D	42.84 %	1.23 %
10	C	49.84 %	1.39 %	20	A	15.19 %	3.25 %	30	C	58.93 %	1.68 %	40	B	76.58 %	0.0 %	50	D	44.28 %	1.55 %	60	C	66.05 %	1.02 %

//Hints and Solutions//

1. During sleep, neural pathways have a run of their own.

"Dreams are both internal and external. Since the ego or the director is absent during sleep the neural pathways have a run of their own. Thus the day-long experiences or the existing memories are the driving force for the internal dreams."

Hence, the correct option is (B).

2. A really restful sleep is deep sleep without dreams.

"Really restful sleep is a deep sleep without dreams. This helps in the flushing out of the toxic material from the major part of the brain. Besides removing the toxins from the brain the increase of synaptic cleft may also help in explaining the dreaming process."

Hence, the correct option is (A).

3. The police caught the thief red-handed is the correct passive.

The given sentence is In Passive Voice of simple past tense. As per the question we have to change it into Active Voice of simple past tense.

The structure of transformation Is as follows:

Structure of simple past:

Subject+V_2+Object. (Active Voice)

Subject (objective case)+was/were+ V_3+ Object (Subjective Case). (Passive Voice)

Subject and the object will interchange places.

'Was caught' will be changed into 'catch' as per the structure.
Hence, the correct option is (B).

4. The jury **has** given its verdict in favor of the victim.

The present perfect tense is used to indicate that an action is completed in the near past.

The structure is: Subject + has/have + V_3 + object.

When the subjects represent a single idea as a whole, the verb used is in the singular form. In the above sentence, the subject the 'jury' has given its decisions as a whole.
Hence, the correct option Is (A).

5. Lethal: Able to cause or causing death; extremely dangerous.

Fatal: causing or ending In death.

Curious: Interested in learning about people or things around you.

Smooth: Having a surface or consisting of a substance that is perfectly regular and has no holes, lumps, or areas that rise or fall suddenly.

Kind: Generous, helpful, and thinking about other people's feelings.
Hence, the correct option is (A).

6. Clinch: To finally get or win something.

Lose: To fail to win.

Clasp: To hold someone or something firmly in your hands or arms.

Seal: To make an agreement more certain or to approve it formally.

Deal: To give or share out something.
Hence, the correct option is (A).

7. The correct speech is: She said to her mother, "I'm doing my work"

While changing the narration of the sentence, we need to follow steps

When converting from indirect to direct speech 'that' is removed and replaced with commas and inverted commas.

'told' is used when two people are mentioned in the reporting speech. 'told' is converted to 'said' in the direct speech.

Indirect speech always undergoes a reverse backshift in tense and so 'was doing' which is in past continuous tense will be converted into 'am doing' which is in present continuous.

'am' is used because 'I' is used.
Hence, the correct option is (C).

8. There is an expression which is used in its original form without any alterations:

Take someone's word for it- to believe that what someone is saying is true.

For example:

If she says she's sick, you have to take her word for it.
Hence, the correct option is (C).

9. The appropriate preposition for the given blank will be "around".

The given sentence is talking about trying the local food of Dal lake, Kashmir.

The preposition 'around' means in or to various places or directions.
Hence, the correct option is (B).

10. The appropriate pronoun for the given blank will be "whom".

whom: used instead of 'who' as the object of a verb or preposition - object pronoun

who: the person that; whoever, (related to persons) - subject pronoun.

which: used for a thing or animal i.e., any non-living entity
Hence, the correct option is (C).

11. The appropriate phrasal verb for the given blank will be "go through"

Go through: search through or examine something, especially methodically

Set out: begin a journey

Lookup: search for and find a piece of information in a book or database

Imagine: form a mental image or concept of
Hence, the correct option is (B).

12. The appropriate preposition for the given blank will be "from".

The preposition 'from' is used for indicating a distinction.

The preposition 'among' is used for indicating a division, choice or differentiation involving three or more participants.

The preposition 'between' is used for indicating a connection or relationship involving two or more parties.

The conjunction 'and' is used for connecting two identical comparatives, to emphasize a progressive change.
Hence, the correct option is (A).

13. The correct answer is: He said, "I do not like video games."

The given sentence is a direct speech, so 'quotation marks' should be used here.

The question mark is used after asking a question.
Example: What is her name?

The exclamation mark is used to express wonder, surprise or to emphasize. Example: I have found the lost photo album!
Hence, the correct option is (D).

14. The appropriate adjective for the given blank will be "many".

The adjective 'many' is used with a countable noun; means a large number of people, things, places, etc.

The adjective 'less is used with an uncountable noun; means a smaller amount of; not as much.

The adjective 'little' is also used with an uncountable noun; means small in size, amount, or degree (often used to convey an appealing diminutiveness or express an affectionate or condescending attitude).

The adjective 'more' is comparative of much or many; means a greater or additional amount or degree.
Hence, the correct option is (A).

15. The appropriate word for the given blanks will be "have been buried".

In the present perfect tense, we make passive verb forms by putting 'has/have + been' before the past participle form of the verb.

Hence, the correct option is (C).

16. Financial Assistance to Non-School Going Disabled Children (less than 18 years) is the Financial Assistance Scheme of Social Justice and Empowerment Department of State Government of Haryana.

The Ministry of Social Justice and Empowerment is a Government of India ministry. It is responsible for welfare, social justice and empowerment of disadvantaged and marginalised sections of society, including scheduled castes (SC), Other Backward Classes (OBC), Manual Scavengers, the disabled, the elderly, and the victims of drug abuse.

Hence, the correct option is (C).

17. Dhauladhar Range forms part of the Lesser Himalayas.

The three major divisions of the Himalayas are:

The Great Himalayas or the Himadri, the Middle Himalayas (Lesser Himalayas) or the Himachal, and the Outer Himalayas or the Shivaliks. Pirpanjal range, Dhauladhar range (Himachal Pradesh), Mussoorie range (Uttarakhand), Nagtibba range (Uttarakhand) are part of the Middle Himalayas. The longitudinal valley lying between the lesser Himalayas and the Shiwaliks is known as Duns. Dehra Dun, Kotli Dun, and Patli Dun are some of the well-known Duns. Most of the world's highest peaks are located in this Inner Himalayan region. Mount Everest, Mount K-2, Mount Kanchenjunga are important peaks located in Inner Himalayas. Purvanchal is the southward extension of the Himalayas running along the northeastern edge of India. They run along the India-Myanmar Border extending from Arunachal Pradesh in the north to Mizoram in the south. Naga Hills, Patkai bum hills, Manipur hills, Mizo hills form part of this Purvanchal.
Hence, the correct option is (A).

18. The quit India movement was launched in response to Cripps Mission.

Cripps Mission was sent by the British government in March 1942. It was aimed to obtain Indian support in the 2nd world war. It was headed by Sir Richard Standford Cripps, who was labour minister in Winston Churchill's government. The Mission was rejected by the INC, the Muslim League and other Indian groups.

Few proposals of Cripps Mission are:

- Dominion status to India after the war.
- Constitution-making body after the war.
- Constitution so framed would be acceptable by the British Government only if certain province desires to stay away from the Union of India. Any province which wouldn't accept the new constitution would have the right to sign a separate agreement with the British.

Gandhi called Cripps Mission 'A post-dated cheque drawn on a failing bank' due to the Cripps offer of Dominion Status after the war.
Hence, the correct option is (C).

19. J. B. Dunlop invented the Pneumatic rubber tyre.

John Boyd (J.B.) Dunlop (5 February 1840 – 23 October 1921) was a Scottish inventor and veterinary surgeon who spent most of his career in Ireland. Familiar with making rubber devices, he re-invented pneumatic tyres for his child's tricycle and developed them for use in cycle racing.
Hence, the correct option is (A).

20. Deodhar Trophy is related to Cricket.

The Deodhar Trophy is a List A cricket competition in Indian domestic cricket. It is a 50 -over tournament which is played annually between 3 teams. These 3 national-level teams are India A, India B, and India C. The first edition was in the year (1973-74).

The Trophy was named after Prof. D.B. Deodhar. He is also known as the Grand Old Man of Indian cricket.
Hence, the correct option is (A).

21. All particles of the compound are of only one type is not a characteristic of a compound.

A compound is a substance formed when two or more elements are chemically bonded together. So, all particles of the compound cannot have the same particles. If it has the same particles, then it will be referred to as an element. The elements of the compound are chemically combined, so they cannot be separated by simple physical methods.
Hence, the correct option is (B).

22. Work done on the object does not depend on the initial velocity of an object.

Work done: Work is said to be done when a force applied to an object moves that object.

Work can be calculated by multiplying the force by the movement of the object. The SI unit of work is the joule (J).

$$W = F \times d\cos\theta$$

where,

$F =$ force applied in Newton

$d =$ displacement in meter

$\theta =$ angle between force and displacement

As work is done on the object and is a product of force and displacement and also related to the angle between force and displacement. It is not dependent on the initial velocity of the object.

Hence, the correct option is (D).

23. The Pitch of sound depends upon Frequency.

Pitch is that characteristic of a musical sound by which a shrill sound can be distinguished from a grave one, even though the two sounds may be of the same intensity. It is also defined as that characteristic of sound by which the ear assigns it a place on a musical scale. When a stretched string is plucked, a sound of a certain pitch sensation is produced. If the tension in the string is increased, the pitch (the shrillness) becomes higher. Increasing the tension also increases the frequency of vibration. Therefore, the pitch is intimately related to frequency. But frequency alone does not determine the pitch. Below 1000 Hz, the pitch is slightly higher than the frequency and above 1000 Hz the position is reversed. The loudness of sound also affects the pitch up to 1000 Hz. An increase in loudness causes a decrease in pitch. From about 1000 to 3000 Hz, the pitch is independent of loudness, while above 3000 Hz an increase in loudness causes an increase in pitch.
Hence, the correct option is (B).

24. $Ni(28) - 1\,s^2, 2\,s^2, 2p^6, 3\,s^2, 3p^6, 3\,d^8, 4\,s^2$

$$Ni^{2+} = 1\,s^2, 2\,s^2, 2p^6, 3\,s^2, 3p^6, 3\,d^8, 4\,s^0$$

$$Cu(29) = 1\,s^2, 2\,s^2, 2p^6, 3\,s^2, 3p^6, 3\,d^{10}, 4\,s^1$$

$$Cu^+ = 1\,s^2, 2\,s^2, 2p^6, 3\,s^2, 3p^6, 3\,d^{10}$$

Hence, the correct option is (A).

25. Both $CaHCO_3$ and $CaCl_2$ is responsible for hardness of water

Temporary hardness of water is due to the presence of bicarbonates of calcium and magnesium while permanent hardness is due to the presence of soluble chlorides and sulphates of calcium and magnesium.
Hence, the correct option is (C).

26. Celsius is a unit of Temperature.

Celsius, also called centigrade, scale based on 0° for the freezing point of water and 100° for the boiling point of water. Invented in 1742 by the Swedish astronomer Anders Celsius, it is sometimes called the centigrade scale because of the 100 - degree interval between the defined points.

Hence, the correct option is (A).

27. Galvanization is a method of protecting iron from rusting, by coating it with a thin layer of zinc.

Galvanization is a process used for the protection of steel or iron objects from rusting by applying a protective zinc layer on the iron surface. Iron metal is dipped in molten zinc to form a protective coating on the surface of the iron.

Hence, the correct option is (C).

28. Given:

$V = 220$ volts, $R = 110\Omega$

The power consumed by electric iron is given by

$$P = \frac{V^2}{R} = I^2R = VI$$

Where,

$V =$ Supply voltage

$I =$ current flowing through the electric iron

$R =$ Resistance of the electric iron

∴ Power consumed by electric iron can be calculated as

$$P = \frac{(220)^2}{110}$$

$\therefore P - 440$ W

Hence, the correct option is (C).

29. Radiation thermometers are known as a pyrometer.

Radiation thermometers:

This type of sensor detects infrared emitted from the object and measures temperature based on the amount of Infrared radiation.

The radiation thermometer cannot be used for measuring the temperature of the inside of the object or the gaseous atmosphere.

Hence, the correct option is (B).

30. The passenger tends to lean forward when a running metro stops suddenly. It is because of inertia of Motion

When the running metro stops suddenly, the passenger tends to lean forward because the lower part of his body comes to rest with the ground but the upper part tends to continue its motion due to inertia of motion.
Hence, the correct option is (C).

31. The logic follows here is :

Sum of place values of alphabets of the given word = Given number.

M + O + N + K = 13 + 15 + 14 + 11

= 53

Similarly,

T + U + T + O + R = 20 + 21 + 20 + 15 + 18

= 94

Hence, the correct answer is (A).

32. The correct order is:

Measure	Marks	Cut	Tailor	Put on
4	3	1	5	2

Hence, the correct option is (D).

33. Given:

A = 4, K = 3, N = 2, P = 1.

Sum of first Set (A) = K + A + N + P +K

= 3 + 4 + 2 + 1 + 3

= 13.

Sum of the second set (B) = N + P + A + K +N

= 2 + 1 + 4 + 3 + 2

= 12

Sum of the third set (C) = P + K + A + N + A

= 1 + 3 + 4 + 2 + 4

= 14

Sum of the fourth set (D) = N + A + K + N + A

= 2 + 4 + 3 + 2 + 4

= 15
Hence, the correct option is (D).

34. The given set of letters: ETTLOB

The only meaningful word that can be made using the given letters is BOTTLE.
Hence, the correct option is (D).

35. After unjumbling the letters, we get

(D): ENAHTME ⇒ METHANE

(A): THLAAPS ⇒ ASPHALT

(B): THANAPH ⇒ NAPHTHA

(C): LESIED ⇒ DIESEL

Except METHANE, all are products obtained from petroleum

Hence, the correct option is (D).

36. The given code are as follows:

Alphabet	C	O	M	M	A	N	D	E	R
Code	5	1	3	3	6	8	9	4	7

Similarly,

Alphabet	C	O	N	D	E	M	N
Code	5	1	8	9	4	3	8

So, the code for CONDEMN is 5189438.
Hence, the correct option is (D).

37.

Symbol	+	-	×	÷
Meaning	-	×	÷	+

Given equation:

24 – 16 + 8 ÷ 4 × 2

On interchanging:

24 × 16 – 8 + 4 ÷ 2

⇒ 384 – 8 + 2 = 378
Hence, the correct option is (C).

38. These units of volume have been written in descending order according to their value in litre.

1. 1 Cubic Metre = 1000 L

5. 1 Gallon = 3.78541 L

2. 1 Litre = 1 L

4. 1 Pint = 0.473176 L

3. 1 Millilitre = 0.001 L
Hence, the correct option is (D).

39.

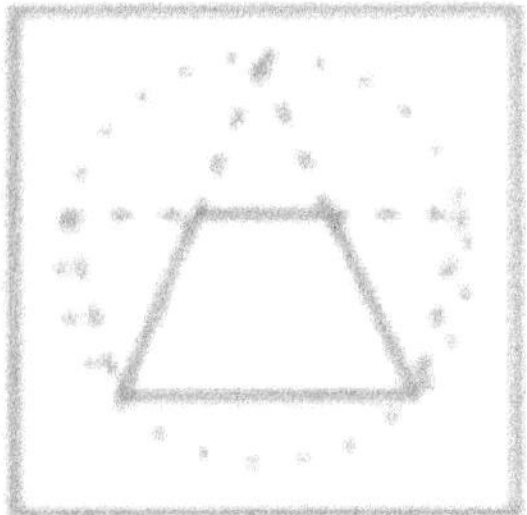

Hence, the correct option is (A).

40. We can conclude that,

1 dot, 4 dots, 2 dots, and 6 dots are adjacent to 5 dots.

Therefore, 3 dots must be opposite to 5 dots.
Hence, the correct option is (B).

41. Let, x = ?

$$(25)^{7.5} \times (5)^{2.5} \div (125)^{1.5} = 5^x$$

Then,

$$\frac{(5^2)^{7.5} \times (5)^{2.5}}{(5^3)^{1.5}} = 5^x$$

$$\Rightarrow \frac{5^{(2\times7.5)} \times 5^{2.5}}{5^{(3\times1.5)}} = 5^x$$

$$\Rightarrow \frac{5^{15} \times 5^{2.5}}{5^{4.5}} = 5^x$$

$$\Rightarrow 5^x = 5^{(15+2.5-4.5)}$$

$$\Rightarrow 5^x = 5^{13}$$

$$\therefore x = 13$$

Hence, the correct option is (B).

42. Given Expression

$$\frac{(243)^{\left(\frac{n}{5}\right)} \times 3^{2n+1}}{9^n \times 3^{n-1}}$$

$$= \frac{(3^5)^{\left(\frac{n}{5}\right)} \times 3^{2n+1}}{(3^2)^n \times 3^{n-1}}$$

$$= \frac{\left(3^{5\times\left(\frac{n}{5}\right)} \times 3^{2n+1}\right)}{(3^{2n} \times 3^{n-1})}$$

$$= \frac{3^n \times 3^{2n+1}}{3^{2n} \times 3^{n-1}}$$

$$= \frac{3^{(n+2n+1)}}{3^{(2n+n-1)}}$$

$$= \frac{3^{3n+1}}{3^{3n-1}}$$

$$= 3^{(3n+1-3n+1)}$$

$$= 3^2$$

$$= 9$$

Hence, the correct option is (C).

43. Let the number of seats for Mathematics, Physics, and Biology be $5x, 7x$ and $8x$ respectively.

Number of increased seats in mathematics $= \frac{5x\times140}{100}$

$$= 7x$$

Number of increased seats in physics $= \frac{7x\times150}{100}$

$$= \frac{21x}{2}$$

Number of increased seats in biology $= \frac{8x\times175}{100}$

$$= 14x$$

$\therefore$ The required ratio

$$= 7x : \frac{21x}{2} : 14x$$

$$= 14x : 21x : 28x$$

$$= 2 : 3 : 4$$

Hence, the correct option is (A).

44. Given:

$$\sqrt{(11x^3 + 6x^2 + 5x + 62)} + \sqrt{(11x^3 + 6x^2 + 5x + 42)} = 10$$

We know that,

$$(a + b)(a - b) = a^2 - b^2$$

Let,

$$\sqrt{(11x^3 + 6x^2 + 5x + 62)} - \sqrt{(11x^3 + 6x^2 + 5x + 42)} = k$$

So,

$$\sqrt{(11x^3 + 6x^2 + 5x + 62)} + \sqrt{(11x^3 + 6x^2 + 5x + 42)} = 10 \quad .....(i)$$

$$\sqrt{(11x^3 + 6x^2 + 5x + 62)} - \sqrt{(11x^3 + 6x^2 + 5x + 42)} = k \quad .....(ii)$$

On multiplying equation (i) and equation (ii),

$$\left(\sqrt{(11x^3 + 6x^2 + 5x + 62)} + \sqrt{(11x^3 + 6x^2 + 5x + 42)}\right) \times \left(\sqrt{(11x^3 + 6x^2 + 5x + 62)} - \sqrt{(11x^3 + 6x^2 + 5x + 42)}\right) = k \times 10$$

$\Rightarrow \left(\sqrt{(11x^3+6x^2+5x+62)}\right)^2 - \left(\sqrt{(11x^3+6x^2+5x+42)}\right)^2 = 10k$

$\Rightarrow (11x^3+6x^2+5x+62) - (11x^3+6x^2+5x+42) = 10k$

$\Rightarrow 20 = 10k$

$\Rightarrow k = 2$

Hence, the correct option is (D).

45. Given:

$x + y + xy = 1, y + z + yz = 7$ and $x + z + xz = 8$

Add 1 to all expressions,

$1 + x + y + xy = 2$

$\Rightarrow 1 + x + y(1 + x) = 2$

$\Rightarrow (1 + x)(1 + y) = 2 \quad .....(i)$

Similarly,

$1 + y + z + yz = 8$

$\Rightarrow (1 + y)(1 + z) = 8 \quad .....(ii)$

Similarly,

$1 + z + x + xz = 9$

$\Rightarrow (1 + z)(1 + x) = 9 \quad .....(iii)$

Now for the value of x multiply equation (i) and (iii) and divide by (ii)

$\frac{[(1+x)(1+y)(1+x)(1+z)]}{(1+y)(1+z)} = \frac{(2\times9)}{8}$

$\Rightarrow (1 + x)^2 = \frac{9}{4}$

$\Rightarrow 1 + x = \frac{3}{2}$

$\Rightarrow x = \frac{1}{2}$

Similarly for y multiply equation (i) and (ii) and divide by (iii)

$\frac{[(1+x)(1+y)(1+y)(1+z)]}{(1+z)(1+x)} = \frac{(2\times8)}{9}$

$(1 + y)^2 = \frac{16}{9}$

$\Rightarrow 1 + y = \frac{4}{3}$

$\Rightarrow y = \frac{1}{3}$

Similarly for z multiply equation (ii) and (iii) and divide by (i)

$\frac{[(1+y)(1+z)(1+z)(1+x)]}{(1+x)(1+y)} = \frac{(8\times9)}{2}$

$(1 + z)^2 = \frac{72}{2}$

$\Rightarrow 1 + z = 6$

$\Rightarrow z = 5$

Now,

$18xyz = 18 \times \left(\frac{1}{2}\right) \times \left(\frac{1}{3}\right) \times 5$

$= 15$

Hence, the correct option is (A).

46. Given:

$\left(x + \frac{1}{x}\right)\left(x - \frac{1}{x}\right)\left(x^2 + \frac{1}{x^2} - 1\right)\left(x^2 + \frac{1}{x^2} + 1\right)$

$= \left(x + \frac{1}{x}\right)\left(x^2 + \frac{1}{x^2} - 1\right)\left(x - \frac{1}{x}\right)\left(x^2 + \frac{1}{x^2} + 1\right)$

$\because (A + B)(A^2 - AB + B^2) = A^3 + B^3$

$\because (A - B)(A^2 + AB + B^2) = A^3 - B^3$

$= \left(x^3 + \frac{1}{x^3}\right)\left(x^3 - \frac{1}{x^3}\right)$

$= x^6 - \frac{1}{x^6}$

Hence, the correct option is (D).

47. Given:

5x - y = 5 ......(i)

⇒ 3x + 2y = 29 ......(ii)

By multiplying 3 with eq (i) and 5 with eq (ii) we get,

15x - 3y = 15 ......(iii)

⇒ 15x + 10y = 145 ......(iv)

By subtracting eq (iv) from eq (iii) we get,

-13y = -130

⇒ y = $\frac{-130}{-13}$

⇒ y = 10

By putting the value of y in eq (i) we get,

5x - 10 = 5

⇒ 5x = 5 + 10

⇒ 5x = 15

⇒ x = $\frac{15}{5}$

⇒ x = 3

So,

$x = 3, y = 10$
Hence, the correct option is (D).

48. Given:

$\cos^2\theta = \frac{(x+y)^2}{4xy}$

We know that,

Max value of $\cos^2\theta = 1$

Therefore,

$1 = \frac{(x+y)^2}{4xy}$

$\Rightarrow 4xy = (x+y)^2$

$\Rightarrow 4xy = x^2 + y^2 + 2xy$

$\Rightarrow 0 = x^2 + y^2 - 2xy$

$\Rightarrow 0 = (x-y)^2$

$\Rightarrow 0 = x - y$

$\Rightarrow x = y$
Hence, the correct option is (C).

49. Given:

Volume $= 924\ m^3$

Curved surface area Of cylinder $= 264\ m^2$

$2\pi rh = 264$

$\Rightarrow 2 \times \frac{22}{7} \times r \times h = 264$

$\Rightarrow rh = 42$ ....(i)

Volume of cylinder $= \pi r^2 h = 924$

$\frac{22}{7} \times r \times rh = 924$

$\Rightarrow \frac{22 \times r \times 42}{7} = 924$

$\Rightarrow r = 7\ m$

Diameter $= 2r = 7 \times 2 = 14m$

Substituting the value of r in question (i). we get,

$\Rightarrow 7 \times h = 42$

$\Rightarrow h = 6\ m$

Diameter: height

$= 14:6$

$= 7:3$

Hence, the correct option is (B).

50. Given:

Data $3,5,1,6,5,9,5,2,8,6$

Mean $= x$, median $= y$, and mode $= z$

Number of terms $= n = 10$

Mean $= \frac{\text{Sum of the terms}}{\text{Total number of terms}}$

Mean $= x = \frac{3+5+1+6+5+9+5+2+8+6}{10}$

$= \frac{50}{10}$

$= 5$

Arrange given data in ascending order: $1,2,3,5,5,5,6,6,8,9$

Here number of terms is even,

So, median will be average of two middle terms

i.e., $y = \frac{5\text{ th term} + 6\text{ th term}}{2}$

$= \frac{5+5}{2}$

$= 5$

Now, mode is the most common number

In given data 5 is the most common number

$\therefore$ Mode $= z = 5$

$\therefore x = y = z$
Hence, the correct option is (D).

51. Let the initial price of oil be $100x$

Price of oil after increment $= 100x \times \frac{125}{100}$

$= 125x$

Ram spends $= 100x \times \left(\frac{110}{100}\right)$

$= 110x$

Decrease in consumption $= 125x - 110x$

$= 15x$

Decrease $\% = \left(\frac{15x}{125x}\right) \times 100$

$= 12\%$

$\therefore$ The percentage decrease in Ram's oil consumption is 12%.

Hence, the correct option is (C).

52. Given:

$\angle PFG = 50^\circ, \angle CDQ = 50^\circ$ and $\angle FGP = 100^\circ$

$\Rightarrow \angle PFG + \angle FGP + \angle GPF = 180^\circ$ (Sum of angles in Δ is 180°)

$\Rightarrow \angle GPF = 180° - 150° = 30°$

Now,

$\angle BPD = \angle FPG = 30°$ (opposite angles)

Now,

$\angle ABP = \angle BPD + \angle CDQ$ (exterior angle is equal to the sum of interior opposite angles)

$\Rightarrow \angle ABP = 80°$

Now,

$\angle PGF + \angle PGH = 180°$ (angle in a straight line)

$\Rightarrow \angle PGH = 80°$

Now,

$\angle CHI = \angle PGH = 80°$

So,

The supplementary angle of $\angle ABP + \angle ABP = 180°$ (sum of angles and its supplementary is $180°$)

The supplementary angle of $\angle ABP = 100°$

Finally,

The supplementary angle of $\angle ABP + \angle CHI = 100° + 80°$

$= 180°$

Hence, the correct option is (A).

53. A and B complete a work in $= 15$ days

One day's work of $(A + B) = \frac{1}{15}$

B complete the work in $= 20$ days

One day's work of $B = \frac{1}{20}$

Then, A's one day's work = $\frac{1}{15} - \frac{1}{20}$

$= \frac{4-3}{60}$

$= \frac{1}{60}$

Therefore, A can complete the one work $= \frac{1}{\left(\frac{1}{60}\right)}$

Thus, A can complete the work in 60 days.

Hence, the correct option is (A).

54. Let the distance travelled by $x\ km$.

Then,

$\frac{x}{10} - \frac{x}{15} = 2$

$\Rightarrow 3x - 2x = 60$

$\Rightarrow x = 60\ km$

Time taken to travel $60\ km$ at $10\ km/hr = \left(\frac{60}{10}\right) hrs = 6\ hr$

So, Robert started $6\ hr$ before $2\ P.M.$ i.e., at $8\ A.M.$

∴ Required speed $= \left(\frac{60}{5}\right) kmph$

$= 12 kmph$

Hence, the correct option is (C).

55. Given:

Principal (P) = Rs. 20000, Rate (r) $= 15\%$, Time (n) $= 2$ years

We know that,

Amount (A) in compund interest.

$A = P\left(1 + \frac{r}{100}\right)^n$

$= 20000 \times \left(1 + \frac{15}{100}\right)^2$

$= 20000 \times \left(\frac{23}{20}\right)^2$

$= 50 \times 23 \times 23$

$A = 26450$

Compound Interest $=$ Amount - Principal

$= 26450 - 20000$

$= 6450$

∴ The compound interest is Rs. 6450

Hence, the correct option is (B).

56. Given:

$\frac{(\cos 12° + \sin 78°)(\sec 12° + cosec 78°)}{\sin 64° \sec 26° + \cos 35° cosec 55°}$

$\Rightarrow \frac{[\cos 12° + \sin(90-12°)][(\sec 12° + cosec(90-12°)]}{\sin 64° \sec(90-64°) + \cos 35° cosec(90-35°)}$

$\Rightarrow \frac{(\cos 12° + \cos 12°)(\sec 12° + \sec 12°)}{\sin 64° cosec 64° + \cos 35° \sec 35°}$

$\Rightarrow \frac{2\cos 12° \times 2\sec 12°}{1+1}$

$\Rightarrow \frac{2 \times 2\cos 12° \times \frac{1}{\cos 12°}}{2}$

$\Rightarrow \frac{4}{2}$

$\Rightarrow 2$

Hence, the correct option is (C).

57. Total selling price of two bullocks $= 8400 + 8400 = Rs. 16800$

$\therefore$ Cost price of first bullock $= 8400 \times \frac{100}{120} = Rs. 7000$

According to the question, there is no profit or loss.

$\therefore$ Cost price of second bullock $= 16800 - 7000 = Rs. 9800$

Selling price of second bullock $= Rs. 8400$

$\therefore$ Loss $= 9800 - 8400 = Rs. 1400$

$\therefore$ Percentage loss on second bullock $= \frac{1400}{9800} \times 100$

$= \frac{100}{7}\%$

$= 14\frac{2}{7}\%$

Hence, the correct option is (C).

58. Given:

$\sin(6\theta + 16^\circ) = \cos(2\theta + 10^\circ)$

We know that,

$\cos\theta = \sin(90^\circ - \theta)$

Therefore,

$\sin(6\theta + 16^\circ) = \sin[90^\circ - (2\theta + 10^\circ)]$

$\Rightarrow 6\theta + 16^\circ = 90^\circ - 2\theta - 10^\circ$

$\Rightarrow 6\theta + 2\theta = 80^\circ - 16^\circ$

$\Rightarrow 8\theta = 64^\circ$

$\Rightarrow \theta = \frac{64^\circ}{8}$

$\Rightarrow \theta = 8^\circ$

Hence, the correct option is (C).

59.

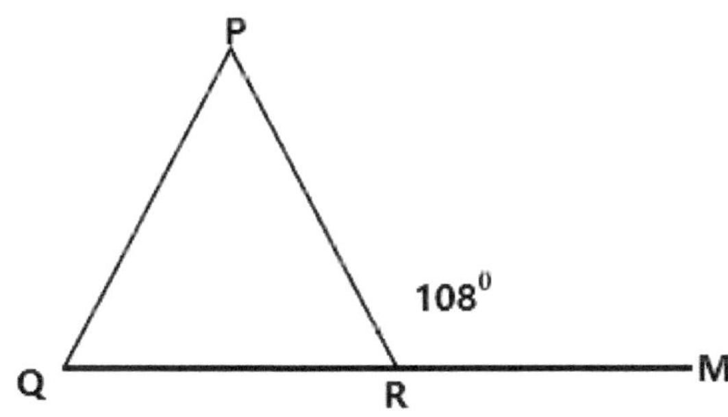

Given:

$\angle PRM = 108^\circ$

$\Rightarrow \angle PRQ = 180^\circ - 108^\circ$

$\Rightarrow \angle PRQ = 72^\circ$

In the triangle $PQR, \angle P + \angle Q = 180^\circ - 72^\circ = 108^\circ [\angle R = 72^\circ$ and sum of all the angles of the triangle is $180^\circ]$

$\frac{4}{5}\angle P + \angle P = 108^\circ$

$\Rightarrow \frac{9}{5}\angle P = 108^\circ$

$\Rightarrow \angle P = 108^\circ \times \left(\frac{5}{9}\right)$

$\Rightarrow \angle P = 60^\circ$

$\Rightarrow \angle Q = \frac{4}{5} \times 60^\circ$

$\Rightarrow \angle Q = 48^\circ$

Hence, the correct option is (D).

60. Given:

Simple Interest $(S.I)$ = Rs. 3200

Compound Interest $(C.I)$ = Rs. 3472

Time (T) = 2 years

We know that,

$S.I = \frac{P \times R \times T}{100}$

$3200 = P \times R \times \frac{2}{100}$

$\Rightarrow PR = 3200 \times 50 \; .....(i)$

$C.I = P\left(\left(1 + \frac{R}{100}\right)^T - 1\right)$

$\Rightarrow 3472 = P\left(\left(1 + \frac{R}{100}\right)^2 - 1\right) \; .....(ii)$

Dividing eq (ii) from eq (i), we get,

$\frac{3472}{3200 \times 50} = \frac{P\left(\left(1+\frac{R}{100}\right)^2 - 1\right)}{P \times R}$

$\Rightarrow \frac{217}{200 \times 50} = \frac{\left(\left(1+\frac{R}{100}\right)^2 - 1\right)}{R}$

$\Rightarrow \frac{217}{200 \times 50} = \frac{1 + \frac{R^2}{10000} + \frac{2R}{100} - 1}{R}$

$\Rightarrow \frac{217}{10000} = \frac{\frac{R^2}{10000} + \frac{2R}{100}}{R}$

$\Rightarrow 217\,R = R^2 + 200R$

$\Rightarrow 217\,R - 200\,R = R^2$

$\Rightarrow 17\,R = R^2$

$\Rightarrow R = 17\ \%$

$\therefore$ The rate percent is 17%.

Hence, the correct option is (C).

Mock Test 10

English

Ques (1-2):Direction: In the following question, a sentence has been given in active/passive voice. Out of the four alternative suggested, select the one which best expresses the same sentence in active/passive voice.

Q.1 Had he touched my bag?

A. Had my bag touched by him?
B. Have my bag been touched by him?
C. Had my bag been touched by him?
D. Has my bag been touched by him?

Q.2 The institute gave me a scholarship.

A. I will be given a scholarship by the institute
B. I was being given a scholarship by the institute
C. I was given a scholarship by the institute
D. I am given a scholarship by the institute

Q.3 Direction: Convert the following sentence into indirect speech.

He said to me, "I am doing my work."

A. He told me that I am doing my work.
B. He told me that I was doing my work.
C. He told me that he was doing his work.
D. He said that he was doing my work.

Q.4 Direction: Select the correct indirect form of the given sentence.

He said to me, "I have a car".

A. He asked me that he had a car.
B. He says to me he has a car.
C. He told me that he had a car.
D. He said to me that he have a car.

Q.5 Direction: Fill in the blank with the correct answer.

Besides his parents, he _____ also present at the function.

A. were **B.** had **C.** have **D.** was

Q.6 Direction: Choose the word that can substitute the given sentence.

One who is unable to pay his debts.

A. Brood **B.** Caucus
C. Insolvent **D.** Bale

Q.7 Direction: In the following question, out of the given four alternatives, select the alternative which best expresses the meaning of the Idiom/Phrase.

Lion's share

A. Totally unaware
B. A major share
C. Completely alone
D. Done for material benefits

Q.8 Direction: Select the most appropriate synonym of the given word.

Hinder

A. Help **B.** Facilitate
C. Obstruct **D.** Assist

Q.9 Direction: Select the most appropriate synonym of the given word.

Imperative

A. Preface **B.** Necessary
C. Epilogue **D.** Prologue

Q.10 Direction: Fill in the blank with the correct tense of the verb choosing from the options given below:

He generally _________ (go) for a walk every morning even now.

A. has gone **B.** went **C.** goes **D.** had gone

Q.11 Which of the following sentence is correctly punctuated?

A. The speaker said, please, lend me your ears.
B. The speaker said please, lend me your ears.
C. The speaker said, Please ! lend me your ears.
D. The speaker said, Please lend me your ears.

Q.12 Direction: Identify the finite as well as non-finite verbs in the sentence.

Jumping over the fence, the boy escaped from the charging bull.

A. Finite-jumping, Non-finite-escaped
B. Finite-escaped, Non-finite-charging
C. Finite-escaped, Non-finite-jumping
D. Finite-escaped, Non-finite-jumping, charging

Ques (13-15):Direction: Read the following passage carefully and answer the question given below.

With the successful pre-dawn launch of RISAT-2B satellite, the Indian Space Research Organization (ISRO) has added another feather to its cap. The satellite will enhance India's capability in crop monitoring during the monsoon season, forestry mapping for forest fires and deforestation, and flood mapping as part of the national disaster management programme. Given that overcast skies are a constant during the monsoon season and during times of flood, the ability to penetrate the cloud cover is essential. While optical remote sensing that relies on visible light for imaging gets obstructed by clouds, RISAT-2B will not. Much like the RISAT-1 satellite that was launched by ISRO in April 2012, RISAT-2B will also use microwave radiation. Unlike visible light, microwaves have longer wavelength and so will not be susceptible to atmospheric scattering. Microwave radiation can thus easily pass through the cloud cover, haze and dust, and image the ground. Hence, RISAT-2B satellite will be able to image under almost all weather and environmental conditions. Since it does not rely on visible light for imaging, it will be able to image the ground during both day and night.

The satellite does not have passive microwave sensors that detect the radiation naturally emitted by the atmosphere or reflected by objects on the ground. Instead, RISAT-2B will be transmitting hundreds of microwave pulses each second towards the ground and receiving the signals reflected by the objects using radar. The moisture and texture of the object will determine the strength of the microwave signal that gets reflected. While the strength of the reflected signal will help determine different targets, the time between the transmitted and reflected signals will help determine the distance to the object.

Q.13 As per the given passage, how RISAT-2B satellite will image in the cloudy weather?

I. With the help of its microwave radiation that can pass through cloud cover and dust easily.

II. With the help of visible light that creates images.

III. With the help of electronic rays that creates image of an object.

A. Only I **B.** Only II
C. Only II and III **D.** Only I and II

Q.14 What does the writer want to convey with the text given in italic – "the Indian Space Research Organization (ISRO) has added another feather to its cap."?

I. ISRO has worked hard on building its rapport among the other space research organizations of the world.

II. ISRO has made an accomplishment that made the nation proud of it.

III. ISRO has become the apex space research institute of the world.

A. Only I **B.** Only II
C. Only II and III **D.** Only I and II

Q.15 Which of the following has a similar meaning to "penetrate" in the context of the passage?

A. Enlarge **B.** Pinch **C.** Excess **D.** Invade

General Knowledge

Q.16 What was the name given for the rescue operations conducted by the Indian Government during Nepal Earthquake Tragedy?

A. Operation Maitri **B.** Operation Nepal
C. Operation Abhaya **D.** Operation Sahay

Q.17 The first nuclear explosion in India was conducted at which of the following?

A. Pokhran **B.** Mumbai
C. Nellie **D.** Sriharikota

Q.18 In which year did Swami Vivekanand participate at the Parliament of Religions held in Chicago?

A. 1891 **B.** 1892 **C.** 1893 **D.** 1895

Q.19 In which of the following states of India, Yakshagana, a dance drama is popular?

A. Tamil Nadu **B.** Karnataka
C. Kerala **D.** Madhya Pradesh

Q.20 Which state has won the UN Award for Performance in Non-Communicable Diseases related SDGs?

A. Karnataka **B.** Kerala
C. Tamil Nadu **D.** Himachal Pradesh

Science

Q.21 The best conductor of heat among liquids is:

[MP Sub Inspector (MPSI), 2017]

A. Alcohol **B.** Ether **C.** Mercury **D.** Water

Q.22 The gravitational force between two objects is F. If masses of both objects are halved without changing distance between them, then the gravitational force would become:

A. $\frac{F}{4}$ **B.** $\frac{F}{2}$ **C.** F **D.** $2F$

Q.23 A ball of mass 2 kg is thrown up with a speed of 10 m/s. find the potential energy of the ball at the highest point?

A. 100 J **B.** 80 J **C.** 70 J **D.** 110 J

Q.24 What does the atomic number represent?

A. Electron number **B.** Number of protons
C. Number of neutrons **D.** Number of atoms

Q.25 Which of the following requires a medium for their propagation?

A. Light wave
B. Electromagnetic wave
C. Microwave
D. Sound wave

Q.26 When a ball drops on the floor it bounces. This is according to:

A. Newton's first law of motion
B. Newton's second law of motion
C. Newton's third law of motion
D. The ball is elastic

Q.27 Butanone is a four-carbon compound with the functional group:

A. Carboxylic acid **B.** Aldehyde
C. Ketone **D.** Alcohol

Q.28 The neutral atoms of all of the isotopes of the same element have:

A. Different numbers of protons
B. Equal numbers of neutrons
C. The same number of electrons
D. The same mass numbers

Q.29 Cinnabar heated in air then it converts into ________.

A. Lead oxide **B.** Potassium oxide
C. Mercury oxide **D.** Sodium oxide

Q.30 Interaction of two waves passing through the same time is called:

A. Interference of waves
B. Reflection of waves
C. Stationary waves
D. None of the above

Reasoning

Q.31 In a certain code language, A11MS is written as E55QW. How will PG1MS be written in the same language?

A. RL5QW **B.** RKSQW **C.** TKSOW **D.** TK5QW

Q.32 If ENGLAND is coded as 1234526 and FRANCE is written as 785291. How will GREECE be written in this coding system?

A. 381191 **B.** 381911 **C.** 394132 **D.** 562134

Q.33 Direction: Two positions of the same dice are given. Which number will be at the top if '3' is at the bottom?

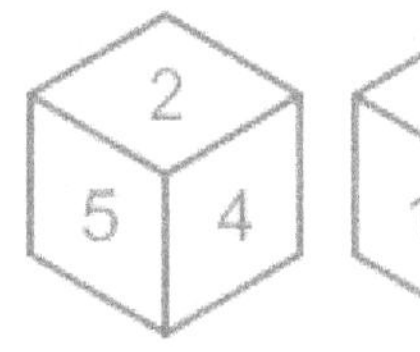

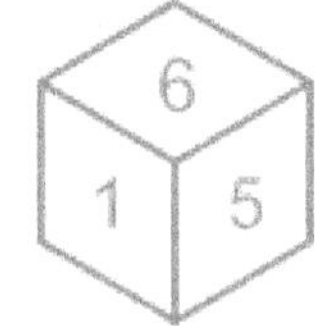

[UP Police Sub Inspector, 2021], [NCERT National Talent Search Exam, 2019]

A. 5 **B.** 6 **C.** 2 **D.** 4

Q.34 Direction: If the given figure is folded to form a cube, which number will be opposite '5'?

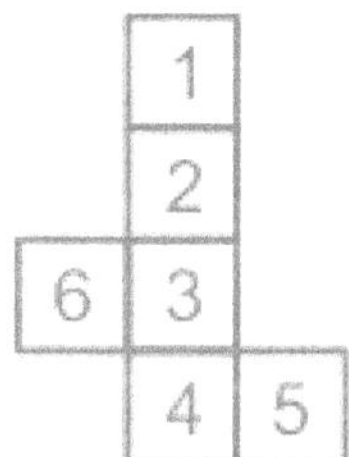

[Delhi Forest Guard, 2020], [NCERT National Talent Search Exam, 2019]

A. 2 **B.** 3 **C.** 6 **D.** 1

Ques (35-36):Direction: In the following question, arrange the given words in a meaningful sequence and thus find the correct answer from alternatives.

Q.35 1. Nation
2. Village
3. City
4. District
5. State

A. 2, 3, 4, 5, 1 **B.** 2, 3, 4, 1, 5
C. 1, 3, 5, 4, 2 **D.** 1, 2, 3, 4, 5

Q.36 1. Caste
2. Family
3. Newly Married Couple
4. Clan
5. Species

A. 2, 3, 1, 4, 5 **B.** 3, 4, 5, 1, 2
C. 3, 2, 1, 4, 5 **D.** 4, 5, 3, 2, 1

Q.37 Unscramble the word:

A. EREEMTURPAT **B.** EMREEUTPRTA
C. TEMPERATURE **D.** EUREEUPTTRA

Q.38 Unscramble the word:

A. NCITNETNO **B.** NICNTTEON
C. NICNTETON **D.** CONTINENT

Ques (39-40):Direction: Study the following table and answer the question given below.

Sector	Male	Female
Voluntary Work	41000	67000
IT	121000	107000
Engineering	398000	105000
Legal Services	273000	251000
Healthcare	227000	271000
Business Services	186000	124000
Self Employed	45000	62000
Unemployed	52000	43000
Total	**1343000**	**1031000**

Q.39 If it is predicted that the number of females employed in IT will rise by 10% every year, but the number of males stays the same, what percent of IT employees would be female after a three year period?

A. 54.1% **B.** 53.5% **C.** 85.0% **D.** 45.5%

Q.40 Approximately what percentage of the people sampled are unemployed?

A. 7% **B.** 5% **C.** 6% **D.** 4%

Mathematics

Q.41 If (a + b) = 16 and ab = 63 such that (a - b) > 0, then find the value of $a^2 - b^2$.

A. 23 **B.** 25 **C.** 52 **D.** 32

Q.42 Simple interest on Rs. 24000 at $8\frac{1}{2}\%$ per annum for 8 months is:

A. Rs. 1560 **B.** Rs. 1620 **C.** Rs. 1480 **D.** Rs. 1360

Q.43 The ratio of the area (in cm^2) to the circumference (in cm) of a circle is 21 : 2. Find the area of the circle.

A. 154 cm^2 **B.** 616 cm^2
C. 346.5 cm^2 **D.** 1386 cm^2

Q.44 Find the total amount for a period of 6 months on the principal amount of Rs. 10000 at 12% p.a. compounded quarterly.

A. Rs. 14652 **B.** Rs. 10609
C. Rs. 12365 **D.** Rs. 11360

Q.45 If $\tan^4\theta + \tan^2\theta = 1$, then the value of $\cos^4\theta + \cos^2\theta = ?$ is

A. 8 **B.** 10 **C.** 1 **D.** 2

Q.46 The interior angles of a pentagon are x°, (x - 10)°, (x + 20)°, (2x - 44)°, and (2x - 70)°. Then find the value of x.

A. 93° **B.** 92° **C.** 104° **D.** 78°

Q.47 The heights of 10 boys were measured in cm and the results are as follows. How many boys' weight more than mean height?

145, 160, 149, 138, 161, 132, 156, 159, 153, 151

A. 7 **B.** 9 **C.** 5 **D.** 6

Q.48 If 3 men or 4 women can plow a field in 86 days, how much time will 14 men and 10 women take?

A. 12 days **B.** 43 days **C.** 86 days **D.** 60 days

Q.49 $\sqrt{196} \times \sqrt{144} \times$ 20% of 500 = ? + 1256

A. 15544 **B.** 15572 **C.** 15589 **D.** 15511

Q.50 This year, the cost of a tomato increased by 20% over that of the last year. Last year a tomato costed Rs.10 and a potato costed Rs. 5. This year it costs Rs. 11 more to buy 5 potato and 3 tomato. Find the percentage increase in the price of the potato.

A. 4% **B.** 15% **C.** 27% **D.** 20%

Q.51 If the radius of a solid sphere is 1.4 cm, then what is the total surface area of the sphere?

A. 31.68 cm^2 **B.** 24.64 cm^2

C. 63.36 cm^2 **D.** 49.28 cm^2

Q.52 Ram can complete work in 20 days by working 5 hours a day, while Suresh can complete that work in 25 days by working 3 hours a day, If they work together $\frac{30}{7}$ hours a day, how many days will Ram and Suresh take to complete the work?

A. 10 days **B.** 15 days **C.** 30 days **D.** 25 days

Q.53 A father distributed some chocolates among his four children and kept some with him. The eldest three children got chocolates in the ratio 3 : 11 : 7. The total number of chocolates with father and youngest child is three times the total chocolates with the three eldest children. The ratio of chocolates with father and that with all the children is 3 : 4. Find the total number of chocolates if the youngest child has 81 chocolates with him?

A. 273 **B.** 252 **C.** 278 **D.** 303

Q.54 Direction: From the following data, what is the value of the median?

20 21 25 26 23 29 32 39 33

A. 26 **B.** 23 **C.** 25.22 **D.** 29

Q.55 What is the remainder if we divide $6x^3 + x^2 - 2x + 4$ by x-2 ?

A. 48 **B.** 52 **C.** -26 **D.** -24

Q.56 If approximate solution of the set of equations, 2x + 2y - z = 6, x + y + 2z = 8 and -x + 3y + 2z = 4, is given by x = 2.8 y = 1 and z = 1.8. Then, what is the exact solution?

A. x = 3 , y = 1 , z = 2 **B.** x = 1 , y = 2 , z = 2

C. x = 2 , y = 3 , z = 1 **D.** x = 1 , y = 3 , z = 2

Q.57 If θ be an acute angle and $7\sin^2\theta + 3\cos^2\theta = 4$, then the value of $\tan\theta$ is:

A. $\sqrt{3}$ **B.** $\frac{1}{\sqrt{3}}$ **C.** 1 **D.** 0

Q.58 6 years ago the ratio of the son and his father was 6 : 11 and 6 years hence their age ratio will be 9 : 14. Find the ratio of their present ages.

A. 6 : 7 **B.** 3 : 5 **C.** 1 : 4 **D.** 4 : 7

Q.59 The income of Adarsh, Satpal and Rahim in the ratio of 12 : 9 : 7 and their spendings are in the ratio 15 : 9 : 8. If Adarsh saves 25% of his income. What is the ratio of the savings of Adarsh, Satpal and Rahim?

A. 15 : 18 : 11 **B.** 5 : 8 : 7

C. 23 : 18 : 11 **D.** 25 : 16 : 13

Q.60 A chord AB of a circle of radius 5.25 cm makes an angle of 600600 at the center of the circle. Find the area of the major segment.

A. 168 cm^2 **B.** 100 cm^2 **C.** 84 cm^2 **D.** 70 cm^2

// Smart Answer Sheet //

Correct Percentage of students who answered correctly. **Skipped** Percentage of students who skipped.

Q.	Ans.	Correct	Skipped	Q.	Ans.	Correct	Skipped	Q.	Ans.	Correct	Skipped	Q.	Ans.	Correct	Skipped	Q.	Ans.	Correct	Skipped	Q.	Ans.	Correct	Skipped
1	C	62.46 %	1.39 %	11	D	41.28 %	1.27 %	21	C	79.54 %	0.0 %	31	D	67.71 %	1.33 %	41	D	56.69 %	1.35 %	51	B	65.53 %	1.06 %
2	C	43.78 %	1.17 %	12	D	26.35 %	3.53 %	22	A	41.7 %	1.48 %	32	A	62.5 %	1.39 %	42	A	62.75 %	1.33 %	52	A	26.67 %	3.59 %
3	C	63.47 %	1.46 %	13	A	17.25 %	3.68 %	23	A	17.87 %	4.18 %	33	A	56.74 %	1.79 %	43	D	41.56 %	1.31 %	53	B	29.24 %	3.13 %
4	C	87.48 %	0.0 %	14	B	41.63 %	1.44 %	24	B	53.28 %	1.68 %	34	C	13.14 %	4.36 %	44	B	69.95 %	1.21 %	54	A	61.22 %	1.52 %
5	D	42.02 %	1.9 %	15	D	88.16 %	0.0 %	25	D	81.9 %	0.0 %	35	A	58.62 %	1.14 %	45	C	86.43 %	0.0 %	55	B	79.43 %	0.0 %
6	C	63.74 %	1.36 %	16	A	32.35 %	4.63 %	26	C	77.33 %	0.0 %	36	C	56.32 %	1.58 %	46	B	16.34 %	3.75 %	56	A	25.88 %	3.57 %
7	B	58.9 %	1.88 %	17	A	65.76 %	1.91 %	27	C	43.86 %	1.44 %	37	C	83.72 %	0.0 %	47	D	64.55 %	1.05 %	57	B	49.8 %	1.36 %
8	C	85.37 %	0.0 %	18	C	43.75 %	1.39 %	28	C	43.33 %	1.93 %	38	D	81.66 %	0.0 %	48	A	41.85 %	1.86 %	58	B	14.83 %	4.46 %
9	B	54.69 %	1.09 %	19	B	60.32 %	1.05 %	29	C	61.44 %	1.02 %	39	A	63.14 %	1.69 %	49	A	83.96 %	0.0 %	59	A	29.85 %	3.27 %
10	C	57.64 %	1.29 %	20	B	88.53 %	0.0 %	30	A	31.28 %	4.61 %	40	D	56.06 %	1.35 %	50	D	52.79 %	1.16 %	60	C	49.1 %	1.14 %

//Hints and Solutions//

1. The correct active/passive voice of given sentence is 'Had my bag been touched by him?'.

The given sentence is in past perfect tense and in active voice. This is an interrogative sentence. The rule for changing a past perfect tense from active voice to passive voice:

Interchange the object and subject with each other, i.e., object of the active sentence become the subject of the passive sentence.

Structure: Had + Subject + V_3 + Object + ? (Active Voice)

Hence, the correct option is (C).

2. The correct active/passive voice of the given sentence is I was given a scholarship by the institute.

The given sentence is in Active Voice. As per the given question we have to change it into Passive Voice.

The process of transformation is as follows:

Subject + V_2+ Object (Active Voice)

Subject (objective case)+ was/were + V_3 + Object (subjective case) (Passive Voice)

Here, in the given question 'The institute' is the subject.

And 'me' is an object.

The subject will be put in place of the object and the object will be put in place of the subject.

And 'gave' will be changed into 'was given'.

The conjunction 'by' will be added.

Hence, the correct option is (C).

3. The indirect speech of the given sentence is 'He told me that he was doing his work.'

While changing the narration of an imperative sentence, we need to follow the given steps-

Change 'said to' in reporting clause into 'told'. Replace comma (,) and inverted commas (" ") with the conjunction 'that'. Present continuous tense is changed into past continuous tense. First-person (I) is changed into the third person (he). Possessive adjective (my) is changed into 'his', i.e., according to the subject of the reporting verb.

Hence, the correct option is (C).

4. The indirect speech of the given sentence is 'He told me that he had a car'.

The given sentence is in direct speech. As per the given question we have to change it into indirect speech.

The process of transformation as follows:

The reporting verb will change because it has an object. Comma and inverted commas will be removed. 'Said to' will be changed into 'told'. The conjunction 'that' will be added. 'have' will be changed into 'had'. (present perfect tense into past perfect tense). 'I' will be changed into 'he' because the first person pronouns are changed according to the subject of the reporting verb.

Hence, the correct option is (C).

5. Besides his parents, he was also present at the function.

In the given sentence, the subject 'he' is singular.

According to the subject-verb-agreement rule, a singular subject should be followed by a singular verb and a plural subject should be followed by a plural verb.

Thus, options 'have' and 'were' get eliminated as they are plural in form.

'had' also gets eliminated as 'has/have' forms are always followed by the V_3 form of the verb whereas we have the V_1 form of the verb (present) in the given sentence.

'was' fits correctly in the given blank as it is a singular verb.

Hence, the correct option is (D).

6. The one word substitution of given sentence is Insolvent.

Insolvent means not having enough money to pay what you owe. A person or firm whose liabilities exceed the value of owned assets is termed as insolvent. It is the inabilities of the company or person to pay liabilities as they become due.

Hence, the correct option is (C).

7. The right meaning of given word is a major share.

Lion's share is an idiomatic phrase which means the largest part of something.

Example:

The Lopez family owns the lion's share of the country's farmland.

Hence, the correct option is (B).

8. The right synonym of Hinder is Obstruct.

Hinder means to limit the ability of someone to do something, or to limit the development of something.

Obstruct means to stop something from happening or somebody/something from moving either by accident or deliberately.

Hence, the correct option is (C).

9. The right synonym of Imperative is Necessary.

Imperative means extremely important, essential or urgent.

Necessary means needed in order to achieve a particular result, essential.

Hence, the correct option is (B).

10. He generally goes (go) for a walk every morning even now.

The simple present tense is used when an action is happening right now, to state or ask about things in general, or when it happens regularly or unceasingly. The structure is given below:

Subject $+V_1+$ object. The verb will take 's/es' if the given noun/pronoun (3rd person) is singular.

Example:

He plays badminton daily. In the given sentence, we need a simple present verb tense as a routine task has been given here. Since 'He' is a singular pronoun, the singular verb i.e., 'goes' will be used.

Hence, the correct option is (C).

11. The correct punctuated sentence is The speaker said, Please lend me your ears.

An exclamation mark after 'please' makes it seem like the speaker is insistent, raising their voice or shouting. Thus, exclamation mark is not used after please.

Direct speech is a sentence in which the exact words spoken are reproduced in speech/quotation marks. A comma is used after the introductory clause, i.e., right before the quoted part-The speaker said, The part that is quoted directly by the speaker needs to be within inverted commas.

Hence, the correct option is (D).

12. The correct non-finite verb of given sentence is Finite-escaped, Non-finite-jumping, charging.

'Escaped' is a finite verb since it has a subject-the boy. The words jumping and charging are present participles, the non-finite verbs.

Hence, the correct option is (D).

13. Microwave radiation can thus easily pass through the cloud cover, haze and dust, and image the ground. Hence, RISAT-2B satellite will be able to image under almost all weather and environmental conditions. Since it does not rely on visible light for imaging, it will be able to image the ground during both day and night.

With the help of underlined text it is clear that only statement I is true.

Statement III is not even mentioned anywhere in the passage.

Hence, the correct option is (A).

14. ISRO has made an accomplishment that made nation proud on it.

"Add a feather to cap" is an idiom that means to accomplish a deed one can proud of. Clearly only statement II renders the same meaning.

Hence, the correct option is (B).

15. Given that overcast skies are a constant during the monsoon season and during times of flood, the ability to penetrate the cloud cover is essential.

In the given scenario penetrate is used to gain access to the cloud cover so that images from each and every angle can be obtained. Thus among the given words only "invade" has the similar meaning.

Hence, the correct option is (D).

16. Operation Maitri was the name given for the rescue operations conducted by the Indian Government during Nepal Earthquake Tragedy.

Operation Maitri (Operation Amity) was a rescue and relief operation in Nepal by the government of India and the Indian armed forces in the aftermath of the April 2015 Nepal earthquake. The Indian government responded within a few minutes of the quake. It started on 26 April 2015 and also involved Nepali ex-servicemen from India's Gurkha Regiments for interface for guidance, relief and rescue.

Hence, the correct option is (A).

17. The first nuclear explosion in India was conducted at Pokhran.

Pokhran was also the first confirmed nuclear weapons test by a nation outside the five permanent members of the UN Security Council. The bomb was detonated on the army base Pokhran test range in Rajasthan. The first nuclear explosion in India was conducted on 18 May 1974. The assigned code name of the first nuclear bomb test was Smiling Buddha.

Hence, the correct option is (A).

18. In 1891 Swami Vivekanand participate at the Parliament of Religions held in Chicago

Swami Vivekanand participated at the Parliament of Religions held in Chicago (USA) on 11th September 1893 and raised the prestige of India and Hinduism very high. He preached Vedantic Philosophy. He condemned the caste system and the current Hindu emphasis on rituals and ceremonies.

Hence, the correct option is (C).

19. In the state of Karnataka, Yakshagana, a dance drama is popular.

Yakshagana is a traditional Indian theatre, developed in the western parts of Dakshina Kannada, Udupi, Uttara Kannada, Shimoga and Chikmagalur districts in the state of Karnataka. Yakshagana is a communal drama and dance form of the Karnataka state. This art is also known by the name "Aat" or Baylat.

Hence, the correct option is (B).

20. Kerala has won the UN Award for Performance in Non-Communicable Diseases related SDGs

Kerala has received the United Nations award for its "outstanding contribution" towards the Non-communicable diseases-related sustainable development goals (SDGs). World Health Organization (WHO) Director-General announced this year's UN Interagency Task Force (UNIATF) award on prevention and control of non-communicable diseases. Kerala is one of the seven ministries of health across the world.

Hence, the correct option is (B).

21. The best conductor of heat among liquids is mercury.

According to the thermal properties of matter, mercury is the only liquid good conductor of heat. That is why it is also used in a mercury thermometer.

We know that most metals are good conductors of heat as solid at room temperature. But mercury is the only good conductor of heat in a liquid state due to its high coefficient of expansion. One more property of mercury that is its high boiling point makes it suitable for measuring high temperatures.

Hence, the correct option is (C).

22. We know that, according to the force of gravitation

$F = \frac{Gm_1m_2}{r^2}$ (G = Gravitational constant)

where m_1 and m_2 are the masses of two objects respectively. And r is the distance between the two masses Now, according to the question, if masses of both objects are halved,

i.e.,

$m_1' = \frac{m_1}{2}$ and $m_2' = \frac{m_2}{2}$

$$F = \frac{Gm_1m_2'}{r^2} = \frac{G\left(\frac{m_1}{2}\right)\left(\frac{m_2}{2}\right)}{r^2}$$

$$= \frac{1}{4}\frac{Gm_1m_2}{r^2} = \frac{F}{4} \text{ where } \frac{Gm_1m_2}{r^2} = F$$

So, new force $F' = \frac{F}{4}$

Thus, the new gravitational force will become $\frac{1}{4}$ times of its original gravitational force.

Hence, the correct option is (A).

23. Given,

m = 2 Kg

v = 10 m/s

We know that when the ball reaches the highest point, its whole kinetic energy is converted into Potential energy.

The formula of kinetic energy is given by

$K = \frac{1}{2} mv^2$

Hence Kinetic energy at the time of throwing is

$K = \frac{1}{2} \times 2 \times 10^2$

= 100 J

The potential energy of the ball at the highest point is 100 J.

Hence, the correct option is (A).

24. The atomic number represents a number of protons.

It is the number of a chemical element in the periodic system, whereby the elements are arranged in order of increasing the number of protons in the nucleus. Accordingly, the number of protons, which is always equal to the number of electrons in the neutral atom, is also the atomic number. The atomic number (Z) of an element is the number of protons in the nucleus of each atom of that element.

Hence, the correct option is (B).

25. Sound wave is mechanical wave, thus it requires a medium for propagation.

Rest all the waves are electromagnetic which do not require any medium for propagation.

Hence, the correct option is (D).

26. When a ball drops on the floor it bounces. This is according to Newton's third law of motion.

Newton's third law implies that for every action there is a reaction. When a ball drops on to the floor it bounces because as Newton's third law implies that for every action there is a reaction.

Examples of Newton's third law of motion are:

- Pulling an elastic band.
- Swimming or rowing a boat.
- Static friction while pushing an object.
- Standing on the ground or sitting on a chair.
- The upward thrust of a rocket.
- Resting against a wall or tree.

Hence, the correct option is (C).

27. Butanone is a four-carbon compound with the functional group ketone.

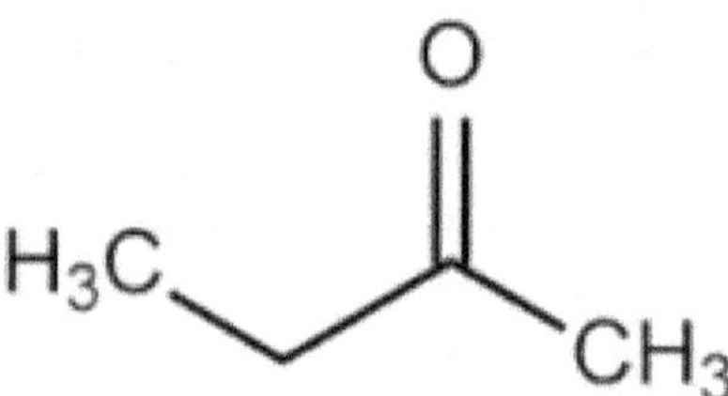

In ketones, the carbonyl group has 2 hydrocarbon groups attached to it. These can be either the ones containing benzene rings or alkyl groups. Ketone does not have a hydrogen atom attached to the carbonyl group. Butanone has a functional group ketonic group (C=O).

Hence, the correct option is (C).

28. The neutral atoms of all of the isotopes of the same element have the same number of electrons.

Atoms of the same element having the same atomic number but different mass are called isotopes. They have same number of protons and electrons but different number of neutrons.

For example:

Hydrogen - protium $({}^1_1H)$, deuterium $({}^2_1H)$ and tritium $({}^3_1H)$ are isotopes.

Hence, the correct option is (C).

29. Cinnabar heated in air then it converts into mercury oxide.

Mercury can be obtained from cinnabar HgS by heating the cinnabar ore in current of air and condensing the mercury vapour formed. Due to its relatively low boiling point, mercury can be easily purified by vaccum distillation.

$$HgS + O_2 \rightarrow Hg + SO_2 \uparrow$$

Hence, the correct option is (C).

30. Interaction of two waves passing through the same time is called interference of waves.

Interference occurs when several waves are added together provided that the phase differences between them remain constant over the observation time. It is sometimes desirable for several waves of the same frequency and amplitude to sum to zero.

Hence, the correct option is (A).

31. PG1MS will be written as TK5QW.

The pattern for this code is as follows,

A	1	1	M	S
+4 ↓	+4 ↓	+4 ↓	+4 ↓	+4 ↓
E	5	5	Q	W

Similarly,

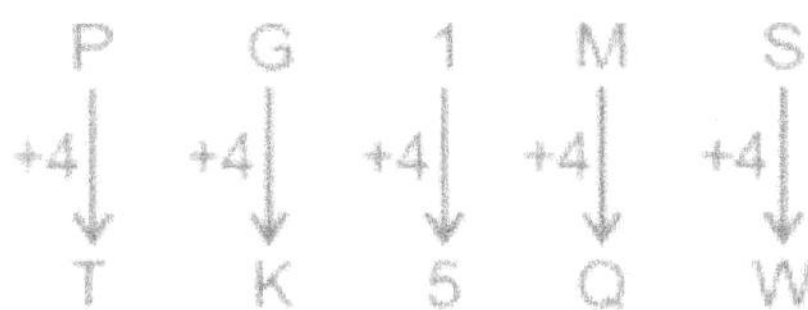

Hence, the correct option is (D).

32. ENGLAND

Word	Code
E	1
N	2
G	3
L	4
A	5
N	2
D	6

FRANCE

Word	Code
F	7
R	8
A	5
N	2
C	9
E	1

From the above table

GREECE

Word	Code
G	3
R	8
E	1
E	1
C	9
E	1

Hence, the correct option is (A).

33. The Logic here is as follows:

As 5 is the common face on both the dice, keeping it constant and then rotating in the clockwise direction, we get the faces opposite to each other.

Dice 1	3	2	4
Dice 2	5	1	6

Therefore, the face opposite to 2 is 1, the face opposite to 4 is 6, and finally, the face opposite to 3 will be 5.

Hence, the correct option (A).

34. If the given figure is folded to form a cube, then the face opposite to that of the number 5 will be 6.

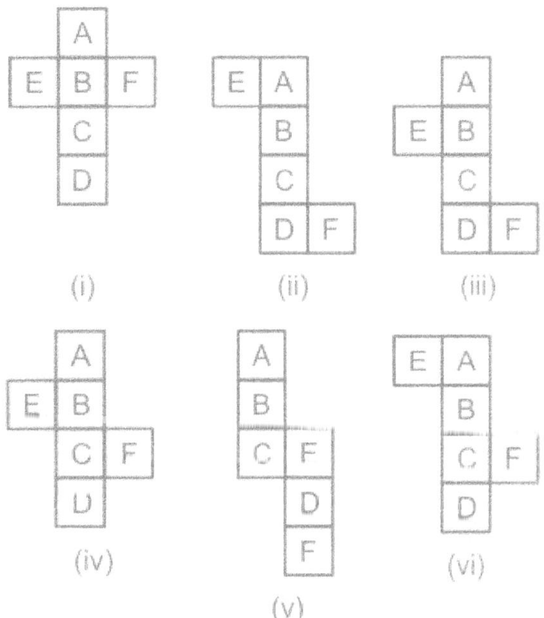

The clearly seen alternate position of the open dice becomes the opposite pair after folding and the two remaining faces also become opposite to each other.

Here, In every figure:

A is opposite to C.

B is opposite to D.

Thus the remaining, E is opposite to F.

The alternate position of faces becomes opposite to each other, as shown below:

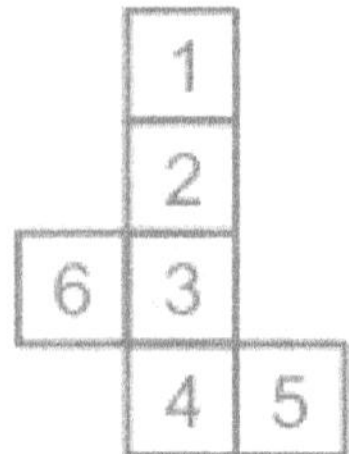

The opposite pairs are (1, 3), (2, 4) and the remaining (5, 6).

Hence, the correct option is (C).

35. The correct order of the sequence is:

Village	City	District	State	Nation
2	3	4	5	1

Hence, the correct option is (A).

36. The correct order of the sequence is:

Newly Married Couple	Family	Caste	Clan	Species
3	2	1	4	5

Hence, the correct option is (C).

37. The correct word is TEMPERATURE.

TEMPERATURE: Temperature is the measure of hotness or coldness expressed in terms of any of several scales, including Fahrenheit and Celsius.

Hence, the correct option is (C).

38. The correct word is CONTINENT.

CONTINENT: A continent is one of Earth's seven main divisions of land. The continents are, from largest to smallest: Asia, Africa, North America, South America, Antarctica, Europe, and Australia.

Hence, the correct option is (D).

39. Step 1- The number of female IT employees starting from the table is 107000.

Step 2- If the number of female employees is increased by 10%, then after three years there are 142417 employees.

$$= 107000 \times 1.10 \times 1.10 \times 1.10$$

= 142417

Step 3- Male IT workforce still stands at 121000.

So, the total employees in IT is now 142417 + 121000 = 263417.

So, 54.1 percent of the 263417 IT employees are 142417.

Hence, the correct option is (A).

40. Step 1

Make sure you add together the male and female figures to arrive at a figure for 'people'. Total number unemployed

= 52000 + 43000

= 95000

Step 2

Total number people sampled = 1343000 + 1031000

= 2374000

Step 3

So now $95000 \div 2374000$ = 4%.

4% of the people sampled are unemployed.

Hence, the correct option is (D).

41. Given:

(a+b) = 16

ab = 63

We know that,

$(a - b)^2 = (a + b)^2 - 4ab$

$\Rightarrow (a - b)^2 = (16)^2 - 4 \times 63$

$\Rightarrow (a - b)^2 = 256 - 252$

$\Rightarrow (a - b)^2 = 4$

$\Rightarrow (a - b) = \sqrt{4}$

$\Rightarrow (a - b) = 2$

Now, $a^2 - b^2 = (a + b)(a - b)$

= 16 × 2

= 32

∴ The value of $a^2 - b^2$ is 32.

Hence, the correct option is (D).

42. Given:

Principle $(P) =$ Rs. 24,000

Rate $(R) = 8\frac{1}{2}\%$

Time $(T) = 8$ months $= \frac{8}{12}$

Simple interest $(SI) = \frac{P \times R \times T}{100}$

$$\Rightarrow SI = \frac{24000 \times \frac{17}{2} \times \frac{8}{12}}{100}$$

$$\Rightarrow SI = \frac{24000 \times 17 \times 8}{100 \times 2 \times 12}$$

$$\Rightarrow SI = 1360$$

∴ Simple interest is Rs. 1360.

Hence, the correct option is (A).

43. Given:

Area: Circumference $= 21:2$

Formula Used:

Area of circle $= \pi r^2$

The circumference of circle $= 2\pi r$

Where,

$r =$ radius of the circle

Let the radius of the circle be ' $r' cm$.

According to the question, we have

$\left(\frac{\pi r^2}{2\pi r}\right) = \frac{21}{2}$

$\Rightarrow \frac{r}{2} = \left(\frac{21}{2}\right)$

$\Rightarrow r = 21\ cm$

Now,

The area of circle $= \left(\frac{22}{7}\right) \times 21 \times 21$

$\Rightarrow 1386\ cm^2$

∴ The area of the circle is $1386\ cm^2$.

Hence, the correct option is (D).

44. Given:

Time = 6 months

Principal = Rs. 10000

Rate of Interest = 12% p.a. compounded quarterly.

Formula Used:

A = P{1 + ($\frac{R}{100}$)}n

Where,

A = Amount,

P = Principal,

R = Rate of Interest

n = Number of times compounding is done

According to the question,

Effective rate of interest = $\frac{R}{4}$

= $\frac{12}{4}$ = 3% ----(Because interest is compounded quarterly)

and n = $\frac{6}{3}$ = 2 quarters ----(Because interest is compounded quarterly)

Now,

A = P{1 + ($\frac{R}{100}$)}n

= 10000 × {1 + ($\frac{3}{100}$)}2

= 10000 × ($\frac{103}{100}$) × ($\frac{103}{100}$)

= Rs. 10609

∴ The total amount is Rs. 10609.

Hence, the correct option is (B).

45. Given,

$= \tan^4\theta + \tan^2\theta = 1$

According to question,

$= \tan^2\theta(\tan^2\theta + 1)$

$\Rightarrow \tan^2\theta \times \sec^2\theta = 1\{\because \sec^2\theta = 1 + \tan^2\theta\}$

$\Rightarrow \left(\frac{\sin^2\theta}{\cos^4\theta}\right) = 1$

$\Rightarrow 1 - \cos^2\theta = \cos^4\theta\{\because \sin^2\theta = 1 - \cos^2\theta\}$

$= \cos^4\theta + \cos^2\theta = 1$

Hence, the correct option is (C).

46. Given:

The angles of a pentagon are x°, (x - 10)°, (x + 20)°, (2x - 44)°, and (2x - 70)°

Sum of all interior angles of a regular polygon = (n - 2) × 180°

For pentagon,

n = 5

∴ Sum of all interior angles of a regular pentagon = (5 - 2) × 180°

⇒ Sum of all interior angles of a regular pentagon = 3 × 180°.

⇒ Sum of all interior angles of a regular pentagon = 540°.

Now,

x + (x - 10)° + (x + 20)° + (2x - 44)° + (2x - 70)° = 540

⇒ x + x - 10° + x + 20° + 2x - 44° + 2x - 70° = 540°

⇒ (x + x + x + 2x + 2x) + (20° - 10° - 44° - 70°) = 540°

⇒ 7x - 104° = 540°

⇒ 7x = 540° + 104°

⇒ 7x = 644°

⇒ x = ($\frac{644°}{7}$)

⇒ x = 92°

Hence, the correct option is (B).

47. Given:

Number of boys = 10

Mean = $\frac{\text{Sum of observation}}{\text{Number of observation}}$

Mean = $\frac{(145+160+149+138+161+132+156+159+153+151)}{10}$

Mean = $\frac{1504}{10}$

Mean = 150.4

The mean of boys weight is 150.4.

∴ 6 boys are heavier than mean weight.

Hence, the correct option is (D).

48. Given:

3 men or 4 women can plow a field in 86 days.

Concept:

If a person completes a task in "d" days, then

N person complete the same task in ($\frac{d}{N}$) days.

According to the question,

3 men = 4 women

1 man = ($\frac{4}{3}$) women

14 men = 14 × ($\frac{4}{3}$) = ($\frac{56}{3}$) women

14 men and 10 women = ($\frac{56}{3}$) + 10 = ($\frac{86}{3}$) women

Again, it is given that 4 women can plow a field in 86 days.

1 woman can plough in = 86 × 4 days.

= ($\frac{86}{3}$) women can plough in:

= $\frac{(86\times4)}{\left(\frac{86}{3}\right)}$

= $\frac{(86\times4\times3)}{86}$

= 12 days

Hence, the correct option is (A).

49. Given,

$\sqrt{196} \times \sqrt{144} \times 20\%$ of $500 = ? + 1256$

$\Rightarrow 14 \times 12 \times \frac{20}{100} \times 500 = ? + 1256$

= $168 \times 100 = ? + 1256$

16800 = ? + 1256

= 16800 - 1256

= 15544

Hence, the correct option is (A).

50. Given:

Cost of the tomato last year = Rs. 10

So, Cost of the tomato this year = 10 + 20% of 10

= Rs. (10 + 2)

= Rs. 12

Cost of the potato last year = Rs. 5.

Let the cost of potato this year be x.

Therefore, cost of 5 potato and 3 tomato this year = 5x + (3 × 12)

= 5x + 36 ..... (i)

Cost of 5 potato and 3 tomato last year = 5 × 5) + (3 × 10

= 55 .... (ii)

This year the cost is Rs.11 more

From (i) and (ii), we get

= 5x + 36 = 55 + 11

⇒ 5x = (66 – 36)

⇒ x = 6

Increase in the cost of potato = (6 – 5) = Rs. 1

Percentage increase = $\frac{1}{5} \times 100$

= 20%

Hence, the correct option is (D).

51. Given:

Radius of a sphere (r) = 1.4 cm

The surface area of a sphere = 4 × π × r^2

= 4 × $\frac{22}{7}$ × $(1.4)^2$

= $\frac{88}{7}$ × 1.4 × 1.4

= 88 × 0.2 × 1.4

= 24.64 cm^2

∴ The total surface area of a sphere is 24.64 cm^2.

Here we can use unit digit to find the answer

After the third step in the calculation, we just have to look for the last digit

= 88 × 0.2 × 1.4

The last digit is 4 (8 × 2 × 4 = 64)

And there is only one option that has the last digit 4

So, our answer will be 24.64 cm^2

Hence, the correct option is (B).

52. Given,

The number of days taken by Ram = 20 days

Working hours of Ram in a day = 5 hours

The number of days taken by Suresh = 25 days

Working hours of Suresh in a day = 3 hours

If someone completes work in x days

∴ Work done in 1 day = $\frac{1}{x}$

∵ Ram takes 20 days by working 5 hours a day to complete the work.

Ram takes 100 hours to complete the work.

Work done by Ram in 1 hour = $\frac{1}{100}$

Suresh takes 15 days by working 3 hours a day to complete the work.

Suresh takes 75 hours to complete the work.

Work done by Suresh in 1 hour = $\frac{1}{75}$

Work done by Ram and Suresh together in 1 hour = $(\frac{1}{100} + \frac{1}{75})$

Let, both together takes x days.

∴ Work done by Ram and Suresh together in x days by working $\left(\frac{30}{7}\right)$ hours = $\left(\frac{30}{7}\right) \times x \times \left(\frac{1}{100}\right) + \left(\frac{1}{75}\right)$

$\Rightarrow \left(\frac{30}{7}\right) \times x \times \left(\frac{1}{100}\right) + \left(\frac{1}{75}\right) = 1$

$\Rightarrow \left(\frac{30}{7}\right) \times x \times \left(\frac{7}{300}\right) = 1$

$\Rightarrow \frac{x}{10} = 1$

$\Rightarrow x = 10$ days

∴ Number of days taken by Ram and Suresh = 10 days

Hence, the correct option is (C).

53. Given:

The eldest three children got chocolates in the ratio 3 : 11 : 7

Let the children be P, Q, R and S and Father be F.

Chocolates with P : Q : R = 3 : 7 : 11

Let the number of chocolates be 3k, 7k and 11k.

Total chocolates with three eldest children = 21k

Chocolate with F and S = 3 × 21k = 63k

Total chocolates = (21k + 63k) = 84k

Chocolate with F : (P + Q + R + S) = 3 : 4

Total 7 units of chocolate = 84 k

1 unit = 12k

Chocolate with F = 3 × 12k = 36k

Chocolate with S = (63k – 36k) = 27k

27 k = 81

k = 3

Total number of chocolates = 84k

= 84 × 3

= 252

Hence, the correct option is (B).

54. If data contains n values and n is odd number, then median is the $\left(\frac{n+1}{2}\right)^{th}$ observation after arranging them in either ascending or descending order.

Hence first, we will arrange the observations in ascending order:

20 21 23 25 26 29 32 33 39

Now, we can see that number of observations are nine, which is odd.

Hence median $= \left(\frac{n+1}{2}\right)^{th}$ observation

$= \frac{(9+1)}{2}$

$= \frac{10}{2}$

= 5th observation

Which is 26.

Hence, the correct option is (A).

55. According to remainder theorem, if p(x) be any polynomial of degree greater than or equal to one and let "a" be any real number. If p(x) is divided by the linear polynomial x-a, then the remainder is p(a).

So to know the value of remainder, we have to find the value of p(2).

$p(2) = 6(2)^3 + (2)^2 - 2(2) + 4$

= 6(8) + 4 – 4 + 4

= 48 + 4

= 52

Hence, the correct option is (B).

56. Substituting the approximate values x′ = 2.8, y′ = 1 z′ = 1.8 in the given equations, we get

2(2.8) + 2(1) – 1.8 = 5.8 ....(i)

2.8 + 1 + 2(1.8) = 7.4 ....(ii)

-2.8 +3(1) + 2(1.8) = 3.8 ....(iii)

Subtracting each equation (i), (ii), (iii) from the corresponding given equations we obtain

2xe + 2ye – ze = 0.2 ....(iv)

xe + ye +2ze = 0.6 ....(v)

-xe + 3ye + 2ze = 0.2 ....(vi)

Where x_e = x – 2.8, y_e = y – 1, z_e = z = 1.8.

Solving the equations (iv), (v), (vi), we get x_e = 0.2, y_e = 0, z_e = 0.2.

This gives the better solution x = 3, y = 1, z = 2, which incidentally is the exact solution.

Hence, the correct option is (A).

57. Given:

$$7\sin^2\theta + 3\cos^2\theta = 4$$

$$\Rightarrow 7\sin^2\theta + 3(1 - \sin^2\theta) = 4$$

$$= 7\sin^2\theta + 3 - 3\sin^2\theta = 4$$

$$= 4\sin^2\theta = 1$$

$$= \sin^2\theta = \frac{1}{4}$$

$$= \sin\theta = \frac{1}{2}$$

$$= \sin\theta = \sin 30°$$

$$\theta = 30°$$

$$\tan 30° = \frac{1}{\sqrt{3}}$$

Hence, the correct option is (B).

58. Given:

6 year ago the ratio of son and his father = 6 : 11

6 year hence their ratio will be = 9 : 14

The difference between their ages will always same.

In a : b and c : d if b - a = d - c then b - d = a - c

6 year ago, Son : Father = 6 : 11

Age difference = 11 - 6 = 5

6 year hence, Son : Father = 9 : 14

Age difference = 14 - 9 = 5

As the age difference is already the same, we can say changes of 3R in son's age as well as father's age is due to the gap of 12 years.

So, 3R = 12 year

R = 4 year

6 year = $(\frac{3}{2})$R

To find their present ratio add the $(\frac{3}{2})$R to the ratio of 6 year ago.

Son : Father = 6 + $(\frac{3}{2})$: 11 + $(\frac{3}{2})$

= $(\frac{15}{2})$: $(\frac{25}{2})$

= 3 : 5

∴ The ratio of their present age is 3 : 5.

Hence, the correct option is (B).

59. Given.

Income = Expenditure + Saving

Adarsh: 12x = 15y + 3x (3x = 25% of 12x)

Satpal: 9x = 9y + (9x – 9y)

Rahim: 7x = 8y + (7x – 8y)

Therefore, 12x – 3x = 15y

$$\Rightarrow \frac{x}{y} = \frac{5}{3}$$

$$y = \frac{3x}{5}$$

Therefore, savings = (income – expenditure)

Adarsh = 12x – 9x

= 3x

Satpal = 9x – 9y

$$= 9x - \frac{27}{5}x$$

$$= \frac{18}{5}x$$

Rahim = 7x – 8y

$$= 7x - \frac{24}{5}x$$

$$= \frac{11}{5}x$$

i.e., the ratio of savings of Adarsh : Satpal : Rahim

$$= 3x{:}\frac{18}{5}x{:}\frac{11}{5}x$$

$$= 15{:}\,18{:}\,11$$

Hence, the correct option is (A).

60. The given circle is an equilateral triangle

Area of the minor sector

$$= \frac{60}{360} \times \pi \times 5.25^2$$

= 14.4375 cm^2

Area of the triangle

$= \frac{\sqrt{3}}{4} \times 5.25^2$

= 11.93 cm^2

Area of the minor segment = Area of the minor sector - Area of the triangle

= 2.5 cm^2

Area of the major segment = Area of the circle - Area of the minor segment

= 86.54 cm^2 - 2.5 cm^2

= 84 cm^2

Hence, the correct option is (C).

Sectional Test 01

Q.1 What is the square root of 640?

A. $8\sqrt{8}$ **B.** $8\sqrt{5}$ **C.** $10\sqrt{8}$ **D.** $8\sqrt{10}$

Q.2 If 20% of x is equal to 40% of 60 , what is the value of x ?

A. 100 **B.** 120 **C.** 80 **D.** 140

Q.3 If $5(x+1)=3(x+2)+11$, then find the valve of x

A. 3 **B.** 5 **C.** 6 **D.** 2

Q.4 The remainder when x^3+x^2-x+1 is divided by $x+2$ is-

A. -1 **B.** 1 **C.** 0 **D.** 2

Q.5 If the ratio of cost price to selling price is $5:3$, then loss percent is:

A. 20% **B.** 40% **C.** 30% **D.** 15%

Q.6 After successive discounts of 20% and 10%, the mobile was sold for Rs. 1710. What was the original price of the mobile?

A. Rs. 2000 **B.** Rs. 2200 **C.** Rs. 2375 **D.** Rs. 2300

Q.7 In what time will Rs. 1000 amounts to Rs. 1331 at 20% per annum, compounded half-yearly?

A. 3 years **B.** 2 years **C.** 1.5 years **D.** 1 years

Q.8 Rs. 7000 becomes Rs. 10360 in 6 years at simple interest. What is the per annum rate of interest?

A. 10% **B.** 9% **C.** 11% **D.** 8%

Q.9 How many small solid balls with diameter $21\ cm$ can be made from a solid big sphere of diameter $84\ cm$?

A. 64 **B.** 48 **C.** 32 **D.** 76

Q.10 $\triangle ABC$ is an equilateral Δ with side $5\ cm$. Area of $\triangle ABC$ is:

A. $\sqrt{3}\times 25$ sq. cm **B.** $\frac{\sqrt{3}}{2}\times 5$ sq. cm

C. $\frac{\sqrt{3}}{4}\times 5$ sq. cm **D.** $\frac{\sqrt{3}}{4}\times 25$ sq. cm

Q.11 If the side of a square is $(2x+5)cm$ and the perimeter is $28\ cm$. Find the value of x ?

A. 1 **B.** 2 **C.** 3 **D.** 4

Q.12 In the given figure, $\angle MON = 116°$. Find the value of $\angle MQN$.

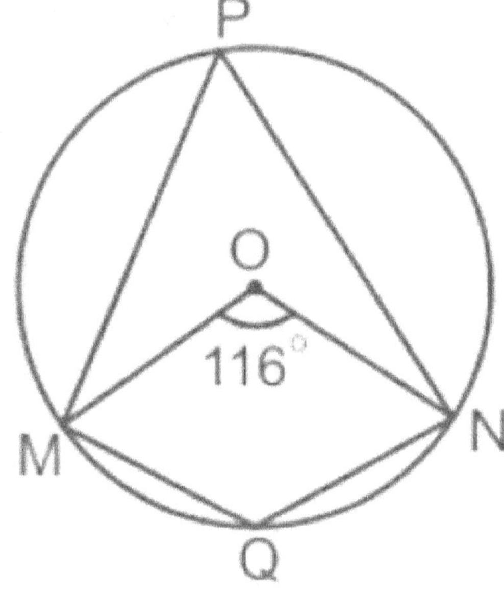

A. 122° **B.** 158° **C.** 126° **D.** 102°

Q.13 What is the value of the expression:

$(\sin 0°\cdot\sin 1°\cdot\sin 2°\cdot\sin 3°\cdot sinn4° \ldots\ldots \sin 89°)$

A. 1 **B.** 0 **C.** $\frac{1}{2}$ **D.** Infinity

Q.14 The value of $\sin 60°\cos 30° - \cos 60°\sin 30°$ is:

A. $\frac{\sqrt{3}}{2}$ **B.** $\frac{1}{2}$ **C.** $\frac{1}{\sqrt{2}}$ **D.** 1

Q.15 The efficiencies of A, B and C are in the ratio $2:3:4$. They together can complete a piece of work in 6 days. In how many days A alone can complete that same piece of work?

A. 30 **B.** 27 **C.** 24 **D.** 25

Q.16 A boy goes to school at a speed of $45\ km/h$ and reaches the school 7 minutes late. If he travels at speed of $60\ km/h$, he reaches the school 8 min early. Find the distance travelled by the boy.

A. 45 km **B.** 60 km **C.** 50 km **D.** 55 km

Q.17 If $a:(b+c)=4:5$ and $c:(a+b)=1:2$, then $b:(a+c)$ is equal to:

A. 4:7 **B.** 2:5 **C.** 2:7 **D.** 1:2

Q.18 If Mode is 15 and mean $-$ median $=25$ then find the value of mean?

A. 92 **B.** 65 **C.** 72 **D.** 90

Q.19 What is the mean of $5,10,15,20,25,30,35,40,45,50$?

A. 26.5 **B.** 27.5 **C.** 28.5 **D.** 29.5

Q.20 If $a + b = 13$ and $ab = 36$, find the value of $a - b$.

A. 5 **B.** 2 **C.** 7 **D.** 9

// Smart Answer Sheet //

Correct — Percentage of students who answered correctly. Skipped — Percentage of students who skipped.

Q.	Ans.	Correct / Skipped	Q.	Ans.	Correct / Skipped	Q.	Ans.	Correct / Skipped	Q.	Ans.	Correct / Skipped	Q.	Ans.	Correct / Skipped	Q.	Ans.	Correct / Skipped
1	D	31.82 % / 4.54 %	5	B	29.55 % / 38.63 %	9	A	22.73 % / 38.63 %	13	B	43.18 % / 22.73 %	17	C	18.18 % / 40.91 %			
2	B	50.0 % / 29.55 %	6	C	27.27 % / 29.55 %	10	D	36.36 % / 29.55 %	14	B	29.55 % / 34.09 %	18	D	20.45 % / 34.1 %			
3	C	45.45 % / 22.73 %	7	C	18.18 % / 38.64 %	11	A	34.09 % / 27.27 %	15	B	29.55 % / 27.27 %	19	B	45.45 % / 18.19 %			
4	A	27.27 % / 38.64 %	8	D	34.09 % / 29.55 %	12	A	20.45 % / 31.82 %	16	A	18.18 % / 25.0 %	20	A	38.64 % / 22.72 %			

//Hints and Solutions//

1. Given: Number=640

The square root of 640= $\sqrt{640}$= $\sqrt{8\times8\times10}$

= 8 $\sqrt{10}$

∴ Square root of 640 is $8\sqrt{10}$

Hence, the correct option is (D).

2. Given: 20% Of $x = 40\%$ of 60

Using the concept of percentage,

$\Rightarrow \frac{20}{100}\times x = \frac{40}{100}\times 60$

$\Rightarrow 20\times x = 40\times 60$

$\Rightarrow x = \frac{2400}{20}$

$\Rightarrow x = 120$

∴ The value of x is 120.

Hence, the correct option is (B).

3. Given: $5(x+1) = 3(x+2)+11$

$\Rightarrow 5x+5 = 3x+6+11$

$\Rightarrow 5x+5 = 3x+17$

$\Rightarrow 5x-3x = 17-5$

$\Rightarrow 2x = 12$

$\Rightarrow x = 6$

∴ The value of x is 6.

Hence, the correct option is (C).

4. Given: $p(x) = x^3+x^2-x+1,\ g(x) = x+2$

Putting, $g(x) = 0$, we get,

$x+2 = 0$

$\Rightarrow x = -2$

Put the value of x in $P(x)$,

$\Rightarrow (-2)^3+(-2)^2-(-2)+1$

$\Rightarrow -8+4+2+1 = -1$

∴ The remainder= -1

Hence, the correct option is (A).

5. Given: Let cost price (C.P.) be $= 5x$ and selling price (S.P.) $= 3x$

We know,

Loss %= $\frac{(C.P.-S.P.)}{S.P.}\times 100$

$\Rightarrow$ Loss % $= \frac{(5x-3x)}{5x}\times 100 = \frac{2x}{5x}\times 100 = 40\%$

∴ $\%$ Loss is 40%

Hence, the correct option is (B).

6. Given: Successive discounts of the mobile was 20% and 10%

Selling Price of the mobile= Rs. 1710

We know,

Single discount $= [a+b-\frac{ab}{100}]\%$

Where, $a =$ first discount rate of the mobile $= 20\%$

$b =$ second discount rate of the mobile $= 10\%$

Let original price of the mobile be Rs. x

$\Rightarrow$ Single discount $= [20+10-\frac{(20\times10)}{100}]\%$

$\Rightarrow$ Single discount $= [30-\frac{200}{100}] = 28\%$

$\Rightarrow$ Original cost of the mobile $\times \frac{(100-single\ discount)}{100} = 1710$

$\Rightarrow x\times\frac{(100-28)}{100} = 1710$

$\Rightarrow x = \frac{1710\times100}{72}$

$= 2375$ Rs.

Hence, the correct option is (C).

7. Given: Principal $(P) =$ RS. 1000,

Amount $(A) =$ Rs. 1331,

Rate $\% = 20\%$

We know,

Compound interest $= P\left(1+\frac{R}{100}\right)^t$

Here, $P =$ Principal, $R =$ Rate, $t =$ Time

According to question,

When interest is compound half -yearly.

Rate $\% = \frac{20}{2} = 10\%$

Time $= 2t$

By using formula,

$\Rightarrow 1331 = 1000\left(1+\frac{10}{100}\right)^{2t}$

$\Rightarrow \frac{1331}{1000} = \left(\frac{11}{10}\right)^{2t}$

$\Rightarrow \left(\frac{11}{10}\right)^3 = \left(\frac{11}{10}\right)^{2t}$

By equating both sides

$\Rightarrow 2t = 3$

$\Rightarrow t = \frac{3}{2}$ years

$\Rightarrow t = 1\left(\frac{1}{2}\right)$ years

∴ Time is 1.5 years

Hence, the correct option is (C).

8. Given: Principal $=$ Rs. 7,000

Amount $=$ Rs. 10,360

Time $= 6$ years

We know,

Amount = S.I.+ P, where S.I. = Simple interest, P= Principal

Also, S.I. = $\frac{PRT}{100}$------(1)

Where, R= Rate, T= Time

Now, S.I. = Amount-P

⇒ S.I.= 10360-7000= 3360

From (1),

R= $\frac{S.I.\times 100}{P\times T}$

⇒ R= $\frac{3360\times 100}{7000\times 6}$= 8%

Therefore, rate of interest is 8%.

Hence, the correct option is (D).

9. Given:

Diameter of small balls $= 21\ cm$

Diameter of big ball $= 84\ cm$

We know,

The volume of a sphere $= \frac{4}{3}\pi r^3$

Now, Diameter of small balls $= 21\ cm$

⇒ Radius of small balls, (r) $= \frac{21}{2}\ cm$

Also, Diameter of big ball $= 84\ cm$

⇒ Radius of big ball, (R) $= 42\ cm$

Let the number of small balls be N

$\Rightarrow N \times \frac{4}{3}\pi r^3 = \frac{4}{3}\pi R^3$

$\Rightarrow N \times \frac{4}{3}\pi \times \frac{21}{2} \times \frac{21}{2} \times \frac{21}{2} = \frac{4}{3}\pi \times 42 \times 42 \times 42$

$\Rightarrow N = \frac{42\times 42\times 42\times 2\times 2\times 2}{21\times 21\times 21}$

$\Rightarrow N = 64$

∴ The number of small balls are 64.

Hence, the correct option is (A).

10. Given: Side of equilateral triangle $= 5\ cm$

We know,

Area of an equilateral triangle $= \frac{\sqrt{3}}{4} \times Side^2$

∴ The area of the equilateral triangle is $= \frac{\sqrt{3}}{4} \times 5^2$

$= \frac{\sqrt{3}}{4} \times 25\ cm^2$

∴ The area of the equilateral triangle is $\frac{\sqrt{3}}{4} \times 25$ sq. cm.

Hence, the correct option is (D).

11. Given: Side $= (2x + 5)cm$

Perimeter $= 28\ cm$

We know,

Perimeter $= 4 \times$ Side

Now,

Side $= (2x + 5)cm$

$\Rightarrow 28 = 4(2x + 5)$

$\Rightarrow 2x + 5 = 7$

$\Rightarrow 2x = 2$

$\Rightarrow x = 1$

∴ The value of x is 1.

Hence, the correct option is (A).

12. Given: $\angle MON = 116°$

From the property:

Angle made by the same chord at the centre is twice of the angle made by the same chord at the circumference and, in a cyclic quadrilateral, the sum of opposite angles is $180°$.

Now, from the figure given,

$\angle MON = 116°$

$\Rightarrow \angle MPN = \frac{\angle MON}{2}$ (Above property)

$\Rightarrow \angle MPN = \frac{116^\circ}{2} = 58^\circ$

Now, In a cyclic quadrilateral, the sum of opposite angles is 180°.

$\Rightarrow \angle MPN + \angle MQN = 180^\circ$

$\Rightarrow 58^\circ + \angle MQN = 180^\circ$

$\Rightarrow \angle MQN = 180^\circ - 58^\circ$

$\Rightarrow \angle MQN = 122^\circ$

$\therefore$ The value of $\angle MQN$ is 122°.

Hence, the correct option is (A).

13. Given: $(\sin 0^\circ \cdot \sin 1^\circ \cdot \sin 2^\circ \cdot \sin 3^\circ sinn4^\circ \ldots\ldots \sin 89^\circ)$

$\Rightarrow \sin 0^\circ \times (\sin 1^\circ \cdot \sin 2^\circ \cdot \sin 3^\circ \cdot \sin 4^\circ \ldots\ldots \sin 89^\circ)$

$\Rightarrow 0 \times (\sin 1^\circ \cdot \sin 2^\circ \cdot \sin 3^\circ \cdot \sin 4^\circ \ldots\ldots \sin 89^\circ)$

$= 0$

Hence, the correct option is (B).

14. Given: $Sin 60^\circ \cos 30^\circ - \cos 60^\circ \sin 30^\circ$

We know,

$\sin(A - B) = \sin A \cos B - \cos A \sin B$

$\because$ The given trigonometric equation is

$\sin 60^\circ \cos 30^\circ - \cos 60^\circ \sin 30^\circ$

It is Written in the form

$\sin A \cos B - \cos A \sin B = \sin(A - B)$

$\therefore \sin 60^\circ \cos 30^\circ - \cos 60^\circ \sin 30^\circ = \sin(60^\circ - 30^\circ)$

$= \sin 30^\circ$

$= \frac{1}{2}$ (since, Trigonometric Value of $\sin 30^\circ = \frac{1}{2}$)

Hence, the correct option is (B)

15. Given: The efficiency of A, B and $C = 2:3:4$

They together can complete in 6 days

According to the formula:

Work done $=$ Time $\times$ Efficiency

Total work is:

$6 \times (2 + 3 + 4) = 54$

A can complete the work in $= \frac{54}{2} = 27$ days

$\therefore$ A can complete the work in 27 days.

Hence, the correct option is (B).

16. Given: Speed of boy $45\ km/h$ and $60\ km/h$ respectively.

We know,

Speed $= \frac{Distance}{Time}$

The ratio of the speed of boy,

$\Rightarrow S_1 : S_2 = 45 : 60$

$\Rightarrow S_1 : S_2 = 3 : 4$

The ratio of time,

$\Rightarrow t_1 : t_2 = 4 : 3$

According to the question, the difference in the according to speed change

$\Rightarrow 1$ unit $= 15$ minutes

$\Rightarrow 4$ units $= 60$ minutes $= 1$ hour

Now, from the relation,

Speed $= \frac{Distance}{Time}$

$\Rightarrow 45 = \frac{Distance}{1}$

$\Rightarrow$ Distance $= 45\ km$

$\therefore$ The distance travel by boy is $45\ km$.

Hence, the correct option is (A).

17. Given: $a : (b + c) = 4 : 5$

$c : (a + b) = 1 : 2$

According to the question:

$\frac{a}{b+c} = \frac{4}{5}$-----(1)

$\Rightarrow a + b + c = 4 + 5 = 9$ uniits

Again,

$\frac{c}{a+b} = \frac{1}{2}$-----(2)

$\Rightarrow c + a + b = 1 + 2 = 3$ units

Now, $a + b + c$ should remain constant (equal) multiply equation (2) by 3 :

It means,

$\frac{c}{a+b} = \frac{1 \times 3}{2 \times 3} = \frac{3}{6}$

$\Rightarrow \frac{a}{b+c} = \frac{4}{5}$

On compairing,

$a = 4, c = 3$

Then, $b = (a + b + c) - (a + c)$

$\Rightarrow 9 - (4 + 3) = 2$

Now, $b: (a + c) = 2: (4 + 3) = 2: 7$

$\therefore b: (a + c)$ is equal to $2: 7$

Hence, the correct option is (C).

18. Given: If mode $= 15$ and mean $-$ median $= 25$

We know that,

Mode $=$ mean -3 (mean -median)

Put the value,

$15 =$ mean $-3(25)$

$\Rightarrow$ Mean $= 75 + 15 = 90$

Hence, the correct option is (D).

19. Given: $5,10,15,20,25,30,35,40,45,50$

We know,

Mean $= \frac{Sum\ of\ numbers}{Total\ Numbers}$

$\Rightarrow$ Sum of numbers $= 5 + 10 + 15 + 20 + 25 + 30 + 35 + 40 + 45 + 50$

$\Rightarrow$ Sum of numbers $= 275$

$\Rightarrow$ Mean $= \frac{275}{10}$

$\Rightarrow$ Mean $= 27.5$

Hence, the correct option is (B).

20. Given: $a + b = 13$

$ab = 36$

We know:

$(a - b)^2 = (a + b)^2 - 4ab$

$\Rightarrow (a - b)^2 = 13^2 - (4 \times 36)$

$\Rightarrow (a - b)^2 = 169 - 144$

$\Rightarrow (a - b)^2 = 25$

$\Rightarrow a - b = \sqrt{25}$

$\Rightarrow a - b = 5$

$\therefore$ The value of $a - b$ is 5.

Hence, the correct option is (A).

Sectional Test 02

Q.1 Given the equation: $\sqrt{\left(1+\frac{27}{169}\right)} = 1+\frac{x}{13}$, then find the value of x.

A. 1 **B.** 5 **C.** 6 **D.** 3

Q.2 In an exam P secures 55% marks and Q secures 105 marks more than P. If the maximum marks were 700, then what is the percentage of Q?

A. 60% **B.** 68% **C.** 70% **D.** 75%

Q.3 What will come in place of question mark:
$(x+1)(x^2-x+1) = ?$

A. x^3+1 **B.** x^3-1
C. x^3 **D.** x^3+x^2+1

Q.4 If $2x+8=5x-1$, then find the value of x.

A. 2 **B.** 3 **C.** 4 **D.** 0

Q.5 If two cows and three horses cost Rs. 4,000 and three cows and two horses cost Rs. 3,500, how much does a cow cost?

A. Rs. 1500 **B.** Rs. 1000 **C.** Rs. 500 **D.** Rs. 2000

Q.6 By selling a chair for Rs. 450 the shopkeeper incurs a loss of 10%, then what will be the selling price of the chair when he gets a profit of 10%?

A. Rs. 550 **B.** Rs. 600 **C.** Rs. 480 **D.** Rs. 650

Q.7 Megha buys a book at 20% discount on its marked price. she makes a profit of 12% by selling it at Rs. 560. What was the marked price of the book?

A. Rs. 625 **B.** Rs. 600 **C.** Rs. 500 **D.** Rs. 700

Q.8 Find the principal when simple interest is Rs. 1800 at 10% per anum for 10 years.

A. Rs. 3600 **B.** Rs. 1800 **C.** Rs. 1000 **D.** Rs. 1500

Q.9 In how many years will Rs. 4000 amount to Rs. 5324 at a rate of 10% compounded annually?

A. 5 years **B.** 3 years **C.** 2 years **D.** 4 years

Q.10 The ratio of the length to the width of a rectangular field is $4:3$. If the width of the ground is 90 meters, then find its length (in meters).

A. 100 **B.** 120 **C.** 140 **D.** 160

Q.11 The lateral surface area of a cube is $144\ cm^2$, then find the volume of the cube.

A. $196\ cm^3$ **B.** $216\ cm^3$ **C.** $256\ cm^3$ **D.** $343\ cm^3$

Q.12 The corresponding sides of two similar triangles are in the ratio of $1:3$. Their altitude will be in the ratio?

A. $1:3$ **B.** $1:2$ **C.** $3:1$ **D.** $1:5$

Q.13 In the given figure, O is the centre of the circle. $AB = 8\ cm$ and $BC = 6\ cm$, then what is the diameter of the circle?

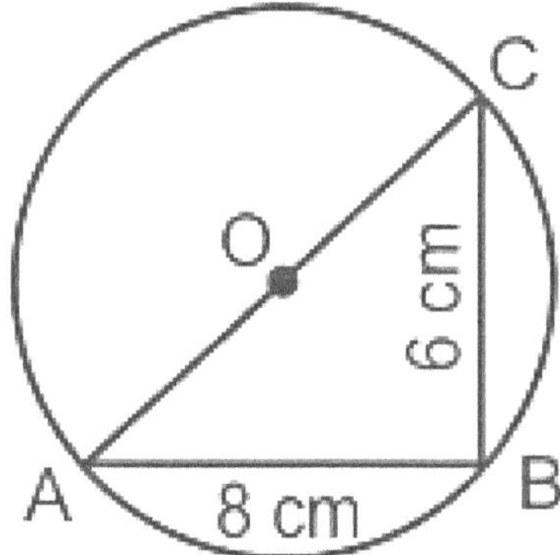

A. 16 cm **B.** 10 cm **C.** 12 cm **D.** 15 cm

Q.14 If $A+B=90°$ and $SinA=\frac{3}{5}$ find the value of $\tan B$.

A. $\frac{3}{4}$ **B.** $\frac{4}{3}$ **C.** $-\frac{3}{4}$ **D.** $-\frac{4}{3}$

Q.15 If $2\cos 3\theta = 1$, then $\theta =$

A. $20°$ **B.** $40°$
C. $25°$ **D.** None of the above

Q.16 If 15 workers can earn in 10 days. Find the earning (in of 5 workers in 8 days.

[SSC Constable (GD), 2019]

A. 400 **B.** 360 **C.** 540 **D.** 480

Q.17 Ramdev covers a distance of $30\ km$ at a speed of $60\ km/hr$ and another $50\ km$ at a speed of $100\ km/hr$, what is his average speed for the whole journey?

A. $100\ km/hr$ **B.** $82\ km/hr$
C. $00\ km/hr$ **D.** $85\ km/hr$

Q.18 The mean and Median of observation is 12 and 17 respectively. What is the mode of this observation?

A. 27 **B.** 29 **C.** 5 **D.** 204

Q.19 The range of the following data, $6,14,20,16,6,5,4,18,25,15$ and 5 is-

A. 21 **B.** 4 **C.** 25 **D.** 20

Q.20 Ratio of two numbers is $3:4$. If we subtract 5 in each number then ratio becomes $5:7$. Find out the numbers?

A. 30, 40 **B.** 40, 44 **C.** 24, 32 **D.** 121, 21

// Smart Answer Sheet //

Correct Percentage of students who answered correctly. **Skipped** Percentage of students who skipped.

Q.	Ans.	Correct / Skipped	Q.	Ans.	Correct / Skipped	Q.	Ans.	Correct / Skipped	Q.	Ans.	Correct / Skipped	Q.	Ans.	Correct / Skipped	Q.	Ans.	Correct / Skipped
1	A	42.89 % / 1.71 %	5	C	46.31 % / 1.98 %	9	B	59.79 % / 1.39 %	13	B	60.63 % / 1.86 %	17	C	44.05 % / 1.02 %			
2	C	67.78 % / 1.34 %	6	A	57.82 % / 1.02 %	10	B	65.94 % / 1.98 %	14	B	44.73 % / 1.67 %	18	A	41.53 % / 1.26 %			
3	A	79.07 % / 0.0 %	7	D	13.29 % / 4.64 %	11	B	40.86 % / 1.16 %	15	A	60.55 % / 1.58 %	19	A	56.89 % / 1.21 %			
4	B	78.08 % / 0.0 %	8	B	78.41 % / 0.0 %	12	A	77.92 % / 0.0 %	16	D	43.29 % / 1.91 %	20	A	69.82 % / 1.48 %			

//Hints and Solutions//

1. Given:

$$\sqrt{\left(1+\frac{27}{169}\right)} = 1+\frac{x}{13}$$

$\Rightarrow \sqrt{\frac{196}{169}} = 1+\frac{x}{13}$

$\Rightarrow \frac{14}{13} - 1 = \frac{x}{13}$

$\Rightarrow \frac{1}{13} = \frac{x}{13}$

$\therefore x = 1$

Hence, the correct option is (A).

2. Given:

Maximum Marks $= 700$

We know,

Percentage = $\frac{Actual}{Total} \times 100$

P secures $= 55\%$ of maximum marks

$\Rightarrow 55\%$ of $700 = 385$=P

Q secures $= 105 + P$ marks

$\Rightarrow 105 + 385 = 490$

$\Rightarrow$ Percentage of $Q = \frac{490}{700} \times 100 = 70\%$

$\therefore$ The required answer is 70%.

Hence, the correct option is (C).

3. Given:

$(x+1)(x^2 - x + 1)$

Multiplying the given terms:

$\Rightarrow ? = (x^3 - x^2 + x + x^2 - x + 1)$

$\therefore ? = (x^3 + 1)$

Hence, the correct option is (A).

4. Given:

$2x + 8 = 5x - 1$

$\Rightarrow 5x - 2x = 8 + 1$

$\Rightarrow 3x = 9$

$\Rightarrow x = 3$

$\therefore$ The value of x is 3.

Hence, the correct option is (B).

5. Given:

Cost of 2 Cows and 3 Horses $=$ Rs. 4000

Costs of 3 Cows and 2 horses $=$ Rs. 3500

Forming the equations with C for cow and H for horses:

$2C + 3H = 4000$----(1)

$3C + 2H = 3500$-----(2)

On solving equation (1) and equation (2) , we get,

$C = 500$ & $H = 1000$

$\therefore$ The cost of one cow is Rs.500.

Hence, the correct option is (C).

6. Given:

S.P. of chair $=$ Rs. 450

Loss $\% = 10\%$

Let the Cost price of chair be Rs. $100x$

Now, after 10% loss

Selling price of chair $= 100x - 10\%$ of $100x$

$= 90x$

And, according to question,

$\Rightarrow 90x = 450$

$\Rightarrow x = \frac{450}{90}$

$= 5$

$\Rightarrow 100x =$ Rs. 500

So, cost price of chair $=$ Rs. 500

Now, after 10% profit

Selling price of chair $= 500 + 10\%$ of $500 = 500 + 50$

$=$ Rs. 550

$\therefore$ The selling price of the chair after 10% profit is Rs. 550.

Hence, the correct option is (A).

7. Given:

The selling price of book $=$ Rs. 560

Profit $= 12\%$

Discount, D $= 20\%$

We know,

S.P.= C.P. (1+ $\frac{P}{100}$), where, P= Profit

$\Rightarrow$ 560= C.P. (1+ $\frac{12}{100}$)

$\Rightarrow$ 560= C.P. ($\frac{28}{25}$)

$\Rightarrow$ C.P.= 560 $\times \frac{25}{28}$

$\Rightarrow$ C.P.= Rs. 500

Now, from the following formula:

$\frac{C.P.}{M.P.} = \frac{100-D\%}{100+P\%}$

$\Rightarrow \frac{500}{M.P.} = \frac{100-20}{100+12}$

$\Rightarrow$ M.P. = $\frac{500\times112}{80}$

$\Rightarrow$ M.P.= Rs. 700

Hence, the correct option is (D).

8. Given:

The simple interest, S.I. = Rs. 1800

Rate of interest $= 10\%$

Time duration $= 10$ year

We know,

Simple Interest= $\frac{PRT}{100}$ where, P= Principal, R= Rate, T= Time

$\Rightarrow 1800 = \frac{P\times10\times10}{100}$

$\Rightarrow P = 1800$

∴ The principal is Rs. 1800 .

Hence, the correct option is (B).

9. Given :

Rs.4000 amounts to Rs.5324 @ 10% compounded annually

We know,

$A = P \times \left(1 + \frac{r}{100}\right)^n$

Where

$A =$ Amount accumulated

$P =$ Principal

$r =$ Rate of interest

$n =$ Time-period

$\Rightarrow 5324 = 4000 \times \left(1 + \frac{10}{100}\right)^n$

$\Rightarrow \frac{5324}{4000} = \left(\frac{11}{10}\right)^n$

$\Rightarrow \frac{1331}{1000} = \left(\frac{11}{10}\right)^n$

$\Rightarrow n = 3$

∴ Rs.4000 will amount to Rs.5324@ 10% in 3 years.

Hence, the correct option is (B).

10. Given:

The ratio of the length and width $= 4:3$

Width $= 90\ m$

length : width $= 4:3$

Let the length and width be $4x$ and $3x$

According to the question, we have

$3x = 90\ m$

$\Rightarrow x = 30\ m$

Now, the length of the rectangle is:

$4x = 4 \times 30$

$= 120\ m$

∴ The length of the rectangle is $120\ m$.

Hence, the correct option is (B).

11. Given:

The lateral surface area of a cube $= 144\ cm^2$

We know,

The lateral surface area of cube $= 4a^2$

The volume of the cube $= a^3$

Where a is the edge length of the cube.

According to the question, we have

The lateral surface area of a cube is $144\ cm^2$

$4a^2 = 144\ cm^2$

$\Rightarrow a^2 = \frac{144}{4}$

$\Rightarrow a^2 = 36$

$\Rightarrow a = \sqrt{36}$

$\Rightarrow a = 6\ cm$

So, Volume of the cube $= a^3$

$\Rightarrow$ Volume $= (6)^3$

$\Rightarrow$ Volume $= 6 \times 6 \times 6 = 216\ cm^3$

∴ The volume of the cube is $216\ cm^3$.

Hence, the correct option is (B).

12. Given: The corresponding sides of two similar triangles are in the ratio of $1:3$.

According to the concept,

The ratio of sides $=$ Ratio of altitudes

$\Rightarrow$ Two similar triangles with their sides of ratio $1:3$ is given in the question,

$\therefore$ Ratio of altitude $= 1:3$

Hence, the correct option is (A).

13. Given:

$AB = 8\ cm, BC = 6\ cm$

From the theorem:

The angle subtended by semicircle at any point of the remaining part of the circle is $90°$.

$\angle PAQ = 90°$ (from the figure)

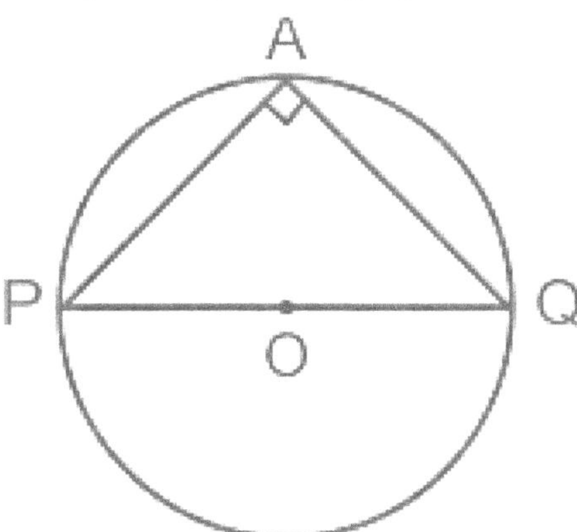

Applying Pythagoras theorem in the triangle inside the circle given:

$AB^2 + BC^2 = AC^2$

$\Rightarrow 8^2 + 6^2 = AC^2$

$\Rightarrow AC^2 = 10^2$

$\Rightarrow AC = \pm 10$

But length of side can not be negative, hence

$AC = 10\ cm$

$\therefore$ The diameter of the given circle will be $10\ cm$.

Hence, the correct option is (B).

14. Given:

$A + B = 90°$ and $SinA = \frac{3}{5}$

We know,

$\sin\theta = \frac{Perpendicular}{Hypotenuse}$

$= \frac{3}{5}$

Now,

Let perpendicular=3k, Hypotenuse=5k, where k is a constant.

We know,

Base = $\sqrt{(Perpendicular^2 + Hypotenuse^2)}$

$\Rightarrow$ Base $= \sqrt{(5k)^2 - (3k)^2}$

$\Rightarrow$ Base $= 4k$

Also, $\tan\theta = \frac{Perpendicular}{Base}$

$\Rightarrow \tan A = \frac{3k}{4k} = \frac{3}{4}$

$\Rightarrow \tan(90° - B) = \frac{3}{4}$

$\Rightarrow \cot B = \frac{3}{4}$

$\Rightarrow \tan B = \frac{4}{3}$

$\therefore \tan B = \frac{4}{3}$

Hence, the correct option is (B).

15. Given:

$2\cos 3\theta = 1$

$\Rightarrow 2\cos 3\theta = 1$

$\Rightarrow \cos 3\theta = \frac{1}{2}$

From the value of angle:

$\cos 60° = \frac{1}{2}$

Using the value of $\cos 60°$

$\Rightarrow \cos 3\theta = \cos 60°$

$\Rightarrow 3\theta = 60°$

$\Rightarrow \theta = 20°$

Hence, the correct option is (A).

16. Given:

Earning of 15 workers in 10 days $=$ Rs. 1800

From the concept:

Earning is directly proportional to the product of the number of workers and time taken.

According to the question,

$15 \times 10 =$ Rs. 1800

Then, $5 \times 8 =$ Rs. $1800 \times \frac{5\times8}{15\times10}$

$\Rightarrow$ Rs. $1800 \times \frac{40}{150} =$ Rs. 480

∴ The earning of 5 workers in 8 days is Rs. 480

Hence, the correct option is (D).

17. Given:

In first case:

$Speed(S_1) = 60\ km/hr$

Distance $(D_1) = 30\ km$

In second case:

$speed(S_2) = 100\ km/hr$

Distance $(D_2) = 50\ km$

∴ Total distance= 30+50

=80 km

We know,

Average speed= $\frac{Total\ Distance}{Total\ Time}$

Time= $\frac{Distance}{Speed}$

According to the question:

In first case:

Time $= \frac{30}{60} = \frac{1}{2} hrs$

In second case,

Time $= \frac{50}{100} = \frac{1}{2} hrs$

∴ Total Time $= \frac{1}{2} + \frac{1}{2} = \frac{2}{2} = 1hrs$

And, Average Speed $= \frac{80}{1} = 80\ km/hr$

∴ The average speed of whole journey is $80\ km/hr$.

Hence, the correct option is (C).

18. Given:

Mean $= 17$, Median $= 12$

According to the formula,

Mode $= 3$ Median - 2 Mean

$\Rightarrow$ Mode $= (3 \times 17) - (2 \times 12)$

$\Rightarrow$ Mode $= 51 - 24$

$\Rightarrow$ Mode $= 27$

∴ The mode is 27.

Hence, the correct option is (A).

19. Given:

6,14,20,16,6,5,4,18,25,15 and 5

From the concept,

The range of a number set is the difference between the maximum and lowest values in the number group.

Now,

Max. value of number set $= 25$

The lowest value of number set $= 4$

∴ Range $= 25 - 4 = 21$

Hence, the correct option is (A).

20. Given:

Ratio of two numbers $= 3:4$

After subtracting 5 the ratio $= 5:7$

Let the two numbers be $3x$ and $4x$.

Subtract 5 from each of these numbers,

We get, $3x - 5$ and $4x - 5$

According to the question,

$\Rightarrow \frac{3x-5}{4x-5} = \frac{5}{7}$

$\Rightarrow (3x - 5) \times 7 = (4x - 5) \times 5$

$\Rightarrow 21x - 35 = 20x - 25$

$\Rightarrow 21x - 20x = -25 + 35$

$\Rightarrow x = 10$

The required numbers are

$3x = 3 \times 10 = 30$

$4x = 4 \times 10 = 40$

∴ The numbers are 30 and 40.

Hence, the correct option is (A).

Sectional Test 03

Q.1 224 is what percent of 320?

A. 80% **B.** 70% **C.** 35% **D.** 65%

Q.2 If the selling price of a bed is Rs. 21384 after allowing two successive discounts of 12% and 10%. Find the market price.

A. Rs. 27,000 **B.** Rs. 25,000
C. Rs. 24,000 **D.** Rs. 14,000

Q.3 If $a^3 + b^3 = 0$, find $a + b$.

A. $\sqrt{3ab}$ **B.** $\sqrt{2ab}$ **C.** $\sqrt{4ab}$ **D.** 1

Q.4 Mr. Thomas invested an amount of Rs. 13,900 divided in two different schemes A and B at the simple interest rate of 14% p.a. and 11% p.a respectively. If the total amount of simple interest earned in 2 years be Rs. 3508, what was the amount invested in Scheme B?

A. Rs. 6400 **B.** Rs. 6500 **C.** Rs. 7200 **D.** Rs. 7500

Q.5 The efficiency of A is 20% more than B and the efficiency of C is 40% less than B. If C alone can complete a task in 24 days, then find in how many days A and C together can complete the whole work?

A. 8 days **B.** 10 days **C.** 15 days **D.** 16 days

Q.6 The speed of Ram is $12\ km/hr$ but he stops at every fifth kilometer for $9\ \text{min}$. Then find the total time taken by Ram to cover $84\ km$?

A. 9 hr 24 minutes **B.** 8 hr 24 minutes
C. 9 hr 12 minutes **D.** 8 hr 12 minutes

Q.7 If $x = 5 + \sqrt{79 + \sqrt{11 - \sqrt{49}}}$, then find $2x + 3$.

A. 31 **B.** 41 **C.** 29 **D.** 37

Q.8 At what rate of Compound Interest per annum will be a sum of Rs. 1000 becomes Rs. 1210 in 2 years?

A. 12% **B.** 15% **C.** 8% **D.** 10%

Q.9 Rs. 6400 is divided among A, B and C in the ratio of $2:9:5$ respectively. What is the difference (in Rs.) between the shares of B and C?

A. Rs. 1600 **B.** Rs. 1800 **C.** Rs. 2700 **D.** Rs. 2800

Q.10 The ratio of the length and breadth of a rectangle is $5:3$ and its perimeter is $64\ cm$, then find the area of the rectangle.

A. 132 cm^2 **B.** 120 cm^2 **C.** 240 cm^2 **D.** 280 cm^2

Q.11 A 50 liters mixture of acid and water is in the ratio of $3:2$. What amount of water must be added to get the ratio $2:3$?

A. 20 liters **B.** 25 liters **C.** 30 liters **D.** 40 liters

Q.12 Find the mean of the given data.
$\{9,2,3,4,2,6,8,7,4,11\}$

A. 5 **B.** 5.4 **C.** 5.6 **D.** 5.7

Q.13 If $\tan^2 A = \frac{9}{16}$. Then find out the value of $Sin^2 A + SinA + 1$.

A. $\frac{36}{25}$ **B.** $\frac{49}{25}$ **C.** $\frac{16}{25}$ **D.** $\frac{9}{25}$

Q.14 If angles of a triangle are in the ratio of $2:3:4$, then the measure of the smallest angle is:

A. 30° **B.** 50° **C.** 40° **D.** 20°

Q.15 The ratio of the radius of two cylinders is $2:3$ and the ratio of their heights is $5:3$. The ratio of their volumes will be-

A. $9:4$ **B.** $27:20$ **C.** $4:9$ **D.** $20:27$

Q.16 Two triangles ABC and PQR are similar to each other in which $AB = 10\ cm, PQ = 8\ cm$. Then the ratio of the areas of triangles ABC and PQR is-

A. $4:5$ **B.** $25:16$ **C.** $64:125$ **D.** $4:7$

Q.17 If $\sin\theta = \frac{3}{5}$, then find the value of $\tan\theta$.

A. $\frac{4}{5}$ **B.** $\frac{3}{5}$ **C.** $\frac{3}{4}$ **D.** $\frac{4}{3}$

Q.18 Find the value of x and y if $x + y = 6$ and $4x + 7y = 36$.

[MP Police (Constable), 2016]

A. 2, 4 **B.** 4, 2 **C.** 1, 1 **D.** 0, 0

Q.19 Find the value of: $12\frac{1}{2} \div 8\frac{1}{3} \times 4 + 6$.

A. 11 **B.** 12 **C.** 13 **D.** 10

Q.20 What should come in place of question mark (?) in the following question:

$$77 \div 7 \times 4 + \left(\frac{1}{5}\right) \text{ of } 15 \times 4 = ?$$

A. 66 **B.** 79 **C.** 56 **D.** 55

// Smart Answer Sheet //

Correct — Percentage of students who answered correctly. Skipped — Percentage of students who skipped.

Q.	Ans.	Correct / Skipped	Q.	Ans.	Correct / Skipped	Q.	Ans.	Correct / Skipped	Q.	Ans.	Correct / Skipped	Q.	Ans.	Correct / Skipped	Q.	Ans.	Correct / Skipped
1	B	86.71 % / 0.0 %	5	A	16.67 % / 3.89 %	9	A	61.29 % / 1.27 %	13	B	10.56 % / 4.3 %	17	C	61.2 % / 1.69 %			
2	A	24.32 % / 3.32 %	6	A	40.22 % / 1.8 %	10	C	50.99 % / 1.43 %	14	C	88.89 % / 0.0 %	18	A	47.65 % / 1.75 %			
3	A	69.46 % / 1.81 %	7	A	40.95 % / 1.72 %	11	B	42.43 % / 1.78 %	15	D	46.55 % / 1.98 %	19	B	53.0 % / 1.05 %			
4	A	29.04 % / 4.66 %	8	D	54.28 % / 1.27 %	12	C	43.03 % / 1.02 %	16	B	60.86 % / 1.36 %	20	C	57.25 % / 1.64 %			

//Hints and Solutions//

1. Given:

Numbers 224 and 320

We know,

Percentage of a number= $\frac{Given\ number}{TotalNumber} \times 100$

$\Rightarrow$ Required percentage= $\frac{224}{320} \times 100$

$= 70$

$\therefore$ 224 is 70% of 320.

Hence, the correct option is (B).

2. Given:

Selling price $=$ Rs. 21384

We know,

Selling price $=$ Market price $(1 - D_1)(1 - D_2)$

Where D_1 and D_2 are discount rate

$\Rightarrow 21384 =$ Market price $[1 - \left(\frac{12}{100}\right)][1 - \left(\frac{10}{100}\right)]$

$\Rightarrow 21384 =$ Market price $\left(\frac{88}{100}\right)\left(\frac{90}{100}\right)$

$\Rightarrow$ Market price $= 21384 \times \frac{100\times100}{88\times90}$

$\Rightarrow$ Market price $=$ Rs. 27,000

$\therefore$ Market price of bed is Rs. 27,000

Hence, the correct option is (A).

3. Given: $a^3 + b^3 = 0$

We know,

$(a+b)^3 = a^3 + b^3 + 3ab(a+b)$

According to given expression:

$a^3 + b^3 = 0$

$\Rightarrow (a+b)^3 = 0 + 3ab(a+b)$

$\Rightarrow 3ab = \frac{(a+b)^3}{a+b}$

$\Rightarrow a + b = \sqrt{3ab}$

$\therefore$ The value of $a + b$ is $\sqrt{3ab}$.

Hence, the correct option is (A).

4. Given:

Amount invested by Mr. Thomas = Rs. 13900, Rates of interest = 14% and 11%

Amount earned in 2 years= Rs. 3508

Let the investment in scheme A be Rs. x

Investment in scheme B be Rs.(13900- x)

We know,

S.I. $= \frac{P\times R\times T}{100}$

Where, S.I.= Simple interest, P=Principal, R=Rate, T= Time

S.I. for Rs. x for 2 years at 14% p.a $= \frac{28x}{100}$

S.I. for Rs. $(13900 - x)$ for 2 years at 11% p.a $= \frac{(13900-x)\times2\times11}{100}$

As per the question,

$\Rightarrow \frac{28x}{100} + \frac{(13900-x)\times2\times11}{100} = Rs. 3508$

$\Rightarrow 28x - 22x = 45000$

$\Rightarrow 6x = 45000$

$\Rightarrow x = 7500$

$\therefore$ Investment in scheme $B = 13900 - 7500$

$=$ Rs.6400

Hence, the correct option is (A).

5. Given:

C alone can complete a work in 24 days

The efficiency of $A 20\%$ more than B

The efficiency of C 40% less than B

We know,

Total work $=$ Efficiency $\times$ Time

Let efficiency of B be 5 units/day.

According to the question, we have

$\Rightarrow$ Efficiency of $A = 5 \times \frac{120}{100} = 6$ units $/$ day

$\Rightarrow$ Efficiency of $C = 5 \times \frac{60}{100} = 3$ units $/$ day

Now, the efficiency ratio of A, B and C

$A : B : C = 5 : 4 : 3$

$\Rightarrow$ Total work $= 3 \times 24 = 72$ units

$\Rightarrow$ Time taken by A and C to complete the work $= \frac{72}{6+3}$

$= \frac{72}{9}$

$= 8$ days

∴ The time taken by A and C to complete the whole work is 8 days.

Hence, the correct option is (A).

6. Given:

The speed of Ram is $12\ km/hr$. Ram stops at every fifth kilometer for 9 min and total distance is $84\ km$.

We know,

Speed= $\frac{Distance}{Time}$

Time taken by Ram to cover $84\ km$ at the speed of $12\ km/hr = \frac{84}{12} hr$

∴ Time $= \frac{84}{12}$

$= 7hr$

Now, he stops at every fifth kilometer for 9 min

∴ Number of times he stop $= \frac{84}{5}$

$= 16.8$ times and for the last kilometers he covers the full distance without any stoppage.

Total stoppage $= 16$ times (since for the last kilometers he covers the full distance without any stoppage.)

⇒Time taken in stops $= 9 \times 16$

$= 144$ minutes

$= 2hr24$ minutes

∴ Total times $= 7hr + 2$ hr 24 minutes

$= 9$ hr 24 minutes

∴ Total time taken by Ram to cover whole distance is 9 hr 24 minutes.

Hence, the correct option is (A).

7. Given:

$$x = 5 + \sqrt{79 + \sqrt{11 - \sqrt{49}}}$$

$$\Rightarrow 5 + \sqrt{79 + \sqrt{11 - 7}}$$

$$= 5 + \sqrt{79 + \sqrt{4}}$$

$$= 5 + \sqrt{79 + 2}$$

$$= 5 + \sqrt{81}$$

$$= 5 + 9$$

$$= 14$$

Now,

$$2x + 3 = 2 \times 14 + 3$$

$$= 31$$

∴ The value of $2x + 3$ is 31 .

Hence, the correct option is (A).

8. Given:

Principal = Rs. 1000

Amount $=$ Rs. 1210

Time $= 2$ years

We know,

Amount $=$ Principal $\left(1 + \frac{Rate}{100}\right)^{Time}$

Where,

Amount $= A$, Principal $= P$

Time $= T$, Rate% $= R$

$$\Rightarrow 1210 = 1000\left(1 + \frac{R}{100}\right)^2$$

$$\Rightarrow \frac{1210}{1000} = \left(1 + \frac{R}{100}\right)^2$$

$$\Rightarrow \left(\frac{121}{100}\right)^{0.5} = \frac{100+R}{100}$$

$$\Rightarrow \frac{11}{10} \times 100 = (100 + R)$$

$$\Rightarrow R = 110 - 100$$

$$\Rightarrow R = 10$$

∴ Rate of interest is 10% per annum.

Hence,the correct option is (D).

9. Given:

The Rs. 6400 is divided among $A, B,$ and C in the ratio of $2:9:5$

Total money $= 6400$

The ratio $A, B,$ and $C = 2:9:5$

Then the difference between the shares of B and $C = \frac{6400}{16} \times (9 - 5)$

The difference between the shares of B and $C = 400 \times 4 = 1600$

∴ The difference between the share of B and C is Rs. 1600.

Hence, the correct option is (A).

10. Given:

The ratio of length and breadth of the rectangle $= 5:3$

The perimeter of rectangle $= 64\ cm$

We know,

Area of rectangle $= l \times b$

Perimeter of rectangle $= 2(l + b)$

Where,

$l =$ length

$b =$ breadth

Let the length and breadth be $5x$ and $3x$

According to the question, we have

$2(5x + 3x) = 64$

$\Rightarrow 16x = 64$

$\Rightarrow x = 4$

$\Rightarrow l = 5x$

$= 5 \times 4$

$= 20\ cm$

$\Rightarrow b = 3x$

$= 3 \times 4$

$= 12\ cm$

Now,

The area of rectangle $= 20 \times 12$

$= 240\ cm^2$

∴ The area of the rectangle is $240\ cm^2$.

Hence, the correct option is (C).

11. Given:

Total amount of mixture $= 50$ liters

The ratio of acid and water $= 3:2$

Let the amount of acid and water be $3x$ and $2x$

Then, according to the question, we have

$3x + 2x = 50$ liters

$\Rightarrow 5x = 50$ liters

$\Rightarrow x = 10$ liters

So, the amount of acid $= 3x$

$= (3 \times 10)$ liters

$= 30$ liters

And, amount of water $= 2x$

$= (2 \times 10)$ liters

$= 20$ liters

Now, let the amount of added water be y

Then, according to the question, we have

$\frac{30}{20+y}$ liters $= 2:3$

$\Rightarrow (30 \times 3)$ liters $= 2(20 + y)$ liters

$\Rightarrow 90$ liters $= 40$ liters $+2y$

$\Rightarrow 2y = (90 - 40)$ liters $= 50$ liters

$\Rightarrow y = \frac{50}{2}$ liters $= 25$ liters

∴ The needed amount of water be 25 liters.

Hence, the correct option is (B).

12. Given: The set of Data $= \{9,2,3,4,2,6,8,7,4,11\}$

We know,

Mean= $\frac{Sum\ of observations}{Total\ observations}$

∴ Mean $= \frac{9+2+3+4+2+6+8+7+4+11}{10}$

$\Rightarrow$ Mean $= \frac{56}{10}$

$\Rightarrow$ Mean $= 5.6$

∴ The required value of mean is 5.6.

Hence, the correct option is (C).

13. Given:

$\tan^2 A = \frac{9}{16}$

We know,

tan A= $\frac{p}{b}$

sin A= $\frac{p}{h}$

h= $\sqrt{p^2 + b^2}$

where, h= Hypotenuse, p= Perpendicular and b=Base

Using all the above formulas,

$\Rightarrow \frac{p}{b} = \frac{3}{4}$

So, $h = \sqrt{3x^2 + 4x^2}$

$\Rightarrow h = \sqrt{9x + 16x}$

$\Rightarrow h = \sqrt{25}x$

$\Rightarrow h = 5x$

$SinA = \frac{p}{h}$

$\Rightarrow SinA = \frac{3x}{5x}$----(1)

$\Rightarrow Sin^2A = \left(\frac{3}{5}\right)^2$

$\Rightarrow Sin^2A = \frac{9}{25}$----(2)

From (1) and (2)

$Sin^2A + SinA + 1$

$= \frac{9}{25} + \frac{3}{5} + 1$

$\therefore \sin^2A + SinA + 1 = \frac{49}{25}$

Hence, the correct option is (B).

14. As we know,

Sum of all three angles of a triangle is $180°$

Ratio of three angles of a triangle $= 2:3:4$

$\Rightarrow 2 + 3 + 4 = 9$ unit

$\Rightarrow 9$ unit $= 180°$

$\Rightarrow 1$ unit $= 20°$

∴ Smallest angle will be:

$\Rightarrow 2$ unit $= 20 \times 2$

$= 40°$

Hence, the correct option is (C).

15. Given:

The ratio of the radius of two cylinders $= 2:3$

The ratio of heights of two cylinders $= 5:3$

We know,

The volume of cylinder $= \pi r^2 h$

Let assume that radius of cylinder $_1 = 2r$

And, the radius of cylinder $_2 = 3r$

Let assume the height of cylinder $_1 = 5h$

And, the height of cylinder $_2 = 3\ h$

The volume of cylinder $_1 = \pi(2r)^2(5h)$

The volume of cylinder $_2 = \pi(3r)^2(3h)$

According to the question:

$\Rightarrow$ The volume of cylinder $_1$: The volume of cylinder $_2$

$\Rightarrow \pi(2r)^2(5h) : \pi(3r)^2(3h)$

$= 20:27$

∴ The volume of cylinder $_1$: The volume of cylinder $_2$ $=$ $20:27$

Hence, the correct option is (D).

16. Given:

Two triangles ABC and PQR are similar to each other in which $AB = 10\ cm, PQ = 8\ cm$.

According to the concept of similarity of triangles:

Ratio of areas of two triangles $=$ Ratio of squares of corresponding sides of triangles

$$\frac{\text{Area of } \Delta ABC}{\text{Area of } \Delta PQR} = \frac{(AB)^2}{(PQ)^2}$$

$$\Rightarrow \frac{\text{Area of } \Delta ABC}{\text{Area of } \Delta PQR} = \frac{(10)^2}{(8)^2}$$

$$\Rightarrow \frac{\text{Area of } \triangle ABC}{\text{Area of } \Delta PQR} = \frac{100}{64}$$

$$\Rightarrow \frac{\text{Area of } \Delta ABC}{\text{Area of } \Delta PQR} = \frac{25}{16}$$

Hence, the correct option is (B).

17. Given:

$\sin\theta = \frac{3}{5}$

In a right-angled triangle

$\sin\theta = \frac{Perpendicular}{Hypotenuse}$

$\tan\theta = \frac{Perpendicular}{Base}$

From Pythagoras theorem,

$H^2 = P^2 + B^2$

Where, H= Hypotenuse, P= Perpendicular, B= Base

$\Rightarrow B^2 = 5^2 - 3^2$

$\Rightarrow B^2 = 25 - 9$

$\Rightarrow B^2 = 16$

$\Rightarrow B = 4$

$\Rightarrow \tan\theta = \frac{3}{4}$

∴ The value of $\tan\theta$ is $\frac{3}{4}$.

Hence, the correct option is (C).

18. Given:

If $x + y = 6$ and $4x + 7y = 36$

According to the question,

$x + y = 6$------(1)

$4x + 7y = 36$------(2)

Multiply by 4 in equation (1)

$\Rightarrow 4x + 4y = 24$------(3)

Subtract equation (2) from equation (3)

$\Rightarrow 4x + 7y - 4x - 4y = 36 - 24$

$\Rightarrow 3y = 12$

$\Rightarrow y = 4$

Putting $y = 4$ in equation (1)

$\Rightarrow x = 6 - 4$

$\Rightarrow x = 2$

∴ The value of x and y is 2 and 4.

Hence, the correct option is (A).

19. Given:

Expression is $12\frac{1}{2} \div 8\frac{1}{3} \times 4 + 6$

By applying the BODMAS rule in expression:

$\frac{25}{2} \div \frac{25}{3} \times 4 + 6$

$= \frac{25}{2} \times \frac{3}{25} \times 4 + 6$

$= \frac{3}{2} \times 4 + 6$

$= 6 + 6 = 12$

∴ The value of $12\frac{1}{2} \div 8\frac{1}{3} \times 4 + 6$ is 12.

Hence, the correct option is (B).

20. Given:

$77 \div 7 \times 4 + \left(\frac{1}{5}\right)$ of $15 \times 4 = ?$

By applying the BODMAS rule in expression:

$\Rightarrow 77 \div 7 \times 4 + 3 \times 4 = ?$

$\Rightarrow 11 \times 4 + 3 \times 4 = ?$

$\Rightarrow 44 + 12 = ?$

Compairing both sides,

$\Rightarrow ? = 56$

∴ The required result will be 56.

Hence, the correct option is (C).

Sectional Test 04

Q.1 Choose the box that is similar to the box formed from the given sheet of paper (X).

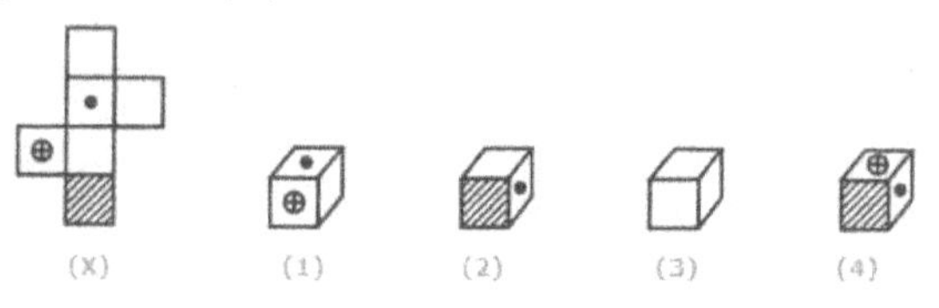

A. (1) only
B. (1) and (3) only
C. (1), (3), and (4) only
D. (1), (2), (3), and (4)

Q.2
Choose the box that is similar to the box formed from the given sheet of paper (X).

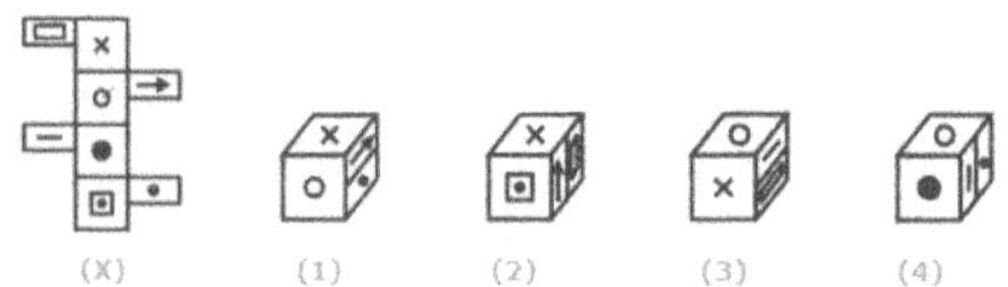

A. (1) and (2) only **B.** (1) and (3) only
C. (3) and (4) only **D.** (1), (2), (3) and (4)

Q.3 In a certain code language, "BANGED" is written as "JJKQCC" and "TILTS" is written as "XXOKU". How is "STRAY" written in that code language?

A. DEUVT **B.** DTEUV **C.** DEUTV **D.** DFTUV

Q.4 If T = 20, MEDIA = 32, then how will you code ELICIT?

A. 57 **B.** 58 **C.** 59 **D.** 60

Ques (5-6): Arrange the words given below in a meaningful sequence.

Q.5 1. Key
2. Door
3. Lock
4. Room
5. Switch on

A. 5, 1, 2, 4, 3 **B.** 4, 2, 1, 5, 3
C. 1, 3, 2, 4, 5 **D.** 1, 2, 3, 5, 4

Q.6 1. Word
2. Paragraph
3. Sentence
4. Letters
5. Phrase

A. 4, 1, 5, 2, 3 **B.** 4, 1, 3, 5, 2
C. 4, 2, 5, 1, 3 **D.** 4, 1, 5, 3, 2

Q.7 By rearranging TUOONRD, what do you get?

[RRB (NTPC), 2017]

A. Name of a river **B.** Name of an animal
C. Name of a flower **D.** Name of a train

Q.8 Rearrange the given letters to form meaningful words and select the option which is different from the other three words.

A. REAYBL **B.** ETWAH
C. EZAMI **D.** SEHCWA

Q.9 If × stands for 'addition', ÷ stands for 'subtraction', + stands for 'multiplication' and-stands for 'division', then 20 × 8 ÷ 8 - 4 + 2 = ?

A. 80 **B.** 25 **C.** 24 **D.** 5

Q.10 Insert the missing number in each of the following :

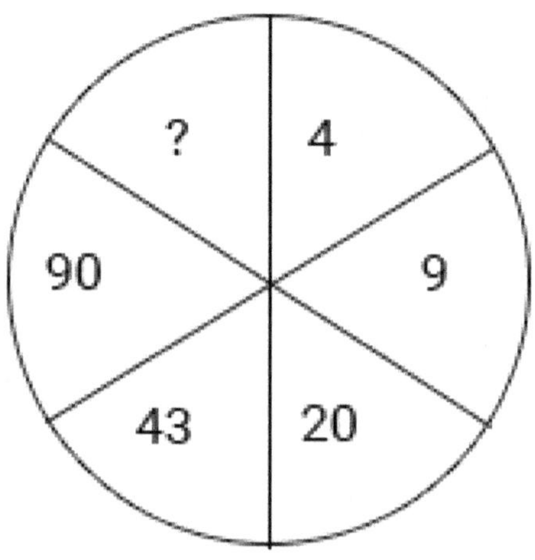

A. 185 **B.** 126 **C.** 239 **D.** 145

// Smart Answer Sheet //

Correct Percentage of students who answered correctly. **Skipped** Percentage of students who skipped.

Q.	Ans.	Correct Skipped	Q.	Ans.	Correct Skipped	Q.	Ans.	Correct Skipped	Q.	Ans.	Correct Skipped	Q.	Ans.	Correct Skipped	Q.	Ans.	Correct Skipped
1	A	23.68 % 0.0 %	3	A	15.79 % 36.84 %	5	C	31.58 % 39.47 %	7	D	21.05 % 36.84 %	9	C	34.21 % 36.84 %			
2	B	26.32 % 36.84 %	4	B	31.58 % 36.84 %	6	D	13.16 % 39.47 %	8	D	5.26 % 36.85 %	10	A	21.05 % 36.84 %			

//Hints and Solutions//

1.

(1)

Figure (X) is similar to Form (1). So, when the sheet shown in figure. (X) is folded to, form a cube, then the face bearing the dot lies opposite to the shaded face, the face bearing a circle (with '+' sign inside it) lies opposite to a blank face and the remaining two blank faces lie opposite to each other. Clearly, the cubes shown in figures (2) and (4) cannot be formed since they have the shaded face adjacent to the face bearing a dot and the cube shown in the figure. (3) cannot be formed since it shows all the three blank faces adjacent to each other. Therefore, only the cube is shown in the figure. (1) can be formed.

Hence, the correct option is (A).

2. By observation and thinking, we get the following two forms,

(1)

(3)

Hence, the correct option is (B).

3. As,

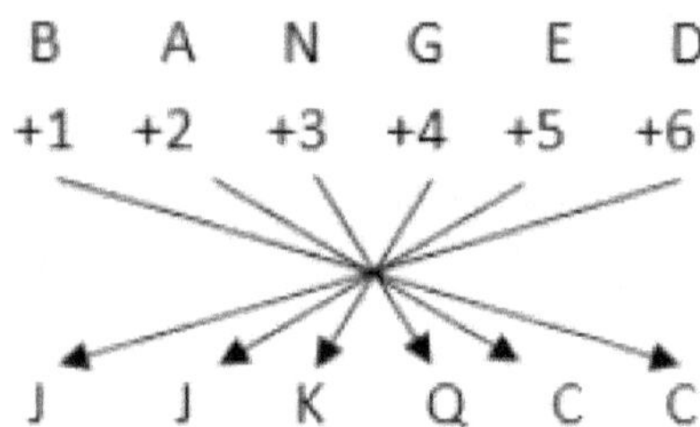

And,

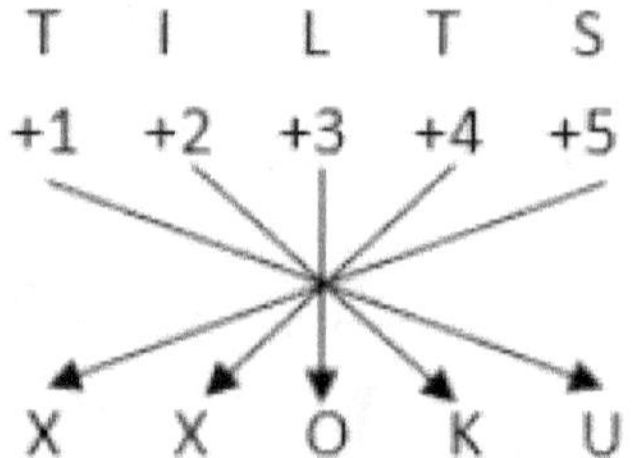

Similarly,

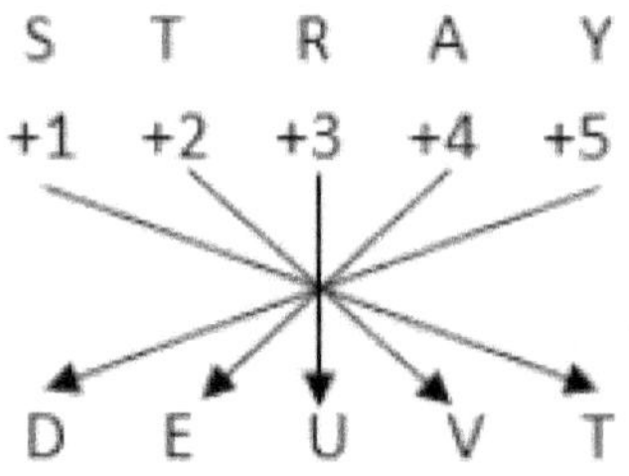

Thus, STRAY is coded as DEUVT.

Hence, the correct option is (A).

4. Here the place value of each letter as per their position in Alphabetical order is taken and then their sum is considered as the number code of respective group of letters.

T = 20,

MEDIA = 13+5+4+9+1 = 32

Similarly,

ELICIT = 5+12+9+3+9+20 = 58

Hence, the correct option is (B).

5. Logically the correct sequence is:

Key - 1

Lock - 3

Door - 2

Room - 4

Switch on - 5

Hence, the correct option is (C).

6. Logically the correct sequence is:

Letters - 4

Word - 1

Phrase - 5

Sentence - 3

Paragraph - 2

Hence, the correct option is (D).

7. After re-arranging the word TUOONRD we get,

DURONTO

Duronto express is a long-distance non-stop source to destination trains run by the Indian Railways.

Hence, the correct option is (D).

8. (A) REAYBL=BARLEY

(B) ETWAH=WHEAT

(C) EZAMI=MAIZE

(D) SEHCWA=CASHEW

Except for CASHEW, all are grain fruit

(D) Cashew is a dry fruit.

Hence, the correct option is (D).

9. Given expression:

20 × 8 ÷ 8 - 4 + 2 = ?

According to the condition given in question for changing signs, the expression is:

20 + 8 - 8 ÷ 4 × 2

= 20 + 8 - 2 × 2

= 20 + 8 - 4 = 24

Hence, the correct option is (C).

10. The pattern followed is:

4 × 2 + 1=9

⇒ 9 × 2 +2 =20

⇒ 20 × 2 +3 =43

⇒ 43 × 2 +4 = 90

⇒ 90× 2 +5= 185

Therefore, the missing number is 185.

Hence, the correct option is (A).

Sectional Test 05

Q.1 In the following question, a matrix of certain characters is given. These characters follow a certain trend, row-wise or column-wise. Find out this trend and choose the missing character accordingly.

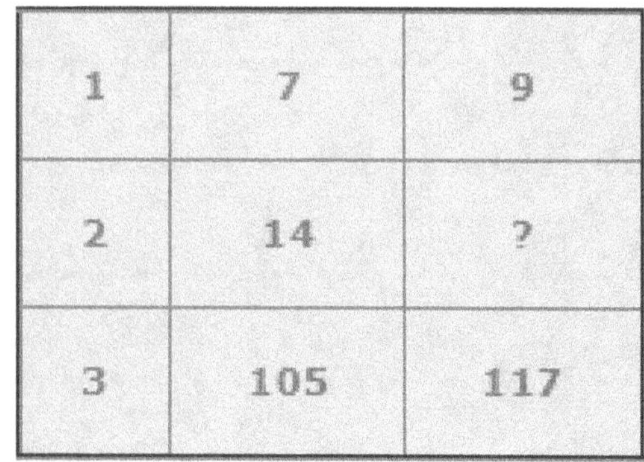

1	7	9
2	14	?
3	105	117

A. 26 **B.** 20 **C.** 16 **D.** 12

Q.2 Given interchanges :

Signs + and - , numbers 4 and 8.

A. 4 + 8 - 12 = 12 **B.** 4 - 8 + 12 = 0
C. 8 + 4 - 12 = 24 **D.** 8 - 4 + 12 = 8

Q.3 From the given alternative words, select the word which CANNOT be formed using the letters of the given word, remember that each letter can be used only once in forming new word.

IMPERIALISM

A. PEARL **B.** MASTER
C. RAMP **D.** REAL

Q.4 In the following question, from the given alternative words, select the word which cannot be formed using the letters of the given word.

Nightwalker

A. Talker **B.** Waller **C.** Tailer **D.** Winer

Ques (5-6): Arrange the words given below in a meaningful sequence.

Q.5 1. Police
2. Punishment
3. Crime
4. Judge
5. Judgement

A. 3, 1, 2, 4, 5 **B.** 1, 2, 4, 3, 5
C. 5, 4, 3, 2, 1 **D.** 3, 1, 4, 5, 2

Q.6 1. Family
2. Community
3. Member
4. Locality
5. Country

A. 3, 1, 2, 4, 5 **B.** 3, 1, 2, 5, 4
C. 3, 1, 4, 2, 5 **D.** 3, 1, 4, 5, 2

Q.7 In a certain code language, "TERMITE" is written as "UDSLJSF". How is "MINISTER" written in that code language?

A. NHOHSTFQ **B.** NHHOTSFQ
C. NHOHTSFQ **D.** NHOHTSQF

Q.8 In a certain code language, "COPIOUS" is written as "2345389" and "GENEROUS" is written as "16760389". How is "PIGEON" written in that code language?

A. 451763 **B.** 451673 **C.** 451637 **D.** 452637

Q.9

How many dots lie opposite to the face having three dots, when the given figure is folded to form a cube?

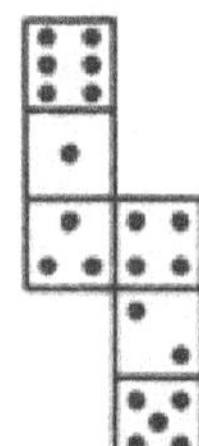

A. 2 **B.** 4 **C.** 5 **D.** 6

Q.10 Choose the box that is similar to the box formed from the given sheet of paper (X).

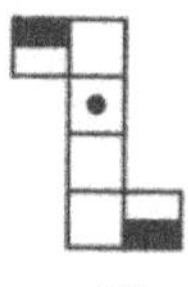

(X) (1) (2) (3) (4)

A. (1) and (2) only **B.** (2) and (3) only
C. (2) and (4) only **D.** (1), (2), (3) and (4)

// Smart Answer Sheet //

Correct — Percentage of students who answered correctly. Skipped — Percentage of students who skipped.

Q.	Ans.	Correct / Skipped	Q.	Ans.	Correct / Skipped	Q.	Ans.	Correct / Skipped	Q.	Ans.	Correct / Skipped	Q.	Ans.	Correct / Skipped	Q.	Ans.	Correct / Skipped
1	D	25.81 % / 0.0 %	3	B	41.94 % / 45.16 %	5	D	35.48 % / 45.17 %	7	C	32.26 % / 45.16 %	9	D	25.81 % / 45.16 %			
2	B	25.81 % / 45.16 %	4	B	41.94 % / 45.16 %	6	A	41.94 % / 45.16 %	8	C	29.03 % / 45.16 %	10	D	3.23 % / 45.16 %			

//Hints and Solutions//

1. According to the matirix given:

In the first column, 2 x 1 + 1 = 3.

In the second column, 14 x 7 + 7 = 105.

Let the missing number in the third column be y.

Then, y x 9 + 9 = 117

Or, 9y = 108

Or, y = 12.

Hence, the correct option is (D).

2. On interchanging + and - and 4 and 8 in (B),

we get the equation as:

8 + 4 - 12 = 0

or 12 - 12 = 0

or 0 = 0, which is true.

By changing the signs in other options we dont get the required solution.

Hence, the correct option is (B).

3. 'MASTER' is the word that cannot be formed as there is no 'T' in the given word. All other words can be formed from the word given.

Hence, the correct option is (B).

4. Since there is only a single 'l' involved in 'Nightwalker' so 'Waller' can't be formed.

Hence, the correct option is (B).

5. Logically the correct sequence is:

Crime - 3

Police - 1

Judge - 4

Judgement - 5

Punishment - 2

Hence, the correct option is (D).

6. Logically the correct sequence is:

Member - 3

Family - 1

Community - 2

Locality - 4

Country - 5

Hence, the correct option is (A).

7. There are 26 alphabets in English and if we assign numbers to each and every alphabet starting from 'A', 'B', 'C etc., it will appear to be:

A = 1, B = 2, C = 3, D = 4....... likewise, till Z = 26

And, the code is like:

T + 1 = U

⇒ E – 1 = D

⇒ R + 1 = S

⇒ M – 1 = L

⇒ I + 1 = J

⇒ T – 1 = S

⇒ E + 1 = F

Likewise,

M + 1 = N

⇒ I – 1 = H

⇒ N + 1 = O

⇒ I – 1 = H

⇒ S + 1 = T

⇒ T – 1 = S

⇒ E + 1 = F

⇒ R – 1 = Q

Hence, the correct option is (C).

8. Code for the word 'COPIOUS' is:

C-2, O-3, P-4, I-5, O-3, U-8, S-9

And,

'GENEROUS' is:

G-1, E-6, N-7, E-6, R-0, O-3, U-8, S-9

Similarly,

'PIGEON' is coded as:

P-4, I-5, G-1, E-6, O-3, N-7

Therefore, the correct code is: 451637

Hence, the correct option is (C).

9. By observation and thinking, we get,

When this figure is folded to form a cube then the face bearing six dots will lie opposite the face bearing three dots.

Hence, the correct option is (D).

10. By observation and thinking we get that,

When a cube is formed by folding the sheet shown in fig. (X), the two half-shaded faces lie opposite to each other and one of the three blank faces appears opposite to the face bearing a dot.

Clearly, each one of the four cubes shown in figures (1), (2), (3) and (4) can be formed by folding the sheet shown in fig. (X).

Hence, the correct option is (D).

Sectional Test 06

Q.1 The six faces of dice have been marked with alphabets A, B, C, D, E, and F respectively. This dice is rolled down three times. The three positions are shown as:

(i)

(ii)

(iii)

Find the alphabet opposite A.

A. C **B.** D **C.** E **D.** F

Q.2 A dice is thrown four times and its four different positions are shown below. Find the number on the face opposite the face showing 2.

(i)

(ii)

(iii)

(iv)

A. 3 **B.** 4 **C.** 5 **D.** 6

Q.3 In the following question, select the word which cannot be formed using the letters of the given word.

PREMONITION

A. PROMINENT **B.** NONMETRO
C. IMPOTENT **D.** NOONTIME

Q.4 In the following question, select the word which cannot be formed using the letters of the given word.

FRAGRANCE

A. GRATE **B.** RANGE **C.** GEAR **D.** EAR

Ques (5-6): Arrange the words given below in a meaningful sequence.

Q.5 1. Leaf
2. Fruit
3. Stem
4. Root
5. Flower

A. 3, 4, 5, 1, 2 **B.** 4, 3, 1, 5, 2
C. 4, 1, 3, 5, 2 **D.** 4, 3, 1, 2, 5

Q.6 1. Nation
2. Village
3. City
4. District
5. State

A. 2, 3, 4, 5, 1 **B.** 2, 3, 4, 1, 5
C. 1, 3, 5, 4, 2 **D.** 1, 2, 3, 4, 5

Q.7 What is the value of P in the following Equation?

$19^{2.5} \times 19^{P} = 19^{7}$

A. 3.9 **B.** 4.1 **C.** 3.7 **D.** 4.5

Q.8 Find the missing number:

13	54	?
7	45	32
27	144	68

A. 42 **B.** 4 **C.** 6 **D.** 36

Q.9 In a certain code language, "SATURN" is written as "JVQXWW" and "URANUS" is written as "OYJENY". How is "JUITER" written in that code language?

A. NIPMQN **B.** NIPMYF
C. NQMPIN **D.** FYLMPI

Q.10 If 'GWEOS' is codded as 'SCUKG', then 'RBETP' will be codded as –

A. HXUFJ **B.** TWQJL **C.** OECYA **D.** ISQMV

// Smart Answer Sheet //

Correct — Percentage of students who answered correctly. Skipped — Percentage of students who skipped.

Q.	Ans.	Correct / Skipped	Q.	Ans.	Correct / Skipped	Q.	Ans.	Correct / Skipped	Q.	Ans.	Correct / Skipped	Q.	Ans.	Correct / Skipped	Q.	Ans.	Correct / Skipped
1	C	50.55 % / 1.41 %	3	C	45.66 % / 1.31 %	5	B	77.94 % / 0.0 %	7	D	60.67 % / 1.25 %	9	A	77.83 % / 0.0 %			
2	C	84.01 % / 0.0 %	4	A	20.42 % / 3.99 %	6	A	56.8 % / 1.9 %	8	B	40.4 % / 1.96 %	10	A	24.7 % / 4.54 %			

//Hints and Solutions//

1. From figures (ii) and (iii), we conclude that the alphabets C, D, B and F appear adjacent to the alphabet E.

Therefore, the alphabet A appears opposite E. Conversely, E appears opposite A.

Hence, the correct option is (C).

2. From figures (i), (ii) and (iv) We conclude that 6, 4, 3 and 1 lie adjacent to 2.

Thus, 5 must lie opposite 2.

Hence, the correct option is (C).

3. IMPOTENT - Can not be made from the word PREMONITION as there is only 1 'T' in the given word.

PROMINENT - Can be made from the word PREMONITION.

NONMETRO - Can be made from the word PREMONITION.

NOONTIME - Can be made from the word PREMONITION.

Hence, the correct option is (C).

4. Letter 'T' is used in option (A) but it is not present in the original word FRAGRANCE. Thus we cannot form the word GRATE.

Hence, the correct option is (A).

5. Logically the correct sequence is:

Root - 4

Stem - 3

Leaf - 1

Flower - 5

Fruit - 2

Hence, the correct option is (B).

6. Logically the correct sequence is:

Village - 2

City - 3

District - 4

State - 5

Nation - 1

Hence, the correct option is (A).

7. Given equation is:

$$19^{2.5} \times 19^{p} = 19^{7}$$

Here it is in the form of $a^m \times a^n = a^{m+n}$

Here $m = 2.5, n = p, m + n = 7$

$\Rightarrow 2.5 + p = 7$

$\Rightarrow p = 7 - 2.5$

$\Rightarrow p = 4.5$

Hence, the correct option is (B).

8. According to the given matrix:

In the first column,

27- 7×2 = 13

In the second column,

144 - 45×2 = 54

So,

in the third column,

68 -32×2 = 4

Hence, the correct option is (B).

9. As,

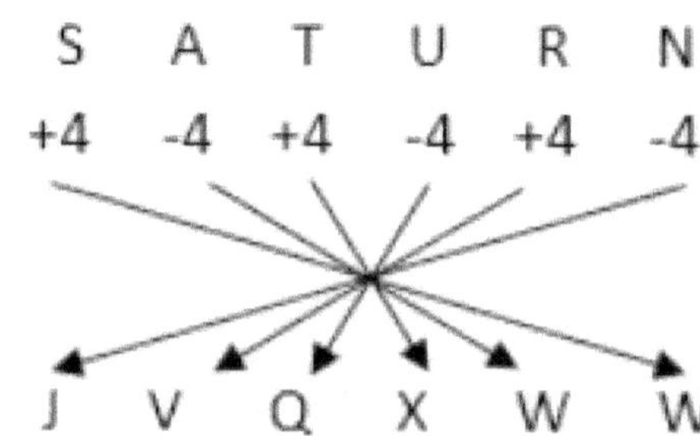

And,

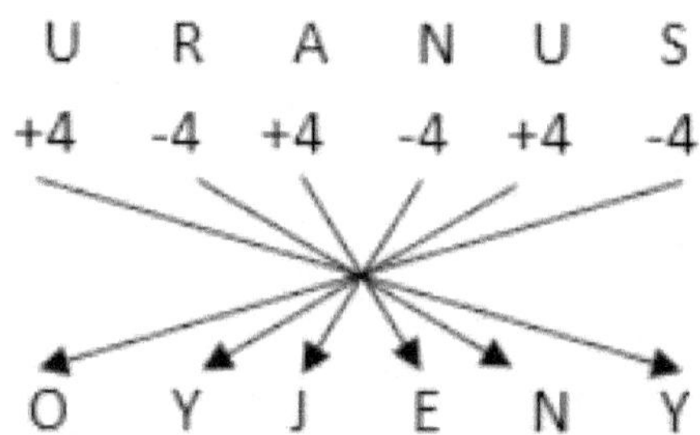

Similarly,

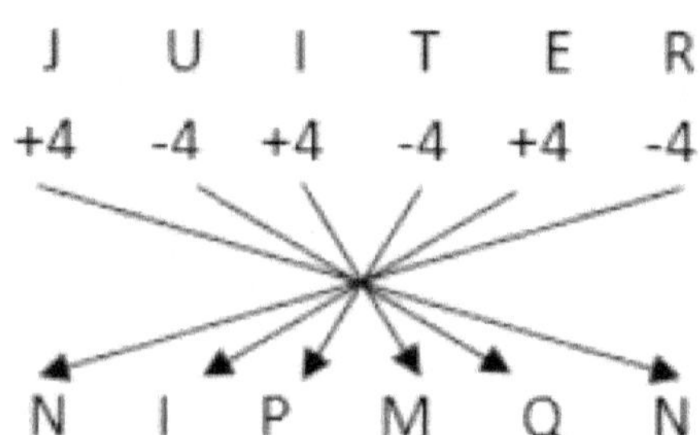

Thus, JUITER is coded as NIPMQN.

Hence, the correct option is (A).

10. Given: 'GWEOS' → 'SCUKG'

26 letters available in English alphabet.

G →S

G is 7th letter in English alphabet, 26-7 = 19, S is 19th letter in English alphabet.

W →C

W is 23th letter in English alphabet, 26-23 = 3, C is 3rd letter in English alphabet.

E →U

E is 5th letter in English alphabet, 26-5 = 21, U is 21th letter in English alphabet.

O →K

O is 15th letter in English alphabet, 26-15 = 11, K is 11th letter in English alphabet.

S →G

S is 19th letter in English alphabet, 26-19 = 7, G is 7th letter in English alphabet.

By the same formula, RBETP ' will be codded as 'HXUFJ'.

Hence, the correct option is (A).

Sectional Test 07

Q.1 Passengers sitting in a stationary car experience a jerk when the car suddenly starts. This is due to ____.

A. Inertia of motion
B. Inertia of rest
C. Inertia of turning
D. Inertia of acceleration

Q.2 If a body is moving in such a way that force acting on it is uniform and perpendicular to the motion of the body, then ________.

A. Only speed will change
B. Speed and direction of the body will change
C. The velocity of the body does not change
D. Speed remains the same, but direction changes

Q.3 In the atmosphere, highest amount of ozone gas is present in:

A. Troposphere **B.** Mesosphere
C. Stratosphere **D.** Thermosphere

Q.4 Gravitational force:

A. Allows us to be in controlled motion
B. Is a dissipative force
C. Strong force
D. None of the above

Q.5 The Work Done by the Centripetal Force for a Body Moving in a Circular Path is ________.

A. Negative **B.** Zero **C.** Constant **D.** Positive

Q.6 Suresh purchases a table lamp for study. The table lamp consumes 960 J of electrical energy in 16s. What is its power?

A. 60W **B.** 45W **C.** 50W **D.** 48W

Q.7 Which planet has the largest number of natural satellites or moons?

A. Jupiter **B.** Mars **C.** Saturn **D.** Venus

Q.8 Which of the following is a conductor?

A. Sugar solution **B.** Plastic, PVC
C. Salt solution **D.** Mica

Q.9 A molecule of Ammonia (NH_3) has:

A. Only single bonds
B. Only double bonds
C. Only triple bonds
D. Two double bonds and one single bond

Q.10 In which of the following, 14 U, will be the differences in the Molecular Formulae and Molecular Masses:

A. CH_3OH and C_2H_5OH
B. C_2H_5OH and C_3H_7OH
C. C_3H_7OH and C_4H_9OH
D. All of the above

// Smart Answer Sheet //

Correct — Percentage of students who answered correctly. Skipped — Percentage of students who skipped.

Q.	Ans.	Correct / Skipped	Q.	Ans.	Correct / Skipped	Q.	Ans.	Correct / Skipped	Q.	Ans.	Correct / Skipped	Q.	Ans.	Correct / Skipped	Q.	Ans.	Correct / Skipped
1	B	37.5 % / 0.0 %	3	C	33.33 % / 33.34 %	5	B	39.58 % / 33.34 %	7	C	37.5 % / 33.33 %	9	A	31.25 % / 33.33 %			
2	D	35.42 % / 33.33 %	4	A	35.42 % / 33.33 %	6	A	54.17 % / 33.33 %	8	C	54.17 % / 33.33 %	10	D	35.42 % / 33.33 %			

//Hints and Solutions//

1. When the car starts, the people sitting in it experience a jerk. This is because, while the car was stationary, the people were stationary with it. Hence, they were having an inertia of rest. When the car starts, the inertia of the car changes from that of rest to that of motion. But the inertia of the people still remains that of rest. Hence, they experience a jerk.

Hence, the correct option is (B).

2. Given that-

Applied force is uniform and perpendicular to the motion.

From the definition of the centripetal force, if a force is perpendicular to the motion, it is a centripetal force and this force makes the body move in a circular motion.

We know F = $\frac{mv^2}{r}$

Since F is uniform, so v will also be uniform. So speed (magnitude of velocity) will not change.

In a circular motion, a body moves in a circle, and in a circle the direction of motion changes at every point.

At point A, the direction of the velocity is in the upward direction.

At point B, the direction of the velocity is in the leftward direction,

At point C, the direction of the velocity is in the downward direction.

The body comes in the initial direction after one complete circle.

So If the force on a moving body is always uniform and perpendicular to its motion, then Speed remains the same, but direction changes.

Hence, the correct option is (D).

3. In the atmosphere, the highest amount of ozone gas is present in the stratosphere. Ozone layer thickness is measured in Dobson units. Ozone is an O_3 molecule. The ozone layer is present mostly in the Stratosphere and partially in the Troposphere.

Hence, the correct option is (C).

4. Gravitational force is responsible of objects falling back on Earth, revolution of Earth around Sun and Moon around Earth. It allows everything in the Universe to be in controlled motion.

Gravity is not a dissipative force since no energy is lost from a system when motion takes place. Further it is also very weak force.

Hence, the correct option is (A).

5. For a body that moves in a circular path, the displacement and the centripetal force are perpendicular to each other. Thus, the work done or accomplished by the centripetal force is zero.

Hence, the correct option is (B).

6. Power – It is defined as the rate of doing work.

$$\therefore P = \frac{W}{t}$$

Where, P = power, W = work done, and t = time

Now,

Time = 16s

Work done = Energy consumed by the lamp = 960 J

Power = $\frac{960}{16}$

= 60 Js-1

= 60W

Hence, the correct option is (A).

7. Saturn has the largest number of natural satellites or moons. It has 82 natural satellites with known orbits. Saturn is the second-largest in the Solar System, after Jupiter. It is a gas giant with an average radius of about nine and a half times that of Earth.

Hence, the correct option is (C).

8. The salt solution is a conductor. Materials that conduct electrical current easily are called conductors. Conductors have a low resistivity. Among the options, only the salt solution is a conductor. Salt solution consists of sodium ions (Na+) and chlorine(Cl-) ions. The flow of ions to the opposite ends of the electrodes allows electric current to flow through the salt solution. Conduction of electricity happens in a substance only if it contains charged particles (electrons/ions) that are free to move around. Silver is the best conductor of electricity.

Hence, the correct option is (C).

9. A molecule of ammonia (NH_3) has only single bonds and these are covalent bonds.

Atomic number of N is 7. Its electronic configuration is 2, 5 so it needs 3 more electrons to complete its "Octet". It gains 3 electrons each from 3 hydrogen atoms. Also, N has one lone pair of electrons. The pair of electrons on the nitrogen atom in NH_3 molecule which is not involved in bond formation is called lone pair.

Hence, the correct option is (A).

10. Here, 14 U, will be the differences in the molecular formulae and molecular masses in all these statements.

You can easily understand by this:

In option (A): The difference in the molecular formulae of CH_3OH and C_2H_5OH is CH_2. The difference in the molecular masses of CH_3OH and C_2H_5OH is 46 – 32 = 14 U.

In option (B): The difference in the molecular formulae of C_2H_5OH and C_3H_7OH is CH_2. And the difference in the molecular masses of C_2H_5OH and C_3H_7OH is 60 – 46 = 14 U.

In option (C): The difference in the molecular formulae of C_3H_7OH and C_4H_9OH is CH_2. And the difference in the molecular masses of C_3H_7OH and C_4H_9OH is 74 – 60 = 14 U.

Hence, the correct option is (D).

Sectional Test 08

Q.1 The work done by the force of friction on a body sliding on a rough horizontal surface will be-

A. Positive **B.** Negative **C.** Zero **D.** Constant

Q.2 After full moon day, the size of the visible part of the moon appears to become thinner and thinner every night, On the fifteenth day, the moon is not visible. This day is known as the:

A. New moon day **B.** Moon day
C. Full moon day **D.** Half-moon day

Q.3 The atmosphere is held on the earth by _____.

A. Gravity **B.** The sun
C. Clouds **D.** None of the above

Q.4 If the velocity of the moving body is doubled (m remaining constant), then the kinetic energy of the body increases by how many times?

A. Increases by 4 times **B.** Increases by 6 times
C. Becomes one-fourth **D.** Remains constant

Q.5 Henry is the unit of:

A. Capacitance **B.** Resistance
C. Inductance **D.** Reactance

Q.6 On which principle is the wire used in an electric circuit?

A. Electromagnetic induction
B. Tensile wire
C. Electromagnetic effect
D. Thermal effect of electricity

Q.7 The coil of wire used in electric heaters is called a/an_______.

A. Filament **B.** Cell **C.** Battery **D.** Element

Q.8 Elements on the right side of the Periodic Table are ____.

A. Metals **B.** Transition Metals
C. Semi Metals **D.** Non Metals

Q.9 Identify the Unsaturated Compounds from the following:

A. Propane, Propene
B. Propene, Chloropropane
C. Propyne, Chloropropane
D. Propene, Propyne

Q.10 The total number of nucleons in the nucleus is called ________.

A. Atomic number **B.** Electric charge
C. Mass number **D.** Periodic number

// Smart Answer Sheet //

Correct Percentage of students who answered correctly. **Skipped** Percentage of students who skipped.

Q.	Ans.	Correct	Skipped	Q.	Ans.	Correct	Skipped	Q.	Ans.	Correct	Skipped	Q.	Ans.	Correct	Skipped	Q.	Ans.	Correct	Skipped	Q.	Ans.	Correct	Skipped
1	B	47.5 %	0.0 %	3	A	62.5 %	25.0 %	5	C	57.5 %	27.5 %	7	D	42.5 %	25.0 %	9	D	45.0 %	25.0 %				
2	A	57.5 %	25.0 %	4	A	65.0 %	25.0 %	6	D	45.0 %	25.0 %	8	D	42.5 %	25.0 %	10	C	32.5 %	25.0 %				

//Hints and Solutions//

1. The work done by the force of friction on a body sliding on a rough horizontal surface will be negative. When a body is sliding on a rough horizontal surface, the force of friction acts in the direction opposite to the direction of motion. Hence, force and displacement are in opposite directions. Therefore, work done by the force of friction on a body sliding on a rough surface is negative.

Hence, the correct option is (B).

2. Every night after the full moon day, the size of the visible part of the moon becomes thinner. It takes a period of 15 days for the moon to become completely invisible. This day is called new moon day.

Hence, the correct option is (A).

3. The earth, because of gravity, pulls all objects into itself. In reality, the air around our planet is kept around by gravity, and the envelope of air around the planet is called the atmosphere. The atmosphere can not be protected by air, clouds, or earth magnetic fields unless and until there is an irresistible force against the surface and that force is the only force of gravitation.

Hence, the correct option is (A).

4. The kinetic energy of an object is defined as the energy that it possesses due to its motion. Thus, an object that has motion possesses kinetic energy. The amount of kinetic energy that an object has depends upon two variables i.e. the mass (m) of the object and the speed (v) of the object. If the velocity of the moving body is doubled, then the kinetic energy becomes 4 times.

This is because the kinetic energy of a body is directly proportional to the square of its velocity when the mass of the body is kept constant.

Hence, the correct option is (A).

5. Henry is the unit of inductance. The henry (symbol: H) is the SI-derived unit of electrical inductance. The henry is named in honor of Joseph Henry (1797-1878) an American physicist who discovered electromagnetic induction. Inductance is the tendency of an electrical conductor to oppose a change in the electric current flowing through it.

Hence, the correct option is (C).

6. When the electric current is passed through a conductor, it generates heat energy due to the electric resistance it offers to the flow of the electric current. The work done in overcoming the resistance is converted to heat.

Applications of the heating effect of electric current include appliances like an electric immersion water heater, electric iron box, Fuse, Fluorescent Tube Light, etc.

Heating elements are generally made of specific alloys like nichrome, manganin, constantan etc.

A good heating element has high resistivity and a high melting point.

Hence, the correct option is (D).

7. An electric room heater or an electric heater used for cooking contains a coil of wire. The coil of wire used in electric heaters is called an element. The heating coil of the electric room heater transfers the electric energy into heat energy. The elements become red hot and give out heat after connecting to the electric supply. The amount of heat produced in a wire depends on its material used, length, and thickness. The coil of the electric heater is made up of nichrome. Nichrome consists of 80% nickel, 20% chromium.

Hence, the correct option is (D).

8. Elements on the right side of the Periodic Table are non metals. A periodic table is an arrangement of elements based on their atomic numbers and chemical properties. It is divided into 18 groups and 7 periods running vertically and horizontally respectively. The periodic table accommodates a discrete combination of metal, non-metals, and metalloids.

Metals- These elements have a tendency to lose one or more electrons to attain a stable electronic configuration. These are placed towards the left side of the periodic table. For example, Sodium (Na), Calcium (Ca), Potassium (K), etc.

Non Metals- These elements have a tendency to gain one or more electrons to attain a stable electronic configuration. These are placed towards the right side of the periodic table. For example, Oxygen (O), Nitrogen (N), Chlorine (Cl), etc.

Metalloids- These elements are characterized by having intermediate properties of metals and non-metal. These are placed towards the middle of the periodic table.

For example, Boron (B), Silicon (Si), Germanium (Ge), etc.

Hence, the correct option is (D).

9. A hydrocarbon in which the two carbon atoms are connected by a "double bond" or a "triple Bond" is called an unsaturated hydrocarbon. Propene, $CH_3CH = CH_2$ and Propyne $CH_3-C \equiv CH$ both have double and triple bonds, respectively hence unsaturated. Propane and chloropropane are saturated hydrocarbons which contain only single bonds.

Hence, the correct option is (D).

10. The mass number (A), also called atomic mass number or nucleon number, is the total number of protons and neutrons (together known as nucleons) in an atomic nucleus. The mass number is different for each different isotope of a chemical element. This is not the same as the atomic number (Z) which denotes the number of protons in a nucleus, and thus uniquely identifies an element. Hence, the difference between the mass number and the atomic number gives the number of neutrons (N) in a given nucleus: N=A−Z.

Hence, the correct option is (C).

Sectional Test 09

Q.1 The smell of perfume spreads out by a process known as:

A. Evaporation **B.** Diffusion
C. Condensation **D.** Fusion

Q.2 Which planet in the Solar System has the highest density?

A. Earth **B.** Uranus **C.** Neptune **D.** Jupiter

Q.3 The rate of flow of electric charges is known as:

A. Electric potential
B. Electric conductance
C. Electric current
D. None of the above

Q.4 A boy is whirling a stone tied with a string in a horizontal circular path. If the string breaks, the stone:

A. Will continue to move in the circular path
B. Will move along a straight line towards the center of the circular path
C. Will move along a straight line tangential to the circular path
D. Will move along a straight line perpendicular to the circular path away from the boy

Q.5 Let two bodies be with masses 2kg and 5kg respectively. Let these bodies be at rest with the same force acting on them. Calculate the ratio of times that is required by both the bodies to reach the final velocity.

A. 25:4 **B.** 5:3
C. 2:5 **D.** None of these

Q.6 Calculate the energy loss in a perfectly inelastic collision if the mass of the object is 40kg with velocity 4m/s hits the object of mass 60kg with velocity 2m/s.

A. 440 J **B.** 110 J **C.** 392 J **D.** 48 J

Q.7 Which of the following represents Saponification reaction?

A. $CH_3COONa + NaOH + CaO \rightarrow CH_4 + Na_2CO_3$
B. $CH_3COOH + C_2H_5OH + H_2SO_4 \rightarrow$ CH3COOC2H5 $+ H_2O$
C. $2CH_3COOH + 2Na \rightarrow 2CH_3COONa + H_2$
D. $CH_3COOC_2H_5 + NaOH \rightarrow CH_3COONa + C_2H_5OH$

Q.8 The process of change of state from solid to liquid is called:

A. Melting **B.** Freezing
C. Boiling **D.** Condensation

Q.9 A key of a mechanical piano struck gently and then struck again but much harder this time. In the second case:

A. Sound will be louder but the pitch will not be different
B. Sound will be louder and the pitch will also be higher
C. Sound will be louder but the pitch will be lower
D. Both loudness and pitch will remain unaffected

Q.10 Which one among the following most correctly determines the atomic number of an element?

A. Number of protons
B. Number of protons and electrons
C. Number of ions
D. Number of nucleons

// Smart Answer Sheet //

Correct — Percentage of students who answered correctly. Skipped — Percentage of students who skipped.

Q.	Ans.	Correct Skipped	Q.	Ans.	Correct Skipped	Q.	Ans.	Correct Skipped	Q.	Ans.	Correct Skipped	Q.	Ans.	Correct Skipped	Q.	Ans.	Correct Skipped
1	B	54.55 % 0.0 %	3	C	57.58 % 24.24 %	5	C	33.33 % 24.25 %	7	D	45.45 % 24.25 %	9	A	42.42 % 24.25 %			
2	A	39.39 % 24.25 %	4	C	60.61 % 24.24 %	6	D	24.24 % 24.24 %	8	A	60.61 % 24.24 %	10	A	51.52 % 24.24 %			

//Hints and Solutions//

1. Diffusion is the tendency of gas molecules to occupy the entire volume available to them. In other words, we can say it's the mixing of two substances on their own. The molecules of perfume diffuse with air and reach us with the movement of air particles.

Hence, the correct option is (B).

2. Earth has the highest density of any planet in the Solar System, at 5.514 g/cm^3. This is considered the standard by which other planet's densities are measured. In addition, the combination of Earth's size, mass, and density also results in a surface gravity of 9.8 m/s^2.

Hence, the correct option is (A).

3. The rate of flow of charge is electric current. An ampere is the flow of one coulomb through an area in one second. Electric current is defined as the rate of flow of electric charges. Electric current I= $\frac{q}{t}$ A, where q is the amount of charge that flows in time t.

Hence, the correct option is (C).

4. When the boy is whirling a stone which is tied with a string covering a circular path, then the centripetal force starts acting towards the center of the circular path. According to the question, while writing the stone the string breaks. The moment the string breaks the centripetal force acting towards the center ceases and hence no force acts on the system. So by Newton's first law of motion, the stone will continue in a straight line and will fly off along the tangent of the circular path.

Hence, the correct option is (C).

5. Given,

Let two bodies be with masses 2kg and 5kg respectively. Let these bodies be at rest with the same force acting on them.

Force (1) = $\frac{F}{2}$

Force (2) = $\frac{F}{5}$

Applying formula:

v = u + at

Finding the ratio for both the forces:

$\Rightarrow v_1 = \frac{F}{2} \times T_1$

$\Rightarrow v_2 = \frac{F}{5} \times T_2$

Using above values:

$\Rightarrow \frac{F}{2} \times T_1 = \frac{F}{5} \times T_2$

$\Rightarrow v_1 : v_2$

$\Rightarrow 2 : 5$

Hence, the correct option is (C).

6. The collision is inelastic implies both masses clump together to one ie the total mass after the collision is $(40 + 60) = 100 \text{ kg}$.

According to conservation of momentum applied to both the bodies under collision the equation is:

$$= 40 \times 4 + 60 \times 2 = 100 \times \text{v}$$

$$= 280 = 100 \text{ v}$$

$$= \text{v} = \frac{280}{100}$$

$$= 2.8 \text{ m/s}$$

So, the energy before collision is:

Using formula,

$$KE = \frac{1}{2} m_1 v_1^2 + \frac{1}{2} m_2 {v_2}^2 = \text{joules}$$

$$= \left(\frac{1}{2}\right) 40 \times 4^2 + \left(\frac{1}{2}\right) 60 \times 2^2 = 320 + 120$$

$$= 440J$$

But energy after collision $= \left(\frac{1}{2}\right) 100 \times 2.8^2$

$$= 392J$$

So, energy loss:

$$= 440 - 392$$

$= 48$ J

Hence, the correct option is (D).

7. In saponification reaction, when an ester is heated with sodium hydroxide solution, ester gets hydrolysed (breaks down) to form the parent alcohol and sodium salt of carboxylic acid.

$CH_3COOC_2H_5 + NaOH \rightarrow CH_3COONa + C_2H_5OH$

Hence, the correct option is (D).

8. The process of a solid becoming a liquid is called melting. Melting is a physical process that results in the phase transition of a substance from a solid to a liquid.

Hence, the correct option is (A).

9. Any sound wave pitch depends on the frequency of the wave. When the mechanical piano is struck harder the second time, we find sound will be louder but the pitch remains the same because the frequency has not changed. The pitch depends on the frequency of the particular key which is being hit and hence there would be no change in the pitch of the sound. Loudness depends on amplitude which will be more if the key is struck harder.

Hence, the correct option is (A).

10. The atomic number or proton number (symbol Z) of a chemical element is the number of protons found in the nucleus of every atom of that element. The atomic number uniquely identifies a chemical element. It is identical to the charge number of the nucleus. In an uncharged atom, the atomic number is also equal to the number of electrons.

Hence, the correct option is (A).

Sectional Test 10

Q.1 Which country has signed a $ 2.25 billion deal with a Russian state-run nuclear energy company 'ASE' in August 2022?

[RBI Assistant, 2020], [UPSSSC Rajasva Lekhpal, 2015]

A. India **B.** China
C. Japan **D.** South Korea

Q.2 Jakarta is the capital of which country?

A. Malaysia **B.** Indonesia
C. Thailand **D.** Mauritius

Q.3 Which ruler had promoted 'Din-i-Ilahi'?

A. Babur **B.** Akbar
C. Aurangzeb **D.** Shah Jahan

Q.4 Elephant festival is celebrated annually in which Indian city?

A. Bhopal **B.** Kota **C.** Jaipur **D.** Udiapur

Q.5 Vinesh Phogat is a great Indian______.

A. Sumo Wrestler **B.** Wrestler
C. Boxer **D.** Runners

// Smart Answer Sheet //

Correct — Percentage of students who answered correctly. Skipped — Percentage of students who skipped.

Q.	Ans.	Correct / Skipped	Q.	Ans.	Correct / Skipped	Q.	Ans.	Correct / Skipped	Q.	Ans.	Correct / Skipped	Q.	Ans.	Correct / Skipped	Q.	Ans.	Correct / Skipped
1	D	78.6 % 0.0 %	2	B	56.44 % 1.85 %	3	B	16.38 % 4.03 %	4	C	69.76 % 1.25 %	5	B	62.64 % 1.59 %			

//Hints and Solutions//

1. South Korea has signed a $ 2.25 billion deal with a Russian state-run nuclear energy company 'ASE'in August 2022.

- It has been signed to provide components for Egypt's first nuclear power plant.
- ASE is a subsidiary of Rosatom, a state-owned Russian nuclear conglomerate.
- South Korea has also signed a $ 20 billion contract to build nuclear power reactors in the UAE.

Hence, the correct option is (D).

2. Jakarta is the capital of Indonesia.

Indonesia, country located off the coast of mainland Southeast Asia in the Indian and Pacific oceans.

It is an archipelago that lies across the Equator and spans a distance equivalent to one-eighth of Earth's circumference.

Hence, the correct option is (B).

3. A new religion called Din-i-Ilahi (Divine faith in one God) was promulgated by Akbar in 1582.

Only 15 followers joined this new religion including Birbal.

The good points of all the religions were included in Din-i-Ilahi. The basic purpose was to bridge the gap between all religions.

Hence, the correct option is (B).

4. Elephant Festival is a festival celebrated in Jaipur city in Rajasthan. It is held on the day of Holi festival, usually in the month of March. For this festival, elephants are nicely groomed and clothed and decorated with heavy ornaments.

Hence, the correct option is (C).

5. Vinesh Phogat is an Indian wrestler.

She became the first Indian woman wrestler to win Gold in both Commonwealth and Asian games (2018).

She was awarded the Arjuna Award in 2016 and Rajiv Gandhi Khel Ratna Award in 2020.

Hence, the correct option is (B).

Sectional Test 11

Q.1 Who has been crowned Miss Universe 2021?

A. Roshanara Ebrahim
B. Noa Kochba
C. Harnaaz Sandhu
D. Nandita Banna

Q.2 Which river is known as 'Dakshin Ganga'?

A. Krishna
B. Mahanadi
C. Godavari
D. Cauvery

Q.3 Which of the following mountain are formed when the great blocks of the earth's crust may be raised of lowered?

A. Fold Mountains
B. Block Mountains
C. Volcanic Mountains
D. Dissected mountains

Q.4 The two natural harbours in India are ________.

A. Mumbai and Kochi
B. Chennai and Paradip
C. Kolkata and Vishakhapatnam
D. Kandla and New Mangalore

Q.5 Which of the following coastal plain is located between the Sahyadri and the Arabian Sea?

A. Gujarat Coastal Plain
B. West Coastal Plain
C. Karnataka Coastal Plain
D. East Coastal Plain

// Smart Answer Sheet //

Correct Percentage of students who answered correctly. Skipped Percentage of students who skipped.

Q.	Ans.	Correct / Skipped	Q.	Ans.	Correct / Skipped	Q.	Ans.	Correct / Skipped	Q.	Ans.	Correct / Skipped	Q.	Ans.	Correct / Skipped	Q.	Ans.	Correct / Skipped
1	C	26.48 % 3.83 %	2	C	48.86 % 1.08 %	3	B	47.01 % 1.45 %	4	A	26.79 % 3.66 %	5	B	67.88 % 1.69 %			

//Hints and Solutions//

1. India's Harnaaz Sandhu, hailing from Chandigarh, has been crowned Miss Universe 2021, two decades after Lara Dutta won the title in 2000.

She beat contestants from Paraguay and South Africa.

She was crowned at the contest held in Eilat, Israel on 13 December 2021.

India had earlier won the coveted crown twice with Sushmita Sen bagging the title in 1994 and Lara Dutta in 2000.

Hence, the correct option is (C).

2. Godavari river is known as the Ganga of South India or 'Dakshin Ganga' because it is the largest river of South India, similarly to Ganga in northern India. It is 1465 km long that makes it the second-largest river of India after Ganga (2525km). Its origin is in Triyambakeswar Maharashtra and merge in the Bay of Bengal after flowing from many states of South India.

Hence, the correct option is (C).

3. Block Mountains are formed when the great blocks of the earth's crust may be raised or lowered during the stages of mountains building. Block Mountains are formed as the result of damage caused by the tensile and compressive forces caused by endogenous forces from the Earth's interior, also known as fault-block mountains.

Hence, the correct option is (B).

4. Mumbai is a natural harbour on the west coast and is also the biggest port of India.

Kochi in Kerala is a natural harbour. It handles the export of tea, coffee and spices and imports of petroleum oil and fertilisers.

Hence, the correct option is (A).

5. West Coastal Plain is located between the Sahyadri and the Arabian Sea. It is mainly characterised by sandy beaches, coastal sand dunes, mud flats, lagoons, alluvial tracts along rivers, estuary, laterite platforms and residual hills.

Hence, the correct option is (B).

Sectional Test 12

Q.1 Who among the followings has been appointed as the Director of the National Council of Educational Research and Training (NCERT) in February 2022?

A. Dinesh Prasad Saklani
B. V. Anantha Nageswaran
C. Dr Shankar Acharya
D. Jaithirth Rao

Q.2 Which among the following is the smallest ocean of the world?

A. Pacific **B.** Indian **C.** Atlantic **D.** Arctic

Q.3 The Chauri Chaura Incident paved the way for end of which among the following movements?

A. Civil Disobedience Movement
B. Non-Cooperation Movement
C. Quit India Movement
D. Kheda Satyagraha

Q.4 Which of the following language is known as the queen of all the languages of the World?

A. Malayalam **B.** Hindi
C. Kannada **D.** Dogri

Q.5 What is the full form of "IRBM"?

A. Intermediate Resource Ballistic Missile
B. Intermediate Range Ballistic Missile
C. Intermediate Range of Ballistic Missile
D. Intermediated Replace Ballistic Missile

// Smart Answer Sheet //

Correct Percentage of students who answered correctly. Skipped Percentage of students who skipped.

Q.	Ans.	Correct / Skipped	Q.	Ans.	Correct / Skipped	Q.	Ans.	Correct / Skipped	Q.	Ans.	Correct / Skipped	Q.	Ans.	Correct / Skipped	Q.	Ans.	Correct / Skipped
1	A	59.0 % / 1.55 %	2	D	77.06 % / 0.0 %	3	B	16.31 % / 5.0 %	4	C	41.39 % / 1.5 %	5	B	52.01 % / 1.23 %			

//Hints and Solutions//

1. Professor Dinesh Prasad Saklani has been appointed as the new Director of the National Council of Educational Research and Training (NCERT).

He has been appointed for a period of five years or till he attains the age of 65 years, whichever is the earliest.

NCERT is an autonomous body, which assists and advises the government on policies for improvement in school education.

Hence, the correct option is (A).

2. The Arctic Ocean is the smallest ocean in the world.

It is the Earth's northernmost body of water.

Most of the Arctic Ocean is covered by ice throughout the year.

The length of the Arctic Ocean is 6.1 million square miles.

The Arctic Ocean is divided by an underwater ocean ridge called the Lomonosov ridge.

Hence, the correct option is (D).

3. The Chauri Chaura incident took place on 4 February 1922 at Chauri Chaura in the Gorakhpur district of the United Provinces (modern-day Uttar Pradesh) in British India. Mahatma Gandhi, who was strictly against violence, halted the non-cooperation movement on the national level on 12 February 1922, as a direct result of this incident.

Hence, the correct option is (B).

4. Kannada is the queen of all the languages of the World. It is the mother of many languages that are spoken now across the globe.

Hence, the correct option is (C).

5. An intermediate-range ballistic missile (IRBM) is a ballistic missile with a range of 3,000–5,500 km (1,864–3,418 miles), between a medium-range ballistic missile (MRBM) and an intercontinental ballistic missile (ICBM).

Hence, the correct option is (B).

Sectional Test 13

Q.1 Direction: Choose the most appropriate synonym-

Toothsome

A. Delicious **B.** Tasty
C. Mouth-watering **D.** All of the above

Q.2 Direction: Select the most appropriate antonym of the given word.

Constrict

A. Diminish **B.** Dilate
C. Downsize **D.** Downturn

Q.3 Direction: Choose the correct form of passive voice from the given alternatives.

Someone has lit the fire.

A. The fire was lit by someone.
B. You are requested to light the fire by someone.
C. The fire has been lit by someone.
D. The fire had been lit by someone.

Q.4 Direction: Choose the correct form of passive voice from the given alternatives.

The boy killed the snake with a stick.

A. The snake was killed by the boy with a stick.
B. A stick was killed by the boys with a snake.
C. A snake with stick was killed by the boy.
D. A snake is killed by the boy with a stick.

Q.5 Direction: In the following question, direct speech sentences are given and you are required to find the correct indirect speech sentence of the same.

The Captain said to his men, "Stand at ease."

A. The Captain urged his men to stand at ease.
B. The Captain wanted his men to stand at ease.
C. The Captain told his men that they should stand at ease.
D. The Captain commanded his men to stand at ease.

Q.6 Direction: In the following question, direct speech sentences are given and you are required to find the correct indirect speech sentence of the same.

The peon said to his officer, "Please forgive me".

A. The peon requests his officer to forgive him.
B. The peon has requested his officer to forgive him.
C. The peon requested his officer to forgive him.
D. The peon has been requesting his officer to forgive him.

Q.7 Direction: In the following question, out of the given four alternatives, select the alternative which best expresses the meaning of the Idiom/Phrase.

Once bitten, twice shy

A. A bad experience cause to believe caution
B. Bitten by an animal
C. Having bad experiences one after the other
D. None of the above

Q.8 Direction- In the following question, out of the given four alternatives, select the alternative which best expresses the meaning of the Idiom/Phrase.

At one's beck and call

A. Matter of dispute **B.** In disorder
C. Under one's control **D.** At risk

Q.9 Direction: Complete the sentence by choosing the appropriate non-finite from the following.

"______ a loud sound, the students rushed out of the auditorium."

A. Hearing **B.** Hear **C.** To hear **D.** Heard

Q.10 Direction: Fill in the blanks with a suitable preposition.

I heard that he died ___ a heart attack.

A. of **B.** for **C.** about **D.** to

Q.11 Which of these is used to separate short co-ordinate clauses of a compound sentence?

A. Semicolon **B.** Comma
C. Full stop **D.** Colon

Q.12 Direction: Select the answer choice that identifies the verb in the sentence.

The interior temperatures of even the coolest stars are measured in millions of degrees.

A. Coolest **B.** Of even
C. Are measured **D.** In millions

Q.13 Direction: Fill in the blanks in the following sentences with the correct pronoun.

He was so afraid that his knees knocked ______ other.

A. Every **B.** One **C.** Each **D.** None

Ques (14-15):Direction- Read the passage carefully and answer the following question.

Organic farming is in a nascent stage in India and was introduced in 2005. About 2.78 million hectares of farmland were under organic cultivation as of March 2020, according to the Union Ministry of Agriculture and Farmers' Welfare. This is two percent of the 140.1 million ha net sown area in the country. Of this, 1.94 million ha is under National Programme for Organic Production (NPOP), 0.59 million ha under Paramparagat Krishi Vikas Yojna (PKVY); 0.07 million ha under Mission Organic Value Chain Development for North Eastern Regions (MOVCDNER) and 0.17 million ha under state schemes or non-schemes. This shows that the NPOP scheme covers about 70 percent of the organic area of the country, of which 30 percent is under conversion.

Q.14 What is the thematic center of the passage?

A. Intensive Farming in India
B. Subsistence Farming In India
C. Shifting Agriculture in India
D. Organic farming in India

Q.15 Which word is similar in meaning to 'nascent'?

A. Developing **B.** Dying

C. Declining **D.** Mature

// Smart Answer Sheet //

Correct Percentage of students who answered correctly. **Skipped** Percentage of students who skipped.

Q.	Ans.	Correct / Skipped	Q.	Ans.	Correct / Skipped	Q.	Ans.	Correct / Skipped	Q.	Ans.	Correct / Skipped	Q.	Ans.	Correct / Skipped	Q.	Ans.	Correct / Skipped
1	D	38.24 % / 0.0 %	4	A	41.18 % / 32.35 %	7	A	23.53 % / 32.35 %	10	A	35.29 % / 32.36 %	13	C	58.82 % / 29.42 %			
2	B	32.35 % / 32.36 %	5	D	29.41 % / 32.35 %	8	C	35.29 % / 32.36 %	11	B	35.29 % / 29.42 %	14	D	41.18 % / 32.35 %			
3	C	26.47 % / 29.41 %	6	C	29.41 % / 29.41 %	9	B	23.53 % / 32.35 %	12	C	38.24 % / 32.35 %	15	A	23.53 % / 32.35 %			

//Hints and Solutions//

1. Toothsome means temptingly tasty.

Delicious means having a very pleasant taste or smell.

Tasty means having a good flavour.

Mouth-watering means (used about food) that looks or smells very good.

Hence, the correct option is (D).

2. Constrict means make narrower, especially by encircling pressure.

Dilate means make or become wider, larger, or more open.

Diminish means to become or to make something smaller or less important, decrease

Downsize means to reduce the number of people who work in a company, business, etc.

Downturn means a drop in the amount of business that is done, a time when the economy becomes weaker.

Hence, the correct option is (B).

3. The fire has been lit by someone.

The given sentence is in active voice and it is in Present Perfect Tense.

Rule:

Subject + (has /have) + been + V^3 + Other agents.

Hence, the correct option is (C).

4. The snake was killed by the boy with a stick.

Given sentence is in Past simple tense.

Rule:

Subject + (was /were) + V^3+ Other agents.

Hence, the correct option is (A).

5. The Captain commanded his men to stand at ease.

This is an imperative sentence. In such sentences, order, request, advise or negative command is given. In negative command, the reported speech starts with Do not or Don't.

Rules for changing imperative sentences in indirect speech:

- "Said" will change to "commanded" as per the sense of the sentence.
- Inverted commas (" ") is removed and 'to' is used before the main verb (stand).

Hence, the correct option is (D).

6. The peon requested his officer to forgive him.

This is an imperative sentence. In such sentences, order, request, advise or negative command is given. In negative command, the reported speech starts with Do not or Don't.

Rules for changing imperative sentences in indirect speech:

- "Said" will change to 'requested' as per the sense of the sentence.
- Inverted commas (" ") is removed and 'to' is used before the main verb.

The pronoun of the reported speech changes accordingly. The first person pronoun 'me' will change according to the subject 'peon'. "Me" will change to "him".

Hence, the correct option is (C).

7. Once bitten, twice shy means "a bad experience cause to believe caution".

Example-

I will never work with Peter again. He expects everyone to do the work on his behalf, once bitten twice shy.

Hence, the correct option is (A).

8. At one's beck and call means ready to do something for someone any time you are asked.

Example-

She was confined to a wheelchair but had a private nurse at her beck and call.

Hence, the correct option is (C).

9. "Hear a loud sound, the students rushed out of the auditorium."

Remember, the non-finite participle is formed by adding '-ing', '-d, '-ed, '-en, '-t or '-n' to the base verb (hear-hearing). In the other options the verbs are the wrong form for a participle.

Hence, the correct option is (B).

10. I heard that he died of a heart attack.

The preposition 'of' is used to establish a connection or relating to somebody or someone with something. For example,

Everyone understands the role of a teacher in our lives.

In this sentence of links, the nouns, role, and teacher. Any other preposition cannot appropriately describe the relationship of the role and teacher of the noun.

Hence, the correct option is (A).

11. The comma is used to separate short co-ordinate clauses of a compound sentence. For example, " She came, she stooped, she conquered."

Hence, the correct option is (B).

12. "Are" is the auxiliary verb for passive voice and "measured" is the past participle of the verb "to measure."

"Coolest" (A) is the superlative form of the adjective "cool," modifying "temperatures."

"Of even" (B) and "in millions" (D) are prepositional phrases

Hence, the correct option is (C).

13. He was so afraid that his knees knocked each other.

From the given options, the correct choice to fill in the blank is 'each.'

We know that each other is used to denote the mutual relationship between two person or things.

Example: The sibling loves each other.

Hence, the correct option is (C).

14. The thematic center of the passage is organic farming in India.

The passage as a whole focuses on Organic farming and the area that is being covered under its umbrella.

The other choices address types of agriculture that are being followed In India but it is not the main idea of the passage.

Hence, the correct option is (D).

15. Nascent: (especially of a process or organization) just coming into existence and beginning to display signs of future potential.

Developing: growing or becoming stronger or more advanced.

Thus, from the above-given explanation, we can say that both 'Nascent' and 'Developing' are synonyms to each other.

Hence, the correct option is (A).

Sectional Test 14

Q.1 Direction: In the following question, out of the given four alternatives, select the alternative which best expresses the meaning of the Idiom/Phrase.

To pick holes

A. To find some reason to quarrel
B. To destroy something
C. To criticize someone
D. To cut some part of an item

Q.2 Direction- In the following question, out of the given four alternatives, select the alternative which best expresses the meaning of the Idiom/Phrase.

To smell a rat

A. To see signs of plague epidemic
B. To get bad small of a bad dead rat
C. To suspect foul dealings
D. To be in a bad mood

Q.3 Direction: Choose the most appropriate synonym-

Berserk

A. Clever **B.** Morose **C.** Cheerful **D.** Wild

Q.4 Direction: Select the most appropriate antonym of the given word.

Impertinent

A. Impressive **B.** Smooth
C. Healthy **D.** Respectful

Q.5 Direction: Choose the correct form of passive voice from the given alternatives.

The boy laughed at the beggar.

A. The beggar was laughed by the boy.
B. The beggar was being laughed by the boy.
C. The beggar was being laughed at by the boy.
D. The beggar was laughed at by the boy.

Q.6 Direction: Choose the correct form of passive voice from the given alternatives.

They drew a circle in the morning.

A. A circle was being drawn by them in the morning.
B. A circle was drawn by them in the morning.
C. In the morning a circle have been drawn by them.
D. A circle has been drawing since morning.

Q.7 Direction: Choose the most appropriate option to change the narration (direct/indirect) of the given sentence.

Kirti asked me if I had watched the movie on television the previous night.

A. Kirti asked me, "Did you watch the movie on television last night?"
B. Kirti asked me, "Had you watched the movie on television last night?"
C. Kirti asked me, "Did I watched the movie on television last night?"
D. Kirti asked me, "You had watched the movie on television last night?

Q.8 Direction: Choose the most appropriate option to change the narration (direct/indirect) of the given sentence.

Experts said that several steps were being taken to promote foreign trade as it constituted 45% of the country's economy.

A. Experts are saying, "Several steps were taken to promote foreign trade as it constituted 45% of the country's economy".
B. Experts said, "Several steps should be taken to promote foreign trade as they constitute 45% of the country's economy".
C. Experts said, "Several steps are being taken to promote foreign trade as it constitutes 45% of the country's economy".
D. Experts said, "Several steps had been taken for promoting foreign trade as it constitute 45% of the country's economy".

Ques (9-11):Direction: Read the passage and answer the question that follow.

If you've ever spent time in the UK, you'll surely have had a nice cuppa. While drinking tea is certainly a centuries-old tradition in the UK, many countries have their own strong cultural practices involving tea. The nation which drinks most tea is Turkey, It is also a popular drink in China and India, where most of the world's tea is grown. Many forms of tea exist around the world. Green tea is popular in China and Japan. In India, tea is often prepared with spices and boiled in both water and milk, and Tibetans commonly drink tea with butter and salt. Many cultures have traditions of people meeting to sit together and drink tea. For example, Japanese tea ceremonies can be formal, elegant affairs that last for hours.

Q.9 According to passage which nation drink tea most?

A. India **B.** China **C.** Turkey **D.** U.K.

Q.10 How Tibetans drink there tea?

A. Boil water and milk **B.** Butter and salt
C. Using spices **D.** Green tea

Q.11 What is the antonym of Elegant?

A. Messy **B.** Graceful
C. Discerning **D.** Sophisticated

Q.12 Which of these is not a punctuation mark?

A. Full stop **B.** Comma **C.** Colon **D.** Hashtag

Q.13 Which of these is used after a nominative absolute?

A. Colon **B.** Comma
C. Full stop **D.** Question mark

Q.14 Complete the sentence by choosing the appropriate non-finite from the following.

"I tried ______ a stain left by coffee from my shirt using the new cleaning agent."

A. clean **B.** to clean
C. to cleaning **D.** to cleaned

Q.15 Choose the synonym of the given word:

Amiable

A. Strict **B.** Unreasonable
C. Aloof **D.** Friendly

// Smart Answer Sheet //

Correct Percentage of students who answered correctly. **Skipped** Percentage of students who skipped.

Q.	Ans.	Correct	Q.	Ans.	Correct	Q.	Ans.	Correct	Q.	Ans.	Correct	Q.	Ans.	Correct	Q.	Ans.	Correct
		Skipped			Skipped			Skipped			Skipped			Skipped			Skipped
1	C	80.99 %	4	D	83.41 %	7	A	55.14 %	10	B	87.91 %	13	B	67.49 %			
		0.0 %			0.0 %			1.93 %			0.0 %			2.0 %			
2	C	78.56 %	5	D	54.74 %	8	C	40.82 %	11	A	64.41 %	14	B	64.24 %			
		0.0 %			1.36 %			1.71 %			1.72 %			1.77 %			
3	D	83.26 %	6	B	53.67 %	9	C	40.68 %	12	D	79.81 %	15	D	86.15 %			
		0.0 %			1.72 %			1.97 %			0.0 %			0.0 %			

//Hints and Solutions//

1. To pick holes means to try and make an idea or piece of work seem bad by finding all the things that are wrong or missing.

Example-

He cross-examined like a trial lawyer and could pick holes in the best of arguments.

Hence, the correct option is (C).

2. To smell a rat means to suspect or realize that something is wrong in a particular situation.

Example-

When I got an e-mail asking for my password, I should have smelled a rat.

Hence, the correct option is (C).

3. Berserk means out of control with anger or excitement, wild or frenzied.

Wild means lacking discipline or restraint.

Clever means quick to understand, learn, and devise or apply ideas, intelligent.

Morose means sullen and ill-tempered.

Cheerful means noticeably happy and optimistic.

Hence, the correct option is (D).

4. Impertinent means not showing proper respect, rude.

Respectful means feeling or showing deference and respect.

Impressive means evoking admiration through size, quality, or skill, grand, imposing, or awesome.

Smooth means having an even and regular surface, free from perceptible projections, lumps, or indentations.

Healthy means in a good physical or mental condition, in good health.

Hence, the correct option is (D).

5. The beggar was laughed at by the boy.

Given sentence is in Past indefinite (Past simple) tense and it is in the active voice.

Rule:

Subject + (was /were) + V^3 + Other Agents.

Hence, the correct option is (D).

6. A circle was drawn by them in the morning.

Given sentence is in Past simple tense and it is in active voice, we need to change it into passive voice.

Rule:

Subject + (was / were) + V^3 + Optional Agents.

Hence, the correct option is (B).

7. Kirti asked me, "Did you watch the movie on television last night?"

The reporting verb 'asked' suggests that the sentence is an interrogative sentence. The reporting verb will be same as in indirect speech. "If" will be removed and "inverted commas" will be introduced. "I" will be converted to "you" acc. to the object "me". The past perfect tense (I had watched) will be converted into the simple past interrogative tense (Did you watch). "Previous" will be converted to "last".

Hence, the correct option is (A).

8. Experts said, "Several steps are being taken to promote foreign trade as it constitutes 45% of the country's economy".

The given sentence is in indirect speech. The reporting verb 'said' will remain unchanged, 'that' will be removed and inverted commas will be introduced. While converting it into the direct speech, 'were' will be converted into 'are' and 'constituted' will be changed into 'constitutes' (past will change to present).

Hence, the correct option is (C).

9. According to the passage, Turkey nation drinks tea most. The given passage is about the Cultural tradition of tea. Each country has a different recipe for making tea.

Let us refer to the passage - While drinking tea is certainly a centuries-old tradition in the UK, many countries have their own strong cultural practices involving tea. The nation which drinks most tea is Turkey.

Hence, the correct option is (C).

10. The given passage is about the Cultural tradition of tea.

Each country has a different recipe for making tea.

Let us refer to the passage - Many forms of tea exist around the world. Green tea is popular in China and Japan. In India, tea is often prepared with spices and boiled in both water and milk, and Tibetans commonly drink tea with butter and salt.

Hence, the correct option is (B).

11. Elegant (adjective): graceful and attractive in appearance or behavior.

Messy (adjective): Producing or causing dirt and untidiness.

Hence, the correct option is (A).

12. The hashtag Isn't a punctuation mark. It is a symbol used in social networks, and it has no relevance in English Grammar. The main punctuation marks are full stop, comma, colon, semicolon, question mark, exclamation mark, a hyphen, dash, brackets, apostrophe.

Hence, the correct option is (D).

13. The comma is used after a nominative absolute. For example, " Once over, she returned home in complete peace."

Hence, the correct option is (B).

14. The correct answer is to clean.

"I tried to clean a stain left by coffee from my shirt using the new cleaning agent."

Remember, the non-finite infinitive is formed by placing 'to' before the base verb. In option (A) 'to' is missing. In options (C) and (D) the base verb changes form.

Hence, the correct option is (B).

15. Amiable means having an easygoing and pleasing manner especially in social situations.

Friendly means- characteristic of or befitting a friend.

Strict means rigidly accurate; allowing no deviation from a standard.

Unreasonable means not being reasonable, not showing good judgment.

Aloof means remote in manner.

Hence, the correct option is (D).

Sectional Test 15

Q.1 Direction: Choose the correct antonym for the given word:

Elevation

A. Reduction **B.** Depression
C. Humiliation **D.** Demotion

Q.2 Direction: Choose the correct antonym of the given word.

Bravery

A. Heroism **B.** Daring
C. Courage **D.** Cowardice

Q.3 Direction: Select the option that means the same as the given idiom.

To eat humble pie

A. To deny desperately **B.** To defend oneself
C. To accept error **D.** To be aggressive

Q.4 Direction: In the following question, a sentence is given in Direct/Indirect speech.

She said, "Mr. Hamel did not scold Franz."

A. She said that Mr. Hamel had not scolded Franz.
B. She informed that Mr. Hamel did scold Franz.
C. She said that Mr. Hamel has not scolded Franz.
D. She told that Mr. Hamel had not scolded Franz.

Q.5 Direction: In the following question, a sentence is given in Direct/Indirect speech. Out of the four alternatives, choose the one which best expresses the sentence in Indirect/Direct speech.

The nurse said, "The patient has been sleeping for the past five hours."

A. The nurse said that the patient had been sleeping for the past five hours.
B. The nurse informed that the patient had been sleeping since the past five hours.
C. The nurse said that the patient has been sleeping for the past five hours.
D. The nurse told us that the patient had been sleeping for the past five hours.

Q.6 Direction: Select the correct passive form of the given sentence.

Raj delivered me a letter.

A. A letter was delivered by me
B. A letter is delivered by Raj
C. A letter was delivered to me by Raj
D. A letter has delivered to me by Raj

Q.7 Select the correct passive form of the given sentence.

Fatima has painted this picture.

A. The picture was painted by her
B. The picture is being painted by him
C. The picture is painted by her
D. This picture has been painted by Fatima

Ques (8-10):Direction: Read the passage and answer the question that follow.

Nowruz means new day in Persian and is the most important festival of the year in Iran. Nowruz marks the spring equinox when night and day are of equal length. It's the day when winter changes into spring in the northern hemisphere, and it feels like a new beginning. People prepare a special table in their homes, where they place small dishes holding seven symbolic foods and spices. The names of these foods all start with the letter 's' in Persian and so the table is called the 'seven s' The seven s's symbolize life, love, health, and prosperity.

Q.8 On which season did Nowruz celebrate?

A. Spring **B.** Summer **C.** Winter **D.** Rainy

Q.9 According to passage, what does 'seven s' symbolize?

A. Family, festival
B. Living, viability, entity
C. Life, love, health, and prosperity
D. Devotion, well being

Q.10 How does the Nowruz feel like?

A. New day **B.** Renewal
C. Awakening **D.** New beginning

Q.11 Direction: In the following question, out of the four alternatives, choose the alternative which best expresses the meaning of the idiom/Phrase.

Something up one's sleeve

A. A grand idea
B. A secret plan
C. A profitable plan
D. Something important

Q.12 Which of the following sentence is written correctly using adjective?

A. Yesterday, I was tireder than you
B. Yesterday, I was the tiredest
C. Yesterday, I was more tired than you
D. Yesterday, I was tired than you

Q.13 Direction: Fill in the blank with an appropriate adjective.

His attitude was the _______ offensive among all the guys.

A. fewest **B.** least **C.** fewer **D.** less

Q.14 Direction: Fill in the blanks in the following sentences with the correct pronoun.

______ of these two boys is guilty.

A. Either **B.** One **C.** Any **D.** None

Q.15 Direction: Fill in the blanks in the following sentence with the correct pronoun.

______, he and I shall prepare for the birthday party.

A. I **B.** you **C.** we **D.** our

// Smart Answer Sheet //

Correct Percentage of students who answered correctly. Skipped Percentage of students who skipped.

Q.	Ans.	Correct / Skipped	Q.	Ans.	Correct / Skipped	Q.	Ans.	Correct / Skipped	Q.	Ans.	Correct / Skipped	Q.	Ans.	Correct / Skipped	Q.	Ans.	Correct / Skipped
1	A	61.13 % / 1.12 %	4	A	11.25 % / 4.1 %	7	D	44.46 % / 1.07 %	10	D	49.48 % / 1.44 %	13	B	82.86 % / 0.0 %			
2	D	88.51 % / 0.0 %	5	A	69.4 % / 1.24 %	8	A	68.82 % / 1.89 %	11	B	53.02 % / 1.22 %	14	A	78.05 % / 0.0 %			
3	C	64.13 % / 1.44 %	6	C	88.07 % / 0.0 %	9	C	60.45 % / 1.19 %	12	C	85.95 % / 0.0 %	15	B	55.38 % / 1.05 %			

//Hints and Solutions//

1. Elevation means the action or fact of raising or being raised to a higher or more important level, state, or position.

Reduction: the action or fact of making something smaller or less in amount, degree, or size.

Drepression: feelings of severe despondency and dejection.

Humiliation: the action of humiliating someone or the state of being humiliated.

Demotion: reduction in rank or status.

Hence, the correct option is (A).

2. Bravery: courageous behaviour or character.

Cowardice: lack of bravery.

Heroism: great bravery.

Daring: (of a person or action) adventurous or audaciously bold.

Courage: the ability to do something that frightens one, bravery.

Hence, the correct option is (D).

3. The given idiom 'to eat humble pie' means to admit that you were wrong.

Example:

After boasting that his company could outperform the industry's best, he's been forced to eat humble pie.

Hence, the correct option is (C).

4. The given sentence is in Direct Speech. As per the question, we have to change it into Indirect Speech.

While changing the narration of an assertive sentence, we make the following changes:

The first person (I/We) changes according to the subject and the second person (You) changes according to the object.

The conjunction 'that' is used in place of commas and inverted commas.

Simple past tense changes to Past perfect tense.

In the given sentence, 'did not scold' changes to 'had not scolded'.

So, the correct indirect speech is She said that Mr. Hamel had not scolded Franz.

Hence, the correct option is (A).

5. The nurse said that the patient had been sleeping for the past five hours.

The given sentence is in Direct Speech. As per the question, we have to change it into Indirect Speech.

While changing the narration of an assertive sentence, we make the following changes:

- 'Said to' is changed to 'told + object'.
- The first person (I/We) changes according to the subject and the second person (You) changes according to the object.
- The conjunction 'that' is used in place of commas and inverted commas.
- Present perfect continuous tense changes to past perfect continuous tense.
- 'has been sleeping' will change to 'had been sleeping'.
- The nurse said that the patient had been sleeping for the past five hours.

Hence, the correct option is (A).

6. A letter was delivered to me by Raj.

First of all, we need to identify (S+V+O) Subject, Verb, and object in the active sentence to convert to passive voice, which is Raj + delivered + a letter in the sentence.

Now, the object (a letter) is interchanged with the subject (Raj), and the verb (delivered) is converted to the third form verb (delivered) which Is followed by (By, With, to, etc). Here we use By.

'Delivered' is followed by 'to' when used in passive voice.

Hence, the correct option is (C).

7. This picture has been painted by Fatima

The sentence is in present perfect.

The rule for transforming into passive form is:

Active: Subject + has/have + v^3 + object

Passive: Object + has/have + been + V^3 + by + subject

Therefore according to this rule, "This picture has been painted by Fatima." is correct.

Hence, the correct option is (D).

8. This passage is about celebrating the Persian festival Nowruz. This festival mostly celebrated in Iran.

Nowruz marks the spring equinox when night and day are of equal length.

Hence, the correct option Is (A).

9. This passage is about celebrating the Persian festival Nowruz. This festival is mostly celebrated in Iran.

The seven s' symbolize life, love, health, and prosperity.

Hence, the correct option is (C).

10. This passage is about celebrating the Persian festival Nowruz. This festival is mostly celebrated in Iran.

Nowruz marks the spring equinox when night and day are of equal length. It's the day when winter changes into spring in the northern hemisphere, and it feels like a new beginning.

Hence, the correct option is (D).

11. Something up one's sleeve: To have a secret plan, idea, or advantage that can be utilized if and when it is required.

Hence, the correct option is (B).

12. The correct way of writing the comparative adjective is to write it as,

Subject + more + Adjective +than

In this statement, the subject; the speaker is more tired than the other person.

In accordance to the rule, the correct way of using the adjective is, I am more tired than you.

So, the correct sentence is: Yesterday, I was more tired than you.

Hence, the correct option is (C).

13. His attitude was the least offensive among all the guys.

The most appropriate adjective of all the options is least. It is a superlative adjective form. Where the attitude of the boy was the least offensive out of other boys.

Hence, the correct option is (B).

14. From the given options, the correct choice to fill in the blank is 'either.'

We know that either is used to denote choice between the two-person or thing.

Example: Either of these two boys is guilty.

Hence, the correct option is (A).

15. From the given options, the correct choice to fill in the blank is 'you.'

We know that, if all the three-person or two out of three come in a single sentence, the order is 231.

Example: He and I shall prepare for the birthday party.

Hence, the correct option is (B).

// Notes //

// Notes //

www.ingramcontent.com/pod-product-compliance
Lightning Source LLC
Chambersburg PA
CBHW081307130726
47998CB00010B/2963

9789391464417